CASES IN
LABOR LAW

GRID SERIES IN LAW

Consulting Editor
THOMAS W. DUNFEE, University of Pennsylvania

Atteberry, Pearson, & Litka, *Real Estate Law*
Dunfee & Gibson, *Modern Business Law: An Introduction to Government and Business,* Second Edition
Erickson, Dunfee, & Gibson, *Antitrust and Trade Regulation: Cases and Materials*
Francois, *Mass Media Law and Regulation*
Litka, *Business Law,* Second Edition
Litka & Inman, *The Legal Environment of Business: Text, Cases, and Readings*
Miller, *Government Policy Toward Labor: An Introduction to Labor Law*
Stern & Yaney, *Cases In Labor Law*
Warren, *Antitrust in Theory and Practice*
Wolfe & Naffziger, *Legal Perspectives of American Business Associations*

OTHER BOOKS IN THE GRID SERIES IN LAW

Naffziger & Knauss, *A Basic Guide to Federal Labor Law*
Zwarensteyn, *Introduction to the Legal System,* Third Edition

CASES IN LABOR LAW

Duke Nordlinger Stern
Executive Director, The West Virginia State Bar
Director of Continuing Legal Education, West Virginia University
Adjunct Professor, West Virginia College of Graduate Studies

Joseph P. Yaney
Chairman, Department of Business Administration
Pennsylvania State University

Grid Inc., Columbus, Ohio

I.S.B.N. 0-88244-110-8
Library of Congress Catalog Card Number 76-5617

1 2 3 4 5 6 ⊠ 2 1 0 9 8 7

CASES IN LABOR LAW

*This book was edited and stylized by Lois Yoakam; Elaine Clatterbuck, production
manager. Cover design by Marcie Clark. The text was set in Times Roman by
Capital Composition Company, Westerville, Ohio.*

To Our Parents

CONTENTS

Editor's Preface   ix

Preface   xii

Reference Chart   xiii

Table of Cases   xv

Chapter
1   Coverage Of The Law   1
    Introduction To The Cases
    Case Questions

2   Union Efforts At Employee Organization   27
    Collective Bargaining
    Introduction To The Cases
    Case Questions

3   Employer Conduct During Unionization   47
    Prohibited Activities
    Introduction To The Cases
    Case Questions

4   Boycotts   79
    Introduction To The Cases
    Case Questions

5   Picketing   109
    Stranger Or Outsider Picketing
    Secondary Picketing
    Introduction To The Cases
    Case Questions

6   Bargaining   139
    Good-faith Bargaining
    Introduction To The Cases
    Case Questions

7   Arbitration And Conflict Resolution   167
    Introduction To The Cases
    Case Questions

8   Civil Rights   191
    Civil Rights Act Of 1866
    National Labor Relations Act
    State Statutes
    Introduction To The Cases
    Case Questions

9   **Fair Employment Practices**   205
      The Employment Setting
      Public Employees
      Administrative Procedures
      Enforcement Procedures
      Introduction To The Cases
      Case Questions

10   **Wage And Hour Laws**   223
      Administrative Procedures
      Equal Pay For Equal Work
      Introduction To The Cases
      Case Questions

11   **Occupational Safety And Health Regulations**   239
      Occupational Safety And Health Act
      Introduction To The Cases
      Case Questions

12   **Public Employees**   263
      Federal Policies
      State Policies
      Political Considerations In Negotiations
      Organizational And Bargaining Rights
      Introduction To The Cases
      Case Questions

13   **Hospitals And Health Care Institutions**   283
      Unionization Drives
      Introduction To The Cases
      Case Questions

14   **Educational Facilities**   303
      Issues
      Future Developments
      Introduction To The Cases
      Case Questions

Appendix A   National Labor Relations Act   331

Appendix B   Labor-Management Reporting and Disclosure Act   361

EDITOR'S PREFACE

Cases In Labor Law is one of several casebooks published in the new Grid Series In Law. This Series is aimed at developing a group of innovative teaching materials designed especially for undergraduate courses in law. The casebooks in the Series are designed to supplement substantively oriented texts by providing primary legal source materials related to particular legal fields.

This book is designed for courses in labor law and industrial relations. To aid the students there is a table which cross-references the coverage of *Cases In Labor Law* with the other basic texts in the field.

Labor law is a complex, evolving field of law. Students need up-to-date primary source materials in order to develop an appropriate appreciation of its complexity and of the underlying policy issues that play such an important role in this field. In addition, students need current materials which indicate the present state of the changing areas of labor law. Using a supplemental casebook is an ideal way for an instructor to insure that these student needs are served. *Cases In Labor Law* is admirably suited for this purpose.

Thomas W. Dunfee
The Wharton School
University of Pennsylvania

PREFACE

Cases In Labor Law is a casebook which deals with people and their problems.

Different people will want to use this book for different purposes. Businessmen who are interested in up-to-date practices will find that the short, important cases presented will brief them on current legal practices. Training directors will find this casebook useful in teaching others about equal employment opportunities, civil rights guarantees, collective bargaining procedures, and grievance processes.

Faculty members will find the casebook an excellent mixture of interest areas; it includes such current topics as unions in health care institutions, educational unions, the Equal Employment Opportunity Commission, and civil rights legislation. *Cases In Labor Law* is designed so that faculty members can teach the basic concepts of the law and then use the cases to illustrate the complexities which develop in real life. Students will find the casebook flows quickly and smoothly from the short introductions of law theory into the text of actual cases.

The brief introductions at the beginning of each chapter explain the basic law. Purposely they are condensed to convey a great deal of information precisely. The teaching cases represent unique situations, and the settings and the decisions are set forth in detail. The cases are varied and have been chosen to hold the student's interest. The self-directed questions at the end of each case help students assess their understanding of the law; they aid students in relating theory to actual practice. These questions will be especially helpful in the industrial or university classroom.

We urge the reader to study the topics presented carefully and do further research for other related current decisions. New cases are listed in many business law publications, and legal services supply weekly updates of these cases. Bear in mind that the law is dynamic, and every day brings new decisions.

In closing, we wish to thank the many people who have helped in the development of the casebook. The opinions expressed by the authors are their own and do not necessarily reflect those of the organizations with which they are affiliated.

REFERENCE CHART OF CASES IN LABOR LAW TO CHAPTERS IN OTHER TEXTS

(Numbers refer to chapters)

Chapters in Cases in Labor Law

Other Texts	1	2	3	4	5	6	7	8	9	10	11	12	13	14
Miller, *Government Policy Towards Labor Relations* (Grid)	1-4, 15-19	5								7,8 10	6		21	
Myers & Twomey, *Labor Law and Legislation* (South-Western)	1-4	7	6	8,9	8,9	5	10		12			13		
Oberer & Hanslowe, *Labor Law* (West)	1-3	5		5	5	4, 6-8								
Taylor & Witney, *Labor Relations Law* (Prentice-Hall)	1-11, 20			17	16,18	12-15							21	
Morris, *The Developing Labor Law* (BNA)	1-4, 28-32	5-6, 20	8-9	21,24	19, 21-22, 25	11-17	18							
Herman & Skinner, *Labor Law: Cases, Text and Legislation* (Random House)	1-4	7	6	9	9	5,8								

TABLE OF CASES

Chapter
1   United States *v.* Hutcheson   3
    NLRB *v.* Jones & Laughlin Steel Corporation   8
    Universal Camera Corporation *v.* NLRB   15
    Truck Drivers Local 413, International Brotherhood of   21
        Teamsters, Chauffeurs, Warehousemen & Helpers of
        America *v.* NLRB

2   NLRB *v.* Local 901, International Brotherhood of Teamsters,   28
        Chauffeurs, Warehousemen & Helpers of America
    B & M Kaufmann *v.* NLRB   30
    Wichita Eagle & Beacon Publishing Co., Inc. *v.* NLRB   33
    NLRB *v.* City Yellow Cab Company   37
    NLRB *v.* Polytech, Inc.   43

3   NLRB *v.* Henriksen, Inc.   48
    Textile Workers Union of America *v.* Darlington   60
        Manufacturing Company
    NLRB *v.* Midwest Hanger Co. & Liberty Engineering   65
        Corporation
    NLRB *v.* Truck Drivers Local 449   72
    NLRB *v.* International Van Lines   76

4   Potter *v.* Houston Gulf Coast Building Trades Council,   80
        AFL–CIO
    NLRB *v.* Local 760, Fruit and Vegetable Packers   83
        and Warehousemen
    C. Comella, Inc. *v.* United Farm Workers Organizing   99
        Committee

5   NLRB *v.* Local 3, International Brotherhood of   110
        Electrical Workers, AFL–CIO
    Local 978, United Brotherhood of Carpenters & Joiners   117
        of America, AFL–CIO *v.* Markwell
    NLRB *v.* Local 182, International Brotherhood of   125
        Teamsters, Chauffeurs, Warehousemen, & Helpers of
        America
    NLRB *v.* Texas Natural Gasoline Corporation   131
    People Acting Through Community Effort *v.* Doorley   135

6   NLRB *v.* Philamon Laboratories, Inc.   140
    International Ladies' Garment Workers' Union, AFL–CIO   146
        v. NLRB
    Firch Baking Company *v.* NLRB   152
    Connecticut Light & Power Company *v.* NLRB   156
    United States Pipe & Foundry Company *v.* NLRB   159

7 Firestone Tire & Rubber Company *v.* Local 887, 168
International Union of the United Rubber, Cork,
Linoleum & Plastic Workers of America, AFL–CIO

International Association of Machinists *v.* Howmet 170
Corporation

Division 85, Amalgamated Transit Union *v.* Port 176
Authority of Allegheny County

Local 6, Bricklayers, Masons and Plasterers International 179
Union of America *v.* Boyd G. Heminger, Inc.

General Dynamics Corporation *v.* Local 5, Industrial 186
Union of Marine and Shipbuilding Workers of America,
AFL–CIO

8 Steele *v.* Louisville & Nashville Railroad 193
Griggs *v.* Duke Power Company 197
Equal Employment Opportunity Commission *v.* 201
Multi-Line Cans, Inc.

9 Dave Van Hoomissen and EEOC *v.* Xerox Corporation 209
Harold Daughtery *v.* Continental Can Company, Inc. 218

10 United States *v.* Darby 225
Walling, U.S. Department of Labor *v.* Jacksonville 228
Paper Company
Maryland *v.* Wirtz, Secretary of Labor 230
Mitchell, Secretary of Labor *v.* C & P Shoe Corporation 233
Breitwieser *v.* KMS Industries, Inc. 236
Brennan, Secretary of Labor *v.* Hatton 236
Hodgson, Secretary of Labor *v.* American Concrete 237
Construction Co., Inc.
Hodgson, Secretary of Labor *v.* Griffin and Brand 237
of McAllen, Inc.

11 Secretary of Labor *v.* Selchow & Righter Company 241
Secretary of Labor *v.* Thorleif Larsen and Son, Inc. 245
Brennan, Secretary of Labor *v.* Interstate Glass Co. 250
Brennan, Secretary of Labor *v.* Occupational Safety and 255
Health Review Commission and Bill Echols Trucking Co.
Secretary of Labor *v.* American Shipbuilding Company 259
Secretary of Labor *v.* Clements Paper Company 259
Secretary of Labor *v.* Walter A. Podpora 260
Secretary of Labor *v.* Arizona Public Service Company 261
Secretary of Labor *v.* C. O. Osborn Contracting Company 261

12 Norwalk Teachers' Association *v.* Board of Education 266
United Federation of Postal Clerks *v.* Blount, Postmaster 272
General
American Federation of State, County, and Municipal 276
Employees, AFL–CIO *v.* Woodward
Shelton *v.* Tucker 279

13   Raymond Convalescent Hospital Inc. *v.* Local 399,   284
         Service & Hospital Employees Union, SEIU, AFL–CIO
      Butte Medical Properties *v.* Local 22, Building Service   294
         Employees' Union, AFL–CIO
      Walters Ambulance Service, Inc. *v.* Association of United   300
         Ambulance Personnel

14   Cornell University *v.* Local 200, Service Employees   305
         International Union, AFL–CIO
      Burlington County College Faculty Association *v.* Board   316
         of Trustees
      Board of Education, Huntington *v.* Associated Teachers   321

The basis for all federal power to regulate labor activities is the United States Constitution. Article III, the Judiciary Article, is the source of one labor statute, the Norris-La Guardia Act of 1932. Almost all other labor legislation flows from the commerce clause of Article I. The commerce clause grants Congress the power to regulate commerce "among the several states," and additional power in Article I provides that Congress can make "all laws" "necessary and proper" to give force and effect to its authority. The question of the boundaries of interstate commerce has been the subject of judicial interpretation; one of the first significant cases was *Gibbons* v. *Ogden* in 1824.

The various labor statutes (see Table 1-1) present a mixed approach to the regulation of employee-employer relations.

TABLE 1-1

DEVELOPMENT OF THE LAW

YEAR	BROAD COVERAGES	RAILWAY	PRIVATE EMPLOYERS
1890	Sherman Act		
1914	Clayton Act		
1926		Railway Labor Act	
1932	Norris-La Guardia Act		
1935			Wagner Act
1947			Taft-Hartley Act
1959			Landrum-Griffin Act
1964	Civil Rights Act		
1970	Occupational Safety and Health Act		
1972	Equal Employment Opportunity Act		
1974			Health Care Amendments

SHERMAN ANTI-TRUST ACT (1890)

This legislation (see Table 1-1) was a reaction to the growth and development of large businesses through trusts and holding companies. To restore effective competition, the Act was designed to "protect trade and commerce against unlawful restraints and monopolies." It declared "[t]hat every contract, combination in the form of trust or otherwise, or conspiracy, in restraint of trade or commerce among the several States, or with foreign nations, is hereby declared to be illegal."

CLAYTON ANTI-TRUST ACT (1914)

This legislation was designed to free labor from the anti-trust restrictions and to permit such activities as strikes, picketing, and boycotts. However, in the *Duplex Printing Press Co. Case* (1921) and successive judicial rulings, the Supreme Court limited such activities to those for the purpose of "lawfully carrying out legitimate objects" and held unions liable for departures from this standard.

RAILWAY LABOR ACT (1926)

Limited to the railroad industry and later extended to airlines, this legislation established protection of employees' right to self-organization and declared that collective bargaining was in the national interest. The Act provided positive measures to avoid wasteful interferences with these carriers of interstate commerce.

NORRIS-LA GUARDIA ACT (1932)

This legislation carried over the spirit of the Railway Labor Act to employees in general. However, it was limited in the protection it afforded, providing only for narrowly limited federal injunctions.

NATIONAL LABOR RELATIONS (WAGNER) ACT (1935)

The Act provided the positive protections for interstate business in general that were granted to the limited areas by the Railway Labor Act. Included in it were protections for employee self-organization and the declaration that employer refusal to bargain collectively in good faith was an unfair labor practice.

LABOR MANAGEMENT RELATIONS (TAFT-HARTLEY) ACT (1947)

While the National Labor Relations Act placed the burden of labor discord in interstate commerce at the door of the employer, the Taft-Hartley amendments recognized that unions could also be guilty of unfair practices. The duty to bargain collectively was also extended to labor.

LABOR-MANAGEMENT REPORTING AND DISCLOSURE (LANDRUM-GRIFFIN) ACT (1959)

These amendments to the Wagner Act reaffirmed the unfair labor practices detailed in the earlier legislation, and went on to bind employers, unions, and their officials to high standards of responsibility and ethical conduct. The Act declares these duties to be critical in maintaining a free flow of commerce.

Additional legislation which is important in labor-management relations is Title VII of the Civil Rights Act of 1964, as amended by the Equal Employment Opportunity Act of 1972, and the Occupational Safety and Health Act of 1970.

INTRODUCTION TO THE CASES

The first case in this chapter, *United States* v. *Hutcheson,* is a landmark decision addressing the issue of union accountability under the Sherman, Clayton, and Norris-La Guardia Acts. (The broad immunization for union activity construed under the *Hutcheson* decision was limited in subsequent cases, including *Mineworkers* v. *Pennington,* 381 U.S. 657 (1965)). The *Jones & Laughlin Steel Corp. Case* is concerned with the applicability and breadth of the Wagner Act.

The extent to which Courts of Appeals can exercise judicial review over National Labor Relations Board decisions was at issue in the *Universal Camera Corp. Case.* Finally, in the *Truck Drivers Union Local No. 413 Case* collective bargaining agreement limitations on employer activities were reviewed by the court.

UNITED STATES v. HUTCHESON
United States Supreme Court
312 U.S. 219 (1941)

• • •

MR. JUSTICE FRANKFURTER delivered the opinion of the Court.

Whether the use of conventional, peaceful activities by a union in controversy with a rival union over certain jobs is a violation of the Sherman Law, Act of July 2, 1890, Stat. 209, as amended, 15 U. S. C. § 1, is the question. It is sharply presented in this case because it arises in a criminal prosecution. Concededly an injunction either at the suit of the Government or of the employer could not issue.

Summarizing the long indictment, these are the facts. Anheuser-Busch, Inc., operating a large plant in St. Louis, contracted with Borsari Tank Corporation for the erection of an additional facility. The Gaylord Container Corporation, a lessee of adjacent property from Anheuser-Busch, made a similar contract for a new building with the Stocker Company. Anheuser-Busch obtained the materials for its brewing and other operations and sold its finished products largely through interstate shipments. The Gaylord Corporation was equally dependent on interstate commerce for marketing its goods, as were the construction companies for their building materials. Among the employees of Anheuser-Busch were members of the United Brotherhood of Carpenters and Joiners of America and of the International Association of Machinists. The conflicting claims of these two organizations, affiliated with the American Federation of Labor, in regard to the erection and dismantling of machinery had long been a source of controversy between them. Anheuser-Busch had had agreements with both organizations whereby the Machinists were given the disputed jobs and the Carpenters agreed to submit all disputes to arbitration. But in 1939 the president of the Carpenters, their general representative, and two officials of the Carpenters' local organization, the four men under indictment, stood on the claims of the Carpenters for the jobs. Rejection by the employer of the Carpenters' demand and the refusal of the latter to submit to arbitration were followed by a strike of the Carpenters, called by the defendants against Anheuser-Busch and the construction companies, a picketing of Anheuser-Busch and its tenant, and a request through circular letters and the official publication of the Carpenters that union members and their friends refrain from buying Anheuser-Busch beer.

These activities on behalf of the Carpenters formed the charge of the indictment as a criminal combination and conspiracy in violation of the Sherman Law. Demurrers, denying that what was charged constituted a violation of the laws of the United States, were sustained. ... and the case came here under the Criminal Appeals Act. ...

In order to determine whether an indictment charges an offense against the United States, designation by the pleader of the statute under which he purported to lay the charge is immaterial. He may have conceived the charge under one statute which would not sustain the indictment, but it may nevertheless come within the terms of another statute. . . . On the other hand, an indictment may validly satisfy the statute under which the pleader proceeded, but other statutes not referred to by him may draw the sting of criminality from the allegations. Here we must consider not merely the Sherman Law but the related enactments which entered into the decision of the district court.

Section 1 of the Sherman Law on which the indictment rested is as follows: "Every contract, combination in the form of trust or otherwise, or conspiracy, in restraint of trade or commerce among the several States, or with foreign nations, is hereby declared to be illegal." The controversies engendered by its application to trade union activities and the efforts to secure legislative relief from its consequences are familiar history. The Clayton Act of 1914 was the result. . . . "This statute was the fruit of unceasing agitation, which extended over more than twenty years and was designed to equalize before the law the position of workingmen and employer as industrial combatants." ... Section 20 of that Act, ... withdrew from the general interdict of the Sherman Law specifically enumerated practices of labor unions by prohibiting injunctions against them—since the use of the injunction had been the major source of dissatisfaction—and also relieved such practices of all illegal taint by the catch-all provision, "nor shall any of the acts specified in this paragraph be considered or held to be violations of any law of the United States." The Clayton Act gave rise to new litigation and to renewed controversy in and out of Congress regarding the status of trade unions. By the generality of its terms the Sherman Law had necessarily compelled the courts to work out its meaning from case to case. It was widely believed that into the Clayton Act courts read the very beliefs which that Act was designed to remove. Specifically the courts restricted the scope of § 20 to trade union activities directed against an employer by his own employees. . . . Such a view it was urged, both by powerful judicial dissents and informed lay opinion, misconceived the area of economic conflict that had best be left to economic forces and the pressure of public opinion and not subjected to the judgment of courts. . . . Agitation again led to legislation, and in 1932 Congress wrote the Norris-La Guardia Act. . . .

The Norris-La Guardia Act removed the fetters upon trade union activities, which according to judicial construction § 20 of the Clayton Act had left untouched, by still further narrowing the circumstances under which the federal courts could grant injunctions in labor disputes. More especially, the Act explicitly formulated the "public policy of the United States" in regard to the industrial conflict, and by its light established that the allowable area of union activity was not to be restricted, . . . , to an immediate employer-employee relation. Therefore, whether trade union conduct constitutes a violation of the Sherman Law is to be determined only by reading the Sherman Law and § 20 of the Clayton Act and the Norris-La Guardia Act as a harmonizing text of outlawry of labor conduct.

Were, then, the acts charged against the defendants prohibited, or permitted, by these three interlacing statutes? If the facts laid in the indictment come within the conduct enumerated in § 20 of the Clayton Act, they do not constitute a crime within the general terms of the Sherman Law because of the explicit command of that section that such conduct shall not be "considered or held to be violations of any law of the United States." So long as a union acts in its self-interest and does not combine with non-labor groups, the licit and the illicit under § 20 are not to be distinguished by any judgment regarding the wisdom or unwisdom, the rightness or wrongness, the selfishness or unselfishness of the end of which the particular union activities are the means. There is nothing remotely within the terms of § 20 that differentiates between trade union conduct directed against an employer because of a controversy arising in the relation between employer and employee, as such, and conduct similarly directed but ultimately due to an internecine struggle between two unions seeking the favor of the same employer. Such strife between competing unions has been an obdurate conflict in the evolution of so-called craft unionism and has undoubtedly been one of the potent forces in the modern development of industrial unions. These conflicts have intensified industrial tension but there is not the slightest warrant for saying that Congress has made § 20 inapplicable to trade union conduct resulting from them.

Insofar as the Clayton Act is concerned, we must therefore dispose of this case as though we had before us precisely the same conduct on the part of the defendants in pressing claims against Anheuser-Busch for increased wages, or shorter hours, or other elements of what are called working conditions. The fact that what was done was done in a competition for jobs against the Machinists rather than against, let us say, a company union is a differentiation which Congress has not put into the federal legislation and which therefore we cannot write into it.

It is at once apparent that the acts with which the defendants are charged are the kind of acts protected by § 20 of the Clayton Act. The refusal of the Carpenters to work for Anheuser-Busch or on construction work being done for it and its adjoining tenant, and the peaceful attempt to get members of other unions similarly to refuse to work, are plainly within the free scope accorded to workers by § 20 for "terminating any relation of employment," or "ceasing to perform any work or labor," or "recommending, advising, or persuading others by peaceful means so to do." The picketing of Anheuser-Busch premises with signs to indicate that Anheuser-Busch was unfair to organized labor, a familiar practice in these situations, comes within the language "attending at any place where any such person or persons may lawfully be, for the purpose of peacefully obtaining or communicating information, or from peacefully persuading any person to work or to abstain from working." Finally, the recommendation to union members and their friends not to buy or use the product of Anheuser-Busch is explicitly covered by "ceasing to patronize . . . any party to such dispute, or from recommending, advising, or persuading others by peaceful and lawful means so to do."

Clearly, then, the facts here charged constitute lawful conduct under the Clayton Act unless the defendants cannot invoke that Act because outsiders to the immediate dispute also shared in the conduct. But we need not determine whether the conduct is legal within the restrictions . . . to the immunities of § 20 of the Clayton Act. Congress in the Norris-La Guardia Act has expressed the public policy of the United States and defined its conception of a "labor dispute" in terms that no longer leave room for doubt. . . . This was done, as we recently said, in order to "obviate the results of the judicial construction" theretofore given the Clayton Act. . . . Such a dispute, § 13 (c) provides, "includes any controversy concerning terms or conditions of employment, or concerning the association or representation of persons in negotiating, fixing, maintaining, changing, or seeking to arrange terms or conditions of employment, regardless of whether or not the disputants stand in the proximate relation of employer and employee." And under § 13 (b) a person is "participating or interested in a labor dispute" if he "is engaged in the same industry, trade, craft, or occupation, in which such dispute occurs, or has a direct or indirect interest therein, or is a member, officer, or agent of any association composed in whole or in part of employers or employees engaged in such industry, trade, craft, or occupation."

To be sure, Congress expressed this national policy and determined the bounds of a labor dispute in an act explicitly dealing with the further withdrawal of injunctions in labor controversies. But to argue, as it was urged before us, that the *Duplex* case still governs for purposes of a criminal prosecution is to say that that which on the equity side of the court is allowable conduct may in a criminal proceeding become the road to prison. It would be strange indeed that although neither the Government nor Anheuser-Busch could have sought an injunction against the acts here challenged, the elaborate efforts to permit such conduct failed to prevent criminal liability punishable with imprisonment and heavy fines. That is not the way to read the will of Congress, particularly when expressed by a statute which, as we have already indicated, is practically and historically one of a series of enactments touching one of the most sensitive national problems. Such legislation must not be read in a spirit of mutilating narrowness. On matters far less vital and far less interrelated we have had occasion to point out the importance of giving "hospitable scope" to Congressional purpose even when meticulous words are lacking. . . . The appropriate way to read legislation in a situation like the one before us, was indicated by Mr. Justice Holmes on circuit: "A statute may indicate or require as its justification a change in the policy of the law, although it expresses that change only in the specific cases most likely to occur in the mind. The Legislature has the power to decide what the policy of the law shall be, and if it has intimated its will, however indirectly, that will should be recognized and obeyed. The major premise of the conclusion expressed in a statute, the change of policy that induces the enactment, may not be set out in terms, but it is not an adequate discharge of duty for the courts to say: We see what you are driving at, but you have not said it, and therefore we shall go on as before." ...

The relation of the Norris-La Guardia Act to the Clayton Act is not that of a tightly drawn amendment to a technically phrased tax provision. The underlying aim of the Norris-La Guardia Act was to restore the broad purpose which Congress thought it had formulated in the Clayton Act but which was frustrated, so Congress believed, by unduly restrictive judicial construction. This was authoritatively stated by the House Committee on the Judiciary. "The purpose of the bill is to protect the rights of labor in the same manner the Congress intended when it enacted the Clayton Act, October 15, 1914 (38 Stat. L., 738), which act, by reason of its construction and application by the Federal courts, is ineffectual to accomplish the congressional intent." ... The *Norris-La Guardia Act was a disapproval of Duplex Printing Press Co.* v. *Deering,* ... and *Bedford Cut Stone Co.* v. *Journeymen Stone Cutters' Assn.* ... as the authoritative interpretation of § 20 of the Clayton Act, for Congress now placed its own meaning upon that section. The Norris-La Guardia Act reasserted the original purpose of the Clayton Act by infusing into it the immunized trade union activities as redefined by the later Act. In this light § 20 removes all such allowable conduct from the taint of being a "violation of any law of the United States," including the Sherman Law.

There is no profit in discussing those cases under the Clayton Act which were decided before the courts were furnished the light shed by the Norris-La Guardia Act on the nature of the industrial conflict. And since the facts in the indictment are made lawful by the Clayton Act in so far as "any law of the United States" is concerned, it would be idle to consider the Sherman Law apart from the Clayton Act as interpreted by Congress. . . . It was precisely in order to minimize the difficulties to which the general language of the Sherman Law in its application to workers had given rise, that Congress cut through all the tangled verbalisms and enumerated concretely the types of activities which had become familiar incidents of union procedure.

Affirmed.

• • •

CASE QUESTIONS

1. How does the Clayton Act differentiate between the purposes of union activities?

2. What effect do the Clayton and Norris-La Guardia Acts have on the determination of criminal liability under the Sherman Act?

NLRB v. JONES & LAUGHLIN STEEL CORPORATION
United States Supreme Court
301 U.S. 1 (1937)

• • •

MR. CHIEF JUSTICE HUGHES delivered the opinion of the Court.

In a proceeding under the National Labor Relations Act of 1935, the National Labor Relations Board found that the respondent, Jones & Laughlin Steel Corporation, had violated the Act by engaging in unfair labor practices affecting commerce. The proceeding was instituted by the Beaver Valley Lodge No. 200, affiliated with the Amalgamated Association of Iron, Steel and Tin Workers of America, a labor organization. The unfair labor practices charged were that the corporation was discriminating against members of the union with regard to hire and tenure of employment, and was coercing and intimidating its employees in order to interfere with their self-organization. The discriminatory and coercive action alleged was the discharge of certain employees.

The National Labor Relations Board, sustaining the charge, ordered the corporation to cease and desist from such discrimination and coercion, to offer reinstatement to ten of the employees named, to make good their losses in pay, and to post for thirty days notices that the corporation would not discharge or discriminate against members, or those desiring to become members, of the labor union. As the corporation failed to comply, the Board petitioned the Circuit Court of Appeals to enforce the order. The court denied the petition, holding that the order lay beyond the range of federal power. . . . We granted certiorari.

The scheme of the National Labor Relations Act—which is too long to be quoted in full—may be briefly stated. The first section sets forth findings with respect to the injury to commerce resulting from the denial by employers of the right of employees to organize and from the refusal of employers to accept the procedure of collective bargaining. There follows a declaration that it is the policy of the United States to eliminate these causes of obstruction to the free flow of commerce. The Act then defines the terms it uses, including the terms "commerce" and "affecting commerce." § 2. It creates the National Labor Relations Board and prescribes its organization. §§ 3—6. It sets forth the right of employees to self-organization and to bargain collectively through representatives of their own choosing. § 7. It defines "unfair labor practices." § 8. It lays down rules as to the representation of employees for the purpose of collective bargaining. § 9. The Board is empowered to prevent the described unfair labor practices affecting commerce and the Act prescribes the procedure to that end. The Board is authorized to petition designated courts to secure the enforcement of its orders. The findings of the Board as to the facts, if supported by evidence, are to be conclusive. If either party on application to the court shows that additional evidence is material and that there were reasonable grounds for the failure to adduce such evidence in the hearings before the Board, the court may order the additional evidence to be taken. Any person aggrieved by a final order of the Board may obtain a review in the designated courts with the same procedure as in the case of an application by the Board for the enforcement of its order. § 10. The Board has broad powers of investigation. § 11. Interference with members of the Board or its agents in the performance of their duties is punishable by fine and imprisonment. § 12. Nothing in the Act is to be construed to interfere with the right to strike. . . .

The procedure in the instant case followed the statute. The labor union filed with the Board its verified charge. The Board thereupon issued its complaint against the respondent alleging that its action in discharging the employees in question constituted unfair labor practices affecting commerce within the meaning of § 8, subdivisions (1) and (3), and § 2, subdivisions (6) and (7) of the Act. Respondent, appearing specially for the purpose of objecting to the jurisdiction of the Board, filed its answer. Respondent admitted the discharges, but alleged that they were made because of inefficiency or violation of rules or for other good reasons and were not ascribable to union membership or activities. As an affirmative defense respondent challenged the constitutional validity of the statute and its applicability in the instant case, notice of hearing was given and respondent appeared by counsel. The Board first took up the issue of jurisdiction, and evidence was presented by both the Board and the respondent. Respondent then moved to dismiss the complaint for lack of jurisdiction; and, on denial of that motion, respondent in accordance with its special appearance withdrew from further participation in the hearing. The Board received evidence upon the merits and at its close made its findings and order.

Contesting the ruling of the Board, the respondent argues (1) that the Act is in reality a regulation of labor relations and not of interstate commerce; (2) that the Act can have no application to the respondent's relations with its production employees because they are not subject to regulation by the federal government; and (3) that the provisions of the Act violate § 2 of Article III and the Fifth and Seventh Amendments of the Constitution of the United States.

The facts as to the nature and scope of the business of the Jones & Laughlin Steel Corporation have been found by the Labor Board and, so far as they are essential to the determination of this controversy, they are not in dispute. The Labor Board has found: The corporation is organized under the laws of Pennsylvania and has its principal office at Pittsburgh. It is engaged in the business of manufacturing iron and steel in plants situated in Pittsburgh and nearby Aliquippa, Pennsylvania. It manufactures and distributes a widely diversified line of steel and pig iron, being the fourth largest producer of steel in the United States. With its subsidiaries—nineteen in number—it is a completely integrated enterprise, owning and operating ore, coal and limestone properties, lake and river transportation facilities and terminal railroads located at its manufacturing plants. It owns or controls mines in Michigan and Minnesota. It operates four ore steamships on the Great Lakes, used in the transportation of ore to its factories. It owns coal mines in Pennsylvania. It operates towboats and steam barges used in carrying coal to its factories. It owns limestone properties in various places in Pennsylvania and West Virginia. It owns the Monongahela connecting railroad which connects the plants of the Pittsburgh works and forms an interconnection with the Pennsylvania, New York Central and Baltimore and Ohio Railroad systems. It owns the Aliquippa and Southern Railroad Company which connects the Aliquippa works with the Pittsburgh and Lake Erie, part of the New York Central system. Much of its product is shipped to its warehouses in Chicago, Detroit, Cincinnati, and Memphis—to the last two places by means of its own barges and transportation equipment. In Long Island City, New York, and in New Orleans it operates structural steel fabricating shops in connection with the warehousing of semi-finished materials sent from its works. Through one of its wholly-owned subsidiaries it owns, leases, and operates stores, warehouses and yards for the distribution of equipment and supplies for drilling and operating oil and gas wells and for pipe lines, refineries and pumping stations. It has sales offices in twenty cities in the United States and a wholly-owned subsidiary which is devoted exclusively to distributing its product in Canada. Approximately 75 percent of its product is shipped out of Pennsylvania.

Summarizing these operations, the Labor Board concluded that the works in Pittsburgh and Aliquippa "might be likened to the heart of a self-contained, highly integrated body. They draw in the raw materials from Michigan, Minnesota, West Virginia, [and] Pennsylvania in part through arteries and by means controlled by the respondent; they transform the materials and then pump them out to all parts of the nation through the vast mechanism which the respondent has elaborated."

To carry on the activities of the entire steel industry, 33,000 men mine ore, 44,000 men mine coal, 4,000 men quarry limestone, 16,000 men manufacture coke, 343,000 men manufacture steel, and 83,000 men transport its product. Respondent has about 10,000 employees in its Aliquippa plant, which is located in a community of about 30,000 persons. . . .

Practically all the factual evidence in the case, except that which dealt with the nature of respondent's business, concerned its relations with the employees in the Aliquippa plant whose discharge was the subject of the complaint. These employees were active leaders in the labor union. Several were officers and others were leaders of particular groups. Two of the employees were motor inspectors; one was a tractor driver; three were crane operators; one was a washer in the coke plant; and three were laborers. Three other employees were mentioned in the complaint, but it was withdrawn as to one of them; and no evidence was heard on the action taken with respect to the other two.

While respondent criticises the evidence and the attitude of the Board, which is described as being hostile toward employers and particularly toward those who insisted upon their constitutional rights, respondent did not take advantage of its opportunity to present evidence to refute that which was offered to show discrimination and coercion. In this situation, the record presents no ground for setting aside the order of the Board so far as the facts pertaining to the circumstances and purpose of the discharge of the employees are concerned. Upon that point it is sufficient to say that the evidence supports the findings of the Board that respondent discharged these men "because of their union activity and for the purpose of discouraging membership in the union." We turn to the questions of law which respondent urges in contesting the validity and application of the Act.

First. The scope of the Act. The Act is challenged in its entirety as an attempt to regulate all industry, thus invading the reserved powers of the States over their local concerns. It is asserted that the references in the Act to interstate and foreign commerce are colorable at best; that the Act is not a true regulation of such commerce or of matters which directly affect it but on the contrary has the fundamental object of placing under the compulsory supervision of the federal government all industrial labor relations within the nation. The argument seeks support in the broad words of the preamble (section one) and in the sweep of the provisions of the Act, and it is further insisted that its legislative history shows an essential universal purpose in the light of which its scope cannot be limited by either construction or by the application of the separability clause.

If this conception of terms, intent and consequent inseparability were sound, the Act would necessarily fall by reason of the limitation upon the federal power which inheres in the constitutional grant, as well as because of the explicit reservation of the Tenth Amendment. . . . The authority of the federal government may not be pushed to such an extreme as to destroy the distinction, which the commerce clause itself establishes, between commerce "among the several States" and the internal concerns of a State. That distinction between what is national and what is local in the activities of commerce is vital to the maintenance of our federal system. . . .

We think it clear that the National Labor Relations Act may be construed so as to operate within the sphere of constitutional authority. The jurisdiction conferred upon the Board, and invoked in this instance, is found in § 10 (a), which provides:

"Sec. 10 (a). The Board is empowered, as hereinafter provided, to prevent any person from engaging in any unfair labor practice (listed in section 8) affecting commerce."

The critical words of this provision, prescribing the limits of the Board's authority in dealing with the labor practices, are "affecting commerce." The Act specifically defines the "commerce" to which it refers (§ 2 (6)):

"The term 'commerce' means trade, traffic, commerce, transportation, or communication among the several States. . . ."

There can be no question that the commerce thus contemplated by the Act (aside from that within a Territory or the District of Columbia) is interstate and foreign commerce in the constitutional sense. The Act also defines the term "affecting commerce" (§ 2 (7)):

"The term 'affecting commerce' means in commerce, or burdening or obstructing commerce or the free flow of commerce, or having led or tending to lead to a labor dispute burdening or obstructing commerce or the free flow of commerce."

. . . Whether or not particular action does affect commerce in such a close and intimate fashion as to be subject to federal control, and hence to lie within the authority conferred upon the Board, is left by the statute to be determined as individual cases arise. We are thus to inquire whether in the instant case the constitutional boundary has been passed.

Second. The unfair labor practices in question. The unfair labor practices found by the Board are those defined in § 8, subdivisions (1) and (3). These provide:

Sec. 8. It shall be an unfair labor practice for an employer—

"(1) To interfere with, restrain, or coerce employees in the exercise of the rights guaranteed in section 7."

"(3) By discrimination in regard to hire or tenure of employment or any term or condition of employment to encourage or discourage membership in any labor organization: . . ."

Section 8, subdivision (1), refers to § 7, which is as follows:

"Sec. 7. Employees shall have the right to self-organization, to form, join, or assist labor organizations, to bargain collectively through representatives of their own choosing, and to engage in concerted activities, for the purpose of collective bargaining or other mutual aid or protection."

Thus, in its present application, the statute goes no further than to safeguard the right of employees to self-organization and to select representatives of their own choosing for collective bargaining or other mutual protection without restraint or coercion by their employer.

That is a fundamental right. Employees have as clear a right to organize and select their representatives for lawful purposes as the respondent has to organize its business and select its own officers and agents. Discrimination and coercion to prevent the free exercise of the right of employees to self-organization and representation is a proper subject for condemnation by competent legislative authority. . . .

Third. The application of the Act to employees engaged in production.—The principle involved. Respondent says that whatever may be said of employees engaged in interstate commerce, the industrial relations and activities in the manufacturing department of respondent's enterprise are not subject to federal regulation. The argument rests upon the proposition that manufacturing in itself is not commerce. . . .

We do not find it necessary to determine whether these features of defendant's business dispose of the asserted analogy to the "stream of commerce" cases. The instances in which that metaphor has been used are but particular, and not exclusive, illustrations of the protective power which the Government invokes in support of the present Act. The congressional authority to protect interstate commerce from burdens and obstructions is not limited to transactions which can be deemed to be an essential part of a "flow" of interstate or foreign commerce. Burdens and obstructions may be due to injurious action springing from other sources. The fundamental principle is that the power to regulate commerce is the power to enact "all appropriate legislation" for "its protection and advancement. . . ."

. . . Although activities may be intrastate in character when separately considered, if they have such a close and substantial relation to interstate commerce that their control is essential or appropriate to protect that commerce from burdens and obstructions, Congress cannot be denied the power to exercise that control. . . . Undoubtedly the scope of this power must be considered in the light of our dual system of government and may not be extended so as to embrace effects upon interstate commerce so indirect and remote that to embrace them, in view of our complex society, would effectually obliterate the distinction between what is national and what is local and create a completely centralized government. The question is necessarily one of degree. . . .

The close and intimate effect which brings the subject within the reach of federal power may be due to activities in relation to productive industry although the industry when separately viewed is local. This has been abundantly illustrated in the application of the federal Anti-Trust Act. ...

It is thus apparent that the fact that the employees here concerned were engaged in production is not determinative. The question remains as to the effect upon interstate commerce of the labor practice involved. ...

Fourth. *Effects of the unfair labor practice in respondent's enterprise.* Giving full weight to respondent's contention with respect to a break in the complete continuity of the "stream of commerce" by reason of respondent's manufacturing operations, the fact remains that the stoppage of those operations by industrial strife would have a most serious effect upon interstate commerce. In view of respondent's far-flung activities, it is idle to say that the effect would be indirect or remote. It is obvious that it would be immediate and might be catastrophic. We are asked to shut our eyes to the plainest facts of our national life and to deal with the question of direct and indirect effects in an intellectual vacuum. Because there may be but indirect and remote effects upon interstate commerce in connection with a host of local enterprises throughout the country, it does not follow that other industrial activities do not have such a close and intimate relation to interstate commerce as to make the presence of industrial strife a matter of the most urgent national concern. When industries organize themselves on a national scale, making their relation to interstate commerce the dominant factor in their activities, how can it be maintained that their industrial labor relations constitute a forbidden field into which Congress may not enter when it is necessary to protect interstate commerce from the paralyzing consequences of industrial war? We have often said that interstate commerce itself is a practical conception. It is equally true that interferences with that commerce must be appraised by a judgment that does not ignore actual experience.

Experience has abundantly demonstrated that the recognition of the right of employees to self-organization and to have representatives of their own choosing for the purpose of collective bargaining is often an essential condition of industrial peace. Refusal to confer and negotiate has been one of the most prolific causes of strife. This is such an outstanding fact in the history of labor disturbances that it is a proper subject of judicial notice and requires no citation of instances. . . . The opinion . . . also points to the large measure of success of the labor policy embodied in the Railway Labor Act. But with respect to the appropriateness of the recognition of self-organization and representation in the promotion of peace, the question is not essentially different in the case of employees in industries of such a character that interstate commerce is put in jeopardy from the case of employees of transportation companies. And of what avail is it to protect the facility of transportation, if interstate commerce is throttled with respect to the commodities to be transported!

These questions have frequently engaged the attention of Congress and have been the subject of many inquires. The steel industry is one of the great basic industries of the United States, with ramifying activities affecting interstate commerce at every point. The Government aptly refers to the steel strike of 1919-1920 with its far-reaching consequences. The fact that there appears to have been no major distrubance in that industry in the more recent period did not dispose of the possibilities of future and like dangers to interstate commerce which Congress was entitled to foresee and to exercise its protective power to forestall. It is not necessary again to detail the facts as to respondent's enterprise. Instead of being beyond the pale, we think that it presents in a most striking way the close and intimate relation which a manufacturing industry may have to interstate commerce, and we have no doubt that Congress had constitutional authority to safeguard the right of respondent's employees to self-organization and freedom in the choice of representatives for collective bargaining.

Fifth. The means which the Act employs—Questions under the due process clause and other constitutional restrictions. Respondent asserts its right to conduct its business in an orderly manner without being subjected to arbitrary restraints. What we have said points to the fallacy in the argument. Employees have their correlative right to organize for the purpose of securing the redress of grievances and to promote agreements with employers relating to rates of pay and conditions of work. . . .

The Act does not compel agreements between employers and employees. It does not compel any agreement whatever. It does not prevent the employer "from refusing to make a collective contract and hiring individuals on whatever terms" the employer "may be unilateral action determine." The Act expressly provides in § 9 (a) that any individual employee or a group of employees shall have the right at any time to present grievances to their employer. The theory of the Act is that free opportunity for negotiation with accredited representatives of employees is likely to promote industrial peace and may bring about the adjustments and agreements which the Act in itself does not attempt to compel. . . . [O]n the other hand, the Board is not entitled to make its authority a pretext for interference with the right of discharge when that right is exercised for other reasons than such intimidation and coercion. The true purpose is the subject of investigation with full opportunity to show the facts. It would seem that when employers freely recognize the right of their employees to their own organizations and their unrestricted right of representation, there will be much less occasion for controversy in respect to the free and appropriate exercise of the right of selection and discharge.

The Act has been criticised as one-sided in its application; that it subjects the employer to supervision and restraint and leaves untouched the abuses for which employees may be responsible; that it fails to provide a more comprehensive plan—with better assurances of fairness to both sides and with increased chances of success in bringing about, if not compelling, equitable solutions of industrial disputes affecting interstate commerce. But we are dealing with the power of Congress, not with a particular policy or with the extent to which policy should go. We have frequently said that the legislative authority, exerted within its proper field, need not embrace all the evils within its reach. The Constitution does not forbid "cautious advance, step by step," in dealing with the evils which are exhibited in activities within the range of legislative power. . . .

The instant case is not a suit at common law or in the nature of such a suit. The proceeding is one unknown to the common law. It is a statutory proceeding. Reinstatement of the employee and payment for time lost are requirements imposed for violation of the statute and are remedies appropriate to its enforcement. The contention under the Seventh Amendment is without merit.

Our conclusion is that the order of the Board was within its competency and that the Act is valid as here applied. The judgment of the Circuit Court of Appeals is reversed and the cause is remanded for further proceedings in conformity with this opinion.

Reversed.

• • •

CASE QUESTIONS

1. What factors did the Court consider in reaching the conclusion that the activities of Jones & Laughlin were interstate in character?

2. What rights of self-organization were granted to employees under the National Labor Relations Act, and what means were established for protection of such rights?

UNIVERSAL CAMERA CORPORATION v. NLRB
United States Supreme Court
340 U.S. 474 (1951)

• • •

MR. JUSTICE FRANKFURTER delivered the opinion of the Court.

The essential issue raised by this case and its companion, *Labor Board* v. *Pittsburgh Steamship Co., . . . ,* is the effect of the Administrative Procedure Act and the legislation colloquially known as the Taft-Hartley Act on the duty of Courts of Appeals when called upon to review orders of the National Labor Relations Board.

The Court of Appeals for the Second Circuit granted enforcement of an order directing, in the main, that petitioner reinstate with back pay an employee found to have been discharged because he gave testimony under the Wagner Act and cease and desist from discriminating against any employee who files charges or gives testimony under that Act. The court below, Judge Swan dissenting, decreed full enforcement of the order. . . . Because the views of that court regarding the effect of the new legislation on the relation between the Board and the Courts of Appeals in the enforcement of the Board's orders conflicted with those of the Court of Appeals for the Sixth Circuit, we brought both cases here . . . The clash of opinion obviously required settlement by this Court.

I.

Want of certainty in judicial review of Labor Board decisions partly ▬ reflects the intractability of any formula to furnish definiteness of content for all the impalpable factors involved in judicial review. But in part doubts as to the nature of the reviewing power and uncertainties in its application derive from history, and to that extent an elucidation of this history may clear them away.

The Wagner Act provided: "The findings of the Board as to the facts, if supported by evidence, shall be conclusive." Act of July 5,1935, § 10(e). ... 29 U. S. C. § 160(e). ... This Court read "evidence" to mean "substantial evidence," . . . , and we said that "[s]ubstantial evidence is more than a mere scintilla. It means such relevant evidence as a reasonable mind might accept as adequate to support a conclusion." . . . Accordingly, it "must do more than create a suspicion of the existence of the fact to be established. ... it must be enough to justify, if the trial were to a jury, a refusal to direct a verdict when the conclusion sought to be drawn from it is one of fact for the jury."

The very smoothness of the "substantial evidence" formula as the standard for reviewing the evidentiary validity of the Board's findings established its currency. But the inevitably variant applications of the standard to conflicting evidence soon brought contrariety of views and in due course bred criticism. Even though the whole record may have been canvassed in order to determine whether the evidentiary foundation of a determination by the Board was "substantial," the phrasing of this Court's process of review readily lent itself to the notion that it was enough that the evidence supporting the Board's result was "substantial" when considered by itself. It is fair to say that by imperceptible steps regard for the fact-finding function of the Board led to the assumption that the requirements of the Wagner Act were met when the reviewing court could find in the record evidence which, when viewed in isolation, substantiated the Board's findings. ... This is not to say that every member of this Court was consciously guided by this view or that the Court ever explicitly avowed this practice as doctrine. What matters is that the belief justifiably arose that the Court had so construed the obligation to review.

Criticism of so contracted a reviewing power reinforced dissatisfaction felt in various quarters with the Board's administration of the Wagner Act in the years preceding the war. The scheme of the Act was attacked as an inherently unfair fusion of the functions of prosecutor and judge. Accusations of partisan bias were not wanting. The "irresponsible admission and weighing of hearsay, opinion, and emotional speculation in place of factual evidence" was said to be a "serious menace." No doubt some, perhaps even much, of the criticism was baseless and some surely was reckless. What is here relevant, however, is the climate of opinion thereby generated and its effect on Congress. Protests against "shocking injustices" and intimations of judicial "abdication" with which some courts granted enforcement of the Board's orders stimulated pressures for legislative relief from alleged administrative excesses. ...

Similar dissatisfaction with too restricted application of the "substantial evidence" test is reflected in the legislative history of the Taft-Hartley Act. The bill as reported to the House provided that the "findings of the Board as to the facts shall be conclusive unless it is made to appear to the satisfaction of the court either (1) that the findings of fact are against the manifest weight of the evidence, or (2) that the findings of fact are not supported by substantial evidence." The bill left the House with this provision. Early committee prints in the Senate provided for review by "weight of the evidence" or "clearly erroneous" standards. But, as the Senate Committee Report relates, "it was finally decided to conform the statute to the corresponding section of the Administrative Procedure Act where the substantial evidence test prevails. In order to clarify any ambiguity in that statute, however, the committee inserted the words 'questions of fact, if supported by substantial evidence *on the record considered as a whole. . . .'*"

This phraseology was adopted by the Senate. The House conferees agreed. ... The Senate version became the law.

It is fair to say that in all this Congress expressed a mood. And it expressed its mood not merely by oratory but by legislation. As legislation that mood must be respected, even though it can only serve as a standard for judgment and not as a body of rigid rules assuring sameness of application. Enforcement of such broad standards implies subtlety of mind and solidity of judgment. But it is not for us to question that Congress may assume such qualities in the federal judiciary.

From the legislative story we have summarized, two concrete conclusions do emerge. One is the identity of aim of the Administrative Procedure Act and the Taft-Hartley Act regarding the proof with which the Labor Board must support a decision. The other is that now Congress has left no room for doubt as to the kind of scrutiny which a Court of Appeals must give the record before the Board to satisfy itself that the Board's order rests on adequate proof.

It would be mischievous word-playing to find that the scope of review under the Taft-Hartley Act is any different from that under the Administrative Procedure Act. The Senate Committee which reported the review clause of the Taft-Hartley Act expressly indicated that the two standards were to conform in this regard, and the wording of the two Acts is for purposes of judicial administration identical. And so we hold that the standard of proof specifically required of the Labor Board by the Taft-Hartley Act is the same as that to be exacted by courts reviewing every administrative action subject to the Administrative Procedure Act.

Whether or not it was ever permissible for courts to determine the substantiality of evidence supporting a Labor Board decision merely on the basis of evidence which in and of itself justified it, without taking into account contradictory evidence or evidence from which conflicting inferences could be drawn, the new legislation definitively precludes such a theory of review and bars its practice. The substantiality of evidence must take into account whatever in the record fairly detracts from its weight. This is clearly the significance of the requirement in both statutes that courts consider the whole record. Committee reports and the adoption in the Administrative Procedure Act of the minority views of the Attorney General's Committee demonstrate that to enjoin such a duty on the reviewing court was one of the important purposes of the movement which eventuated in that enactment.

To be sure, the requirement for canvassing "the whole record" in order to ascertain substantiality does not furnish a calculus of value by which a reviewing court can assess the evidence. Nor was it intended to negate the function of the Labor Board as one of those agencies presumably equipped or informed by experience to deal with a specialized field of knowledge, whose findings within that field carry the authority of an expertness which courts do not possess and therefore must respect. Nor does it mean that even as to matters not requiring expertise, a court may displace the Board's choice between two fairly conflicting views, even though the court would justifiably have made a different choice had the matter been before it *de novo.* Congress has merely made it clear that a reviewing court is not barred from setting aside a Board decision when it cannot conscientiously find that the evidence supporting that decision is substantial, when viewed in the light that the record in its entirety furnishes, including the body of evidence opposed to the Board's view.

There remains, then, the question whether enactment of these two statutes has altered the sope of review other than to require that substantiality be determined in the light of all that the record relevantly presents. A formula for judicial review of administrative action may afford grounds for certitude but cannot assure certainty of application. Some scope for judicial discretion in applying the formula can be avoided only by falsifying the actual process of judging or by using the formula as an instrument of futile casuistry. It cannot be too often repeated that judges are not automata. The ultimate reliance for the fair operation of any standard is a judiciary of high competence and character and the constant play of an informed professional critique upon its work.

Since the precise way in which courts interfere with agency findings cannot be imprisoned within any form of words, new formulas attempting to rephrase the old are not likely to be more helpful than the old. There are no talismanic words that can avoid the process of judgment. The difficulty is that we cannot escape, in relation to this problem, the use of undefined defining terms.

Whatever changes were made by the Administrative Procedure and Taft-Hartley Acts are clearly within this area where precise definition is impossible. Retention of the familiar "substantial evidence" terminolgy indicates that no drastic reversal of attitude was intended. ...

We conclude, therefore, that the Administrative Procedure Act and the Taft-Hartley Act direct that courts must now assume more responsibility for the reasonableness and fairness of Labor Board decisions than some courts have shown in the past. Reviewing courts must be influenced by a feeling that they are not to abdicate the conventional judicial function. Congress has imposed on them responsibility for assuring that the Board keeps within reasonable grounds. That responsibility is not less real because it is limited to enforcing the requirement that evidence appear substantial when viewed, on the record as a whole, by courts invested with the authority and enjoying the prestige of the Courts of Appeals. The Board's findings are entitled to respect; but they must nonetheless be set aside when the record before a Court of Appeals clearly precludes the Board's decision from being justified by a fair estimate of the worth of the testimony of witnesses or its informed judgment on matters within its special competence or both.

From this it follows that enactment of these statutes does not require every Court of Appeals to alter its practice. Some—perhaps a majority—have always applied the attitude reflected in this legislation. To explore whether a particular court should or should not alter its practice would only divert attention from the application of the standard now prescribed to a futile inquiry into the nature of the test formerly used by a particular court.

Our power to review the correctness of application of the present standard ought seldom to be called into action. Whether on the record as a whole there is substantial evidence to support agency findings is a question which Congress has placed in the keeping of the Courts of Appeals. This Court will intervene only in what ought to be the rare instance when the standard appears to have been misapprehended or grossly misapplied.

II.

Our disagreement with the view of the court below that the scope of review of Labor Board decisions is unaltered by recent legislation does not itself, as we have noted, require reversal of its decision. The court may have applied a standard of review which satisfies the present Congressional requirement. ...

III.

The Court of Appeals deemed itself bound by the Board's rejection of the examiner's findings because the court considered these findings not "as unassailable as a master's." They are not. Section 10 (c) of the Labor Management Relations Act provides that "If upon the preponderance of the testimony taken the Board shall be of the opinion that any person named in the complaint has engaged in or is engaging in any such unfair labor practice, then the Board shall state its findings of fact. ..." The responsibility for decision thus placed on the Board is wholly inconsistent with the notion that it has power to reverse an examiner's findings only when they are "clearly erroneous." Such a limitation would make so drastic a departure from prior administrative practice that explicitness would be required.

The Court of Appeals concluded from this premise "that, although the Board would be wrong in totally disregarding his findings, it is practically impossible for a court, upon review of those findings which the Board itself substitutes, to consider the Board's reversal as a factor in the court's own decision. This we say, because we cannot find any middle ground between doing that and treating such a reversal as error, whenever it would be such, if done by a judge to a master in equity." ... Much as we respect the logical acumen of the Chief Judge of the Court of Appeals, we do not find ourselves pinioned between the horns of his dilemma.

We are aware that to give the examiner's findings less finality than a master's and yet entitle them to consideration in striking the account, is to introduce another and an unruly factor into the judgmatical process of review. But we ought not to fashion an exclusionary rule merely to reduce the number of imponderables to be considered by reviewing courts.

The Taft-Hartley Act provides that "The findings of the Board with respect to questions of fact if supported by substantial evidence on the record considered as a whole shall be conclusive," . . . Surely an examiner's report is as much a part of the record as the complaint or the testimony. According to the Administrative Procedure Act, "All decisions (including initial, recommended, or tentative decisions) shall become a part of the record. . . ." We found that this Act's provision for judicial review has the same meaning as that in the Taft-Hartley Act. The similarity of the two statutes in language and purpose also requires that the definition of "record" found in the Administrative Procedure Act be construed to be applicable as well to the term "record" as used in the Taft-Hartley Act.

It is therefore difficult to escape the conclusion that the plain language of the statutes directs a reviewing court to determine the substantiality of evidence on the record including the examiner's report. The conclusion is confirmed by the indications in the legislative history that enhancement of the status and function of the trial examiner was one of the important purposes of the movement for administrative reform. . . .

We do not require that the examiner's findings be given more weight than in reason and in the light of judicial experience they deserve. The "substantial evidence" standard is not modified in any way when the Board and its examiner disagree. We intend only to recognize that evidence supporting a conclusion may be less substantial when an impartial, experienced examiner who has observed the witnesses and lived with the case has drawn conclusions different from the Board's than when he has reached the same conclusion. The findings of the examiner are to be considered along with the consistency and inherent probability of testimony. The significance of his report, of course, depends largely on the importance of credibility in the particular case. To give it this significance does not seem to us materially more difficult than to heed the other factors which in sum determine whether evidence is "substantial."

The direction in which the law moves is often a guide for decision of particular cases, and here it serves to confirm our conclusion. However halting its progress, the trend in litigation is toward a rational inquiry into truth, in which the tribunal considers everything "logically probative of some matter requiring to be proved." . . . This Court has refused to accept assumptions of fact which are demonstrably false, . . . , even when agreed to by the parties. . . . Machinery for discovery of evidence has been strengthened; the boundaries of judicial notice have been slowly but perceptibly enlarged. It would reverse this process for courts to deny examiners' findings the probative force they would have in the conduct of affairs outside a courtroom.

We therefore remand the cause to the Court of Appeals. On reconsideration of the record it should accord the findings of the trial examiner the relevance that they reasonably command in answering the comprehensive question whether the evidence supporting the Board's order is substantial. But the court need not limit its reexamination of the case to the effect of that report on its decision. We leave it free to grant or deny enforcement as it thinks the principles expressed in this opinion dictate.

Judgment vacated and cause remanded.

● ● ●

CASE QUESTIONS

1. Why did the Supreme Court not review the facts to determine whether they supported the NLRB's findings and order?

2. What weight should be given by the reviewing court to the findings of the trial examiner?

TRUCK DRIVERS LOCAL 413, INTERNATIONAL BROTHERHOOD OF TEAMSTERS, CHAUFFEURS, WAREHOUSEMEN & HELPERS OF AMERICA v. NLRB
United States Court of Appeals, District of Columbia Circuit
334 F.2d 539 (D.C. Cir. 1964), *cert. denied* 85 S.Ct. 264

● ● ●

J. SKELLY WRIGHT, Circuit Judge:

The National Labor Relations Board has found certain Picket Line, Struck Goods, Subcontracting, and Hazardous Work clauses in the collective bargaining agreements of petitioner unions void under Section 8(e) of the Labor Act. In their Petition to Review and Set Aside, the unions contend that these provisions are outside the prohibitions of § 8(e) because their aim is benefit to the employees of the bargaining unit, not control of, or interference with, the contracting employer's third-party relationships. The Board cross-petitions for enforcement.

A preliminary issue is whether it is the *object,* the *effect,* or the express or implied *terms* of the challenged clauses which are relevant to the § 8(e) charge. The unions suggest an object test, by parity of reasoning with § 8(b) (4) (B)'s secondary boycott provisions. The Trial Examiner, in one of these companion cases, No. 17,663, considered the effect of the clauses to be relevant to their validity under § 8(e), and took extensive evidence of their effect. The Board, however, at the instance of its General Counsel, held that the implementation of a contract was not relevant to its validity under § 8(e), that extrinsic evidence of object alone was not determinative, and that the contract must be tested by its terms, express or implied. ...

The Picket Line Clause

A key provision in the union contracts protects the right of individual employees to refuse to cross picket lines by immunizing them against employer discipline. This picket line clause is broadly worded to achieve maximum application permitted by the law. The Board held that under § 8(e) of the Act the clause may validly apply only to certain types of picket lines; the union apparently would apply it to all. ...

The Board concedes that the contract clause may permissibly operate to protect refusals to cross a picket line where the line is in connection with a *primary* dispute at the *contracting* employer's *own premises.* This seems clearly correct. Employees who refuse to cross such a line are entitled to the same protection as strikers under Sections 7 and 13 of the Act. ... The refusal to cross being a protected activity, the union and the employer may provide by contract that such refusal shall not be grounds for discharge. ...

A different result must be reached where the picket line at the contracting employer's own premises is itself in promotion of a *secondary* strike or boycott. Refusal to cross that line would itself be secondary activity. To the extent that the clause would protect such refusal to cross, it would then be authorizing a secondary strike, and would *pro tanto* be void under § 8(e) of the Act. There is no merit to the unions' suggestion that this clause is outside the reach of § 8(e) because it protects *individual* refusals, not *union*-induced refusals. We read our own cases as having rejected this argument. ...

The Board also held that the clause may validly protect refusals to cross a picket line at the premises of *another* employer if that picket line meets the conditions expressed in the *proviso* to § 8(b) (4) of the Act. Clearly this is the law. ...

The remaining question concerns refusals to cross a picket line at *another* employer's premises where that line does *not* meet the conditions of the § 8(b) (4) *proviso*. The unions maintain that refusal to cross any lawful primary picket line is primary activity under the Act and that protection thereof in the bargaining agreement falls outside the ambit § 8(e). The Board held that refusal to cross a non-*proviso* picket line constitutes secondary activity, and that contractual protection of such activity violates § 8(e).

A useful approach to this question is through the legislative history of the 1959 amendments which incorporated § 8(e) into the Act. The House Labor Committee report stated: "It is settled law that the National Labor Relations Act does not require a truckdriver to cross a primary picket line. ... [T]he employer could agree that he would not require the driver to enter the strikebound plant." ...

It is also clear "that the right to refuse to cross a primary picket line would not be affected by" the hot cargo ban in the bill passed by the Senate. ... "However, in order to set at rest false apprehensions on this score, the [House] committee appended the disclaimer proviso" which appears in the bill as reported by the House Committee. This disclaimer explicitly protected the right of refusal to cross primary picket lines, and the right to sign contracts immunizing such refusals from employer discipline. The entire House Committee bill, however, including this disclaimer, was replaced by the Landrum-Griffin substitute on the floor of the House. But the Landrum-Griffin substitute was unacceptable to the Senate conferees because: "[T]he House [Landrum-Griffin] bill apparently destroys the right to picket a plant and to honor a picket line even in a strike for higher wages. This change in the present law is entirely unacceptable." 1708(3). It seems clear that, at least on this point, the Senate viewpoint was adopted in conference, modifying the Landrum-Griffin version. The Senate conferees secured the insertion of the following broad and all-encompassing declaration of congressional policy in the bill: "*Provided,* That nothing contained in this clause (B) shall be construed to make unlawful, where not otherwise unlawful, any primary strike or primary picketing." Section 8(b) (4) (B). ...

LEGISLATIVE HISTORY OF THE LABOR-MANAGEMENT RE-PORTING AND DISCLOSURE ACT OF 1959 AT 1432-1433.

[The then] Senator Kennedy further stated in a report to the Senate on the Conference: "We have protected the right of employees of a secondary employer, in the case of a primary strike, to refuse to cross a primary strike picket line." 1389(1). This stated effect of the Senate-House Conference action seems to have been generally accepted. A speech of Senator Douglas inserted in the Congressional Record shortly afterward explained:

> "Under the compromise, we also protected the right of employees of a secondary employer to refuse to cross a picket line in the case of a primary strike. The Landrum-Griffin bill, as written, appeared to take this right away."

In addition, Professor Cox, now the Solicitor General, who was one of the principal architects of the legislation, has confirmed that the intendment of the Act is that "section 8(e) would not prohibit agreements sanctioning refusal to cross a lawful primary picket line. ..."

Similar conclusions are suggested. ... Since "appealing to neutral employees whose tasks aid the employer's everyday operations" is a "traditional primary activity," ... primary picketing retains its primary characteristic even though it induces deliverymen to refuse to cross the line. Thus it seems clear that refusal to cross a lawful primary picket line, absent demonstrated secondary intent, is itself primary, and as such falls outside the Act's proscriptions against secondary activity. ... Since § 8(e) is limited to secondary activity, a provision in the bargaining agreement immunizing the exercise of this protected right against employer discipline does not violate it.

The Struck Goods Clause

A second section of the collective bargaining agreement which is in dispute concerns Struck Goods. ...

In considering clause (a) of this section, the Board acknowledged that it may lawfully apply where the relationship between the contracting employer and the employer with a labor dispute is so close as to render them "allies." The present state of the struck work—ally doctrine is outlined in [four cases]. ... These cases are specifically cited in the conference report on the 1959 amendments, as representing the existing law which Congress did not intend to supersede. ... Under these decisions, an employer is characterized as an "ally" of the struck firm "when he knowingly does work which would otherwise be done by the striking employees of the primary employer and where this work is paid for by the primary employer pursuant to an arrangement devised and originated by him to enable him to meet his contractual obligations. The result must be the same whether or not the primary employer makes any direct arrangement with the employers providing the services." ...

Judge Learned Hand phrased the test: "One does not make oneself a party to the dispute with a primary employer by taking over the business that the strike has prevented him from doing. On the other hand if a secondary employer, knowing of the strike, not only accepts the customer of the primary employer but takes his pay, not from the customer but from the primary employer . . . [then he has] made common cause with the primary employer." . . .

We agree with the Board that to the extent clause (a) protects refusals to work beyond the scope of the ally doctrine, it authorizes a secondary boycott, and so is *pro tanto* void under § 8(e) of the Labor Act. We refrain from defining the exact limits of the ally doctrine, however, and do not decide whether the tests are adequate for all variations in factual situations. Such spelling out is best left for the elucidating process of gradual inclusion and exclusion provided by specific cases.

Clause (b) of the Struck Goods section, set out above, seems to be a typical hot cargo clause, prohibited by § 8(e) of the Act. The unions contend, however, that this clause—like others in the contract—is immune from § 8(e)'s prohibition because it protects the freedom of decision of the individual laborer, rather than creates a power of decision in the union itself. Since few workers will exercise their rights under these clauses, the unions argue, there will be no substantial interference with the business of the employer, particularly in view of the provisions of clause (c). The short answer to this contention is that it has already been rejected by this court. ... Moreover, the legislative history of the 1959 amendments equates these "employee-rights" clauses with other hot cargo clauses. It is clear that § 8(e) was aimed, among other targets, at provisions in contracts under which an employer agrees: he cannot "require his employees to handle any [goods] which . . . came from an employer engaged in a labor dispute," . . . he cannot "require his employees to handle goods or provide other services for the benefit of an employer who is involved in a labor dispute," . . . "that his employees do not have to handle goods which the union labels as 'hot,' " . . . "his employees do not have to handle or work on goods produced or handled by another employer who happens to be in disfavor with the union," . . . he will "not . . . carry the goods and not . . . require his employees to handle them. . . ."

We must conclude, therefore, as did the Board, that this clause (b) is void under § 8(e) of the Act and that clause (c) does not save it.

The Subcontracting Clause

The third major challenged provision of the collective bargaining agreements here concerns Subcontracting:

> "The Employer agrees to refrain from using the services of any person who does not observe the wages, hours and conditions of employment established by labor unions having juridsiction over the type of services performed."

The Board found this clause was secondary, and therefore void under § 8(e) of the Act. It reasoned:

"Like the typical hot cargo clause itself, a subcontractor clause is secondary where it limits, *not the fact of subcontracting*—either prohibiting it outright or conditioning it upon, e. g., current full employment in the unit—but the *persons with whom* the signatory employer may subcontract. ...."

This Board position groups together, as secondary, contract clauses which impose boycotts on subcontractors not signatory to union agreements, and those which merely require subcontractors to meet the equivalent of union standards in order to protect the work standards of the employees of the contracting employer. But the distinction between these two types of clauses is vital. Union-signatory subcontracting clauses are secondary, and therefore within the scope of § 8(e), while union-standards subcontracting clauses are primary as to the contracting employer. We so held. ...

This clause would be a union-signatory clause if it required subcontractors to have collective bargaining agreements with petitioner unions or their affiliates, or with unions generally. We interpret it, however, as merely requiring that subcontractors observe the equivalent of union wages, hours, and the like. Since we find that this clause only requires union standards, and not union recognition, we follow the line of cases in this court cited above to rule it primary, and thus outside § 8(e)'s prohibitions. ...

We therefore conclude that a decree should be drafted condemning the challenged contract clauses only to the extent found unlawful by this court.

Enforced in part and set aside in part.

• • •

CASE QUESTIONS

1. What statutory criteria determines whether a labor contract is valid where it prohibits the discharge of employees who refuse to cross picket lines?

2. What factors determine the validity of a labor contract that prohibits an employer from dealing with a subcontractor?

UNION EFFORTS AT EMPLOYEE ORGANIZATION

2

Section 8(b)(1) of the National Labor Relations Act declares that it is an unfair labor practice for a labor organization or its agents to restrain or coerce (1) employees in the exercise of their rights to engage in or refuse to engage in concerted activities, and (2) employees in the selection of their representatives for collective bargaining or the adjustment of grievances. While the Act prohibits the threatening of physical violence and the actual committing of such acts, it also makes unlawful lesser forms of coercion. As with other areas of the Act, action for remedying unfair practices in this context has been vested in the National Labor Relations Board. The Board is empowered to take reasonable steps including injunctive relief.

COLLECTIVE BARGAINING

The Act provides that "representatives designated or selected for the purpose of collective bargaining by the majority of the employees in *a unit appropriate for such purposes,* shall be the exclusive representative of all the employees in such units. ..." (Emphasis added.) In practice what is the "appropriate" bargaining unit is often subject to dispute between unions, and between a particular union and the employer. The importance of such determination is easily realized in the situation where, if a union is able to confine the unit to a small size, it will have majority status and recognition; but if the bargaining unit is larger, the union will only represent a minority of employees.

If the parties are unable to determine the parameters of the bargaining unit, then the question must be resolved by the Board. It has established a rule of *community of interests* in making such determinations, but in practice the application of this standard can be difficult. Factors which the Board considers are (1) the bargaining history of the industry and the parties, (2) the organizational structure of the employer, (3) the other interests of the labor organization, (4) the desires of the employees, (5) the extent and type of previous organization of the employees, and (6) similarities in the employees' skills, interests, duties, wages, and working conditions. The Board's obligation is made easier because while it must find an appropriate unit, the grouping need not be the ultimate or *most* appropriate.

The Taft-Hartley amendments excluded supervisors from coverage under the Act. Although employees may be classified or titled as supervisors, it is their duties that determine their status. The determining factors include the exercise or authority to exercise independent judgment, and the power to act as an agent for the employer in relations with other employees—whether or not such power is exercised.

INTRODUCTION TO THE CASES

The cases in this chapter explore the areas of union threats or coercion, the certification of the bargaining unit, the exclusion of certain types of individuals from the bargaining unit, and the duration of union representation. In the *Teamsters Case* the question was whether the union's statements and activities were threats or coercions to the employer. Whether certification of a union should be denied on the ground of the union's conflict of interest between its status as a trade association for independent contractors and its proposed representation of organized employees in the same occupation was at issue in *B & M Kaufmann.*

The *Wichita Eagle & Beacon Publishing Co.* and *City Yellow Cab Co.* cases addressed the determination of individuals as supervisors who would be excluded from the bargaining unit. In *Polytech, Inc.* the issue was the continued recognition of a union by a successor employer.

NLRB v. LOCAL 901, INTERNATIONAL BROTHERHOOD OF TEAMSTERS, CHAUFFEURS, WAREHOUSEMEN & HELPERS OF AMERICA
United States Court of Appeals, First Circuit
314 F.2d 792 (1st Cir. 1963)

• • •

ALDRICH, Circuit Judge.

Respondent, Local 901, the Puerto Rico local of the International Brotherhood of Teamsters, Chauffeurs, Warehousemen and Helpers of America, was found by the Board to have violated sections 8(b) (4) (i) and (ii) (C) of the National Labor Relations Act, in that it "induce[d] or encourage[d]" the employees of Valencia Baxt Express, Inc., hereinafter the employer, to engage in a strike, and "threaten[ed]" the employer, with the object of forcing the employer to recognize respondent, when another union, Seafarers International Union of North America, etc., hereinafter SIU, had been previously certified by the Board. Respondent denies that the evidence warrants a finding that it either induced or encouraged the employees, or that it threatened the employer. It further asserts that, even if it did, the statute did not forbid its so doing after the one year presumption period following certification had expired where it appeared that the certified union was in fact no longer the choice of a majority of the employees, and where it had ceased to represent the employees in any substantial manner.

SIU was certified by the Board to represent the Company's employees on November 4, 1960. Early in the morning of November 6, 1961, respondent's pickets appeared outside the plant carrying a sign, "On strike for recognition—Teamsters Local 901." In fact no strike or interruption of work occurred, nor did the pickets speak to the employees. The Board found that later in the morning respondent's president, one Amador, stated to the officials of the employer, "The men are very itchy; they want to strike. I know of the condition of the company and I know that a work stoppage would kill you, but you have to recognize us because we have the cards and you have to sign a contract with us." The employer replied that it believed respondent had a majority, but declined to deal with it before consulting counsel. Thereupon respondent filed with the Board a request for an election, but did not withdraw the pickets. On November 7 the employer filed an 8(b) (7) (C) charge against respondent and later that day the picketing ceased. The following day SIU filed the instant charge. As a result the Board considered this charge rather than the election petition.

We have serious doubts about the violation of section 8(b) (4) (i). Obviously respondent did not "induce" the employees to strike. We agree that even an unsuccessful attempt may "encourage" employees to strike., . . . but having in mind the rather clear evidence that the great majority of the employees were disgruntled with SIU, and that many had signed respondent's cards, it is hard to say this is what happened here. If respondent already had the men, it would seem that a bona fide encouragement would have been readily successful. Hence there must be doubt whether a real attempt was made. Rather, the thrust of respondent's activities seems to have been directed at threatening the employer, a violation of section 8(b) (4) (ii). On this we see no question.

Respondent asserts that picketing alone is not a threat, . . . and that Amador's oral remarks to the employer were merely a "warning" or prediction. However, in order not to be a threat a prediction must relate to an event over which the speaker has no control. Respondent is logically on the horns of a dilemma. We could disagree with the Board's finding that the placard and the picketing were not an encouragement of the employees to strike only because there was no strike when respondent controlled a majority. But if a union with the votes talking strike if its demands are not acceded to is not a threat, it is difficult to think what would be.

We turn to respondent's defenses. Section 8(b) (4) (ii) (C) made respondent's threats illegal "if another labor organization has been certified as the representative . . . ." Respondent asks us to modify "certified" by adding, in effect, "under such circumstances that the employer is obligated to recognize it." More specifically if, because a year had elapsed since the certification and the employer had cause to doubt that the union still represented its employees, and therefore might decline to recognize the certification. . . . Respondent contends that it was free to threaten the employer as a means of obtaining recognition.

If Congress meant by "certified" only unions with whom the employer had an undisputable duty to bargain, it could easily have said so. Failing this, we do not find such an exception easy to imply. Very different considerations may affect an employer's right to conclude that a union no longer represents its employees from those which would permit an outside union to come in and by threats seek to compel the employer to do so. Respondent denies that it has put the employer "in the middle" in this particular case because it says that in fact it had already acquired SIU's majority. However, an employer is not obligated to deny recognition to a certified union after the end of the first year even if it believes it may then lack a majority. The employer may still respect the certification. . . . For reasons set forth in Parks v. Atlanta Printing Pressmen and Assistant's Union, . . . we believe that if Congress intended to allow a competing union, by threats, to derogate from that principle it would have set out the exception. We will not assume it.

Respondent makes a more appealing agrument when it suggests there should be an implied exception in section 8(b) (4) (C) if the certified union has "abandoned" its certification and in effect become "defunct." . . . However, we agree with the Board that there is a vital difference between this and simply abandoning some of its duties towards its members. ... SIU is not a union that has become defunct as such. It is undisputed that it has at all times been vigorously pursuing what it believes are its contractual rights resulting from arbitration. It has also performed some routine services for the employees. It may well be thought that this performance should have been better, or more extensive, but this is normally what is believed whenever a union loses its majority. We will not read an exception into the statute broad enough to meet respondent's attempt to equate inefficiency or ineffectiveness with abandonment of a certification. There were other roads open to respondent.

We confess that for reasons previously stated it is difficult to think of respondent as having simultaneously violated section 8(b) (4) (i) and section 8(b) (4) (ii). However, under the circumstances of this case, we think that within the principle of fitting an order to a respondent's demonstrated predisposition the Board did not exceed its jurisdiction in making the order broad enough to cover what is, essentially, two sides of the same coin.

A decree will be entered enforcing the order of the Board.

● ● ●

CASE QUESTIONS

1. Under the court's interpretation of the Act, what is the primary distinction between a threat and a prediction?

2. When does a certified union's activities become so defunct that recognition of it is invalid?

B & M KAUFMANN v. NLRB
United States Court of Appeals, Seventh Circuit
471 F.2d 301 (7th Cir. 1972), *cert. denied,* 93 S.Ct. 1529 (1973)

● ● ●

PER CURIAM.

The National Labor Relations Board seeks enforcement of a bargaining order based on its findings that the employer (Kaufmann) violated §§ 8(a)(1) and 8(a)(5) of the National Labor Relations Act by refusing to bargain with the union (District 65). The question presented is whether District 65 merits certification as the collective bargaining representative of Kaufmann's employees despite its close relationship and affiliation with the National Association of Women's and Children's Apparel Salesmen, Inc. (NAWCAS), an organization previously denied certification by the Board on conflict of interest grounds. We also hold that the Board's reasons for disqualifying NAWCAS also disqualify District 65; it is not sufficiently independent of NAWCAS to insure good faith representation of the employees in the bargaining unit.

District 65 is a long established labor union presently representing almost 30,000 members under more than 2,000 individual collective bargaining agreements. Prior to its affiliation with NAWCAS, however, it had never represented traveling apparel salesmen who participate in trade shows organized and conducted by NAWCAS and its affiliate members. The majority of NAWCAS' members are independent contractors and are not entitled to union representation under § 2(3) of the Act. The rest are protected by the Act as employee traveling salesmen for individual apparel manufacturers.

Starting in 1965, NAWCAS sought to achieve union status with the help of District 65. The two organizations originally operated under an informal working arrangement; a formal affiliation agreement was signed on July 20, 1967. Under the agreement, District 65 carries on essentially all the "union" functions of NAWCAS. NAWCAS, on its part, collects dues for District 65 from its members, continues to carry on its trade association activities, and retains the right "to make all decisions affecting the interests of its members in accordance with its constitution and by-laws."

The first attempts by the NAWCAS—District 65 combination to organize employee traveling salesmen were frustrated by the Board's decision in Bambury Fashions, Inc., 179 NLRB 447, 72 LRRM 1350 (1969). There, a joint NAWCAS—District 65 certification petition was denied on the ground that NAWCAS was disqualified by its conflict of interest. The Board properly recognized that NAWCAS might subordinate the interests of the employee traveling salesmen (who composed the units in question) to those of the independent contractors. Similarly, NAWCAS, whose primary activity is the operation of trade shows, might oppose joint manufacturer-employee salesmen interests in manufacturer-operated trade shows. Disqualification because of such conflicting interests is a necessary measure to assure good faith representation in collective bargaining. Neither this principle nor the holding of Bambury is questioned in this proceeding.

NAWCAS and District 65 jointly conducted the Kaufmann organizing campaign during the pendency of Bambury in 1969. Kaufmann's employee-salesmen were asked to sign two different representation cards— one designating "NAWCAS—District 65" as the bargaining agent (apparently following the Bambury pattern) and the other designating only "District 65." The stated reason for the use of two cards was to avoid "entanglements" at the Labor Board. . . .

On March 26, 1969, NAWCAS—District 65 jointly requested a meeting with management. On April 18, Kaufmann responded that in view of the Bambury proceeding, it doubted whether NAWCAS—District 65 could represent the unit. The joint campaign continued until May 22, when NAWCAS—District 65 withdrew its request for recognition. At the same time, District 65 individually sought recognition, relying on the alternate representation cards. This change in form was not accompanied by any change in substance. NAWCAS and District 65 remained affiliated, and NAWCAS officers still were capable of influencing if not controlling District 65.

In the subsequent certification proceeding, Kaufmann argued that the union's close ties with NAWCAS barred certification. The Board rejected the defense and ordered an election which District 65 won. Following Kaufmann's renewed refusal to bargain, the Board again rejected Kaufmann's arguments and ordered it to bargain with District 65. Kaufmann then petitioned for review in this court, and the Board cross-petitioned for enforcement of its bargaining order.

The Board argues that District 65's established history as an independent labor union and its expressed intent to act independently in representing the bargaining unit are controlling in a certification proceeding. If these arguments were sufficient, potential conflicts of interest would seldom, if ever, be disqualifying. The Board suggests, however, that ample protection is afforded by the availability of decertification. If District 65 "refuses to maintain an independent course in representing unit employees, or if in bargaining the Employer has grounds for believing that District 65 is acting as an agent for another organization, the Board, pursuant to its authority to police its certifications, may examine Petitioner's conduct when the Board's established procedures are appropriately invoked for such purpose." ...

Under the Board's suggested procedure, the employer would have to challenge the union in a decertification context with proof of actual misconduct by the bargaining representative. Postponing any protection against the risk that conflicting interests may infect the bargaining process until actual damage has been done is inconsistent with the Board's proper evaluation of the potential for harm evidenced by its decision in *Bambury*. Disqualification of a bargaining representative whose independence and loyalty are properly drawn into question should not await proof of actual misconduct. Rather, the Board must focus on the potential for such misconduct before the union is certified.

We agree with Judge Coffin's criticism of the test applied by the Board:

"The principles attaching to the concept of conflicts of interest in the fiduciary field generally, and also in the field of collective bargaining, look to the prevention and forestalling of conditions which are likely to divide loyalties. Were proof of union 'betrayal' required to trigger the application of sanctions, this constructive operation of the law would be largely nullified. We therefore take issue, not with the interpretation of the testimony, nor, of course, with the facts as revealed by the documentary evidence, but rather with the test or standard applied and the application of the undisputed facts to such standard. ..."

As the Board recognized in *Bambury*, "what disqualifies a union from acting . . . is the latent danger that it may bargain, not for the benefit of unit employees, but for the protection and enhancement of [other interests]." ...

The record is replete with proof of the close relationship between NAWCAS and District 65. Mere assertions that they have acted or will act independently are not material even if believable; their continued close relationship in and of itself creates the danger that District 65 "may bargain, not for the benefit of unit employees, but for the protection and enhancement of" NAWCAS. ... We conclude that the same conflict of interest which disqualified NAWCAS in *Bambury* also disqualifies District 65, which owes loyalties both to NAWCAS and to the employees in the bargaining unit.

Employer's petition for review is granted; the Board's cross-petition for enforcement is denied.

• • •

CASE QUESTIONS

1. What facts were cited by the court as the basis for the union's potential conflict of interest?

2. Why did the court side with Kaufmann even though there was no evidence that District 65's activities would benefit NAWCAS over its members?

WICHITA EAGLE & BEACON PUBLISHING CO., INC. v. NLRB
United States Court of Appeals, Tenth Circuit
480 F.2d 52 (10th Cir. 1973)

• • •

SETH, Circuit Judge.

Wichita Eagle & Beacon Publishing Co., Inc. petitions this court, pursuant to 29 U.S.C. § 160(f), to review and set aside an order of the National Labor Relations Board (199 NLRB No. 50). The Board cross-petitions for enforcement of its order.

The Board has found that the newspaper had engaged in unfair labor practices within the meaning of sections 8(a)(1) and (3) of the Act, by transferring employee, Dorothy Wood, against her will, from the editorial page department to the Sunday magazine department because of the said Wood's union activities, and by telling employee Wood that consequences of her union membership and activity might be severe.

The record shows that the newspaper is engaged in the publishing, sale, and distribution of daily newspapers in Wichita, Kansas. In August 1970, the Wichita Newspaper Guild, affiliated with The Newspaper Guild, AFL—CIO, filed a petition with the Board seeking certification as the collective bargaining agent of the newspaper's employees. The Board conducted a hearing on the petition and issued a Decision and Direction of Election. In connection therewith, the Board found that two "editorial writers," Dorothy Wood and Theodore Blankenship, should be included in the bargaining unit as they did not "possess indicia of managerial employees."

The newspaper filed a request for review of the Decision and Direction of Election with the Board, limited to the inclusion of the two editorial employees in the bargaining unit, but the Board denied the request for review.

An election was conducted by the Board among the unit that it had determined was appropriate and the Union was certified as the collective bargaining agent for the bargaining unit. Contract negotiations between the newspaper and the Union were begun; and at the time of the hearing of the unfair labor practice complaint, the parties had not reached a contract.

As to Mrs. Wood, the Union filed charges and a hearing was held before a trial examiner. The trial examiner found that the newspaper had violated section 8(a)(1) and (3) of the Act by transferring Mrs. Wood from the editorial page department to the Sunday magazine department because of her union activities. He recommended that she be reinstated in the editorial page department and that she be awarded any back pay that she would have been entitled to; including increases in salary, but for her transfer. The newspaper filed exceptions to the trial examiner's Decision. The Board issued its Decision and Order, adopting the trial examiner's Decision and adopting his recommended Order.

Mrs. Wood's position prior to her transfer to the Sunday magazine department was that of an editorial writer. As the trial examiner's Decision states, the editorial page department of the newspaper consisted of three people. Charles Pearson, editor of the editorial page, was the acknowledged supervisor of the two employees in the editorial page department, Mrs. Wood and Mr. Blankenship. He was excluded from the collective bargaining unit at the representation hearing by the Board. In the words of the trial examiner, John H. Colburn, editor and publisher of the newspaper, was also part of the editorial page department "in a real but perhaps ex officio sense." The Trial Examiner's Decision, Findings, and Conclusions includes this description of the relationship of the positions:

> "Normal day-to-day procedure, in the editorial page department, was the holding of a midmorning conference, with Colburn, Pearson, Wood, and Blankenship participating. In turn, at the conference, Pearson, Wood, and Blankenship would be asked what he or she had in mind for an editorial. Wood, . . . might say that she had in mind writing a piece on ecology. Colburn or Pearson might say . . . water pollution last week so we will not go on ecology again at this time. That would dispose of Wood's proposal. Or, for instance, Colburn might have responded to Wood's proposal . . . What particular aspect of ecology do you have in mind? Wood would respond . . . the matter would then be discussed by those present. Colburn might then say to Wood, all right, give it a try. On some other subject thus raised, Colburn might make it clear that there were certain specific things that he wished to be stated in the particular proposed editorial, e. g., the theme of the editorial should be that. . . . The editorial write would follow such a directive.
>
> "Following the foregoing type of daily conference with Colburn, Pearson, Wood, and Blankenship would return to their offices. They would then get together in Pearson's office and discuss at greater length topics that had received tentative approval at the conference with Colburn. Views and possibly conflicting contentions would be exchanged

and argued. In most instances it would be at this tripartite conference that definite editorial topics would be assigned by Pearson to Wood, Blankenship, or himself.

"After a writer drafted or wrote an editorial, it was then submitted to Pearson. He might approve it, disapprove it, or prescribe changes or revision. If the editorial cleared Pearson, it would then go to Colburn. Again, the editorial might be approved, rejected, or rejected subject to some particular revision being made." Trial Examiner's Decision, Findings and Conclusions.

Whenever a particular member of the editorial department was assigned a topic which he or she felt unable to write upon, either for reasons of personal conviction or otherwise, upon request the writer would be excused from the assignment. However, as the trial examiner found, ". . . every witness in this case, including Wood, agrees that the editorials of the newspaper function as the voice of [the newspaper's] ownership and management. What appears in an editorial is the subjective viewpoint of management." . . .

Petitioner newspaper contends that editorial writers have the essential characteristics of managerial and confidential employees and therefore the two editorial writers in question, Mrs. Wood and Mr. Blankenship, were improperly included in the collective bargaining unit to begin with, and the newspaper's action in transferring Mrs. Wood was not properly subject to the Act's coverage. On the particular facts of this case, as brought out in the trial examiner's Decision and from an extensive reading of the record, we agree.

We recognize that the task of determining the application of the term *employee* ". . . has been assigned primarily to the agency created by Congress to administer the Act." . . . The courts, however, ". . . have never immunized Board judgments from judicial review in this respect." . . . The court said in NLRB v. North Arkansas Electric Cooperative, Inc., 412 F.2d 324 (8th Cir.):

> "The term 'managerial employee' is not used in the National Labor Relations Act, nor is provision made in the Act for the inclusion or exclusion of such employees in bargaining units. The Act is silent as to whether this type of employee is entitled to the protection of the Act for union activities or membership. The Board, however, has long followed the practive of excluding employees, designated as 'managerial,' from bargaining units in representation elections. It does so on the premise that certain non-supervisory employees are so closely allied with management that they should be excluded from employee bargaining units."

Although the Board considers editorial writers such as Mrs. Wood to be employees within the meaning of the Act, . . . and there does seem to be some language in the case of Associated Press v. NLRB, 301 U.S. 103, . . . which could support this position, a closer reading of the latter case in view of its facts leads us to another conclusion.

Associated Press dealt not with a person who was actively engaged in the "formulating, determining and effectuating" of the employer's policies. . . . Rather, that case dealt with a person who, although characterized as an "editor" or "editorial employee," was employed

". . . to determine the news value of items received and speedily and accurately to rewrite the copy delivered to [him], so that the rewritten matter [should] be delivered to the various filing editors . . . responsible for its transmission, if appropriate, to the areas reached by their circuits."

Regardless of which appellation is given to the employee in Associated Press, whether it be "editor," "editorial employee," or a member of the "news department," his position was much more akin to that of the employees in the news department of the petitioning Wichita Eagle & Beacon Publishing Co., Inc., in the instant case than to that of Mrs. Wood. The hierarchy of personnel in Associated Press was such that the aggrieved employee was responsible, in turn, to a filing editor, various "editorial employees," "supervising editors," and an "executive news editor" in the "news department" of the Associated Press.

Although Mrs. Wood was responsible to the editorial page editor, Mr. Pearson, and in turn to the editor and publisher of the newspaper, Mr. Colburn, as concerns the content and direction of the newspaper's editorials, she nevertheless was an active participant in "formulating, determining and effectuating" the newspaper's journalistic policies. The daily conferences between Colburn, Pearson, Wood, and Blankenship attest to this relationship. While subject to supervision in her writing by the editorial page editor and the editor and publisher, Mrs. Wood could, and did, propose topics for editorials, propound her own viewpoint in an effort to influence editorial policy on various subjects, and was, in sum, an integral participant in the newspaper's subjective voice, its editorials. Whether termed a managerial employee, a confidential employee, or whatever, Mrs. Wood's relationship to the newspaper and its staff placed her in a position where she was intimately involved in "formulating, determining and effectuating" her employer's policies. . . .

Mrs. Wood may not have been a "Chief" (in the words of the trial examiner), but she was certainly a member of the Chief's council in the formulation of editorials. We recognize that she had no formal hand in determining wages, hours, and working conditions for employees on the newspaper, nor did she participate in such matters as basic ownership and management policies in the area of profit and loss and the like. . . . There is, however, a distinction between the reporting of news and the creation and expression of subjective opinion on behalf of a newspaper. To hold that a person who was involved in the formulation of editorial content of a newspaper is not aligned with the newspaper's management would come perilously close to infringing upon the newspaper's First Amendment guarantee of freedom of the press.

The business of the newspaper is not immune from the Act's coverage merely because it is an agency of the press. . . . The newspaper is not contesting the Board's determination that its news department employees are a proper collective bargaining unit and come within the Act's protections. Although the Board's ruling in this case does not have any relation to the impartial distribution of news, per se, nor to the newspaper's ability and freedom to publish the news as it desires it published . . . it does infringe upon the newspaper's freedom to determine the content of its editorial voice in an atmosphere of free discussion and exchange of ideas.

We therefore reject the Board's determination that the two editorial writers, Mrs. Wood and Mr. Blankenship, were "employees" under the National Labor Relations Act. Rather, we hold that they were so closely aligned with the newspaper's management in the formulation, determination, and effectuation, not to mention expression, of the newspaper management's policies through its editorials as to be properly excluded from the collective bargaining unit of news department employees.

As the Supreme Court has noted:

> ". . . [I] n the normal course of events Board orders in certification proceedings under § 9(c) are not directly reviewable in the courts. This Court held as long ago as American Federation of Labor v. Labor Board, 308 U.S. 401, 60 S.Ct. 300, 84 L.Ed. 347, that the 'final order[s]' made reviewable by §§ 10(e) and (f) in the Courts of Appeals do not include Board decisions in certification proceedings. Such decision, rather, are normally reviewable only where the dispute concerning the correctness of the certification eventuates in a finding by the Board that an unfair labor practice has been committed as, for example, where an employer refuses to bargain . . . In such a case, § 9(d) of the Act makes full provision for judicial review of the underlying certification order by providing that 'such certification and the record of such investigation shall be included in the transcript of the entire record required to be filed' in the Court of Appeals."

. . . This is the situation in this case. The newspaper has duly filed objections to and requests for review of the collective bargaining unit determination at every step in this controversy. On the facts here present we find that the Board's Decision and Order are not supported by "substantial evidence on the record considered as a whole." National Labor Relations Act, § 10(e). 29 U.S.C. § 160(e). *Accordingly, the petition for review is granted, and the Decision and Order of the National Labor Relations Board, filed September 29, 1972, is vacated.*

● ● ●

CASE QUESTIONS

1. What factors did the court consider in determining whether the employee was includable in the bargaining unit?

2. What is the basis for the exclusion of managerial employees from a bargaining unit?

NLRB v. CITY YELLOW CAB COMPANY
United States Court of Appeals, Sixth Circuit
344 F.2d 575 (6th Cir. 1965)

● ● ●

Before MILLER, PHILLIPS and EDWARDS, Circuit Judges.

PHILLIPS, Circuit Judge.

The National Labor Relations Board has filed a petition for enforcement of its order, which is reported at 144 NLRB 994. The labor organization involved is Taxicab Drivers Union Local No. 345, affiliated with the Teamsters. Respondents, who operate taxicabs in Akron, Ohio, contend that enforcement of the Board's order should be denied, raising four questions:

(1) Whether the Board properly treated the two respondents as a single employer; (2) whether the Board has jurisdiction over respondents; (3) whether the Board was correct in holding that switchboard operators employed by respondents are not supervisors; and (4) whether the Board was correct in holding that the discharge of two non-union taxicab drivers was a violation of § 8(a) (3) and (1) of the Act, 29 U.S.C. § 158(a) (3) and (1).

1) Relationship between the two companies

Respondents are two Ohio corporations, one known as City Yellow Cab Company and the other as G.I. Cab Company. First we consider the action of the Board in treating respondents as a single employer for jurisdictional purposes.

The record demonstrates that the two corporations have substantially the same management, and that the same four stockholders who own all the stock of City Yellow Cab also own ninety-four percent of the stock of G.I. Cab.

The Board further found additional joint operations by the two companies as follows: The offices of both respondents have been in the same building since July 1962; the taxicabs of both companies are garaged and maintained at the same location; gasoline used by the cabs of both companies comes from the same pumps and parts for cabs are taken from a common source, regardless of which cabs are being repaired; swithboard operators for both companies sit at one continuous switchboard panel in the same room, taking telephone calls for cab service and relaying the requests by radio to cabdrivers; Bryon W. Fry, an officer and director of both companies, makes major personnel decisions, such as the disciplining, hiring, and discharging of employees, and makes purchases for both companies; the same person is the immediate supervisor of the switchboard operators for both companies; and the same person supervises the mechanics for both.

Respondents contend that the two companies in fact compete with each other; that all records and financial transactions are kept separate; that their labor policies are different (primarily in that employees of G. I. Cab are not unionized and employees of City Yellow Cab are represented by a union); that the cabs are dispatched somewhat differently; that there is some variance in fringe benefits; and that the companies have separate bank accounts, social security, internal revenue, and unemployment compensation accounts, and separate Ohio workmen's compensation accounts.

We conclude that under the foregoing findings of the Board, which are supported by substantial evidence, the Board was justified in treating the two corporations as a single employer for jurisdictional purposes. . . .

2) Jurisdiction

The trial examiner made the following findings of fact relative to the gross receipts and interstate commerce links of respondents:

"The gross volume of business of Respondent G.I. Cab and Respondent Yellow Cab was $293,835.45 and $780,160.05, respectively, during 1961, and $281,521.75 and $765,986.10, respectively, during 1962. In 1962, Respondent G.I. Cab received automobiles valued in excess of $24,000, and Respondent Yellow Cab received automobiles valued in excess of $43,000, directly from points outside the State of Ohio. Approximately 5 percent of the trips of both Respondents involve conveyance of passengers between links and channels of interstate commerce such as depots, terminals, airports, and hotels." ...

Although part of the testimony concerning the purchase of automobiles is confusing, we hold that the findings of the Board are supported by substantial evidence on the record as a whole, and that under these facts the Board was authorized to exercise jurisdiction. ...

3) Whether switchboard operators are supervisors

Respondents do not dispute that their conduct toward the switchboard operators violated Section 8(a) (1) and (3) of the Act, 29 U.S.C. § 158(a) (1) and (3), if they were employees as defined in Section 2(3), 29 U.S.C. § 152(3). The only issue as to the unfair labor practices with respect to the switchboard operators is whether or not the Board was correct in finding that they were "employees" rather than "supervisors." It is contended by respondents that the Board was in error in holding that switchboard operators were "employees" and not "supervisors" as defined by Section 2(11) of the Act, 29 U.S.C. § 152 (11). If the operators are supervisors, Section 14(a) of the Act, 29 U.S.C. § 164(a), relieves the respondents of the duty to bargain with a union as their representative.

The facts concerning the switchboard operators in the present case are set forth in detail in the decision of the Board at 144 NLRB 994, and will not be repeated here except in summary. During the summer of 1962, all of the switchboard operators except two signed and mailed to Bryon W. Fry, President of City Yellow Cab and Vice President of G.I. Cab, a petition demanding an improvement in their pay and working conditions. On the next pay day Mr. Fry called two of the switchboard operators to his office, told them that he did not like the word "demand" in their petition, and that "their demands were silly, asinine and ridiculous." Thereafter one switchboard operator was demoted to driver and then fired, and another was discharged upon grounds of "economy." A representative of management stated that "the rest of the people that signed the petition will rue the day they put their names on that paper." Thereupon the switchboard operators asked the assistance of the union, and eight of the ten operators signed union cards. The union demanded recognition and respondents refused on the basis that the switchboard operators were supervisors. Mr. Fry told one of the operators that "they couldn't tolerate a unionized switchboard." It is uncontradicted that the majority of the switchboard operators signed cards authorizing the union to represent them.

On October 28, two switchboard operators and a few drivers began picketing respondents' premises, carrying signs: "ON STRIKE FOR UNION RECOGNITION." The strike ended after respondents obtained two temporary restraining orders from Ohio courts. Ultimately four switchboard operators and two drivers for G.I. Cab were discharged.

The Board ordered all six employees reinstated, with back pay plus interest.

The primary function and duty of the switchboard operators was to receive telephone calls from customers for taxicab service and to relay these requests to available cabdrivers. . . .

This court recently considered the statutory definition of "supervisor" in our decision in Eastern Greyhound Lines v. NLRB, 337 F.2d 84 (C.A. 6), in which we held that dispatchers for the bus company were supervisors. There we applied the definition of the term "supervisor" as set forth in 29 U.S.C. § 152 (11). We followed the well-established rule that this statute is to be read disjunctively and that if a bus company dispatcher possessed any one of the powers described in the act, to be exercised as a matter of independent judgment on the part of the dispatcher, rather than as a matter of a mere routine or of a clerical nature, he was a supervisor within the meaning of the Act. We found that bus company dispatchers under the facts of that case had the power to suspend bus drivers and effectively to recommend discipline. We pointed out that:

> "The evidence showed that in some places Eastern's terminals and its buses are in operation all day and all night. Dispatchers operate in three shifts so that one of them is in service at all hours. In the late night and the early morning hours there are generally no personnel with authority higher than that of a dispatcher on duty. If dispatchers are not supervisors, this multistate transportation system operates a substantial part of the time without supervision. . . ."

We recognized the rule that the statute does not require that the powers described therein be exercised during any definite part of the supervisor's time, and that it is the existence of the power that determines the classification.

Although the switchboard operators involved in the instant case are sometimes called "dispatchers," we find that substantial evidence on the record considered as a whole supports the Board's conclusion that they did not possess the authority to suspend and effectively to recommend discipline of drivers, using independent judgment, as did the bus company dispatchers in Eastern Greyhound Lines v. NLRB, supra.

It is clear that the switchboard operators did not recommend disciplinary action. If a company rule was violated by a cabdriver, the switchboard operator made a verbal report to management, which did not contain any recommendation for discipline. To the contrary, in Eastern Greyhound Lines v. NLRB, supra, a company rule applicable to dispatchers provided that the dispatcher:

> "Maintains discipline and order among drivers; removes drivers from service for infraction of company policies rules and regulations; recommends disciplinary action to be taken for such infractions. . . ."

Greyhound dispatchers were furnished with forms for reporting infractions of driver rules, with a space for recommending discipline. Dispatchers regularly made recommendations concerning discipline which the proof in that case showed to be effective.

Further, in Eastern Greyhound Lines v. NLRB the dispatchers had the authority to suspend a bus driver by ordering him off a bus for misconduct, intoxication or insubordination, thereby removing the driver from service and suspending him pending final determination of appropriate discipline by higher officials.

In the present case the disciplinary authority of the switchboard operators was limited to calling a cabdriver "in off the road" for failure to notify the swithboard each time he dropped off a passenger, each time he picked up a passenger, and before entering the downtown area. Upon being "called in," the driver did not report to the switchboard operator but went directly to Mr. Edick or Mr. Fry. The switchboard operator did nothing more than to make an oral report, without recommendation. Mr. Edick or Mr. Fry then would make an independent investigation and decide whether to send the driver back to work or to discipline him, without consultation with the switchboard operator. It appears that this decision would be made promptly and there was no substantial period of suspension unless imposed by Mr. Edick or Mr. Fry. This authority of switchboard operators to call in drivers off the road is not shown to constitute the power to suspend as was found to be the case in Eastern Greyhound Lines v. NLRB, supra.

It is contended that the switchboard operators "direct" cabdrivers, by telling the driver by radio to pick up a passenger at a given location. This "direction" consisted of nothing more than the relaying by radio of a message received by telephone. The responsibility of making assignments in a routine fashion does not transform an employee into a supervisor. . . .

The switchboard operators had no authority to schedule the hours of drivers or their cabs. This was done on a "trip board" on a seniority basis. Switchboard operators did not participate in preparation of the "trip board."

It is noted that the Board held switchboard operators or dispatchers for a taxicab company to be employees and not supervisors, under facts similar to those presented here, in Yellow Cab, Inc., 131 NLRB 239. We are cited to no decision to the contrary. We hold that under the record in the present case, whatever powers the switchboard operators had to "direct" cabdrivers or to call them in off the job were of a merely routine nature, not requiring the use of independent judgment, and did not come within the powers set forth in the statutory definition of supervisor. . . .

It is significant that the switchboard operators did not consider themselves to be supervisors nor were they so considered by the drivers. New drivers were instructed that their supervisors were Mr. Edick and Mr. Fry. Switchboard operators were never informed by management that they had any authority to discipline drivers. They were never told that they were supervisors until after the beginning of the labor dispute involved in this case.

The fact that at night and at other times no representatives of management were present at respondents' offices, as was also true in Eastern Greyhound Lines v. NLRB, supra, does not necessarily mean that the switchboard operators were supervisors and a part of management. The record shows that all the officers of respondents lived in the city of Akron and could be reached by telephone, and that if a serious situation arose at night, they were called out of bed.

We hold that there is substantial evidence on the record supporting the decision of the board that the switchboard operators did not responsibly direct cabdrivers, did not have the authority to discipline them or effectively to recommend discipline and did not exercise any other authority set forth in § 2(11) of the Act, 29 U.S.C. § 152(11) in other than a routine or clerical nature, not requiring the use of independent judgement. This case therefore is distinguishable on its facts from Eastern Greyhound Lines v. NLRB, supra.

4) Section 8(a) (3) Violations as to cabdrivers

Two cabdrivers for G.I. Cab were discharged because they joined the switchboard operators in picketing. Respondents contend that these drivers were discharged for engaging in an unprotected activity, the employees of G.I. Cab not being represented by a union.

The Board rejected this contention, finding that the drivers for G.I. Cab were also being organized and the picket signs simply demanded recognition, this being true even if it be assumed that the operators were supervisors. We find no evidence on the record to support this holding of the Board, but nevertheless we conclude that the Board reached the correct result in ordering the reinstatement of the two cabdrivers.

The cabdrivers testified that they went on strike and engaged in picketing because they were in sympathy with the demand of the switchboard operators for recognition. The Act protects the rights of employees "to engage in . . . concerted activities for the purpose of . . . mutual aid or protection." . . .

As said by Judge Learned Hand in NLRB v. Peter Cailler Kohler Swiss Chocolates Co., 130 F.2d 503, 505 (C.A. 2):

> "Certainly nothing elsewhere in the act limits the scope of the language to 'activities' designed to benefit other 'employees'; and its rationale forbids such a limitation. When all the other workmen in a shop make common cause with a fellow workman over his separate grievance, and go out on strike in his support, they engage in a 'concerted activity' for 'mutual aid or protection,' although the aggrieved workman is the only one of them who has any immediate stake in the outcome. The rest know that by their action each one of them assures himself, in case his turn ever comes, of the support of the one whom they are all then helping; and the solidarity so established is 'mutual aid' in the most literal sense, as nobody doubts."

. . .In NLRB v. Guernsey-Muskingum Electric Co-op, Inc., 285 F.2d 8, 12 (C.A. 6), this court quoted with approval the following language from NLRB v. Phoenix Mutual Life Insurance Co., 167 F.2d 983, . . . (C.A. 7), cert. denied, 335 U.S. 845: . . .

> "A proper construction is that the employees shall have the right to engage in concerted activities for their mutual aid or protection even though no union activity be involved, or collective bargaining be contemplated. . . . [and] a legitimate interest in acting concertedly in making

known their views to management without being discharged for that interest."

Enforcement granted.

• • •

CASE QUESTIONS

1. What factors did the court consider in determining whether the switchboard operators were employees or supervisors?

2. On what basis did the cab drivers have the right to strike on behalf of the non-union switchboard operators?

NLRB v. POLYTECH, INC.
United States Court of Appeals, Eighth Circuit
469 F.2d 1226 (8th Cir. 1972)

• • •

STEPHENSON, Circuit Judge.

The NLRB applies for enforcement of its order, reported at 186 NLRB No. 148. The Board found respondent Polytech, Incorporated in violation of Sections 8(a)(5) and (a)(1) of the National Labor Relations Act, 29 U.S.C. § 151 et seq. In view of the Supreme Court's recent decision in NLRB v. Burns Int'l Securtiy Services, 406 U.S. 272 . . . (1972), the Board is not seeking enforcement of its order insofar as it requires respondents to abide by the provisions of the collective bargaining agreement in effect at the time respondent took over its business. The principal question presented on review is whether respondent Polytech, Incorporated was a successor company to Polytech Company and thus obligated to recognize the incumbent union and bargain collectively with them. More particularly, questions raised are whether: (1) the Polytech Company ever lawfully recognized the union; (2) there was a "continuity of operations" following the takeover and (3) respondent violated § 8(a)(1) by unlawfully promising benefits to its employees.

In 1966 Terence McGowan organized and incorporated an enterprise known as Polytech Company. In August, 1968, Arundale Manufacturers, Inc., purchased a controlling interest in Polytech Company. McGowan retained a 49% interest, served as its president and actively worked as an instructor or advisor in production processes. Polytech continued to engage in its business of casting sheet plastic and the fabrication of plastic parts. Most of the fabricating was carried on at ECM, a Polytech facility operating at another site. The sheet plastic was fabricated into green filter plates and cover plates for arc welder's helmets, each of which constituted about 40% of Polytech Company's sales during the last 6 months of its existence.

Polytech Company recognized the International Association of Machinists and Aerospace Workers Union as the bargaining representative of all of its production employees in November 1968. The Union was already the bargaining representative of Arundale employees. Polytech Company and the Union entered into a contract covering these employees which was to run from January 1, 1969 through December 31, 1970. This contract was negotiated with the Union by someone other than McGowan. However, in March or April of 1969 McGowan signed a letter agreeing to representation of the employees by the Union at the ECM facility.

Several weeks before June 15, 1969, the operations of ECM Manufacturing Company terminated and on June 15, 1969 all operations of Polytech Company ceased. At this time Polytech Company had 13 production employees, all of whom were discharged.

On July 12, 1969, McGowan and his wife Joyce entered into an agreement with Arundale and Polytech Company pursuant to which the McGowans exchanged their stock interest in Polytech Company for most of the machinery and equipment of Polytech Company. Arundale agreed to lease the real property on which Polytech Company was located to the McGowans.

On July 12, 1969, McGowan commenced operations at the same site under the name Polytech Incorporated. McGowan solicited former employees of Polytech Company to come to work for Polytech, Inc. and hired all of those he reached who wanted jobs. On July 22, 1969 McGowan had hired 8 production employees, 5 of whom were former Polytech Company employees. One of these worked only one day. By July 31, 1969 Polytech, Inc. had 10 employees, 4 of whom were former Polytech Company employees.

Polytech, Inc. concentrated its efforts on the casting of plastic sheets. Almost all of the equipment used in this process had been included in the transfer of July 12 from Arundale and Polytech Company to McGowan. About 90 percent of the transferred equipment is presently in use at Polytech, Inc. Polytech, Inc. does not manufacture the green filter plate which Polytech Company did, but does make the cover plate and sells it to the same customers. Through November 1969, the cover plate sales represented 78% of Polytech, Inc.'s total sales. The sale of unfabricated sheet plastic represents 13% of Polytech, Inc.'s sales volume while it was only 1% of Polytech Company's sales. Most of the fabrication process carried on by Polytech Company has not been carried on by Polytech, Inc.

On July 23, 1969, Union representative James Bagwell visited Polytech, Inc. requesting recognition, and that Polytech, Inc. honor the union—Polytech Company contract. McGowan refused both requests. The next day the charge in this case was filed.

On August 4, 1969, immediately following a second attempt at recognition by Bagwell, McGowan held a meeting with his employees. While no concrete offers of specific benefits were made to the employees by McGowan, he did tell them that he did not intend to take things away from them that they had in the past. Mrs. McGowan, in response to a question by an employee, indicated that if the employees were to receive certain benefits, they would not need a union.

The Board found that Polytech, Inc. was a successor-employer to Polytech Company and that by refusing to recognize the union as the representative of the employees it violated Section 8(a)(5) of the Act. The Board also found that on August 4, 1969, respondent violated § 8(a) (1) by conveying promises of benefits to employees to discourage them from engaging in union activities.

I.

Respondent contends that it should not be required to recognize the Union because there was no showing of legal recognition of the Union by Polytech Company. Thus, even if successorship is found, there would be no duty to recognize an illegally recognized Union. This claim was not raised until April, 1971, in a Petition to Reopen the Record Based on Newly Discovered Evidence. Respondent clearly failed to comply with § 10(e) by not showing that the "newly discovered evidence" was not available at the time of the hearing before the Board or that it could not have been obtained and adduced with the exercise of reasonable diligence by Respondents' former attorney. . . .

II.

Respondent asserts that the Board's determination that Polytech, Inc. was a successor to the Polytech Company is not supported by substantial evidence. Polytech, Inc. argues that there was no continuity of operations because (1) there was no employee identity between the work force composition of Polytech, Inc. and Polytech Co.; (2) there was an approximately 4 week hiatus between operations, and (3) the nature of Polytech, Inc.'s business was substantially different from that of Polytech Company.

When employees have bargained collectively with an employer and there occurs a change of ownership not affecting the essential nature of the enterprise, the successor employer must recognize the incumbent union and deal with it as the bargaining representative. . . . A mere change of employers or of ownership in the employing industry is not a circumstance which will affect the bargaining relationship *if a majority of employees after the change of ownership or management were employed by the preceding employer*. . . . However, where a substantial change in the nature of the business operations is affected as a result of the changed ownership, the new employer need not bargain with the union. . . .

The test is whether there was continuity in the nature and functions between the predecessor and the successor, and the critical question in determining if the employer is a "successor," is whether the employing industry is substantially the same after transfer of ownership. . . .

At the time of the Union's request for recognition, Polytech, Inc. had 7 production employees, 4 of whom were formerly employed by Polytech Company. Under *Burns* it is the number of new employees and whether they are a majority that is important. The fact that the four employees were not a majority of the 13 employees who were discharged when Polytech Company went out of business is persuasive but not decisive. The fact that McGowan attempted to contact and hire all of Polytech Company's former employees shows at least a desire to retain employee identity. Furthermore, where a majority of the new employees are employed by the predecessor, this has been held to constitute a retention of employee identity. . . .

Respondent points to the four week interruption as evidence of non-successorship. In *Burns* and other cases cited by Respondent there was no such gap. This, too, does not persuade us. Respondent cites no cases nor have we found any which make an interruption of operations between employers a determining factor in finding nonsuccessorship. Indeed, the Board has recently found that a break as long as four and one-half months did not determine that the new employer was not a successor. ... A time lapse between the close of business and the takeover is only one factor to be considered in determining successorship. Here we are satisfied that it was insignificant.

Polytech, Inc. urges that there was no continuity of operations because its business was substantially different from that of Polytech Company. Discontinuation of some products by Polytech, Inc. is cited. Polytech Company casted and fabricated sheet plastic. Essentially, Polytech, Inc. continued doing the same thing. Although Polytech, Inc. does not produce the green filter plate, the "essential nature of the enterprise"—that of casting and fabricating sheet plastic—is the same. Indeed, one of Polytech Company's former products (cover plates) now represents 78% of respondent's sales by volume.

Perhaps most persuasive in finding successorship is the purchase by McGowan of Polytech Company's physical assets. Other Courts have consistently found successorship where the new employer purchases a part of all of the assets of the predecessor employer. ... When this is accompanied with a continuation of the same types of product lines, employee identity, and job functions, there is strong evidence of successorship. ... We are satisfied the evidence in this record amply supports the Board's finding that Polytech, Inc. was a "successor" to Polytech Co. We enforce the bargaining order.

III.

Respondent further contends that the statements made by McGowan and his wife at the August 4, 1969 meeting did not violate Section 8(a) (1) of the Act because they were (1) not made during an organizing campaign by the union and (2) protected free speech under Section 8(c) of the Act. Mr. McGowan's statement that he did not intend to take any benefits away from the employees that they had obtained from Polytech Co., and Mrs. McGowan's comment that if the employees received similar benefits they would not need a union, fall within the "promise of benefit" clause of 8(c). The statements implicitly promised that the employees would receive benefits at least equal to those under the Polytech Company's contract with the union. . . .

The Board's order is hereby enforced, except with respect to its finding of violation of Section 8(a) (5) by respondent in refusing to honor the collective bargaining agreement.

• • •

CASE QUESTIONS

1. What test was used by the court to determine whether Polytech, Inc. was a successor employer?

2. What factors did the court use in applying the test?

EMPLOYER CONDUCT DURING UNIONIZATION

3

Historically, most employers have resented union organization of their employees. This feeling appears to be founded on the ideas that (1) since the employers have treated their employees fairly, there is no need for union representation, and (2) unions do not consider management problems and their presence can only distract from the goals of the firm. In some situations these conclusions have proved erroneous, and in others they carry a measure of truth.

Often employers attempt to prevent union organizing. The methods used vary; some amount to illegal unfair labor practices while others may very well be legal. The types of illegal activities are fairly well defined, but problems arise in attempting to determine whether a particular act would fall into an illegal category.

PROHIBITED ACTIVITIES

Those activities of employers which constitute prohibited conduct include (1) misrepresentations in communications to employees, (2) threats of loss of benefits, (3) promises or grants of benefits, (4) unreasonable polling and interrogation, (5) violence, (6) illegal surveillance, (7) discrimination, and (8) interference with the election process. In addition, anti-union employee activities can occur after union recognition has come about, and can be in the form of lockouts, shutdowns, and "runaway shops," those instances when the employer moves his business to discourage union membership or collective bargaining.

Specifically, the National Labor Relations Act defines six employer unfair labor practices in this area. Five are found in Sections 8(a) (1)-(5), and one in Section 8(e). Section 8(a) (1) generally prohibits the interference, restraint or coercion of employees in the exercise of their right to organize. Activities that have been found to be unfair labor practices under this section are wide in scope. Sections 8(a) (2)-(5) deal with management domination of unions, discrimination in employment which is intended to discourage or encourage unionization, discrimination for participation in NLRB proceedings, and refusal to bargain collectively with a duly authorized union. Section 8(e) is concerned with union-employer agreements whereby the employer agrees to or actually ceases or refrains from doing business with other parties.

INTRODUCTION TO THE CASES

The cases in this chapter are concerned with the areas of (1) employer communications, (2) interference, restraint or coercion of employees, (3) employer discrimination, and (4) shutdowns, lockouts, and non-reinstatements. The *Henriksen Case* dealt with employer speeches during a union organizing campaign. The decision in *Darlington Manufacturing* concerned the right of an employer to terminate his business in response to a pro-union employee vote.

In *Midwest Hanger* the court addressed the issue of whether the discharges of a number of employees during a union organizing campaign resulted in an unfair labor practice. The question of whether a temporary lockout by nonstriking members of a multi-employer bargaining association was a lawful practice in response to a union's whipsaw strike against one member-employer was considered in the *Truck Drivers Case.*

Finally, *International Van Lines* was concerned with the issue of whether striking employees were entitled to reinstatement with back pay, irrespective of whether they were characterized as economic strikers or unfair-labor-practice strikers.

NLRB v. HENRIKSEN, INC.
United States Court of Appeals, Fifth Circuit
481 F.2d 1156 (5th Cir. 1973)

• • •

SIMPSON, Circuit Judge:

National Labor Relations Board (Board) pursuant to Section 10(e) of the National Labor Relations Act, Title 29, U.S.C. Sec. 151 et seq., applies to us for enforcement of its order of June 28, 1971, finding that Henriksen, Inc., d/b/a Gibson Discount Center (Company), in violation of Section 8(a)(1) and Section 8(a)(3) and (1) of the Act, committed unfair labor practices at its Port Arthur, Texas, franchised retail merchandise store. We enforce the Board's decision and order as to the Section 8(a)(1) violations, and enforce in part and refuse enforcement in part as to the claimed Sections 8(a)(3) and (1) violations, for the reasons stated below.

The Board found that in the first half of 1969 the Retail, Wholesale, and Department Store Union, AFL-CIO, (Union) began to organize the approximately one hundred employees at the Company's Port Arthur store. The Company actively responded to these efforts mainly in the form of four separate speeches to various groups of employees by Company president, chief operating officer and part-owner Mrs. Clarice Henriksen in November and early December when the Union had gained sufficient support to petition the Board for a representation election. ... [These speeches] were found by the Board to have had such an effect on the Company's employees as to tend to interfere with and coerce them in the exercise of their Section 7 rights under the Act, thus constituting a Section 8(a)(1) unfair labor violation. The Board also found the Company had violated Section 8(a)(1) of the Act because three different departmental managers, one of whom was Mrs. Henriksen's son, placed individual employees, either directly or by inference, in fear of economic reprisal, retaliatory action, loss of employment tenure and curtailment of advancement opportunities as a result of their specific involvement in the union's organizing drive or in the event of the union becoming successful in its organizing efforts. Finally, the Board found that the Company further violated Secs. 8(a)(3) and (1) of the Act by making a special investigative check on employee Violet Smith and then discharging her all because she spearheaded the Union's organizational efforts, and further by imposing more onerous working conditions upon employee Maggie McDaniel.

"[N]ow Congress has left no room for doubt as to the kind of scrutiny which a court of appeals must give the record before the Board to satisfy itself that the Board's order rests on adequate proof." ...

The whole record must be considered, including contradictory evidence or evidence from which conflicting inferences could be drawn, and the Board's finding is not to be set aside if, on the basis of that consideration, substantial evidence exists to support the Board's conclusions. The Board's findings will be set aside only "when the record before a Court of Appeals clearly precludes the Board's decision from being justified by a fair estimate of the worth of the testimony of witnesses or its informed judgment on matters within its special competence or both. ..."

We turn to the record before us.

I   The Speeches

All employees were required to attend the first speech which the Board found to have been violative of the Act. Relevant portions of Mrs. Henriksen's speech on November 14, 1969, to all employees of the Company included the following:

> I want to talk to you for a few minutes about something that has come up here in the store that is very important to me and very important to each of you. What I am refering to is this talk that I heard around the store about a union and the fact that a union is trying to get into our store here. I want each and every one of you to understand just how serious this is. I also want to be sure that I have done my part in explaining just how I feel about a union coming into our store here, because I feel that it would be very unfortunate if some one made a serious mistake. ...
>
> I want to be completely frank and honest with you now and tell you exactly how I feel about the union—the only reason that I am talking to you is that I am concerned for you and your welfare, and your future, and the future of our store. I don't want anyone coming to me later and saying, "Mrs. Henriksen, I just didn't understand how you felt about the union or I wouldn't have made that mistake." I am going to tell you right now in clear and unmistakable terms exactly how I feel so if any of you go ahead and make a mistake despite what I tell you, then I won't have it on my conscience.
>
> This is exactly how I feel: I do not want any union outsiders in this store. I believe it would be a very serious mistake for you, for our families, and for the company for a union to be here, and I intend to do everything possible to protect you and to protect our good jobs here. ...
>
> It may be that some of you have already been misled into signing a union card. Remember, those cards are dangerous as long as they are in effect, and they stay in effect until you do something to cancel them.
>
> I am not going to criticize anybody for making the mistake of signing a union card. As I said before, I have made mistakes—we all do, and I don't hold a grudge against anyone for an honest mistake. But now you know the facts. It is no sin to make an honest mistake, but it is mighty unfortunate if a person makes a mistake does not take some action to correct that mistake when they find out what the true facts are.

As I mentioned before, I have had occasion to sit down with many of you and help you work out your problems. I have helped you arrange your work schedules so that you could continue working and still take care of your families. I have even lingered and held your job and waited for you to come back, some of you, when you were sick.

I didn't do all those things because some one told me I had to do them. I didn't do all those things because some one was standing next to me holding a gun to my head or threatening me. I did those things simply because it was the right thing to do, and I wanted to do it.

Now, I understand that some of the people that I have helped out through some very difficult times are running around behind my back working against me and against the store—and worse of all, this person or these people are working against their fellow employees. This hurts me deeply, and I cannot express my hurt feelings any better than by just simply telling you that I am disappointed. I worked hard in this store, every bit as hard and probably harder than anyone else. I don't have to work here—I could take off every day and just travel or have a good time somewhere else. But I don't want to do that. I want to be here in the store with my people. I want to be here with you in case any of you need me.

I thought this was what you wanted, and I thought I was doing some good. But it really makes me think twice when I learn of someone literally running behind my back and working to tear down all of the good that I have worked so hard to build up. ...

Mrs. Henriksen began her prepared text by impressing upon the employees the serious nature of the Union activity around the store and by stating that she felt that "it would be very unfortunate if some one made a serious mistake." She explicitly stated her adamant opposition to "any Union outsiders" in her store and then announced her determination to do "everything" possible to "protect you and to protect our good jobs here." She extolled what she considered to be the apparently warm and friendly atmosphere and relationship of her store and its employees and contrasted this to the atmosphere in another store in the same town which had become unionized by the same Union seeking to gain a foothold at the Company's store. She proceeded to criticize the Union and to attribute sinister motives to it. Having thus laid out to the employees what she deemed to be the "facts," Mrs. Henriksen's key subsequent comments were:

> "I am not going to criticize anybody for making the mistake of signing a union card. As I said before, I have made mistakes—we all do, and I don't hold a grudge against anyone for an honest mistake. But now you know the facts. It is no sin to make an honest mistake, but it is mighty unfortunate if a person makes a mistake does not take some action to correct that mistake when they find out what the true facts are."

It was primarily from this passage that the Trial Examiner concluded, and the Board agreed, that Mrs. Henriksen had implied that she would hold a grudge against employees who failed to take action to cancel the Union cards they had signed. This threat was found to coerce and restrain the employees in the exercise of their Section 7 rights not to cancel their Union cards and to engage in Union activity. The remaining portion of that speech was found to have been the explication of the various forms which Mrs. Henriksen's grudges might take should they be visited upon her employees. Work schedules would no longer be adjusted to conform to family duties nor would jobs be held open during an illness. Moreover, the spector of closing the store outright was raised when Mrs. Henriksen reminded the employees that she really "didn't have to work here. ..."

In sum, as to this speech, it was the finding of the Trial Examiner, adopted by the Board that:

> "... Respondent threatened to bear a grudge against employees who did not renounce the Union, to withhold from such employees assistance with respect to working conditions and tenure of employment which it would normally give, to close the store, thereby causing the employees to lose their jobs, and to visit other reprisals upon employees, if they persisted in adhering to or assisting the Union or if they voted the Union in." It is found that Respondent thereby violated Sec. 8(a)(1) of the Act.

The second speech which the Board found to have violated the Act was about December 4 delivered to invited employees deemed not to be of pro-union sentiment. Relevant portions of the second speech are: ...

> The union may have made a lot of promises about what it can get for you. Remember this—there are no limits and no legal restrictions on what the union can claim or promise you. When it comes to making big promises the sky is the limit (sic)—they can promise you the moon with a fence around it and they probably will—but it is one thing for them to make those claims and promises and it is another thing for them to deliver on those promises.
>
> In the election you will not be voting on whether or not you want all of the big things that the union pushers have been talking about. You will be voting only on whether you want the union to become your *legal* and *binding* representative, and whether you want to *give up* your right to speak and act for yourself in all matters affecting your job, your pay, and turn this right over to the union.
>
> The union will try to make you believe that if the union should be voted in the signing of a contract with them is automatic. This is *not the truth,* and you should clearly understand that. There is nothing automatic about signing a contract with the union, even if the union should win an election here. If the union should be voted in, this means one thing and one thing only. It means that the union would have the opportunity to sit down and bargain with me concerning your wages, benefits, working conditions, terms and privileges of employment. That's all it means—it does not mean anything else. Everything that you presently have—your pay—your benefits such as holidays, vacations, profit-sharing plan and hospitalization insurance would go on the bargaining table. *Everything* would be subject to negotiation.
>
> And you must remember this: bargaining is just what it says it is. It's a matter of give and take. Bargaining is tough business—it's cold business—it's impersonal business and oftentimes it's "dog eat dog."
>
> Well, I can tell you one thing right now: if the union should win an election in this store, I would bargain with them—and I would bargain with them in good faith—but I would bargain cold with them, and I would bargain tough with them. I would bargain with them just like I do some of the cutthroat suppliers that we have who are always trying to take us to the cleaners. Believe me, I know what bargaining, is, and I do it everyday in connection with this business. I have no intention of letting

this union or anybody else run all over us or tell us what to do. We know our rights, and we intend to stand up for those rights; and if anybody is thinking anything different, they are badly mistaken.

I do not know if you know it or not, but not one paragraph, not one sentence, not one word goes into a contract with a union unless the company agrees that it should be in there. We have to reach an agreement on every paragraph, and every phrase, and every term and condition of that agreement, or it is not included in the agreement. It does not matter if the union has promised you $2.00 an hour, or $3.00 an hour, or $5.00 an hour. If we don't agree to pay those wages—they don't get paid. Remember this—it's the company that pays your wages, not the union; it is the company that provides you with your fringe benefits, not the union; it is the company who provides you with your job here, and for as long as you work here it will be because the company keeps you on the payroll, not the union. The union did not hire you and they cannot fire you. The union does not pay your wages or provide your benefits. The union has never given you anything—and it never will.

So no matter what the union organizers have been promising it doesn't amount to a hill of beans unless the company agrees to it and it goes into the contract. And I'll tell you something else right now—if I were bargaining with the union I would take a close look at everything they said they wanted in a contract. I would have lawyers go over every paragraph that they intended to put in there to be sure it was just right. And further than that I can tell you now that I would not agree to anything in a contract with the union which was not to the *best interest* of this company and *all* of our employees here. The National Labor Relations Act specifically gives the company the legal right to say *no* to any union demand or proposal made during bargaining. This is the law, and we fully intend to exercise our rights under the law. Now that is the way I feel about this matter, and nobody should make any mistake about it.

What would happen if the union made demands on the company during bargaining that the company was not willing to agree to? If no agreement was reached during bargaining, there is only one thing that the union could do about it and that would be to call you out on strike. That is the only weapon the union would have to use. Remember, the union organizers would not go out on strike—they would continue to collect their pay and draw their salaries during the strike. They have nothing at stake, but you and I, and all of us here at Gibson's have everything at stake. In a strike here, nobody would win; everybody would lose.

Here are a few things you should know about a strike. If the union called you out on strike to try to make the company sign its contract, you could lose your job, because economic strikers can be replaced with new workers. Once a striker has been replaced with a new worker, the company is under no obligation to give him his job back even if the strike is later settled. I want to repeat that because it is so important. Employees called out on strike by the union to try to make the company sign its contract can lose their jobs, because those employees can be replaced during the strike with new workers.

And here is something else—people out on strike do not get paid. The store is certainly not going to pay you wages, and the union would not even attempt to meet our payroll here. Now the union may make all kinds of promises about how they will pay you something if they call you out on strike, but you better get them to *guarantee you in writing* exactly what they are going to pay you. Usually unions do not pay strike benefits to people who have just joined. Strike benefits are normally paid to people who have been in a union for a long, long time, like the union members at Gulf and Texaco around here, who have been paying dues and fees to the union for years and years.

And there is a third thing about this strike business—under Texas law, people out on a union strike are not allowed to collect unemployment money. So don't think that you can get unemployment money if the union calls a strike here, because you can't.

The Board found that Mrs. Henriksen's representation of the nature of the collective bargaining process was a distortion. The speech tended to undermine the employer's obligation to bargain in good faith. Mrs. Henriksen indulged in an objectionable analogy when she compared the Union to the ordinary supplier of the store. The analogy was false in that there was no legal duty on Mrs. Henriksen's part to bargain with a supplier whereas there would be a legal duty to bargain if the Union succeeded in becoming the employee's bargaining representative. . . .

The evidence adduced by the Board here need not be overwhelming. But difficulty is necessarily encountered in investigating and proving by inference threats of retaliatory action in labor-management relations. For that reason we are required to give great deference to the Board's expertise in this highly sensitive area. . . . Conceding this special insight to the Board, it was not unreasonable that from the evidence before it the Board determined that the first speech was a threat to visit economic reprisals upon those employees who would not conform to Mrs. Henriksen's desire that "union outsiders" be kept from establishing a foothold in her Company. . . .

Nor can we find substantial error in the Board's conclusion that the faulty analogy employed by Mrs. Henriksen in the second speech was calculated to convey to the listening employees a distorted view of the Company's obligation to bargain in good faith with the Union if it was selected as the bargaining agent. The effect of such distortion upon the employees' minds would reasonably be the conclusion that their bargaining as a Union would be futile. . . .

By this decision, no First Amendment rights of the Company have been infringed upon. In *Gissel Packing Co.,* . . . , the Supreme Court noted that the balancing of the conflicting rights of the employer to free speech and that of the employees to engage in protected activities:

"must take into account the economic dependence of the employees on their employers, and the necessary tendency of the former, because of that relationship, to pick up intended implications of the latter that might be more readily dismissed by a more disinterested ear. . . ."

II   Coercion Based Upon Individual Conversations

The Board found that at various times supervisory personnel had threatened individual employees with economic reprisal, retaliatory action and loss of employment tenure. For instance, an assistant store manager told an employee, Cheryl LeBouef, in response to a request for time off to tend to personal business, that her request would be granted but that things would be much different if the Union succeeded in organizing the Company employees. The manager of the shoe department told another employee, Rosemary Houst, that Union success would result in a cut of employees' hours. Other supervisory personnel attempted to elicit from employees Rita Combs and Khristy Smithhart the names of their co-workers who were Union supporters, the effect of which, found the Board, was to induce fear of retaliatory action by the Company against Union adherents. Young Mr. Henriksen vilified Mrs. McDaniel, as described in Part IV of this opinion.

The conclusion that these instances happened as described was a legitimate credibility choice of the Board. We do not find that any incontrovertible documentary evidence or physical fact contradicts the Board's findings in this respect. ... Accepting the Board's view of the facts, these instances coupled with the Company's expressed anti-union attitude were violations of Section 8(a)(1). ...

III   Special Check and Discharge of Violet Smith

Violet Smith was among those employees of oldest Company service. Her employment dated back to 1965, a year after the store's opening. Due to apparently unsatisfactory performance she was transferred from department to department until she finally was made a checker in September, 1968. The following September she was placed at the somewhat isolated Register No. 1 allegedly because she talked too much with other checkers.

The cash registers were audited daily to ensure that they contained the money from the day's sales as reflected by the registers' tapes. Although accuracy to the penny was achieved only 25 percent of the time, Mrs. Smith's record was substantially worse than those of the other checkers with similar experience, and included daily discrepancies of rather significant amounts of money. In order to assure that discrepancies in the registers were not the result of pilfering by cashiers, the Company engaged an independent survey systems firm to make routine checks of all cashiers four times a year and special checks of designated employees upon request. Such routine evaluations were conducted on October 3, 1968, and January 19, 1969. The results in both instances were favorable to Mrs. Smith.

In April, 1969, apparently dissatisfied with the Company's wage scales, Mrs. Smith contacted the Union and began distributing union authorization cards. She continued these activities into July, when she executed her own card, and into September. She was one of the most active union advocates in the Company's employment. The record shows that Company officials were aware of Mrs. Smith's pro-union actions.

In November and December, 1969, a clerk in the soft goods department noted that a regular customer named Esther Suire visited the store two or three times each week, purchasing $20.00 to $45.00 worth of merchandise each trip. She often selected duplicate items. This clerk's curiosity was aroused because three or four times a week she was called to the information desk of the store to take back goods she had previously helped Mrs. Suire select for purchase. She noticed further that many items returned to her department for reshelving were also items she had helped Mrs. Suire select. At various times also when Mrs. Suire or one of her relatives returned merchandise, they received cash refunds without presenting a sales slip. This was perhaps a result of employees failing to carry out Company policy of requiring a refund slip to be presented, when the customer was a regular like Mrs. Suire. Finally, this clerk observed that

Mrs. Suire appeared always to check out her purchases through Mrs. Smith's register.

Other clerks corroborated these observations concerning Mrs. Suire's frequent visits, duplicate purchases of expensive items and extraordinary number of returns and reported them to the assistant manager of the store. Although the Trial Examiner, after making the necessary determinations of credibility found that the evidence did not establish that Mrs. Suire's returns were "suspiciously excessive," the store manager concluded that Mrs. Smith might be involved in a scheme with Mrs. Suire to defraud the Company by allowing Mrs. Suire to take duplicate items through her register while paying for only one, with Mrs. Suire thereafter returning one of the items with the paid receipt for a refund while keeping the duplicate. The independent survey systems firm was informed as to these matters with the request that it make a special report. This special check was conducted on December 17, 1969, six days before the union representation election. Purchases were checked through Mrs. Smith's register by an investigator posing as a customer. On three of six transactions Mrs. Smith did not tender a receipt, and she failed to ring up the sale at all in one transaction. At the investigator's suggestion, the tape from Mrs. Smith's cash register was removed and found to contain no record of the investigator's purchase. Moreover, the total recorded on the tape was $2.81 less than was actually contained in the register's cash drawer. The investigator told the store manager that he felt there was a "strong indication" that Mrs. Smith might be "building a drawer." This was a shorthand description of a practice of overcharging customers or not recording sales until the amount of cash "over" reaches five or ten dollars at which time the checker removes that amount from the drawer.

The Trial Examiner concluded that this special check, which was imposed on the Union's most active supporter six days prior to the election, was not made on the basis of any suspicion as to Mrs. Smith's honesty, but because she headed the Union's organizational efforts and Company officials were seeking a pretext for her discharge. For this reason the special check was found by the Trial Examiner and the Board to have constituted a violation of Sections 8(a)(3) and (1) of the Act.

Another claimed violation of Sections 8(a)(3) and (1) of the Act was the illegal discharge of employee Violet Smith. Again Mrs. Suire was involved. This incident in reality was a continuation of the previous events involving the register check.

On December 24, 1969, Christmas Eve and exactly one week after the special check was performed on Mrs. Smith and one day after the Union representation election, Mrs. Suire and her sixteen-year-old daughter, Vicki, were in the Company store. Mrs. Suire obtained a small television set in the jewelry-camera department and offered to pay for it there, but the clerk instructed her to pay at the front of the store. She then placed the television set in her shopping cart and proceeded to the rug department, where she placed a large rug in the cart, over the television set. Vicki then wheeled the cart to a position near register No. 3, where she left it. Vicki then got two other carts, one for herself and one for her mother, and both did some additional shopping. When Vicki was ready to leave, she rolled her cart to register No. 1, where Mrs. Smith proceeded to ring up her purchases. During the progress of this check-out Vicki got the cart containing the rug and television set from register No. 3 and rolled it through Mrs. Smith's check-out station, leaving it near, but beyond, her counter. Vicki then paid for the merchandise in the first cart and left the store.

Throughout this time the store manager was aware of Mrs. Suire's presence in the store and the location and the contents of the shopping cart containing the television set and the rug. He alerted the store's security officers and asked them to watch the cart, which they did including Vicki's re-positioning of it from near register No. 3 through the aisle past Mrs. Smith's register No. 1 to rest immediately beyond the counter. One of the security officers followed Vicki outside the store and demanded to see a receipt. She showed him the receipt for the goods in her possession. He checked her merchandise against the receipt and found nothing out of order.

While Vicki was thus engaged with the security officer outside the store, a second security officer observed the unattended shopping cart containing the television set and the rug in the exit area. Since one of his duties was to watch merchandise and people going out, he walked over to investigate. He asked Mrs. Smith, who was in the process of checking out a disinterested customer, if she knew to whom the articles belonged. She replied that she did not know.

Mrs. Suire, still inside the store, proceeded to register No. 1 where she paid Mrs. Smith for the purchases in her cart and pushed them out to her car. Upon learning that Vicki had been questioned about stealing by a security officer, she took all but one of her purchases back into the store and obtained a refund as her means of demonstrating her anger. Mrs. Suire protested that Vicki was not stealing the rug and television set because she had not taken them out of the store. Rather, Mrs. Suire insisted she had asked Vicki to leave the television set and rug with one of the checkers and to explain that she would pay for it later. As Mrs. Suire and Vicki further explained, Vicki had asked Mrs. Smith to watch the items until her mother, who was still in the store, arrived to pay for them, and that meanwhile Vicki went to the car to obtain her mother's checkbook and that Mrs. Smith agreed. Mother and daughter said that it was while Vicki was performing this errand that the security officer stopped and questioned Vicki outside the store.

Soon after this tableau the store manager obtained accounts of what had happened from the various store security officers. He testified that he learned from this questioning of some highly suspicious behavior on the part of Mrs. Smith and Mrs. Suire of sufficient gravity in his judgment to support disciplinary action against Mrs. Smith. The Trial Examiner credited only the testimony by the single security officer who investigated the presence of the shopping cart in the exit area of the store and received a negative reply when he inquired of Mrs. Smith if she knew to whom its contents belonged. The manager questioned Mrs. Smith in his office a few minutes after the incident, again at 5:30 that afternoon, and again on December 26, the first day the store was open after Christmas.

The testimony was in conflict as to what occurred between the store manager and Mrs. Smith at these meetings. However, at the December 26 meeting Mrs. Smith was discharged in the main for the stated reason that she had allowed a shopping cart full of merchandise worth over $125.00 to leave the last point of being checked out, a clear violation of Company policy. Additional causative factors were asserted in the hearing including her poor overall work record, the numerous irregularities on her register, the possibility that she was allowing Mrs. Suire to remove merchandise by the duplicate purchase method, and the December 17, incident in which she might have been "building a drawer."

The Trial Examiner refused to credit the testimony that a violation of the store's policy of not allowing unpaid for merchandise to go past the check-out counter was grounds for discharge, characterizing the manager's and Mrs. Henriksen's testimony to that effect as "self-serving." He regarded Mrs. Smith's action as a mere rule violation, quite independent of any question of dishonesty. Mrs. Smith's negative reply to the security officer's inquiry about the shopping cart containing the television set and the rug parked next to her register was viewed by the examiner as not indicative of an attempt to conceal since there existed a possibility of a misunderstanding because of Mrs. Smith's preoccupation at the moment with checking out another customer. Concerning the other unfavorable aspects of Mrs. Smith's record, the Trial Examiner held that either the Company had failed to substantiate their existence or that they had been tolerated for so long without any conclusion that Mrs. Smith was dishonest that they should not be determinative now. Thus, finding no grounds for harboring a suspicion as to Mrs. Smith's honesty, the Trial Examiner viewed the decision to examine her specially on December 17, as merely an additional pretext for her discharge. "In view of the discriminatory determination thus displayed" by the Company he concluded "that it was Smith's union activities, and not the rug and TV incident or any of Smith's shortcoming," that motivated the Company in discharging Mrs. Smith in violation of Sections 8(a)(3) and (1) of the Act.

We have recited the record regarding the Smith discharge in unusual detail, because, even accepting the credibility determinations made by the Trial Examiner, we find that the record does not support the finding by the Trial Examiner adopted by the Board that Mrs. Smith was discharged because of her union activities. We think this is so despite the Company's avowed anti-union animus and its acknowledged awareness of Mrs. Smith's vigorous activities in promoting the union beginning with her organizational efforts in April, 1969 and continuing through the election in December.

By December, 1969, when the Company was found to have violated the Act with regard to Mrs. Smith, her work record left much to be desired. Her work was unsatisfactory in other departments of the store. Even as a checker she was purposely moved to the register located so as to least encourage distractive conversation with other employees. The record of her accuracy in using the register was insufficient to demonstrate dishonesty but it compared unfavorably with the performance of other checkers with similar or less experience.

Mrs. Suire's frequent duplicate purchases of expensive items through Mrs. Smith's check out line and their later return to the store formed a suspiciously unusual shopping pattern, sufficient motivation for ordering the special check on Mrs. Smith on December 17. The Trial Examiner found that the number of returns was not established to be "suspiciously excessive," but the sole basis for this finding was the failure of the Company's refund voucher books to reflect Mrs. Suire's signature. The record, however, demonstrated the inaccuracy of the Company's refund voucher books for this evidentiary purpose. Mrs. Suire herself testified that both she and others had returned items of her purchase to the store for refund. Clerks from the store offered uncontradicted and disinterested testimony that sometimes Mrs. Suire herself and at other times members of her family returned merchandise for refund. In short, the trial examiner's finding that the evidence did not establish that Mrs. Suire's returns were "suspiciously excessive" is undermined by his faulty methodology.

The coincidence of the Company ordered special check of Mrs. Smith occurring in near proximity to the union representation election required appraisal, of course. But Mrs. Suire's shopping habits, suspicious to the extent that they were noticed by other clerks in the store, coupled with Mrs. Smith's employment history were a reasonable basis for the Company in good faith to investigate the matter furhter by asking for the special check on Mrs. Smith. Further steps by the Company were dependent upon the results of that survey. The record does not support the Board's conclusion that the Company was motivated by anti-union animus in ordering the special check. The record indeed justifies the steps taken to check Mrs. Smith. . . .

Nor do we think that the record supports the Board's ultimate conclusion that the outright discharge of Mrs. Smith was motivated by her union activities. To recapitulate, by that time (a) the Company had the professional opinion of the independent survey systems firm that Mrs. Smith might be "building a drawer" from which to steal money; (b) Mrs. Smith had violated a Company rule which prohibited allowing unpaid merchandise to pass beyond the check-out counter; and (c) also to be weighed was Mrs. Smith's denial to the security officer of knowledge of the ownership of the shopping cart with the television set and the rug, as conflicting with Mrs. Smith's statement (as found by the Trial Examiner) to the store manager that she knew Vicki had placed the television set and rug near her check-out counter and that Vicki's mother was going to pay for them.

We note also that the Company waited until three days *after* the union representation election on December 23, 1969 to discharge Mrs. Smith. In the light of her previous conduct, this fact indicates the Company's cognizance of the possibility of an unfair labor practice charge if she was discharged before the election.

The Board emphasizes on brief that Mrs. Smith was discharged without being informed of the reason for such action and that this fact alone would be "enough to support an inference that the [discharge] was discriminatory. . . ." Those cases, however, are distinguishable in that in each instance the employee discharged had no reasonable basis for knowledge of the cause of discharge. Here Mrs. Smith had been questioned three times within the space of two days on the direct violation of the Company rule prohibiting unpaid merchandise to go beyond the check-out station and the attendant circumstances.

The Board's conclusion that employee Violet Smith was discharged because of her pro-union activities is rejected as not based upon substantial evidence. Her involvement in protected activities was shown to be no more than coincidental to the real reasons for her discharge, which were lawful. . . . We refuse enforcement of the Board's decision and order in respect to this claimed violation of Sections 8(a)(3) and (1).

IV

Also found by the Board to be a violation of Sections 8(a)(3) and (1) of the Act was the imposition of more onerous working conditions on employee Maggie McDaniel because she had engaged in protected prounion activity. The representation election petitioned for by the Union was held December 23, 1969. Mrs. McDaniel served as a Union observer at the election. The Union lost the election.

Two incidents involving Mrs. McDaniel occurred the following day, December 24. She was advised by Charles Brown, an Assistant Store Manager "that he would not assign . . . a boy to help [her] when [she] had any heavy work to do," such as lifting large size rugs. Later the same day Richard Henriksen, the son of the Company President and a department manager, asked Mrs. McDaniel, according to her testimony, "if I was happy that I had ruined everybody's Christmas. I said I didn't know I had ruined everybody's Christmas. He said, 'Well, you sure have . . . you are a Communist just like all the other . . . unionists' ".

The Trial Examiner, as to the first incident, inferred that Brown had previously provided such assistance, and that McDaniel's known support of the Union was the reason for Brown's statement that such help would no longer be afforded. We consider the Examiner's (and the Board's) inferences to be permissible credibility choices, and the Board decision and order in this respect is ordered enforced.

Relief granted as to the second McDaniel incident of December 24, involving young Mr. Henriksen's claimed remark was covered by at least one paragraph of the Notice required to be posted by the Company; viz: "We will not vilify you because you support the Union or any labor organization." We think the finding of unfair labor practice for violation of Section 8(a)(1) and the relief prescribed as to this incident are justified under the evidence. Enforcement in this respect is covered by Part II of this opinion.

V

Finally, we find no merit in the Company's argument generally that it was error for the Board to adopt findings of violations of the Act which were neither alleged in the complaint nor litigated at the hearing. The Company's position comes from an unduly restrictive interpretation of "notice pleading. . . ." It did not litigate in ignorance, but was fully apprised of each issue and litigated each issue fully and without being prejudiced by the absence of more precise notice. . . .

Enforced in part; Enforcement denied in part.

• • •

CASE QUESTIONS

1. How did the court interpret each of the employer's speeches and other activities during the organization campaign?

2. Why did the court hold that the discharge of the female employee was not an unfair labor practice?

TEXTILE WORKERS UNION OF AMERICA
v. DARLINGTON MANUFACTURING COMPANY
United States Supreme Court
380 U.S. 263 (1965)

● ● ●

MR. Justice HARLAN delivered the opinion of the Court.

We here review judgments of the Court of Appeals setting aside and refusing to enforce an order of the National Labor Relations Board which found respondent Darlington guilty of an unfair labor practice by reason of having permanently closed its plant following petitioner union's election as the bargaining representative of Darlington's employees.

Darlington Manufacturing Company was a South Carolina corporation operating one textile mill. A majority of Darlington's stock was held by Deering Milliken, a New York "selling house" marketing textiles produced by others. Deering Milliken in turn was controlled by Roger Milliken, president of Darlington, and by other members of the Milliken family. The National Labor Relations Board found that the Milliken family, through Deering Milliken, operated 17 textile manufacturers, including Darlington, whose products manufactured in 27 different mills, were marketed through Deering Milliken.

In March, 1956, petitioner Textile Workers Union initiated an organizational campaign at Darlington which the company resisted vigorously in various ways, including threats to close the mill if the union won a representation election. On September 6, 1956, the union won an election by a narrow margin. When Roger Milliken was advised of the union victory, he decided to call a meeting of the Darlington board of directors to consider closing the mill. Mr. Milliken testified before the Labor Board:

> "I felt that as a result of the campaign that had been conducted and the promises and statements made in these letters that had been distributed [favoring unionization], that if before we had had some hope, possible hope of achieving competitive [costs] . . . by taking advantage of new machinery that was being put in, that this hope had diminished as a result of the election because a majority of the employees had voted in favor of the union. . . ."

The board of directors met on September 12 and voted to liquidate the corporation, action which was approved by the stockholders on October

17. The plant ceased operations entirely in November, and all plant machinery and equipment were sold piecemeal at auction in December.

The union filed charges with the Labor Board claiming that Darlington had violated §§ 8(a) (1) and (3) of the National Labor Relations Act by closing its plant, ... and § 8(a) (5) by refusing to bargain with the union after the election. The Board, by a divided vote, found that Darlington had been closed because of the antiunion animus of Roger Milliken, and held that to be a violation of § 8(a) (3). The Board also found Darlington to be part of a single integrated employer group controlled by the Milliken family through Deering Milliken; therefore Deering Milliken could be held liable for the unfair labor practices of Darlington. Alternatively, since Darlington was a part of the Deering Milliken enterprise, Deering Milliken had violated the Act by closing part of its business for a discriminatory purpose. The Board ordered back pay for all Darlington employees until they obtained substantially equivalent work or were put on preferential hiring lists at the other Deering Milliken mills. Respondent Deering Milliken was ordered to bargain with the union in regard to details of compliance with the Board order. ...

On review, the Court of Appeals, sitting *en banc,* set aside the order and denied enforcement by a divided vote. ... The Court of Appeals held that even accepting *arguendo* the Board's determination that Deering Milliken had the status of a single employer, a company has the absolute right to close out a part or all of its business regardless of antiunion motives. The court therefore did not review the Board's finding that Deering Milliken was a single integrated employer. We granted certiorari, ..., to consider the important questions involved. We hold that so far as the Labor Relations Act is concerned, an employer has the absolute right to terminate his entire business for any reason he pleases, but disagree with the Court of Appeals that such right includes the ability to close part of a business no matter what the reason. We conclude that the cause must be remanded to the Board for further proceedings.

Preliminarily it should be observed that both petitioners aruge that the Darlington closing violated § 8(a) (1) as well as § 8(a) (3) of the Act. We think, however, that the Board was correct in treating the closing only under § 8(a) (3). Section 8(a) (1) provides that it is an unfair labor practice for an employer "to interfere with, restrain, or coerce employees in the exercise of" § 7 rights. Naturally, certain business decisions will, to some degree, interfere with concerted activities by employees. But it is only when the interference with § 7 rights outweighs the business justification for the employer's action that § 8(a) (1) is violated. ...

A violation of § 8(a) (1) alone therefore presupposes an act which is unlawful even absent a discriminatory motive. Whatever may be the limits of § 8(a) (1), some employer decisions are so peculiarly matters of management prerogative that they would never constitute violations of § 8(a) (1), whether or not they involved sound business judgment, unless they also violated § 8(a) (3). Thus it is not questioned in this case that an employer has the right to terminate his business, whatever the impact of such action on concerted activities, if the decision to close is motivated by other than discriminatory reasons. But such action, if discriminatorily motivated, is encompassed within the literal language of § 8(a) (3). We therefore deal with the Darlington closing under that section.

I.

We consider first the argument, advanced by the petitioner union but not by the Board, and rejected by the Court of Appeals, that an employer may not go completely out of business without running afoul of the Labor Relations Act if such action is prompted by a desire to avoid unionization. Given the Board's findings on the issue of motive, acceptance of this contention would carry the day for the Board's conclusion that the closing of this plant was an unfair labor practice, even on the assumption that Darlington is to be regarded as an independent unrelated employer. A proposition that a single businessman cannot choose to go out of business if he wants to would represent such a startling innovation that it should not be entertained without the clearest manifestation of legislative intent or unequivocal judicial precedent so construing the Labor Relations Act. We find neither.

So far as legislative manifestation is concerned, it is sufficient to say that there is not the slightest indication in the history of the Wagner Act or of the Taft-Hartley Act that Congress envisaged any such result under either statute.

As for judicial precedent, the Board recognized that "[t]here is no decided case directly dispositive of Darlington's claim that it had an absolute right to close its mill, irrespective of motive." The only language by this Court in any way adverting to this problem is found in Southport Petroleum Co. v. National Labor Relations Board, . . . , where it was stated:

> "Whether there was a *bona fide* discontinuance and a true change of ownership—which would terminate the duty of reinstatement created by the Board's order—or merely a disguised continuance of the old employer, does not clearly appear. . . ."

The courts of appeals have generally assumed that a complete cessation of business will remove an employer from future coverage by the Act. Thus the Court of Appeals said in these cases: The Act "does not compel a person to become or remain an employee. It does not compel one to become or remain an employer. Either may withdraw from that status with immunity, so long as the obligations of any employment contract have been met. . ."

The Eighth Circuit, in National Labor Relations Board v. New Madrid Mfg. Co., . . . , was equally explicit:

> "But none of this can be taken to mean that an employer does not have the absolute right, at all times, to permanently close and go out of business . . . for whatever reason he may choose, whether union animosity or anything else, and without his being thereby left subject to a remedial liability under the Labor Management Relations Act for such unfair labor practices as he may have committed in the enterprise, except up to the time that such actual and permanent closing . . . has occurred."

The AFL-CIO suggests in its *amicus* brief that Darlington's action was similar to a discriminatory lockout, which is prohibited " 'because designed to frustrate organizational efforts, to destroy or undermine bargaining representation, or to evade the duty to bargain.'" One of the purposes of the Labor Relations Act is to prohibit the disciminatory use of economic weapons in an effort to obtain future benefits. The discriminatory lockout designed to destroy a union, like a "runaway shop," is a lever which has been used to discourage collective employee activities in the future. But a complete liquidation of a business yields no such future benefit for the employer, if the termination is bona fide. It may be motivated more by spite against the union than by business reasons, but it is not the type of discrimination which is prohibited by the Act. The personal satisfaction that such an employer may derive from standing on his beliefs and the mere possibility that other employers will follow his example are surely too remote to be considered dangers at which the labor statutes were aimed. Although employees may be prohibited from engaging in a strike under certain conditions, no one would consider it a violation of the Act for the same employees to quit their employment *en masse,* even if motivated by a desire to ruin the employer. The very permanence of such action would negate any future economic benefit to the employees. The employer's right to go out of business is no different.

We are not presented here with the case of a "runaway shop," whereby Darlington would transfer its work to another plant or open a new plant in another locality to replace its closed plant. Nor are we concerned with a shutdown where the employees, by renouncing the union, could cause the plant to reopen. Such cases would involve discriminatory employer action for the purpose of obtaining some benefit in the future from the employees in the future. We hold here only that when an employer closes his entire business, even if the liquidation is motivated by vindictiveness toward the union, such action is not an unfair labor practice.

II.

While we thus agree with the Court of Appeals that viewing Darlington as an independent employer the liquidation of its business was not an unfair labor practice, we cannot accept the lower court's view that the same conclusion necessarily follows if Darlington is regarded as an integral part of the Deering Milliken enterprise.

The closing if an entire business, even though discriminatory, ends the employer-employee relationship; the force of such a closing is entirely spent as to that business when termination of the enterprise takes place. On the other hand, a discriminatory partial closing may have repercussions on what remains of the business, affording employer leverage for discouraging the free exercise of § 7 rights among remaining employees of much the same kind as that found to exist in the "runaway shop" and "temporary closing" cases. ... Moreover, a possible remedy open to the Board in such a case, like the remedies available in the "runaway shop", and "temporary closing" cases, is to order reinstatement of the discharged employees in the other parts of the business.

No such remedy is available when an entire business has been terminated. By analogy to those cases involving a continuing enterprise we are constrained to hold, in disagreement with the Court of Appeals, that a partial closing is an unfair labor practice under § 8(a) (3) if motivated by a purpose to chill unionism in any of the remaining plants of the single employer and if the employer may reasonably have foreseen that such closing would likely have that effect.

While we have spoken in terms of a "partial closing" in the context of the Board's finding that Darlington was part of a larger single enterprise controlled by the Milliken family, we do not mean to suggest that an organizational integration of plants or corporations is a necessary prerequisite to the establishment of such a violation of § 8(a) (3). If the persons exercising control over a plant that is being closed for antiunion reasons (1) have an interest in another business, whether or not affiliated with or engaged in the same line of commercial activity as the closed plant, of sufficient substantiality to give promise of their reaping a benefit from the discouragement of unionization in that business; (2) act to close their plant with the purpose of producing such a result; and (3) occupy a relationship to the other business which makes it realistically foreseeable that its employees will fear that such business will also be closed down if they persist in organizational activities, we think that an unfair labor practice has been made out.

Although the Board's single employer finding necessarily embraced findings as to Roger Milliken and the Milliken family which, if sustained by the Court of Appeals, would satisfy the elements of "interest" and "relationship" with respect to other parts of the Deering Milliken enterprise, that and the other Board findings fall short of establishing the factors of "purpose" and "effect" which are vital requisites of the general principles that govern a case of this kind.

Thus, the Board's findings as to the purpose and foreseeable effect of the Darlington closing pertained *only* to its impact on the Darlington employees. No findings were made as to the purpose and effect of the closing with respect to the employees in the other plants comprising the Deering Milliken group. It does not suffice to establish the unfair labor practice charged here to argue that the Darlington closing necessarily had an adverse impact upon unionization in such other plants. We have heretofore observed that employer action which has a foreseeable consequence of discouraging concerted activities generally does not amount to a violation of § 8(a) (3) in the absence of a showing of motivation which is aimed at achieving the prohibited effect. ... In an area which trenches so closely upon otherwise legitimate employer prerogatives, we consider the absence of Board findings on this score a fatal defect in its decision. The Court of Appeals for its part did not deal with the question of purpose and effect at all, since it concluded that an employer's right to close down his entire business because of distaste for unionism, also embraced a partial closing so motivated.

Apart from this, the Board's holding should not be accepted or rejected without court review of its single employer finding, judged, however, in accordance with the general principles set forth above. Review of that finding, which the lower court found unnecessary on its view of the cause, now becomes necessary in light of our holding in this part of our opinion, and is a task that devolves upon the Court of Appeals in the first instance. . . .

In these circumstances, we think the proper disposition of this cause is to require that it be remanded to the Board so as to afford the Board the opportunity to make further findings on the issue of purpose and effect. ... This is particularly appropriate here since the cases involve issues of first impression. If such findings are made, the cases will then be in a posture for further review by the Court of Appeals on all issues. Accordingly, without intimating any view as to how any of these matters should eventuate, we vacate the judgments of the Court of Appeals and remand the cases to that court with instructions to remand them to the Board for further proceedings consistent with this opinion. It is so ordered.

Judgments of Court of Appeals vacated and cases remanded with instructions.

Mr. Justice STEWART took no part in the decision of these cases.

Mr. Justice GOLDBERG took no part in the consideration or decision of these cases.

● ● ●

CASE QUESTIONS

1. Under what conditions may an employer lawfully terminate his business operations in response to a pro-union election?

2. What was the Supreme Court's final ruling in this case?

NLRB v. MIDWEST HANGER CO. & LIBERTY ENGINEERING CORPORATION
United States Court of Appeals, Eighth Circuit
474 F.2d 1155 (8th Cir. 1973)

● ● ●

GIBSON, Circuit Judge.

The National Labor Relations Board seeks enforcement of its decision and order reported at 193 NLRB No. 85. The Board found that Midwest Hanger Company and Liberty Engineering Corporation committed unfair labor practices in (1) coercive interrogation of one employee, (2) discriminatory discharge of 18 employees during a union organizing campaign, (3) threatening striking employees with discharge or other reprisal, and (4) discharge of one employee at the conclusion of an unfair labor practices strike upon his unconditional offer to return to work.

Although an election petition was filed, no election has yet been held. The Board ordered reinstatement with back pay for all concerned employees and further entered a bargaining order based upon its finding that the employer's actions precluded the holding of a valid election.

The Factual Background: The United Steelworkers of America, AFL-CIO, began its campaign to obtain recognition as the bargaining representative for the employees of the Company on June 1, 1970, when four employees signed authorization cards. The campaign reached its peak on June 11 and 12, when the Union mailed a letter to the president of the Company requesting recognition and offering to prove its majority status by submitting the signed authorization cards to a neutral party for inspection and verification. The Company received the letter on Monday, June 15; it made no reply.

During the intervening weekend the Company, which manufactures laundry and dry cleaning products, had selected 22 employees for discharge. These terminations were attributed to an expected decline in business due to a previously announced price increase effective as of June 15. Jones, the President of the Company, testified that their customers built up large inventories between the announcement and the effective date of the price increase. This had two effects: first, it caused an increase in work load over normal levels during the period just prior to the date of increase as customers built up their stock at the lower price, and second, it caused a decrease in business after the date of the increase as these customers reduced their inventories to normal levels. The standard which the Company claimed to have used in selecting the employees to be terminated was the efficiency of the employee based on skills, attendance habits, and ability. The Company contends that the employees discharged were the least efficient of its employees.

The Discriminatory Discharge: The General Counsel charges that the Company violated Section 8(a) (1) and (3) by the discharge of 18 named employees during the weekend of June 13 and 14 and thereafter. Seven of the employees were discharged during the weekend, six on Monday, June 15, and two on Tuesday, June 16. Two of the other three were discharged on July 1 and the other on August 11.

The discharge of a large number of employees including some union leaders during a union organizing campaign would appear to be "inherently destructive of employee interests," thus placing the burden on the Company of explaining away or justifying its action. As said in NLRB v. Great Dane Trailers, 388 U.S. 26, 34 . . . (1967):

> "From this review of our recent decisions, several principles of controlling importance here can be distilled. First, if it can reasonably be concluded that the employer's discriminatory conduct was 'inherently destructive' of important employee rights, no proof of an antiunion motivation is needed and the Board can find an unfair labor practice even if the employer introduces evidence that the conduct was motivated by business considerations."

Though a reduction in work force was clearly in order, the manner in which the Company made the reduction gave rise to a finding by the Board that the stated reasons given were pretextual.

Even though the employer may reduce its number of employees, it may not discriminate because of union activity in the selection of those to be terminated. The General Counsel relied initially on a percentage test to show that the selection procedures had been used to discriminate against the union employees. Of the 18 discharged employees, all but one had signed authorization cards. This presented a telling percentage of 95 per cent discharge of union adherents while the percentage of union employees in the plant as a whole was 70 percent. This on its face would indicate a discriminatory discharge violative of the Act. . . . The Company challenges these statistics by countering that other discharges of non-union adherents during the same period of time as the discharges in question would alter the figures. This may be correct, but there still exists substantial evidence in the record from which the Board could infer that the discharges questioned were discriminatory, and the Board can properly consider in context the discharges made during a crucial period of the organizing campaign.

As stated by Judge Lay in NLRB v. The Freeman Company, 471 F.2d 708 (8th Cir. 1972):

> "The rule is generally recognized that where the company demonstrates a proper business reason which standing alone would justify the company's action affecting employees, the Board has the burden to overcome this fact and demonstrate that the reasons exercised by the company were pretextual. ..."

We feel the Board here has carried, with exceptions later discussed, its burden of proof. Although evidence of a proper business purpose was supplied by the Company, the record contains substantial evidence to overcome the prima facie business purpose and to warrant an inference of discrimination. The most persuasive of this evidence is the showing by General Counsel that while these employees were discharged rather than laid off, the Company continued to advertise in a local newspaper for new employees, and that within a month after the discharge of these employees the Company began to hire new employees to maintain the work force at the new reduced level.

These discharges must be considered along with the Company's assertion that its biggest problem was employee turnover and the resulting inexperience of its work force. The Company alleged that the employees selected for termination were so selected because they were the least efficient of the Company's work force. This explanation implied that the employees met the minimum level of competency required to perform the work. The Company chose to ignore this ready pool of at least minimally qualified persons when it needed additional employees to replace the normal turnover occurring after the reduction in force. Instead of utilizing previously experienced employees, it recruited new, untrained personnel. This action was inconsistent with both the reasonable needs of the business and, more importantly, with the employer's past practice during slack business periods.

While we recognize that the National Labor Relations Act does not give the Board license to dictate the method by which an employer must reduce his work force, the Board may consider the method selected just as it does any employer action affecting employees where it finds that the action was taken for a prohibited purpose. The method selected for the reduction in work force may in itself be evidence of a discriminatory purpose when considered in light of the surrounding circumstances. The Act protects employees' rights to organize and bargain collectively and any action taken by management to thwart that right is violative of the Act.

Majestic Molded Products, Inc. v. NLRB, 330 F.2d 603 (2d Cir. 1964), presents a factual situation sufficiently analogous to the instant case to lend authoritative support to the Board's position. In Majestic two related companies had the same officers and shareholders and shared the same building. Both companies were unionized. During a period when a rival union was trying to gain recognition as the bargaining representative in one of the companies, Lucky Wish Products, Inc., a substantial number of employees were laid off. The company alleged that the layoff was due to a decline in business. At the same time, however, the sister company, Majestic Molded Products, Inc., increased its work force. The Court held that Majestic's failure to hire the employees laid off by Lucky Wish, in the absence of credible evidence other than the bare statements of management that the employees laid off by Lucky Wish were not qualified to perform the work done at Majestic, would support an inference that the layoff had been made because of the union activity and not for the reasons advanced by the employer.

The Company's failure here to preserve this group of experienced employees in combating normal attrition of workers, indicates a desire to permanently disassociate these employees from the Company, a desire which would be consistent with an anti-union motivation in the terminations. The Board, at least, could draw this permissible inference of illegal discrimination from the factual situation presented. Also casting doubt on the Company's explanation that the employees selected for termination were the least efficient employees in the plant is the fact that the selections were made without consulting the foreman who, as members of management, could best evaluate job performance of the employees. Although it was proper for the Company officials to reserve to themselves the decision on the dischargees, their failure to consult with the supervisors who best know the efficiency of each employee indicates that the criteria which was followed in making the selections was focused on some other aspect of the employee's conduct rather than efficiency.

Although the evidence in this case is conflicting on the charge of discrimination in the discharge of the named employees, there is substantial evidence from which the Board could permissibly infer discriminatory motives in the discharges, and we must enforce the Board's Order providing for reinstatement and back pay for these employees.

Two other employees were discharged on about July 1, allegedly for excessive absences. Elaine Peukert was absent 55.5 hours between January 1 and June 16, and she had received several warnings. She was not absent from June 16 to the time of her discharge. Kim Bristow was absent on June 16 and the next day was given a written warning. On June 29, she requested the next day off to go to the doctor and received permission. On her return to work on the following day, she was informed that she was discharged for repeated absenteeism. She was not absent between June 17 and June 29. During this period both employees had engaged in overt union activities which had come to the attention of management.

The Hearing Examiner found that these two employees had been discharged in violation of the Act and the Board ordered their reinstatement with back pay. Due to the prior discharges which we have found to be an unfair labor practice, the intervening union activity and the length of time between any unexcused absence and the discharge, there is substantial evidence to support the Board's findings, and the Order will be enforced as to those two employees.

Betty Johnson was discharged on August 11 for excessive absences. The General Counsel concedes that she had been "frequently absent prior to June 6." On June 16, she received a written warning concerning absences. She refused to sign the warning. On July 13, after several more absences, she was again given a written warning. After four more absences she was discharged.

Conceding that she was active in the union organization drive, it is obvious that the employer had ample cause to discharge her for aggravated and continued absenteeism; and, in the absence of any evidence that this discharge was motivated by any prohibited purpose, we hold that the finding that the discharge was in violation of the Act is not supported by substantial evidence. We, therefore, will not order enforced that portion of the Board's Order which required her reinstatement and back pay.

The Coercive Interrogation: John Sells applied for employment with Liberty Engineering in February, 1970. At the employment interview, Sells was asked how he felt about unions. He replied that in theory unions were "one of the greatest things that had ever been brought about," but that sometimes they get misused. The interviewer told him that they might have some union trouble. Sells replied that since the plant was located in an area where most of the companies were non-union he wouldn't have anticipated any trouble at all. Sells was hired about one week after the interview.

On June 15, the General Manager came to Sells at work and asked him if he had heard any union talk around the plant. Sells answered that he had and upon being asked how long he had heard the talk, replied, "At least a couple of weeks." The General Manager asked Sells to inform him if he heard anything else. Later that afternoon Sells was discharged.

Under the criteria set out in NLRB v. Ritchie Mfg. Co., 354 F.2d 90, 99 (8th Cir. 1966), we find there is substantial evidence in the whole record to support the Board's finding of coercive interrogation. Under *Ritchie* we look not only to the questioning itself but also at the circumstances surrounding the interrogation. *Ritchie* pointed out five circumstances which should receive close attention. These are:

> "[A] history of employer hostility and discrimination, the nature of the information sought (e.g., was the interrogator seeking information from which he could take action against individual employees), the identity of the questioner (i.e., what was his position in the company), the place and method of interrogation, and the truthfulness of the reply (e.g., did the interrogation inspire fear leading to evasive answers). . . ."

These standards had been previously enunciated by the Second Circuit in Bourne v. NLRB, 332 F.2d 47, 48 (2d Cir. 1964).

In the instant case certain of the circumstances point to the interrogation as having a coercive effect. The interrogation occurred against the background of a substantial discharge of employees at the time of the interrogation. The questioner, Ward, was the General Manager of the Company. Although the questioning took place at Sells' work area, it was under circumstances by which Sells might think that Ward had sought him out for questioning rather than having the questions occur in a casual conversation. Finally, Sells' answers, while not untruthful, were evasive. Sells was one of the instigators of the union movement and was well aware of the extent of the union campaign at the time of the questioning.

He did not, however, volunteer this information or any information to Ward. Management could and probably did view his answers as unsatisfactory; hence, his discharge.

These facts constitute substantial evidence to support the Board's conclusion that the questioning was coercive and therefore constituted an unfair labor practice under 29 U.S.C. § 158(a) (1).

The Letter to the Strikers: It is disputed whether a letter sent by the Company to the striking workers was found to be a violation of the Act. The letter was dated October 30, and informed the employees that the plant would reopen on Monday, November 2, and that employees who did not "wish to report to work as scheduled [would] be given until Wednesday, November 4, to seriously consider [their] decision."

In the amended complaint the General Counsel alleged that this letter contained the threat of discharge or other reprisal directed at the striking employees. No other activity of the Company which could be construed as such a threat was litigated. The Hearing Examiner found that "by threatening employees with discharge or other reprisals for engaging in a strike, the [Company] violated Section 8(a) (1) of the Act." While the decision is not pinpointed with regard to this letter, in the context of the entire record the finding can only be construed to relate to the letter. The letter can certainly be viewed as coercive and as an illegal interference with the employees' right to organize.

That portion of the Order which requires the employer to cease and desist threatening the employees with discharge or other reprisals is ordered enforced.

Termination of Grover Speck: On October 22, 1970, the employees on the second shift picketed the plant demanding the reinstatement of the employees discharged since June 12. They were later joined by employees from the other two shifts. Grover Speck, a long-haul truck driver for the Company, was scheduled to haul a load out that evening. He arrived at the plant about 5:00 p.m. but upon the request of the strikers, refused to cross the picket line. When the strike ended and the other employees returned to work, Speck was discharged. The Company alleged that the discharge was for cause, putting forward four independent grounds as giving cause for discharge. These were: (1) failure of Speck to return a telephone call from the Company president relating to loads delivered before the strike, (2) uncomplimentary remarks made about the Company president during a job interview, (3) misconduct during the strike, and (4) abuse of leased equipment.

The latter two of these reasons, if true, give adequate cause for discharge. The misconduct which was alleged was that during the strike Grover Speck had followed a replacement driver, who was then operating a company truck, in an unsafe manner, at high speeds on a narrow winding road. The employer presented the testimony of the truck driver as to the occurrence of this event, and it was corroborated by the Company president who saw Speck's car leave following the truck and another Company employee who testified that he saw Speck's car following the truck. Speck denied that the incident occurred.

The Board has held that "admitted reckless driving in pursuit of an employee in another automobile during the strike was conduct which justified [the employer] in denying his request for reinstatement." . . . This

Court has held that if the employer had reasonable cause to believe that the striking employee had been engaging in unprotected strike activities and, in reliance on that belief, refused to reinstate him, no violation of the Act results. . . .

The Hearing Examiner found that the record did not support this defense, but no explanation of this finding was made. Although the reckless driving was not admitted by Speck, there was no finding of a lack of credibility of the three Company witnesses who testified concerning the incident. There was no finding supported by substantial evidence, or any evidence at all, that the reason for discharge was pretextual and that the true motive for Speck's discharge was his union activities. The record clearly supports the occurrence of the incident.

Another ground which would justify the Company's refusal to reinstate Speck was the alleged abuse of equipment used by Speck. Midwest Hanger does not own its trucks; they are leased from Schock Leasing, Incorporated. Under the terms of the lease, Midwest furnished the drivers and Schock performed all maintenance and repairs. In the case of abuse of equipment by the drivers, Schock may require the Company to replace a driver. If Midwest does not do so, Schock can shift the cost of repairs to Midwest. The president of Schock Leasing testified that the equipment assigned to Speck had been abused, that he had been observed operating it in an improper manner, that his equipment required excessive repairs, and that the engine governor had been tampered with, allowing the engine to overrun, resulting in damage. The president of Schock Leasing contacted President Jones of Midwest Hanger and told him that Speck would have to be replaced. The Hearing Examiner did not credit this testimony because no documentary evidence was produced to support the testimony of the president of Schock Leasing.

There appears to be no reason to discredit the testimony of the president of Schock Leasing for failing to bring in books and records to support his testimony. The "best evidence" rule is not applicable here; he did not testify as to the contents of the records. If there was any doubt in the mind of the General Counsel, the records were equally available to him through the use of the discovery procedures provided. There is no reason to believe that the witness was other than a disinterested third party. It is also relevant to note that the central thrust of the testimony, the fact that Schock Leasing told Midwest Hanger that Speck would have to be replaced, would not be found in the records.

The Board's decision that Grover Speck was discharged because of his union activities is not supported by substantial evidence on the record considered as a whole. While we recognize that strikers are generally entitled to reinstatement upon their unqualified offer to return to work, subject to the availability of a job in the case of an economic striker, such a right is not absolute; there are certain recognized exceptions to the rule. Both of the reasons which we have discussed fall within such exceptions. After the employer has offered legitimate business reasons which would justify his actions, the Board plainly has the burden of going forward and offering evidence that the reasons advanced were pretextual. . . .

The General Counsel's bare contention that this discharge was motivated by Speck's union activity is unsupported by any evidence whatsoever and further is refuted by the record; no other striking employees were discharged, and this discharge was isolated by more than four months from the other discharge associated with union activity in the plant. That portion of the Board's order which requires reinstatement and back pay for Grover Speck is denied enforcement.

The Bargaining Order: On the basis of the unfair labor practices which had been found, the Board concluded that since the Union had acquired cards from a majority of the employees and since the employer's conduct had tended both to destroy that majority and to negate the likelihood of a future fair election, a bargaining order would be appropriate. The employer challenges this bargaining order on the sole grounds that it committed no unfair labor practices. We have found substantial evidence to support the findings of unfair labor practices as to all those charges except the discharge of Grover Speck and Betty Johnson. In view of these findings the contention of the employer is without merit, and the bargaining order is granted enforcement.

The Board's Order is enforced except for that portion which requires reinstatement and back pay for Grover Speck and Betty Johnson.

• • •

CASE QUESTIONS

1. On what basis did the court affirm the Board's finding of employer discriminatory practices?

2. What criteria may be considered by the Board in determining discriminatory discharges?

NLRB v. TRUCK DRIVERS LOCAL 449
United States Supreme Court
353 U.S. 87 (1957)

• • •

Mr. Justice BRENNAN delivered the opinion of the Court.

The question presented by this case is whether the nonstruck members of a multi-employer bargaining association committed an unfair labor practice when, during contract negotiations, they temporarily locked out their employees as a defense to a union strike against one of their members which imperiled the employers' common interest in bargaining on a group basis.

The National Labor Relations Board determined that resort to the temporary lockout was not an unfair labor practice in the circumstances. The Court of Appeals for the Second Circuit reversed. This Court granted certiorari to consider this important question of the construction of the amended National Labor Relations Act, and also to consider an alleged conflict with decisions of Courts of Appeals of other circuits.

Eight employers in the linen supply business in and around Buffalo, New York, comprise the membership of the Linen and Credit Exchange. For approximately 13 years, the Exchange and the respondent Union, representing the truck drivers employed by the members, bargained on a multi-employer basis and negotiated successive collective bargaining agreements signed by the Union and by the eight employers. Sixty days before such an agreement was to expire on April 30, 1953, the Union gave notice of its desire to open negotiations for changes.

The Exchange and the Union began negotiations some time before April 30, but the negotiations carried past that date and were continuing on May 26, 1953, when the Union put into effect a "whipsawing" plan by striking and picketing the plant of one of the Exchange members, Frontier Linen Supply, Inc. The next day, May 27, the remaining seven Exchange members laid off their truck drivers after notifying the Union that the lay-off action was taken because of the Frontier strike, advising the Union that the laid-off drivers would be recalled if the Union withdrew its picket line and ended the strike. Negotiations continued without interruption, however, until a week later when agreement was reached upon a new contract which the Exchange members and the Union approved and signed. Thereupon the Frontier strike was ended, the laid-off drivers were recalled, and normal operations were resumed at the plants of all Exchange members.

The Union filed with the National Labor Relations Board an unfair labor practice charge against the seven employers, alleging that the temporary lockout interfered with its rights guaranteed by § 7, thereby violating § 8(a) (1) and (3) of the Act. A complaint was issued, and after hearing a trial examiner found the employers guilty of the unfair labor practice charged. The Board overruled the trial examiner, finding that "the more reasonable inference is that, although not specifically announced by the Union, the strike against the one employer necessarily carried with it an implicit threat of future strike action against any or all of the other members of the Association," with the "calculated purpose" of causing "successive and individual employer capitulations." The Board therefore found that "in the absence of any independent evidence of antiunion motivation, ... the Respondent's [sic] action in shutting their plants until termination of the strike at Frontier was defensive and privileged in nature, rather than retaliatory and unlawful." The Board, citing Leonard v. National Labor Relations Board, 9 Cir., 205 F.2d 355, concluded "that a strike by employees against one employer-member of a multiemployer bargaining unit constitutes a threat of strike action against the other employers, which threat, per se, constitutes the type of economic or operative problem at the plants of the nonstruck employers which legally justifies their resort to a temporary lockout of employees."

The Court of Appeals agreed "that the Board reasonably inferred" a threat of strike action against the seven employers because there were "no peculiar facts concerning the Union's relations with that single member." The Court of Appeals thus implicitly found that the only reason for the strike against Frontier was the refusal of the Exchange to meet the Union's demands. But the court held that a temporary lockout of employees on a "mere threat of, or in anticipation of a strike," could be justified only if there were unusual economic hardship, and because "the stipulated facts show no economic justification for the lockout, ... the lockout of non-striking employees constituted an interference with their statutory right to engage in concerted activity in violation of § 8(a) (1) of the Act, and also constituted discrimination in the hire and tenure of employment of the employees because of the Union's action, thereby discouraging membership in the Union in violation of § 8(a) (3) of the Act."

Although, as the Court of Appeals correctly noted, there is no express provision in the law either prohibiting or authorizing the lockout, the Act does not make the lockout unlawful *per se*. Legislative history of the Wagner Act, 49 Stat. 449, indicates that there was no intent to prohibit strikes or lockouts as such. The unqualified use of the term "lock-out" in several sections of the Taft-Hartley Act is statutory recognition that there are circumstances in which employers may lawfully resort to the lockout as an economic weapon. This conclusion is supported by the legislative history of the Act.

We are not concerned here with the cases in which the lockout has been held unlawful because designed to frustrate organizational efforts, to destroy or undermine bargaining representation, or to evade the duty to bargain. Nor are we called upon to define the limits of the legitimate use of the lockout. The narrow question to be decided is whether a temporary lockout may lawfully be used as a defense to a union strike tactic which threatens the destruction of the employers' interest in bargaining on a group basis.

The Court of Appeals rejected the preservation of the integrity of the multiemployer bargaining unit as a justification for an employer lockout. The Court founded this conclusion upon its interpretation of the Taft-Hartley Act and its legislative history. After stating that "[m]ulti-employer bargaining has never received the express sanction of Congress," the court reasoned that because at the time of the enactment of the Taft-Hartley Act the Board had never "gone to the extreme lengths to which it now seeks to go in order to maintain the 'stability of the employer unit,'" Congress cannot be said to have given legislative approval to the present Board action. The court concluded that "Congress must have intended that such a radical innovation be left open for consideration by the joint committee it set up under § 402 of the Act [29 U.S.C.A. § 192] to study, among other things, 'the methods and procedures for best carrying out the collective-bargaining processes, with special attention to the effects of industrywide or regional bargaining upon the national economy.'"

We cannot subscribe to this interpretation. Multi-employer bargaining long antedated the Wagner Act, both in industries like the garment industry, characterized by numerous employers of small work forces, and in industries like longshoring and building construction, where workers change employers from day to day or week to week. This basis of bargaining has had its greatest expansion since enactment of the Wagner Act because employers have sought through group bargaining to match increased union strength. Approximately four million employees are now governed by collective bargaining agreements signed by unions with thousands of employer associations. At the time of the debates on the Taft-Hartley amendments, proposals were made to limit or outlaw multi-employer bargaining. These proposals failed of enactment. They were met with a storm of protest that their adoption would tend to weaken and not strengthen the process of collective bargaining and would conflict with the national labor policy of promoting industrial peace through effective collective bargaining.

The debates over the proposals demonstrate that Congress refused to interfere with such bargaining because there was cogent evidence that in many industries the multi-employer bargaining basis was a vital factor in the effectuation of the national policy of promoting labor peace through strengthened collective bargaining. The inaction of Congress with respect to multi-employer bargaining cannot be said to indicate an intention to leave the resolution of this problem to future legislation. Rather, the compelling conclusion is that Congress intended "that the Board should continue its established administrative practice of certifying multi-employer units, and intended to leave to the Board's specialized judgment the inevitable questions concerning multi-employer bargaining bound to arise in the future."

Although the Act protects the right of the employees to strike in support of their demands, this protection is not so absolute as to deny self-help by employers when legitimate interests of employees and employers collide. Conflict may arise, for example, between the right to strike and the interest of small employers in preserving multi-employer bargaining as a means of bargaining on an equal basis with a large union and avoiding the competitive disadvantages resulting from nonuniform contractual terms. The ultimate problem is the balancing of the conflicting legitimate interests. The function of striking that balance to effectuate national labor policy is often a difficult and delicate responsibility, which the Congress committed primarily to the National Labor Relations Board, subject to limited judicial review.

The Court of Appeals recognized that the National Labor Relations Board has legitimately balanced conflicting interests by permitting lockouts where economic hardship was shown. The court erred, however, in too narrowly confining the exercise of Board discretion to the cases of economic hardship. We hold that in the circumstances of this case the Board correctly balanced the conflicting interests in deciding that a temporary lockout to preserve the multi-employer bargaining basis from the disintegration threatened by the Union's strike action was lawful.

Reversed.

Mr. Justice WHITTAKER took no part in the consideration or decision of this case.

• • •

CASE QUESTION

1. What is the statutory basis for interpretation of the legality of lockouts, and when is this an acceptable labor practice?

NLRB v. INTERNATIONAL VAN LINES
United States Supreme Court
93 U.S. 74 (1972)

• • •

Mr. Justice STEWART delivered the opinion of the Court.

The respondent is a moving and storage company based in Santa Maria, California. In August, 1967, Local 381 of the International Brotherhood of Teamsters, Chauffeurs, Warehousemen, and Helpers of America began a campaign to organize the employees of moving and storage firms in the area. By September 21, five of the respondent's employees had signed union authorization cards; it is undisputed that they constituted a clear majority of what would be an appropriate bargaining unit. Instead of demanding recognition by the respondent, the Union on September 21, 1967, petitioned the National Labor Relations Board for certification as the exclusive bargaining agent of the respondent's employees.

Shortly thereafter, on October 2 and 3, the Union held meetings where it was announced that the respondent had at first consented to a representation election but had later withdrawn its consent. It was decided at the October 3 meeting that all of the moving and storage companies involved in the Union organization campaign should be struck; and on October 4, picketing commenced at the respondent's place of business.

Four of the respondent's employees, Robert and Manuel Vasquez, Richard Dicus, and Salvador Casillas, were present at the respondent's premises on the morning when picketing commenced. They refused to cross the picket line. The next morning, Robert and Manuel Vasquez and Richard Dicus received identical telegrams which read: "For failure to report to work as directed at 7 a.m. on Wednesday morning, Oct. 4, 1967, you are being permanently replaced. [Signed] International Van Lines." It is undisputed that at the time of the discharges, the respondent had not in fact hired permanent replacements.

Casillas sought reinstatement in late November, and the other three discharged employees made unconditional offers to return to work on December 12. At least as to these three, the respondent refused reinstatement, claiming that it had at that point hired permanent replacements. The Union then went to the National Labor Relations Board with unfair labor practice charges against the respondent.

The Board determined that the labor picketing that commenced on October 4 was activity protected under § 7 of the National Labor Relations Act, 29 U.S.C. § 157, and concluded that the subsequent discharges of striking employees discriminated against lawful union activity and were unfair labor practices under §§ 8(a) (1) and 8(a) (3) of the Act, 29 U.S.C. §§ 158(a) (1), (a) (3).

It is settled that an employer may refuse to reinstate economic strikers if in the interim he has taken on permanent replacements. ... It is equally settled that employees striking in protest of an employer's unfair labor practices are entitled, absent some contractual or statutory provision to the contrary, to unconditional reinstatement with back pay, "even if replacements for them have been made." ... Since the strike in the instant case continued after the unfair labor practices had been committed by the employer, the Board reasoned that the original economic strike became an unfair labor practice strike on October 5, when the three telegrams werewere sent. The Board held the four employees to be unfair labor-practice strikers and, accordingly, ordered their unconditional reinstatement with back pay.

The Board then sought enforcement of its order in the Court of Appeals for the Ninth Circuit. The Court of Appeals agreed that the labor picketing was a lawful economic strike, and that the discharges of the striking employees were unfair labor practices. ... Nevertheless, the Court of Appeals reversed the portion of the Board's order providing for reinstatement with back pay, reasoning as follows:

"The strikers whose discharges constituted the unfair labor practice were, at the time of their discharges, protesting only the original grievance. Any strikers subsequently discharged might legitimately be considered unfair labor practice strikers, for they would be protesting not only the original grievance but also the subsequent unfair labor practice. The initially discharged strikers were obviously not protesting their own discharges, which had not yet occurred. To assimilate their status to that of their co-workers who had not yet been discharged would eliminate the distinction between .[the] economic-striker-reinstatement rule *(Mackay Radio & Telegraph)* and the unfair-labor-practice-reinstatement rule *(Mastro Plastics)* in cases like this one. ..."

Consistent with its determination that the discharged employees were economic strikers entitled to reinstatement only if the employer could not show legitimate and substantial business justifications for refusing to take them back, the Court of Appeals remanded the case for further findings concerning the reasons for the employer's refusal to rehire them. ... Because this decision appeared to involve principles important to the administration of the National Labor Relations Act as amended, we granted the Board's petition for certiorari, 405 U.S. 953,. ...

Both the Board and the Court of Appeals have agreed that the labor picketing was a lawful economic strike, and the validity of that conclusion is not before us. Given that hypothesis, the Board and the Court of Appeals were clearly correct in concluding that the respondent committed unfair labor practices when it fired its striking employees. "[T]he discharge of economic strikers prior ... to the time their places are filled constitutes an unfair labor practice." ... We need not decide, however, whether the Board was correct in determining that the discharged employees assumed the status of unfair labor practice strikers on October 5, 1971, to reach the conclusion that the Court of Appeals erred in refusing to enforce the Board's order of reinstatement with back pay.

Unconditional reinstatement of the discharged employees was proper for the simple reason that they were the victims of a plain unfair labor practice by their employer. Quite apart from an characterization of the strike that continued after the wrongful discharges occurred, the discharges *themselves* were a sufficient ground for the Board's reinstatement order. "Reinstatement is the conventional correction for discriminatory discharges." ...

It would undercut the remedial powers of the Board with respect to § 8 violations, and subvert the protection of § 7 of the Act, to hold that the employees' rights to reinstatement arising from the discriminatory discharges were somehow forfeited merely because they continued for a time to engage in their lawful strike after the unfair labor practices had been committed.

The judgment of the Court of Appeals is reversed insofar as it refused to enforce the Board's order that the discharged employees be reinstated with back pay.

It is so ordered. Judgment reversed in part.

Mr. Justice BLACKMUN, concurring in the judgment.

The result mandated by the narrow factual situation presented in this case need not be automatically imposed whenever an economic striker is discharged before being permanently replaced. Although the Court's opinion speaks only of permanent replacement as a justification for refusal to reinstate an economic striker, the Court has recognized in the past that, in addition to permanent replacement, other "legitimate and substantial business justifications" for not reinstating an economic striker may exist. . . .

The Court is not faced in the present case with other "legitimate and substantial business justifications" because the employer, who bears the burden of proof, asserted only the permanent-replacement justification. The finding of an unfair labor practice here is not to be read, therefore, as necessarily precluding an employer from reliance on appropriate justifications other than permanent replacement.

Since the employer failed to show any business justification arising before the discharges, these workers enjoyed reinstatement rights when they were discriminatorily discharged. I concur in the reversal of the Court of Appeals' judgment because preservation of the rights existing before the workers were discharged is the appropriate remedy to provide "a restoration of the situation, as nearly as possible, to that which would have obtained but for the illegal discrimination. . . ."

• • •

CASE QUESTIONS

1. What is the effect of the distinction between economic strikers and unfair labor practice strikers on the issue of reinstatement?

2. Why did the Supreme Court refuse to determine the character of the strikers in this case?

BOYCOTTS   4

Section 8(b) (4) of the National Labor Relations Act declares certain types of secondary activities by labor to be unfair labor practices. Secondary activities are directed by a union against an employer's customers or suppliers. Under Section 10(1), the NLRB is required to seek, and the federal district courts are authorized to grant, temporary injunctions against an alleged violation of 8(b) (4) pending disposition by the Board. Under Section 303 of the Labor Management Relations Act a private remedy for damages is afforded for injury from a prohibited secondary labor action.

In essence, Section 8(b) (4) (B) prohibits labor organizations or their agents from (1) actual work stoppages or refusals to work, (2) encouraging or inducing any individual to engage in work stoppages or refusals to work, and (3) threats, coercion, or restraint of any person engaged in a business covered by the Act, where the purpose of such activity is to force or require any person to cease doing business with or dealing with any other person. A situation necessitating the prohibition arises where a union places pressure on a neutral employer—one who is not engaged in the labor dispute—to force him to cease doing business with the primary employer with whom the union has the dispute. The pressure can be in the form of picketing to force the neutral's employees to strike. Or, it can be where the union threatens, coerces, or restrains the neutral employer or his employees.

The ultimate purpose, then, of secondary activity is to bring about a termination of business between the neutral and primary employers. As a result, it is hoped by the union that the economic pressure on the primary employer will cause him to agree to the union's demands. Therefore, the Act seeks (1) to limit the scope of the labor dispute to the primary employer and the union, and (2) to prevent the neutral employer from becoming involved in a labor dispute which does not concern him or his employees.

INTRODUCTION TO THE CASES

The *Potter Case* is concerned with union boycotts of the primary employer. The legality of consumer boycotts is discussed in the *Tree Fruits Case*. The *Comella Case* describes an illegal secondary boycott and shows how a state court treats this problem.

POTTER v. HOUSTON GULF COAST BUILDING TRADES COUNCIL, AFL—CIO
United States Court of Appeals, Fifth Circuit
482 F.2d 837 (5th Cir. 1973)

● ● ●

Before GEWIN, THORNBERRY, and SIMPSON, Circuit Judges.

GEWIN, Circuit Judge:

In this case we are concerned solely with the scope of the equitable relief granted by the district court, 363 F. Supp. 1. Appellants are several unions all members of the Houston Gulf Coast Building and Trades Council. They contend that the relief fashioned by the court below is unnecessarily broad insofar as it bars them from engaging in peaceful primary picketing. We conclude that the scope of the injunctive relief granted is overbroad and should be modified; otherwise we affirm the order of the district court.

This litigation arose out of a labor dispute between appellants and two construction companies, Bullen Corporation (Bullen) and Boley Construction Company (Boley). The case was submitted to the district court upon the following stipulated facts. Bullen is a general contractor engaged in and supervising three separate construction projects in Houston, Texas. In November of 1972 appellant, Houston Gulf Coast Building and Trades Council and its component unions, commenced efforts to organize Bullen's employees. Pickets were established at each of Bullen's three jobsites; they carried signs protesting the allegedly substandard wages paid by Bullen. Bullen immediately notified the unions that a reserve gate for the exclusive use of its employees would be set aside at each jobsite.

While at two of the jobsites appellants confined their picketing to the gates reserved for Bullen's employees, at the third, picketing continued at entrances and other places used by the employees of union subcontractors. In addition, union business agents visited each jobsite and advised employees of the various union subcontractors working at the same jobsites that they should not cross the picket lines. Employees who did not follow this advice were informed that union charges would be filed against them. As a result of these threats and other union activities, employees of the union business agents visited each jobsites stopped working, and Bullen's construction projects were brought to a standstill.

Like Bullen, Boley is a general contractor operating in the Houston area. At one of its construction projects a subcontractor was using non-union labor. A union of sheet metal workers not involved in this appeal began picketing to protest the wages paid by this subcontractor. When a reserve gate was established for the use of the offending subcontractor's employees, picketing was confined to it. But some of appellant's business agents visited the jobsite and ordered all union employees to cease working behind the picket line. Union charges were served upon those who continued to work contrary to this order. As a result the several union subcontractors on the Boley jobsite were all forced to stop work even though they had no dispute with appellants.

Thus at all of the construction sites in question the unions exerted pressure on Boley and Bullen by inducing members who were employed by neutral subcontractors to strike. Both companies filed charges with the National Labor Relations Board alleging that appellants were engaging in unfair labor practices violative of § 8 (b) (4) (i) (ii) (B) of the National Labor Relations Act, the section proscribing secondary boycotts. Following a preliminary investigation, the regional director of the NLRB concluded that there was reasonable cause to believe the companies' allegations. A complaint against the unions was issued. Pursuant to § 10(*l*) of the Act, the regional director petitioned the district court for appropriate interim injunctive relief pending a final disposition of the charges before the Board.

The district court reviewed the stipulation of facts submitted by the parties and determined that the regional director did have reasonable cause to believe that appellants were violating the Act as charged. Appellants do not contest this determination. The facts to which the parties stipulated provide more than ample cause to believe that the unions were engaged in illegal secondary activity violative of § 8(b) (4). Although the line between primary and secondary activity is often especially difficult to draw when two employers are performing separate tasks on common premises, the courts have held time and again that tactics such as those employed by the unions in this case fall on the secondary side of the line.

Having properly concluded that the regional director's petition was meritorious, the district court proceeded to fashion interim injunctive relief. The unions were enjoined from further picketing at any of the Bullen or Boley jobsites and from in any other manner inducing neutral employees to exert pressure upon their employers so as to force them to cease doing business with Bullen or Boley. In addition, the unions were required to notify all members employed by neutral subcontractors that the unions had no objection to their returning to work and that they were expected to man their jobs upon the request of their employers.

Appellants contend that the injunctive relief granted by the district court is overbroad insofar as it prohibits them from engaging in peaceful picketing in front of gates reserved for the exclusive use of the employees of the employers with whom they are at odds. They also protest the portion of the district court decree requiring them to order their striking members to report to work upon request. The regional director, on the other hand, takes the position that here the peaceful primary picketing was so enmeshed with the illegal secondary activity as to be inseparable from it. He argues that to enjoin the latter without at the same time enjoining the former would be useless since the picketing serves as a signal to all union employees to remain on strike until otherwise directed. In considering remedies the district court felt compelled to defer to the expertise of the regional director, and, relying primarily upon the authority of Milk Wagon Drivers v. Meadowmoor Dairies—a case in which the Supreme Court affirmed an injunction against picketing which was accompanied by flagrant violence—it adopted the board decree he recommended.

It has often been said that the provisions of § 8(b) (4) reflect "the dual congressional objectives of preserving the right of labor organizations to bring pressure to bear on offending employers in primary labor disputes and of shielding unoffending employers and others from pressures in controversies not their own." The statute prohibits all union activity "where . . . an object thereof is forcing or requiring" an employer to cease doing business with "any person." Although the language of § 8(b) (4) is quite broad, it bans only secondary activity. Peaceful primary activity and its normal incidents are not forbidden and, in fact, are specifically exempted from the section's coverage.

Thus, whenever possible, a grant of equitable relief should be carefully tailored so as to permit the continuation of primary activities while stamping out the illegal secondary conduct and its deleterious impact. This principle was implicitly recognized by the Supreme Court in Youngdahl v. Rainfair, a case involving a union which had combined picketing with threats, intimidation, and acts of violence. A state court had enjoined all union activity for the immediate future, but the Supreme Court set aside the injunction insofar as it prohibited peaceful picketing. The Court plainly indicated that at least initially the lower court should have halted only the illegal activity; further relief could then be granted if proven necessary. Although there was no secondary activity in the case, *Youngdahl* nevertheless suggests that, if possible, equitable relief in a labor dispute should not be drawn so broadly as to limit the statutorily protected right of unions to bring peaceful primary pressure to bear on employers with whom they have grievances. By proceeding in this manner the courts will insure that both congressional objectives embodied in § 8(b) (4) will be recognized, namely, that of prohibiting secondary activity while permitting primary activity to continue.

In this case there is no evidence of the kind of violence condemned in *Meadowmoor Dairies* or indeed of any violence at all. Appellants' activities, including both the primary picketing and the exertion of secondary pressures, were all peacefully conducted. In these circumstances we believe the district court abused its discretion in ordering a halt to peaceful primary picketing. As long as the unions restrict their picketing to the immediate vicinity of the reserve gates set aside for the use of the employees of the employers against whom their protests are directed, it should be allowed to continue in the absence of violence.

On the other hand insofar as the district court's decree enjoined other union activity designed to coerce neutral employees and ordered the unions to inform these employees that the union no longer objected to a return to work, it constituted a proper exercise of the court's discretion and is affirmed. This part of the decree was intended to halt the illegal secondary activity and to remedy its effects. In the first instance it should have been sufficient. If subsequent events demonstrate this relief to be inadequate—for instance if it becomes clear that the primary picketing operates as nothing more than a signal to neutral employees to remain on strike—then the district court can always respond in an appropriate manner.

Under the facts and in the circumstances disclosed by the record now before us, we modify the injunctive relief ordered by this district court insofar as it prohibits peaceful primary picketing, and that portion of the order is vacated and set aside. The remainder of its order is left intact, and the case is remanded to the district court for further proceedings not inconsistent with this opinion.

Modified, affirmed and remanded.

• • •

CASE QUESTIONS

1. Who is the Appellee, Potter, and why is he a party to this case?

2. Why did the National Labor Relations Board and the district court fail to distinguish between the two types of union activities? What restrictions did the court of appeals place upon the primary activities?

3. How does injunctive relief apply in this case?

NLRB v. LOCAL 760, FRUIT AND VEGETABLE PACKERS AND WAREHOUSEMEN
United States Supreme Court
377 U.S. 58 (1964)

• • •

Mr. Justice BRENNAN delivered the opinion of the Court.

Under § 8(b) (4) (ii) (B) of the National Labor Relations Act, as amended, it is an unfair labor practice for a union "to threaten, coerce, or restrain any person," with the object of "forcing or requiring any person to cease using, selling, handling, transporting, or otherwise dealing in the products of any other producer . . . or to cease doing business with any other person . . ." A proviso excepts, however, "publicity, *other than picketing,* for the purpose of truthfully advising the public . . . that a product or products are produced by an employer with whom the labor organization has a primary dispute and are distributed by another employer, as long as such publicity does not have an effect of inducing any individual employed by any person other than the primary employer in the course of his employment to refuse to pick up, deliver, or transport any goods, or not to perform any services, at the establishment of the employer engaged in such distribution." (Italics supplied.) The question in this case is whether the respondent unions violated this section when they limited their secondary picketing of retail stores to an appeal to the customers of the stores not to buy the products of certain firms against which one of the respondents was on strike.

Respondent Local 760 called a strike against fruit packers and warehousemen doing business in Yakima, Washington. The struck firms sold Washington State apples to the Safeway chain of retail stores in and about Seattle, Washington. Local 760, aided by respondent Joint Council, instituted a consumer boycott against the apples in support of the strike. They placed pickets who walked back and forth before the customers' entrances of 46 Safeway stores in Seattle. The pickets—two at each of 45 stores and three at the 46th store—wore placards and distributed handbills which appealed to Safeway customers, and to the public generally, to refrain from buying Washington State apples, which were only one of numerous food products sold in the stores.

Before the pickets appeared at any store, a letter was delivered to the store manager informing him that the picketing was only an appeal to his customers not to buy Washington State apples, and that the pickets were being expressly instructed "to patrol peacefully in front of the consumer entrances of the store, to stay away from the delivery entrances and not to interfere with the work of your employees, or with deliveries to or pickups from your store." A copy of written instructions to the pickets—which included the explicit statement that "you are also forbidden to request that the customers not patronize the store"—was enclosed with the letter. Since it was desired to assure Safeway employees that they were not to cease work, and to avoid any interference with pickups or deliveries, the pickets appeared after the stores opened for business and departed before the stores closed. At all times during the picketing, the store employees continued to work, and no deliveries or pickups were obstructed. Washington State apples were handled in normal course by both Safeway employees and the employees of other employers involved. Ingress and egress by customers and others were not interfered with in any manner.

A complaint was issued on charges that this conduct violated § 8(b) (4) as amended. The case was submitted directly to the National Labor Relations Board on a stipulation of facts and the waiver of a hearing and proceedings before a Trial Examiner. The Board held, following its construction of the statute in Upholsterers Frame & Bedding Workers Twin City Local No. 61, that "by literal wording of the proviso [to Section 8(b) (4)] as well as through the interpretive gloss placed thereon by its drafters, consumer picketing in front of a secondary establishment is prohibited." . . . Upon respondents' petition for review and the Board's cross-petition for enforcement, the Court of Appeals for the District of Columbia Circuit set aside the Board's order and remanded. The court rejected the Board's construction and held that the statutory requirement of a showing that respondents' conduct would "threaten, coerce, or restrain" Safeway could only be satisfied by affirmative proof that a substantial economic impact on Safeway had occurred, or was likely to occur as a result of the conduct. Under the remand the Board was left "free to reopen the record to receive evidence upon the issue whether Safeway was in fact threatened, coerced, or restrained." . . .

The Board's reading of the statute—that the legislative history and the phrase "other than picketing" in the proviso reveal a congressional purpose to outlaw all picketing directed at customers at a secondary site —necessarily rested on the finding that Congress determined that such picketing always threatens, coerces or restrains the secondary employer. We therefore have a special responsibility to examine the legislative history for confirmation that Congress made that determination. Throughout the history of federal regulation of labor relations, Congress has consistently refused to prohibit peaceful picketing except where it is used as a means to achieve specific ends which experience has shown are undesirable. "In the sensitive area of peaceful picketing Congress has dealt explicitly with isolated evils which experience has established flow from such picketing. . . ." We have recognized this congressional practice and have not ascribed to Congress a purpose to outlaw peaceful picketing unless "there is the clearest indication in the legislative history," that Congress intended to do so as regards the particular ends of the picketing under review. Both the congressional policy and our adherence to this principle of interpretation reflect concern that a broad ban against peaceful picketing might collide with the guarantees of the First Amendment.

We have examined the legislative history of the amendments to § 8(b) (4), and conclude that it does not reflect with the requisite clarity a congressional plan to proscribe all peaceful consumer picketing at secondary sites, and, particularly, any concern with peaceful picketing when it is limited, as here, to persuading Safeway customers not to buy Washington State apples when they traded in the Safeway stores. All that the legislative history shows in the way of an "isolated evil" believed to require proscription of peaceful consumer picketing at secondary sites was its use to persuade the customers of the secondary employer to cease trading with him in order to force him to cease dealing with, or to put pressure upon, the primary employer. This narrow focus reflects the difference between such conduct and peaceful picketing at the secondary site directed only at the struck product. In the latter case, the union's appeal to the public is confined to its dispute with the primary employer, since the public is not asked to withhold its patronage from the secondary employer, but only to boycott the primary employer's goods. On the other hand, a union appeal to the public at the secondary site not to trade at all with the secondary employer goes beyond the goods of the primary employer, and seeks the public's assistance in forcing the secondary employer to cooperate with the union in its primary dispute. This is not to say that this distinction was expressly alluded to in the debates. It is to say, however, that the consumer picketing carried on in this case is not attended by the abuses at which the statute was directed.

The story of the 1959 amendments, which we have detailed at greater length in our opinion filed today in National Labor Relations Board v. Servette, Inc., 377 U.S. 46, begins with the original § 8(b) (4) of the National Labor Relations Act. Its prohibition, in pertinent part, was confined to the inducing or encouraging of "the employees of any employer to engage in a strike or a concerted refusal . . . to . . . handle . . . any goods . . ." of a primary employer. This proved to be inept language. Three major loopholes were revealed. Since only inducement of "employees" was proscribed, direct inducement of a supervisor or the secondary employer by threats of labor trouble was not prohibited. Since only a "strike or a concerted refusal" was prohibited, pressure upon a single employee was not forbidden. Finally, railroads, airlines and municipalities were not "employers" under the Act and therefore inducement or encouragement of their employees was not unlawful.

When major labor relations legislation was being considered in 1958 the closing of these loopholes was important to the House and to some members of the Senate. But the prevailing Senate sentiment favored new legislation primarily concerned with the redress of other abuses, and neither the Kennedy-Ives bill, which failed of passage in the House in the Eighty-fifth Congress, nor the Kennedy-Ervin bill, adopted by the Senate in the Eighty-sixth Congress, included any revision of § 8(b) (4). Proposed amendments of § 8(b) (4) offered by several Senators to fill the three loopholes were rejected. The Administration introduced such a bill, and it was supported by Senators Dirksen and Goldwater. Senator Goldwater, an insistent proponent of stiff boycott curbs, also proposed his own amendments. We think it is especially significant that neither Senator, nor the Secretary of Labor in testifying in support of the Administration's bill, referred to consumer picketing as making the amendments necessary. Senator McClellan, who also offered a bill to curb boycotts, mentioned consumer picketing but only such as was "pressure in the form of dissuading customers *from dealing with* secondary employers." (Emphasis supplied.) It was the opponents of the amendments who, in expressing fear of their sweep, suggested that they might proscribe consumer picketing. Senator Humphrey first sounded the warning early in April. Many months later, when the Conference bill was before the Senate, Senator Morse, a conferee, would not support the Conference bill on the express ground that it prohibited consumer picketing. But we have often cautioned against the danger, when interpreting a statute, of reliance upon the views of its legislative opponents. In their zeal to defeat a bill, they understandably tend to overstate its reach. "The fears and doubts of the opposition are no authoritative guide to the construction of legislation. It is the sponsors that we look to when the meaning of the statutory words is in doubt." Schwegmann Bros. v. Calvert Distillers Corp., 341 U.S. 384, 394-395. ...

The silence of the sponsors of amendments is pregnant with significance since they must have been aware that consumer picketing as such had been held to be outside the reach of § 8(b) (4). We are faithful to our practice of respecting the congressional policy of legislating only against clearly identified abuses of peaceful picketing when we conclude that the Senate neither specified the kind of picketing here involved as an abuse, nor indicated any intention of banning all consumer picketing.

The House history is similarly beclouded, but what appears confirms our conclusion. From the outset the House legislation included provisions concerning secondary boycotts. The Landrum-Griffin bill, which was ultimately passed by the House, embodied the Eisenhower Administration's proposals as to secondary boycotts. The initial statement of Congressman Griffin in introducing the bill which bears his name, contains no reference to consumer picketing in the list of abuses which he thought required the secondary boycott amendments. Later in the House debates he did discuss consumer picketing, but only in the context of its abuse when directed against shutting off the patronage of a secondary employer.

In the debates before passage of the House bill he stated that the amendments applied to consumer picketing of customer entrances to retail stores selling goods manufactured by a concern under strike, if the picketing were designed to "coerce or to restrain the employer of [the] second establishment, to get him not to do business with the manufacturer... ," and further that, "of course, this bill and any other bill is limited by the constitutional right of free speech. If the purpose of the picketing is to *coerce the retailer not to do business* with the manufacturer,—then such a boycott could be stopped. (Italics supplied.)

The relevant changes in former § 8(b) (4) made by the House bill substituted "any individual employed by any person" for the Taft-Hartley wording, "the employees of any employer," deleted the requirement of a "concerted" refusal, and made it an unfair labor practice "to threaten, coerce, or restrain any person" where an object thereof was an end forbidden by the statute, e.g., forcing or requiring a secondary employer to cease handling the products of, or doing business with, a primary employer. There is thus nothing in the legislative history prior to the convening of the Conference Committee which shows any congressional concern with consumer picketing beyond that with the "isolated evil" of its use to cut off the business of a secondary employer as a means of forcing him to stop doing business with the primary employer. When Congress meant to bar picketing *per se,* it made its meaning clear; for example, § 8(b) (7) makes it an unfair labor practice, "to picket or cause to be picketed . . . any employer . . . ." In contrast, the prohibition of § 8(b) (4) is keyed to the coercive nature of the conduct, whether it be picketing or otherwise.

Senator Kennedy presided over the Conference Committee. He and Congressman Thompson prepared a joint analysis of the Senate and House bills. This analysis pointed up the First Amendment implications of the broad language in the House revisions of § 8(b) (4) stating,

> "The prohibition [of the House bill] reaches not only picketing but leaflets, radio broadcasts and newspaper advertisements, thereby interfering with freedom of speech. . . .

> ". . . one of the apparent purposes of the amendment is to prevent unions from appealing to the general public as consumers for assistance in a labor dispute. This is a basic infringement upon freedom of expression."

This analysis was the first step in the development of the publicity proviso, but nothing in the legislative history of the proviso alters our conclusion that Congress did not clearly express an intention that amended § 8(b) (4) should prohibit all consumer picketing. Because of the sweeping language of the House bill, and its implications for freedom of speech, the Senate conferees refused to accede to the House proposal without safeguards for the right of unions to appeal to the public, even by some conduct which might be "coercive." The result was the addition of the proviso. But it does not follow from the fact that some coercive conduct was protected by the proviso, that the exception "other than picketing" indicates that Congress had determined that all consumer picketing was coercive.

No Conference Report was before the Senate when it passed the compromise bill, and it had the benefit only of Senator Kennedy's statement of the purpose of the proviso. He said that the proviso preserved "the right to appeal to consumers by methods other than picketing asking them to refrain from buying goods made by nonunion labor *and* to refrain from trading with a retailer who sells such goods. . . . We were not able to persuade the House conferees to permit picketing in front of that secondary shop, but were able to persuade them to agree that the unions shall be free to conduct informational activity short of picketing. In other words, the union can hand out handbills at the shop . . . and can carry on all publicity short of having ambulatory picketing . . . ." (Italics supplied.) This explanation does not compel the conclusion that the Conference Agreement contemplated prohibiting any consumer picketing at a secondary site beyond that which urges the public, in Senator Kennedy's words, to "refrain from trading with a retailer who sells such goods." To read into the Conference Agreement, on the basis of a single statement, an intention to prohibit all consumer picketing at a secondary site would depart from our practice of respecting the congressional policy not to prohibit peaceful picketing except to curb "isolated evils" spelled out by the Congress itself.

Peaceful consumer picketing to shut off all trade with the secondary employer unless he aids the union in its dispute with the primary employer, is poles apart from such picketing which only persuades his customers not to buy the struck product. The proviso indicates no more than that the Senate conferees' constitutional doubts led Congress to authorize publicity other than picketing which persuades the customers of a secondary employer to stop all trading with him, but not such publicity which has the effect of cutting off his deliveries or inducing his employees to cease work. On the other hand, picketing which persuades the customers of a secondary employer to stop all trading with him was also to be barred.

In sum, the legislative history does not support the Board's finding that Congress meant to prohibit all consumer picketing at a secondary site, having determined that such picketing necessarily threatened, coerced, or restrained the secondary employer. Rather, the history shows that Congress was following its usual practice of legislating against peaceful picketing only to curb "isolated evils."

This distinction is opposed as "unrealistic" because, it is urged, all picketing automatically provokes the public to stay away from the picketed establishment. The public will, it is said, neither read the signs and handbills, nor note the explicit injunction that "This is not a strike against any store or market." Be that as it may, our holding today simply takes not of the fact that Congress has never adopted a broad condemnation of peaceful picketing, such as that urged upon us by petitioners, and an intention to do so is not revealed with that "clearest indication in the legislative history," which we require.

We come then to the question whether the picketing in this case, confined as it was to persuading customers to cease buying the product of the primary employer, falls within the area of secondary consumer picketing which Congress did clearly indicate its intention to prohibit under § 8(b) (4) (ii). We hold that it did not fall within that area, and therefore did not "threaten, coerce, or restrain" Safeway. While any diminution in Safeway's purchases of apples due to a drop in consumer demand might be said to be a result which causes respondents' picketing to fall literally within the statutory prohibition, "it is a familiar rule that a thing may be within the letter of the statute and yet not within the statute, because not within its spirit nor within the intention of its makers." Holy Trinity Church v. United States, 143 U.S. 457, 459. ...

When consumer picketing is employed only to persuade customers not to buy the struck product, the union's appeal is closely confined to the primary dispute. The site of the appeal is expanded to include the premises of the secondary employer, but if the appeal succeeds, the secondary employer's purchases from the struck firms are decreased only because the public has diminished its purchases of the struck product. On the other hand, when consumer picketing is employed to persuade customers not to trade at all with the secondary employer, the latter stops buying the struck product, not because of a falling demand, but in response to pressure designed to inflict injury on his business generally. In such case, the union does more than merely follow the struck product; it creates a separate dispute with the secondary employer.

We disagree therefore with the Court of Appeals that the test of "to threaten, coerce, or restrain" for the purposes of this case is whether Safeway suffered or was likely to suffer economic loss. A violation of § 8(b) (4) (ii) (B) would not be established, merely because respondents' picketing was effective to reduce Safeway's sales of Washington State apples, even if this led or might lead Safeway to drop the item as a poor seller.

The judgment of the Court of Appeals is vacated and the case is remanded with direction to enter judgment setting aside the Board's order. It is so ordered.

Judgment of Court of Appeals vacated and case remanded with directions.

APPENDIX TO OPINION OF THE COURT.

Mr. Justice DOUGLAS took no part in the consideration or decision of this case.

"Notice to Storage [sic] Manager and Store Employees.

"We are advised that you are presently engaged in selling Washington State Apples.

"The 1960 crop of Washington State Apples is being packed by non-union firms, including 26 firms in the Yakima Valley. Prior to this year, the 26 Yakima Valley firms had been parties to a collective bargaining contract with Teamsters Union Local 760 of Yakima, Washington, but this year, when a new contract was being negotiated, the employers took the position that many of the basic provisions of the prior contract, such as seniority, overtime, protection against unjust discharge, grievance procedure and union security, should be weakened or eliminated entirely. These extreme demands plus a refusal to bargain in good faith led to a strike against the employer. The union made all possible efforts to avoid this strike as did outside agencies who were assisting in the negotiations. Even the Governor of the State of Washington, the Honorable Albert D. Rosellini, intervened and suggested that the parties agree to a fact finding committee or arbitration. The union agreed to these proposals but the employers declined.

"The employer's refusal to bargain in good faith has caused the Seattle office of the National Labor Relations Board to prepare a complaint against the employers, charging them with unfair labor practices in violation of federal law.

"The strike at Yakima is still continuing and in order to win this strike, we must ask the consuming public not to purchase Washington State Apples.

"Therefore, we are going to place peaceful pickets at the entrances to your store for the purpose of trying to persuade the public not to buy Washington Apples. These pickets are being instructed to patrol peacefully in front of the consumer entrances of the store, to stay away from the delivery entrances and not to interfere with the work of your employees, or with deliveries to or pickups from your store. A copy of the instructions which have been furnished to the pickets is attached herewith.

"We do not intend that any of your employees cease work as a result of the picketing. We ask that you advise your employees of our intentions in this respect, perhaps by posting this notice on your store bulletin board.

"If any of your employees should stop work as a result of our program, or if you should have any difficulties as far as pickups and deliveries are concerned, or if you observe any of the pickets disobeying the instructions which they have been given, please notify the undersigned union representative at once and we will take steps to see that the situation is promptly corrected.

"As noted above, our information indicates that you are presently selling Washington State Apples. If, however, this information is not correct and you are selling apples exclusively from another state, please notify the undersigned and we will see that the pickets are transferred to another store where Washington State Apples are actually being sold.

"Thank you for your cooperation."

The instructions to pickets read as follows: ...

"Dear Picket:

"You are being asked to help publicize a nationwide-consumer boycott aimed at non-union Washington State Apples. To make this program a success your cooperation is essential. Please read these instructions and follow them carefully.

"1. At all times you are to engage in peaceful picketing. You are forbidden to engage in any altercation, argument, or misconduct of any kind.

"2. You are to walk back and forth on the sidewalk in front of the consumer entrances to the grocery stores. If a particular store is located toward the rear of a parking lot, you are to ask the store manager for permission to walk back and forth on the apron or sidewalk immediately in front of the store; but if he denies you this permission, you are to picket only on the public sidewalk at the entrances to the parking lot. As far as large shipping centers are concerned, you will be given special instruction for picketing in such locations.

"3. You are not to picket in front of or in the area of any entrance to the store which is apparently set aside for the use of store employees and delivery men. As noted above, you are to limit your picketing to the consumer entrances to the store.

"4. This union has no dispute with the grocery stores, and you are forbidden to make any statement to the effect that toe store is unfair or on strike. You are also forbidden to request that the customers not patronize the store. We are only asking that the customers not buy Washington State apples, when they are shopping at the store.

"5. Similarly, you are not to interfere with the work of any employees in the store. If you are asked by these employees what the picketing is about, you are to tell them it is an advertising or consumer picket and that they should keep working. Likewise if you are asked by any truck drivers who are making pickups or deliveries what the picket is about, you are to advise that it is an advertising or consumer picket and that it is not intended to interfere with pickups or deliveries (i. e. that they are free to go through).

"6. If you are given handbills to distribute, please distribute these handbills in a courteous manner and if the customers throw them on the ground, please see that they are picked up at once and that the area is kept clean.

"7. You are forbidden to use intoxicating beverages while on duty or to have such beverages on your person.

"8. If a state official or any other private party should complain to you about the picketing, advise them you have your instructions and that their complaints should be registered with the undersigned union representative.

"9. These instructions should answer most of your questions concerning this program. However, if you have any additional questions or if specific problems arise which require additional instructions, please call the undersigned."

Mr. Justice BLACK, concurring.

Because of the language of § 8(b) (4) (ii) (B) of the National Labor Relations Act and the legislative history set out in the opinions of the Court and of my Brother HARLAN, I feel impelled to hold that Congress, in passing this section of the Act, intended to forbid the striking employees of one business to picket the premises of a neutral business where the purpose of the picketing is to persuade customers of the neutral business not to buy goods supplied by the struck employer. Construed in this way, as I agree with Brother HARLAN that it must be, I believe, contrary to his view, that the section abridges freedom of speech and press in violation of the First Amendment.

"Picketing," in common parlance and in § 8(b) (4) (ii) (B), includes at least two concepts: (1) patrolling, that is, standing or marching back and forth or round and round on the street, sidewalks, private property, or elsewhere, generally adjacent to someone else's premises; (2) speech, that is, arguments, usually on a placard, made to persuade other people to take the picketers' side of a controversy. . . . While "the dissemination of information concerning the facts of a labor dispute must be regarded as within that area of free discussion that is guaranteed by the Constitution," Thornhill v. Alabama, 310 U.S. 88, 102, . . . patrolling is, of course, conduct, not speech, and therefore is not directly protected by the First Amendment. It is because picketing includes patrolling that neither Thornhill nor cases that followed it lend "support to the contention that peaceful picketing is beyond legislative control." Giboney v. Empire Storage & Ice Co., 336 U.S. 490, 499-500. . . . However, when conduct not constitutionally protected, like patrolling, is intertwined, as in picketing, with constitutionally protected free speech and press, regulation of the non-protected conduct may at the same time encroach on freedom of speech and press. In such cases it is established that it is the duty of courts, before upholding regulations of patrolling, "to weigh the circumstances and to appraise the substantiality of the reasons advanced in support of the regulation of the free enjoyment of the rights" of speech and press. Schneider v. State, 308 U.S., at 161. . . .

Even assuming that the Federal Government has power to bar or otherwise regulate patrolling by persons on local streets or adjacent to local business premises in the State of Washington, it is difficult to see that the section in question intends to do anything but prevent dissemination of information about the facts of a labor dispute—a right protected by the First Amendment. It would be different (again assuming federal power) if Congress had simply barred or regulated all patrolling of every kind for every purpose in order to keep the streets around interstate business open for movement of people and property. Schneider v. State, supra, 308 U.S. at 160-161; ... or to promote the public safety, peace, comfort, or convenience, Cantwell v. Connecticut, 310 U.S. 296, ... or to protect people from violence and breaches of the peace by those who are patrolling, Thornhill v. Alabama, supra, 310 U.S. at 105. ... Here the section against picketing was not passed for any of these reasons. The statute in no way manifests any government interest against patrolling as such, since the only patrolling it seeks to make unlawful is that which is carried on to advise the public, including consumers, that certain products have been produced by an employer with whom the picketers have a dispute. All who do not patrol to publicize this kind of dispute are, so far as this section of the statute is concerned, left wholly free to patrol. Thus the section is aimed at outlawing free discussion of one side of a certain kind of labor dispute and cannot be sustained as a permissible regulation of patrolling. ...

Nor can the section be sustained on the ground that it merely forbids picketers to help carry out an unlawful or criminal undertaking. For the section itself contains a proviso which says that it shall not be construed "to prohibit publicity, other than picketing, for the purpose of truthfully advising the public, including consumers . . . that a product or products are produced by an employer with whom . . . [the picketers have] a primary dispute . . ." Thus, it is clear that the object of the picketing was to ask Safeway customers to do something which the section itself recognizes as perfectly lawful. Yet, while others are left free to picket for other reasons, those who wish to picket to inform Safeway customers of their labor dispute with the primary employer, are barred from picketing—solely on the ground of the lawful information they want to impart to the customers.

In short, we have neither a case in which picketing is banned because the picketers are asking others to do something unlawful nor a case in which *all* picketing is, for reasons of public order, banned. Instead, we have a case in which picketing, otherwise lawful, is banned only when the picketers express particular views. The result is an abridgment of the freedom of these picketers to tell a part of the public their side of a labor controversy, a subject the free discussion of which is protected by the First Amendment.

I cannot accept my Brother HARLAN's view that the abridgment of speech and press here does not violate the First Amendment because other methods of communication are left open. This reason for abridgment strikes me as being on a par with holding that governmental suppression of a newspaper in a city would not violate the First Amendment because there continue to be radio and television stations. First Amendment freedoms can no more validly be taken away by degrees than by one fell swoop.

For these reasons I concur in the judgment of the Court vacating the judgment of the Court of Appeals and remanding the case with directions to enter judgment setting aside the Board's order.

Mr. Justice HARLAN, whom Mr. Justice STEWART joins, dissenting.

The question in this case is whether a union involved in a labor dispute with an employer may lawfully engage in peaceful picketing at the premises of another employer in order to dissuade its customers from purchasing products of the first employer dealt in by the picketed establishment. Such activity, in the parlance of labor law, is known as secondary consumer picketing, the picketed employer being called the "secondary employer" and the other the "primary employer."

The question is controlled by § 8(b) of the National Labor Relations Act which makes it an unfair labor practice for a union

"(4) . . . (ii) to threaten, coerce, or restrain any person engaged in commerce . . . where . . . an object . . . is . . . (B) forcing or requiring any person to cease using, selling . . . or otherwise dealing in the products of any other producer, processor, or manufacturer, or to cease doing business with any other person . . . .

with a proviso that

"nothing contained in . . . [the above provisions] shall be construed to prohibit publicity, *other than picketing,* for the purpose of truthfully advising the public, including consumers . . . that a product or products are produced by an employer with whom . . . [the union] has a primary dispute and are distributed by another employer, as long as such publicity does not have an effect of inducing any individual employed by an person other than the primary employer in the course of his employment to refuse to pick up, deliver, or transport any goods, or not to perform any services, at the establishment of the employer engaged in such distribution . . ." (Emphasis added.)

The Labor Board found the Union's picketing at Safeway stores, though peaceful, unlawful *per se* under § 8(b) (4) (ii) (B), and issued an appropriate order. The Court of Appeals reversed, holding the picketing lawful in the absence of any showing that Safeway had *in fact* been "threatened, coerced, or restrained," . . . and remanded the case to the Board for further proceedings. This Court now rejects (correctly, I believe) the Court of Appeals' holding, but nevertheless refuses to enforce the Board's order. It holds that although § 8(b) (4) (ii) (B) does automatically outlaw peaceful secondary consumer picketing aimed at *all* products handled by a secondary employer, Congress has not, with "the requisite clarity," . . . evinced a purpose to prohibit such picketing when directed *only* at the products of the primary employer. Here the Union's picketing related only to Washington apples, not to all products carried by Safeway.

Being unable to discern in § 8(b) (4) (ii) (B) or in its legislative history any basis for the Court's subtle narrowing of these statutory provisions, I must respectfully dissent.

I.

The Union's activities are plainly within the letter of subdivision (4) (ii) (B) of § 8(b), and indeed the Court's opinion virtually concedes that much. . . . Certainly Safeway is a "person" as defined in those subdivisions; indubitably "an object" of the Union's conduct was the "forcing or requiring" of Safeway, through the picketing of its customers, "to cease . . . selling, handling . . . or otherwise dealing in" Washington apples, "the products of" another "product"; and consumer picketing is expressly excluded from the ameliorative provisions of the proviso. . . .

Nothing in the statute lends support to the fine distinction which the Court draws between general and limited product picketing. The enactment speaks pervasively of threatening, coercing, or restraining any person; the proviso differentiates only between modes of expression, not between types of secondary consumer picketing. For me, the Court's argument to the contrary is very unconvincing.

The difference to which the Court points between a secondary employer merely lowering his purchases of the struck product to the degree of decreased consumer demand and such an employer ceasing to purchase one product because of consumer refusal to buy any products, is surely too refined in the context of reality. It can hardly be supposed that in all, or even most, instances the result of the type of picketing involved here will be simply that suggested by the Court. Because of the very nature of picketing, there may be numbers of persons who will refuse to buy at all from a picketed store, either out of economic or social conviction or because they prefer to shop where they need not brave a picket line. Moreover, the public can hardly be expected always to know or ascertain the precise scope of a particular picketing operation. Thus in cases like this, the effect on the secondary employer may not always be limited to a decrease in his sales of the struck product. And even when that is the effect, the employer may, rather than simply reducing purchases from the primary employer, deem it more expedient to turn to another producer whose product is approved by the union.

The distinction drawn by the majority becomes even more tenuous if a picketed retailer depends largely or entirely on sales of the struck product. If, for example, an independent gas station owner sells gasoline purchased from a struck gasoline company, one would not suppose he would feel less threatened, coerced, or restrained by picket signs which said, "Do not buy X gasoline" than by signs which said, "Do not patronize this gas station." To be sure Safeway is a multiple article seller, but it cannot well be gainsaid that the rule laid down by the Court would be unworkable if its applicability turned on a calculation of the relation between total income of the secondary employer and income from the struck product.

The Court informs us that "Peaceful consumer picketing to shut off all trade with the secondary employer unless he aids the union in its dispute with the primary employer, is poles apart from such picketing which only persuades his customers not to buy the struck product." . . . The difference was, it is stated, "well established in the state cases by 1940. . . ." that is, before the present federal enactment. In light of these assertions, it is indeed remarkable that the Court not only substantially acknowledges that the statutory language does not itself support this distinction . . . but cites no report of Congress, no statement of a legislator, not even the view of any of the many commentators in the area, in any way casting doubt on the applicability of § 8(b) (4) (ii) (B) to picketing of the kind involved here.

II.

The Court's distinction fares no better when the legislative history of § 8(b) (4) (ii) (B) is examined. Even though there is no Senate, House, or Conference Report which sheds light on the matter, that hardly excuses the Court's blinding itself to what the legislative and other background materials do show. Fairly assessed they, in my opinion, belie Congress' having made the distinction upon which the Court's thesis rests. Nor can the Court find comfort in the generalization that " 'In the sensitive area of peaceful picketing Congress has dealt explicitly with isolated evils which experience has established flow from such picketing' "; . . . in enacting the provisions in question Congress *was* addressing itself to a particular facet of secondary boycotting not dealt with in prior legislation, namely, peaceful secondary consumer picketing. I now turn to the materials which illuminate what Congress had in mind.

It is clear that consumer picketing in connection with secondary boycotting was at the forefront of the problems which led to the amending of the Taft-Hartley Act by the Labor-Management Reporting and Disclosure Act of 1959. . . . During Senate debate before passage of the Kennedy-Ervin bill, Senator Humphrey criticized an amendment proposed by Senator Goldwater to § 8(b) (4) of the Taft-Hartley Act, which reflected the position of the Administration and was incorporated in substance in the Landrum-Griffin bill passed by the House. He said:

> "To distribute leaflets at the premises of a neutral employer to persuade customers not to buy a struck product is one form of consumer appeal. To peacefully picket the customer entrances, with a placard asking that the struck product not be bought, is another form. I fear that consumer picketing may also be the target of the words 'coerce, or restrain.' I fear that, in addition to the existing foreclosure of the union on strike from making any effective appeal to the employees of the so-called neutral employer, the union by this amendment is now to be effectively sealed off from even an appeal to the consumers."

Reporting on the compromise reached by the Conference Committee on the Kennedy-Ervin and Landrum-Griffin bills, Senator Kennedy, who chaired the Conference Committee, stated:

> "[T]he House bill prohibited the union from carrying on any kind of activity to disseminate informational material to secondary sites. They could not say that there was a strike in a primary plant. . . . Under the language of the conference, [ultimately resulting in present § 8(b) (4) (ii) (B)] we agreed there would not be picketing at a secondary site. What was permitted was the giving out of handbills or information through the radio, and so forth."

Senator Morse, one day later, explained quite explicitly his objection to the relevant portion of the bill reported out of the Conference Committee, of which he was a member:

> "This bill does not stop with threats and with illegalizing the hot cargo agreement. It also makes it illegal for a union to 'coerce, or restrain.' This prohibits consumer picketing. What is consumer picketing? A shoe

manufacturer sells his product through a department store. The employees of the shoe manufacturer go on strike for higher wages. The employees, in addition to picketing the manufacturer, also picket at the premises of the department store with a sign saying, 'Do not buy *X* shoes.' This is consumer picketing an appeal to the public not to buy the product of a struck manufacturer. ..."

Later the same day, Senator Kennedy spoke further on the Conference bill and particularized the union rights protected by the Senate conferees:

"(c) The right to appeal to consumers by methods other than picketing asking them to refrain from buying goods made by non-union labor and to refrain from trading with a retailer who sells such goods.

"Under the Landrum-Griffin bill it would have been impossible for a union to inform the customers of a secondary employer that that employer or store was selling goods which were made under racket conditions or sweatshop conditions, or in a plant where an economic strike was in progress. We were not able to persuade the House conferees to permit picketing in front of that secondary shop, but we were able to persuade them to agree that the union shall be free to conduct informational activity short of picketing. In other words, the union can hand out handbills at the shop, can place advertisements in newspapers, can make announcements over the radio, and can carry on all publicity short of having ambulatory picketing in front of a secondary site. ..."

The Court does not consider itself compelled by these remarks to conclude that the Conference Committee meant to prohibit *all* secondary consumer picketing. A fair reading of these comments, however, can hardly leave one seriously in doubt that Senator Kennedy believed this to be precisely what the Committee had done; the Court's added emphasis on the word "and" .... is, I submit, simply grasping at straws, if indeed the phrase relied on does not equally well lend itself to a disjunctive reading. ...

The complicated role the Court assigns to the publicity proviso ... makes even less understandable its failure to accord to the remarks of Senator Kennedy their proper due. The proviso, according to the Court's interpretation, is unnecessary in regard to picketing designed to effect a boycott of the primary product and comes into play only if a complete boycott of the secondary employer is sought. Had this ingenious interpretation been intended, would not Senator Kennedy, who was at pains to emphasize the scope of activities still left to unions, have used it to refute the criticisms of Senator Morse made only shortly before?

Further, Senator Goldwater spoke in favor of the Conference bill and pointed out that in contrast to the Senate bill, which he had opposed, "[t]he House bill . . . closed up every loophole in the boycott section of the law including the use of a secondary consumer picket line...."

The Court points out that the Senate had no Conference Report when it passed the compromise bill and that it had only Senator Kennedy's statement of the purpose of the proviso. ... But I am wholly at a loss to understand how on that premise (particularly when Senator Kennedy's remarks are supplemented by the comments of one Senator (Morse) who thought the final bill too harsh and those of another (Goldwater) who believed the Senate bill too weak) one can conclude that the members of the Senate did not mean by their vote to outlaw all kinds of secondary consumer picketing.

A reading of proceedings in the House of Representatives leads to a similar conclusion regarding the intent of that body. In criticism of the Landrum-Griffin bill, Congressman Madden stated, "It would prohibit any union from advising the public that an employer is unfair to labor, pays substandard wages, or operates a sweatshop. . . ." Since the theory of the majority regarding the publicity proviso adopted by the Conference is that it is redundant in situations where the union seeks only a boycott of the struck product, the sweep of Congressman Madden's comment is plainly at odds with the Court's view of § 8(b) (4) (ii) (B).

Indicative of the contemporaneous understanding is an analysis of the bill prepared by Congressmen Thompson and Udall and inserted in the Congressional Record, in which a hypothetical case, as directly in point as the department store example used by Senator Morse, is suggested:

> "Suppose that the employees of the Coors Brewery were to strike for higher wages and the company attempted to run the brewery with strikebreakers. Under the present law, the union can ask the public not to buy Coors beer during the strike. It can picket the bars and restaurants which sold Coors beer with the signs asking the public not to buy the product. It can broadcast the request over the radio or in newspaper advertisements.
>
> "The Landrum bill forbids this elementary freedom to appeal to the general public for assistance in winning fair labor standards." . . .

The majority . . . relies on remarks made by Congressman Griffin, the bill's co-sponsor. When read in context what seems significant about them is that the Congressman nowhere suggests that there can be some kind of consumer picketing which does not coerce or restrain the secondary employer. Nor does he intimate any constitutional problem in prohibiting picketing that follows the struck product.

After passage of the Landrum-Griffin bill, Congressman Thompson presented to the House an analysis of the differences between the House and Senate bills prepared by Senator Kennedy and himself. This described the nature of secondary boycotts:

> "In all cases of secondary boycotts two employers are involved. The union brings pressure upon the employer with whom it has a dispute (called the 'primary' employer) by inducing the employees of another employer (called the 'secondary' employer) to go on strike—or the customers not to patronize—until the secondary employer stops dealing with the primary employer. Or the union may simply induce the employees of the secondary employer to refuse to handle or work on goods —*or the customers not to buy*—coming from the primary employer as a way of putting pressure upon him." . . .

The prepared analysis then discusses the effect of the House bill on consumer picketing. . . . To describe activities outlawed by the House bill, it uses the same "Coors beer" hypothetical which the earlier analysis had employed. This analysis shows beyond peradventure that Senator

Kennedy did believe the language of the bill to proscribe *all* consumer picketing and indicates that this view was squarely placed before the House. The Court adverts to this analysis, ... as the genesis of the publicity proviso, but fails to acknowledge the difficulty of squaring the great concern of the Senate conferees to protect freedom of communication with the Court's supposition that the House bill closed off no lines of communication so long as the union appeal was limited to boycott of the struck products.

Congressman Griffin placed in the Congressional Record . . . a preliminary report on the Conference agreement. A summary analysis of Taft-Hartley amendments states that the House bill "Prohibits secondary customer picketing at retail store which happens to sell product produced by manufacturer with whom union has dispute." The Conference agreement, according to this summary, "Adopts House provision with clarification that other forms of publicity are not prohibited; also clarification that picketing at primary site is not secondary boycott."

When Congressman Thompson spoke to the Conference agreement, he reiterated his view of the House bill and of its modification. Specifically he stated, "All appeals for a consumer boycott would have been barred by House bill."

In the light of the foregoing, I see no escape from the conclusion that § 8(b) (4) (ii) (B) does prohibit *all* consumer picketing. There are, of course, numerous times in the debates of both houses in which consumer picketing is referred to generally or the reference is made with an example of an appeal to consumers not to purchase at all from the secondary employer. But it is remarkable that every time the possibility of picketing of the sort involved in this case was considered, it was assumed to be prohibited by the House bill. Admittedly, in the House, appeals to refrain from purchase of the struck product were discussed only by opponents of the House bill; however, only one of two inferences can be drawn from the silence of the bill's supporters. Either the distinction drawn by this Court was not considered of sufficient significance to require comment, or the proponents recognized a difference between the two types of consumer picketing but assumed that the bill encompassed both. Under either supposition, the conclusion reached by the Court in regard to the picketing involved here is untenable.

III.

Under my view of the statute the constitutional issue is therefore reached. Since the Court does not discuss it, I am content simply to state in summary form my reasons for believing that the prohibitions of § 8(b) (4) (ii) (B), as applied here, do not run afoul of constitutional limitations. This Court has long recognized that picketing is "in separably something more [than] and different" from simple communication. ... Congress has given careful and continued consideration to the problems of labor-management relations, and its attempts to effect an accommodation between the right of unions to publicize their position and the social desirability of limiting a form of communication likely to have effects caused by something apart from the message communicated, are entitled to great deference. The decision of Congress to prohibit secondary consumer picketing during labor disputes is, I believe, not inconsistent with the protections of the First Amendment, particularly when, as here, other methods of communication are left open.

Contrary to my Brother BLACK, I think the fact that Congress in prohibiting secondary consumer picketing has acted with a discriminating eye is the very thing that renders this provision invulnerable to constitutional attack. That Congress has permitted other picketing which is likely to have effects beyond those resulting from the "communicative" aspect of picketing does not, of course, in any way lend itself to the conclusion that Congress here has aimed to "prevent dissemination of information about the facts of a labor dispute. ..." Even on the highly dubious assumption that the "non-speech" aspect of picketing is always the same whatever the particular context, the social consequences of the "non-communicative" aspect of picketing may certainly be thought desirable in the case of "primary" picketing and undesirable in the case of "secondary" picketing, a judgment Congress has indeed made in prohibiting secondary but not primary picketing.

I would enforce the Board's order.

• • •

CASE QUESTIONS

1. Why did the Supreme Court devote a substantial portion of its decision to interpreting congressional intent in enacting the Landrum-Griffin Amendments to the National Labor Relations Act?

2. On what basis did the Supreme Court determine the intent of the Congress?

3. When is secondary picketing illegal?

4. What is the basis for the dissenting opinion?

C. COMELLA, INC. v. UNITED FARM WORKERS ORGANIZING COMMITTEE
Court of Appeals of Ohio, Cuyahoga County
292 N.E.2d 647 (Ohio Ct. App. 1972)

• • •

KRENZLER, Judge.

This case involves a labor dispute, wherein the parties are C. Comella, Inc. (hereinafter referred to as "plaintiff" or "Comella"), a Cleveland wholesaler of produce whose place of business is at the Northern Ohio Food Terminal (hereinafter referred to as "NOFT"); United Farm Workers Organizing Committee (hereinafter referred to as "defendant" or "UFWOC"), a labor organization which is part of the AFL-CIO, and which represents California agricultural workers; also named as defendants were Mack Lyons and Diana Lyons, coordinators of UFWOC activity in the Cleveland area; other participants in the labor dispute but not parties to the action are Bud Antle, Inc., a California lettuce grower (hereinafter referred to as "Antle"); various retailers who are customers of Comella and who sell Antle produce; various other individuals representing UFWOC; and the Western Conference of Teamsters.

Antle would not recognize UFWOC as the bargaining agent for its agricultural workers in California and a labor dispute developed between UFWOC and Antle. UFWOC followed Antle's product (lettuce) to Cleveland to Comella's place of business at the NOFT and there engaged in various activities. UFWOC also followed Antle's product (lettuce) from Comella's place of business to various retailers who are customers of Comella and engaged in various activities there.

Comella brought an injunction action in the Common Pleas Court of Cuyahoga County, and the substance of its complaint is as follows.

Defendant union is seeking to force the plaintiff to cease buying lettuce from or handling the produce of Antle. The defendant, its officers, agents, and members entered upon its premises at the NOFT and picketed said premises. The picketing has taken the form of numerous persons blocking the loading dock of plaintiff, blocking trucks that are hauling plaintiff's produce. Defendant has also interfered with plaintiff's business by harassing customers of plaintiff who purchase lettuce, harassing plaintiff by telephone calls, and trespassing upon plaintiff's property, as well as the property of the NOFT.

The substance of the defendants' answer was an admission that Comella is engaged in the business of selling wholesale fresh produce to grocery stores and purchases lettuce from Antle, and that the defendant is a labor union of farm workers. The defendants deny the balance of plaintiff's allegations.

The trial court issued a temporary restraining order against the defendants and enjoined them from interfering with plaintiff's business and interfering with ingress and egress from plaintiff's premises, congregating, loitering, assembling, or picketing anywhere on the premises of the plaintiff or upon the premises of NOFT, harassing or interfering with plaintiff and its customers by telephone calls, letters or otherwise. Defendants were granted the right to picket, by no more than one person at any time, at the East 40th Street entrance or gate to the NOFT.

A hearing was held for a permanent injunction and restraining order and the testimony of twenty-two witnesses was presented to the court. In addition, the following written stipulation was entered into by and between the parties:

The United Farm Workers Organizing Committee is engaged in a labor dispute with certain producers of lettuce in California and Arizona, including Bud Antle, Inc., claiming that UFWOC represents a majority of the agricultural employees of each of those producers.

On July 23, 1970, UFWOC asserted such representation and demanded recognition of certain of them, including Bud Antle, Inc., for purposes of collective bargaining on behalf of their employees.

Those producers of whom the demand for recognition had been made declined to recognize UFWOC on the ground that they had executed contracts with the Western Conference of Teamsters providing for recognition of the Teamsters as collective bargaining agent on behalf of the producers' respective agricultural employees.

UFWOC is not able to obtain assistance under the National Labor Relations Act to establish either than an unfair labor practice has been committed by those producers, or that the UFWOC represents a majority of their employees, respectively, because agricultural employees are not covered by the Act. It therefore has initiated a boycott of the lettuce produced by those employers in order to apply economic pressure to induce recognition of UFWOC.

Following the hearing the trial court made these findings of fact:

(1) Northern Ohio Food Terminals, Inc., is the owner of 216,318 square feet of land containing buildings, with said buildings divided into units, and the units leased to businesses for use and occupancy for Produce Market Purposes.

(2) The area referred to above is used only for Wholesale Produce and is not generally open to the public.

(3) Plaintiff is the lessee of two units from Northern Ohio Food Terminals, Inc.

(4) At the rear of plaintiff's unit there is a loading dock platform having a width of three feet and in the front of plaintiff's units there is a loading platform eight feet in width.

(5) In the first week of December, 1970, the defendants contacted the plaintiff and, after explaining their purpose and the background of their problem, requested the plaintiff to cease purchasing Bud Antle products.

(6) When plaintiff refused to cease purchasing and selling Bud Antle products, the defendants placed observers on the front platform of plaintiff's business and when these observers saw someone purchase Bud Antle lettuce they followed that person to his retail store.

(7) Prior to the issuance of the Temporary Restraining Order there would be as many as fifteen persons from defendants' organization in the Northern Ohio Food Terminal and as many as eight of those persons would be on the front platform of plaintiff's units at one time with a constant surveillance crew of four persons.

(8) The presence of even one person on the front platform for a continuous period during the busy hours of the morning would, due to the tremendous business activity and the limited space of eight feet in width, be an interference with plaintiff's business for it is virtually impossible to stay out of the way of trucks used to transport the produce on the front platform and these trucks would frequently have to wait until the observer moved from one location to another so that they could pass.

(9) Leaflets were passed out at the Northern Ohio Food Terminal, being defendants' Exhibit A and plaintiff's Exhibit 6.

(10) The defendants contacted the retail stores purchasing Bud Antle lettuce from the plaintiff, and asked those store operators not to buy from the plaintiff. Usually five members of the defendants' organization would go to a store to talk with the manager or owner.

(11) The defendants contacted some store operators as many as six times and they returned to those stores with the same requests even though they had previously been asked by the store operators not to return again.

(12) Defendants and their associates told the retail store operators

they would be picketed if they continued to sell Bud Antle lettuce.

(13) Some of the plaintiff's retail store customers were picketed as a result of selling Bud Antle lettuce, and the number of pickets was as high as fifteen. Pickets passed out leaflets, plaintiff's Exhibit 3, and carried signs some of which read, "PLEASE DON'T SHOP AT THIS STORE. UFWOC, AFL-CIO."

(14) During the picketing and on some of the numerous visits by defendants to the retail stores there was violence.

The Court also made the following conclusions of law:

(1) This case is not pre-empted by the National Labor Relations Act.

(2) Defendants' actions to stop the plaintiff and its customers from selling But Antle products is a secondary boycott and may be prohibited under Ohio law.

(3) The defendants' conduct in attempting to persuade others not to purchase any items from plaintiff is illegal conduct under the U.S. Supreme Court's view of secondary boycotts.

(4) The defendants' conduct in telling the members of the public not to shop at the retail stores of plaintiff's customers is an illegal type of secondary boycott under Federal laws.

(5) The movement of the defendant upon the premises of the Northern Ohio Food Terminal grounds may be enjoined on the basis that said grounds are not ordinarily open to the public.

(6) This is an action in equity and under Ohio law, and the new Ohio Rules of Procedure, adopted July 1, 1970, the Court should grant all appropriate relief for the facts pleaded in the complaint.

The Court then enjoined and restrained the defendants from committing, attempting to commit or causing to be committed, any of the following acts:

(1) Interfering with plaintiff's officers, agents, employees, representatives and others having business with the plaintiff;

(2) Interfering with ingress to, or egress from plaintiff's premises, or with vehicular traffic in or about said premises, including the delivery, unloading, loading, and dispatching of produce to and from plaintiff's business;

(3) Congregating, loitering, assembling or picketing anywhere on the premises of plaintiff or on the premises of the Northern Ohio Food Terminal;

(4) Harassing or interfering with the plaintiff and its customers by telephone calls, letters, or otherwise;

(5) Picketing of the plaintiff or any of its retail customers;

(6) Giving any speeches, distributing handbills, or in any other manner advising the general public not to buy Bud Antle lettuce or other products from the named plaintiff, or mentioning the name of its customers in an effort to stop the general public from buying Bud Antle products from said customers.

The Court further added the provision that the injunction should not be construed as prohibiting the defendants from mailing notices to the general public, nor from passing out leaflets to the general public, as a means of expressing their thoughts about Bud Antle products, so long as those expressions are general in nature and do not mention plaintiff or its customers, and so long as such expressions are not generally aimed at the plaintiff or its customers or their business establishments.

Defendants have taken this appeal and list nine assignments of error as follows:

(1) The Trial Court erred in finding that the Northern Ohio Food Terminal is not open to the public and that the appellants therefore do not have a right of access to it for the exercise of First Amendment rights.

(2) The Trial Court erred in finding that there was interference by defendants with plaintiff's business.

(3) The Trial Court erred in finding that the defendants asked retail store operators not to buy from the plaintiff.

(4) The Trial Court erred in finding that defendant's conduct to persuade others not to purchase any item from retailers selling Antle lettuce is illegal conduct under the Federal law and the U.S. Supreme Court's view of secondary boycotts.

(5) The Trial Court erred in finding that the defendants' actions were illegal in requesting retail customers of stores selling Bud Antle lettuce not to patronize those stores although the actions consisting solely of peaceful comunications to persons whom the defendants could not coerce.

(6) The Trial Court erred in excluding evidence of the refusal of Bud Antle, Inc., to recognize and negotiate with UFWOC as the representatives of the majority of Bud Antle employees and in failing to regard such a refusal as justification for secondary boycotts otherwise illegal.

(7) The Trial Court erred in excluding from the Record Defendants' oral and written proffer of evidence that Bud Antle, Inc., refused to recognize and negotiate with UFWOC as the representatives of a majority of Bud Antle employees.

(8) The Trial Court erred in issuing an injunction so overbroad as to bar the defendants from advocating a consumer's boycott of Bud Antle lettuce at the premises of retail sellers of it.

(9) The Trial Court erred in enjoining defendants, its [sic] officers, agents and associates from committing any certain specified acts.

Defendants' nine assignments of error may be divided into four categories.

(1) Assignments of error one and two deal with the question whether the defendants interfered with the plaintiff's business and whether the NOFT was open to the public to such an extent that the defendants have a right of access to it for the exercise of their rights under the First Amendment to the United States Constitution.

The record contains testimony which sufficiently establishes that the NOFT is occupied by produce wholesalers and is not open to the public generally. The testimony also shows that the loading platforms of plaintiff's premises at the NOFT are relatively small, that defendants stationed observers on these platforms, sometimes in groups, and that this caused congestion of plaintiff's premises and made operation of plaintiff's business difficult or impossible. The trial court therefore did not err in finding that the NOFT is not open to the public, and in finding that defendants interfered with plaintiff's business.

Defendants do not have a right of access to the NOFT for the purpose of picketing because it is not a place normally open to the public. A denial of such access does not violate a person's first amendment rights to freedom of speech. ... It is noted that the trial court's injunction does not prohibit picketing in the public areas surrounding the NOFT.

Findings of facts 1 through 9 relating to the defendants' activities at the NOFT are supported by the record; conclusions of law 2, 3, and 5 are correct statements of the law applicable to these facts; and the court properly enjoined defendant from committing the acts listed in items 1, 2, 3, 4, and that part of 5 applicable to plaintiff.

(2) Assignments of error three, four and five are concerned with defendants' actions relating to the plaintiff's customers who are retail store operators and whether these actions were an illegal secondary boycott or part of a lawful primary labor dispute between Antle and UFWOC.

Assignments of error three, four, and five are not well taken. There was testimony before the trial court that numerous members of defendant organization contacted retail stores who purchased Antle lettuce from plaintiff, and on repeated occasions requested those stores not to buy Antle lettuce; that defendants warned the retail stores they would be picketed if they continued to buy Antle lettuce; and that defendants did, in fact, picket the retail stores, and passed out leaflets requesting retail customers not to shop at those stores. Findings of facts 10 through 14 thus have support in the record. The trial court also correctly stated in its conclusions of law 2, 3, and 4 that defendants' activity was a secondary boycott, which is prohibited under both Federal and state law. ...

There will be additional discussion concerning secondary boycotts later in this opinion.

(3) Assignments of error six and seven deal with the refusal of the trial court to admit into evidence or receive the defendants' proffer of evidence regarding the refusal of Antle to recognize and negotiate with UFWOC as a representative of the majority of Antle employees.

Assignments of error six and seven are not well taken. These assignments of error deal with the refusal of Antle (the primary employer) to negotiate and enter into a labor agreement with UFWOC, whose members work for Antle. Inasmuch as both Antle and its employees are located in California, this court does not have jurisdiction of those issues.

Further, the trial court refused to accept defendants' proffer, but it is included as part of the record on this appeal. We have reviewed defendant's proffer, and the material contained therein is not material or relevant to the issues in this case. We cannot say that the trial court erred in not admitting the proffer. In addition, the trial court's refusal to admit the defendant's proffer does not prejudice defendants in this case.

Appellants also seek to have this court rule on the validity of a contract between Antle and the Western Conference of Teamsters as the representative of Antle's field workers. We do not have jurisdiction to decide that issue because the parties to the contract, namely, Antle and the Western Conference of Teamsters, are not before this court. The only issues to be decided in this case are those presented by the complaint of the plaintiff in the trial court and the errors assigned by the appellant in this appeal. The validity of the contract is not an issue in this case.

(4) Assignments of error eight and nine attack the trial court's injunction as being overbroad in that it does not allow a consumer boycott of Antle lettuce at the retail stores of customers of Comella.

As stated above, the trial court's injunction, items 1 through 4, and part of 5, which restrains the defendants from the activities enumerated therein, is valid. However, the balance of the trial court's injunction, as it relates to items 5 and 6, will require further discussion.

The remaining portion of this opinion will be devoted to a discussion of the subject of consumer boycotts at secondary sites, which the defendants claim should be legal under Ohio law.

Generally, issues involving unfair labor practices are brought before the National Labor Relations Board and Federal courts because the Federal government has preempted this area of labor law. However, this case is in a state court because it involves agricultural workers who are exempt from the provisions of the National Labor Relations Act.

Labor law has developed in the United States through many stages, including common law decisions; Sherman and Clayton Antitrust Acts (1890 and 1914); Railway Labor Act (1926); Norris-LaGuardia Act (1932); Wagner Act (1935, the National Labor Relations Act); Taft-Hartley Act (1947, amending the National Labor Relations Act); Landrum-Griffin Act (1959).

The national policy established by the Congress was that the status of labor must be improved as to working conditions and pay, and that the activities of the workers in organizing and unionizing to accomplish these objectives must be protected. Legislation was enacted to protect the rights of both employers and employees in the field of collective bargaining and this legislation spells out the rights, obligations and responsibilities of employers, employees and unions.

The constitutionality of the National Labor Relations Act has been upheld. ... Some states have enacted legislation similar to the National Labor Relations Act which controls labor disputes in which the National Labor Relations Act is not applicable. Ohio has not enacted such legislation; therefore, common law and case decision will control when the National Labor Relations Act is not applicable.

Labor law has a terminology all its own, and in order for those not knowledgeable in the field of labor law to fully understand this case it will require an explanation of some basic labor terms such as the following:

Boycott — Refusal to work for, purchase from or handle the products of an employer.

Picketing — The presence at an employer's business by one or more employees and/or other persons to publicize a labor dispute, influence employees or customers to withhold their work or business, respectively, or show the union's desire to represent the employees. This is usually accompanied by patrolling with signs.

Mass Picketing — Concentrations of large numbers of employees (pickets) at entrances to a plant or business making it difficult or impossible for anyone to enter or leave.

Primary Activity — Action such as a strike or picketing directed against the employer with whom there is a labor dispute.

Primary Employer — The employer with whom the union has a labor dispute.

Secondary Employer — A neutral person or business who has no labor dispute with a union, or one who cannot or will not take the action which the union wants to accomplish its objective.

Secondary Activity — Actions such as a strike or picketing against a secondary or neutral employer with an object of forcing this employer to stop doing business with the primary employer.

Secondary Boycott — Refusal to work for, purchase from or handle products of a secondary employer with whom the union has no dispute with an object of forcing that employer to stop doing business with the primary employer with whom the union has a dispute.

Strike — A concerted refusal of employees to perform work which they have been assigned.

Labor's weapons in industrial and commercial struggles are the strike, picketing, boycott and other similar activities. However, these activities must be peaceful and carried on without violence. Peaceful picketing is protected by the constitutional guarantee of freedom of speech under the First and Fourteenth Amendments to the United States Constitution and Section 11, Article I, Ohio Constitution. . . .

These activities are permissible in order that a union may acquaint the public with the fact that a labor dispute exists, and the nature of such dispute. . . .

As noted above, if there is a dispute between a primary employer and his employees and/or union, peaceful strikes, picketing and boycotting directed against the employer are legal and permitted. . . . Such activity may be undertaken at the employer's site.

However, a question is presented as to how far the area of activity of the union in striking, picketing and boycotting will be permitted to expand beyond the primary employer's site of business.

If a union expands its activity by following the product of the primary employer to a secondary source such as a wholesaler, distributor or retailer doing business with the primary employer, and the union conducts a strike against or boycotts or pickets a secondary employer, this may or may not be legal, depending on the type of activity and the jurisdiction of the dispute, whether Federal or state.

Secondary activities may take several forms, including strikes by secondary employees, refusal to handle non-union merchandise carried by secondary employers, picketing, solicitation, boycotting of the secondary employer generally, or boycotting of only the non-union product. There also may be pickets with signs and handbills, telephone calls and personal calls, letters, advertisements in newspapers, radio and television.

Whenever the union activity expands beyond the two primary participants such as the employer and the employees and/or union, we get into an area of secondary activity which may lead to either an illegal secondary boycott or a legal product boycott, or secondary consumer boycott, which will be discussed hereafter.

A secondary boycott is union pressure directed at a neutral employer or secondary employer to induce or coerce him to cease doing business with a primary employer with whom the union is engaged in a labor dispute. . . .

A secondary boycott has been declared illegal by the Congress of the United States, and this legislation has been held constitutional. The theory of enacting such legislation is that a secondary employer who is neutral or innocent should not suffer because he is not part of the primary labor dispute. . . .

State courts have declared secondary boycotts illegal, either upon the ground that they constitute unlawful coercion or upon the broad principle that one not a party to an industrial dispute cannot, against his will, be made an ally of one of the parties. The common law rule in a majority of states is that a secondary boycott is unlawful and may be enjoined. Secondary boycotts have been held illegal in Ohio. ...

However, Congress has not outlawed every type of secondary activity and the line between legitimate primary activity and banned secondary activity is not absolutely clear. ...

While Section 158(b) (4), makes a secondary boycott an unfair labor practice and unlawful, it is not intended that this section interfere with lawful primary activity, Section 158(b) (4). ...

It must be determined how far the courts will go in protecting the rights of a neutral secondary employer and his right not to be intimidated and harassed, where he does not have a labor dispute of his own. These rights must be balanced with the right of the union and employees to express their grievances against the primary employer and to advise the public concerning these grievances.

It has been held that the union in the primary labor dispute may follow the product of the primary employer and let the public know in a peaceful manner that there is a dispute between the primary employer and the union. This has been allowed in cases where there is a unity of interest between the primary employer and the product and its sale to the secondary employer. Under such facts, what may be called "product picketing" is considered to be a part of the primary labor dispute and therefore valid, the theory being that the activity is directed against the product and therefore against the primary employer, and not against the secondary employer. Some courts have even held that a secondary employer is not really neutral or innocent because when he carries certain non-union products, he is getting the benefits of the lower wages and prices paid by the primary employer and therefore, there is a unity of interest between the primary and secondary employer, and picketing and boycotting at the secondary employer's establishment should be permitted. ...

State courts thus recognized the distinction between picketing a secondary employer merely to follow the struck goods and picketing designed to result in a generalized loss of patronage. This same distinction was recognized by the United States Supreme Court in NLRB v. Fruit and Vegetable Packers Local 760 (1964), 377 U.S. 58, ... hereinafter referred to as the *Tree Fruits* case.

Because of the importance of *Tree Fruits,* it is necessary to look at the facts and the activities of the union in that case. ...

We also note that Justice Black concurred in the judgment of the Court on the grounds that product picketing or consumer picketing as occurred in *Tree Fruits* was protected by the First Amendment guarantee of freedom of speech. ...

The Supreme Court of the United States, in interpreting Section 158(b) (4), ... (the secondary boycott provision), made a distinction between an unlawful secondary boycott and a secondary consumer boycott, including picketing, deciding that the latter, as defined in *Tree Fruits,* was primary in nature and thus valid and lawful. As we have already noted, this is also the position of numerous state courts.

Because the Congress of the United States pre-empted the field of labor law, and since Ohio does not have similar legislation to control in cases that are exempt from the National Labor Relations Act, we will adopt and follow the principle of *Tree Fruits* and recognize the distinction between an unlawful secondary boycott and a lawful secondary consumer boycott.

A peaceful product or secondary consumer boycott that is educational, informational and considered part of the primary labor dispute is valid and lawful. Such boycott must not be forceful, coercive, conducted under restraint and directed against the secondary employer to such an extent that it is considered a traditional secondary boycott.

UFWOC should therefore be allowed to publicize its dispute with Antle by the use of picketing, signs, leaflets, handbills, speeches, advertisements in newspapers and on radio and television, and to generally seek support from the public not to buy Antle lettuce. But defendant's activities should be directed only against Antle and its products and not against plaintiff and its customers.

The trial court therefore properly restrained UFWOC from conducting any forceful or coercive activities directly against the plaintiff and its customers. The injunction should not enjoin all boycott activity by the defendants, only such activity which is directed against the plaintiff and its retail customers.

Defendants argue that the trial court's injunction is so overbroad as to bar the defendants from advocating a consumer boycott of Antle lettuce at the premises of retail sellers.

A careful reading of the trial court's injunction and restraining order might lead one to conclude that the court's order *does permit* a lawful secondary consumer boycott. However, this interpretation is not stated in the court's order (paragraphs 5 and 6) with requisite clarity.

In order to avoid any misinterpretation or misunderstanding of the court's order, this opinion is written to clarify and modify said order to conform with our holding that a secondary consumer boycott, as defined in *Tree Fruits,* is valid and lawful. Paragraphs 5 and 6 of the injunction and restraining order are hereby modified to be consistent with the Supreme Court's ruling in *Tree Fruits* and the holding of this court.

The judgment of the trial court is affirmed, as modified.

Judgment affirmed as modified.

SILBERT and JACKSON, JJ., concur.

• • •

CASE QUESTIONS

1. Why was this case heard by the state court and not a federal court?

2. How can the instant case be distinguished from the *Tree Fruits Case?*

3. Did the court enjoin all activities of the union?

PICKETING 5

There are various types of picketing, and a picketing strategy may be used for a number of purposes or reasons. Picketing does not always occur in conjunction with a strike. Although the basic right to picket has been legally recognized, there appears to be a trend toward stricter regulation of this form of union activity.

A basic form of picketing is that by a union directly against the bargaining employer. Usually workers patrol their employer's place of business, and either carry placards or pass out handbills to inform other workers and/or the public of their grievances. However, neither patrolling nor carrying placards is a requisite to picketing, and other methods of conveying information have been used. Cases which have considered the legality of handbilling as form of picketing have held both ways.

In 1940 the Supreme Court in *Thornhill* v. *Alabama* held that where picketing was identified with the exercise of free speech, it was entitled to the same protections as are afforded to speech. "In the circumstances of our times the dissemination of information concerning the facts of a labor dispute must be regarded as within that area of free discussion that is guaranteed by the Constitution. ..." However, picketing is subject to the same legislative restrictions as are applied to other forms of speech.

STRANGER OR OUTSIDER PICKETING

The same constitutional protections apply to *stranger or outsider picketing* in which persons not connected with to the employer are involved in the activity. In *AFL* v. *Swing*, a 1941 case, the Supreme Court held that it was unconstitutional for the Illinois courts to injoin such picketing ". . . by drawing the circle of economic competition between employers and workers so small as to contain only an employer and those directly employed by him."

SECONDARY PICKETING

Secondary picketing, which usually occurs at a site other then the employer's, is not given the same protections as primary and stranger picketing. In fact, this type of picketing is similar to secondary boycotts. This picketing is usually aimed at an other employer so that he will apply pressure on the primary employer with whom the union has its dispute.

In the 1942 case of *Carpenters & Joiners* v. *Ritter's Cafe,* the Supreme Court defined the *criteria of acceptable secondary picketing* in terms of (1) interdependence of economic interest among persons engaged in the same industry, and (2) limitation of the picketing to the area of the industry within which the dispute giving rise to the picketing occurred.

Regardless of the types of picketing used, however, picketing is generally illegal where either its object or method is unlawful.

INTRODUCTION TO THE CASES

Recognitional and organizational picketing are discussed in the *Local 3 Case.* The *Local 978 Case* is concerned with the situs of picketing. Whether post-election picketing is an unfair labor practice is analyzed in the *Local 182 Case.* Picketing by discharged employees is the subject of the *Texas Natural Gasoline Case.* Finally, state regulation of picketing is discussed in the *Doorley Case.*

NLRB v. LOCAL 3, INTERNATIONAL BROTHERHOOD OF ELECTRICAL WORKERS, AFL—CIO
United States Court of Appeals, Second Circuit
317 F.2d 193 (2d Cir. 1963)

• • •

Before CLARK and WATERMAN, Circuit Judges, and ANDERSON, District Judge.

ANDERSON, District Judge.

This case is before the court on the petition of the National Labor Relations Board for enforcement of an order issued against the respondent Union on July 18, 1962 directing it to cease and desist from picketing the United States Post Office Building in Brooklyn, New York, with the object of forcing a contractor to recognize Local 3 as the representative of its employees in violation of § 8(b) (7) (C) of the National Labor Relations Act.

The Board found the facts to be substantially as follows: In the summer of 1961, one Picoult was awarded a contract by General Services Administration to renovate the Federal Building in Brooklyn. He thereafter entered into a prehire agreement with Local 199 of Industrial Workers of Allied Trades to cover the needed electrical employees.

Prior to the final award, Local 3 had sent a telegram to General Services Administration, protesting the award of the contract to Picoult and requesting that General Services Administration give support and assistance to the preservation of the terms and conditions of employment of members of Local 3.

On November 24, 1961, Local 3 began picketing at the Post Office; its signs read:

ELECTRICIANS
WORKING ON THIS JOB
EMPLOYED BY
PICOULT
ARE NOT MEMBERS
OF THE
ELECTRICAL WORKERS
LOCAL UNION NO. 3

ESTABLISHED 1891
INTERNATIONAL BROTHERHOOD OF
ELECTRICAL WORKERS

AFFILIATED WITH THE
A.F.L—C.I.O.

Call GRamercy 5-3260
Union Label No. 194

Once before and once after the commencement of the picketing, Dobbins, the Local 3 business agent, demanded that Picoult make a contract with Local 3.

About December 15, 1961 Local 3 changed its signs to read:

ELECTRICIANS
WORKING FOR PICOULT
ON THIS JOB RECEIVE
SUB-STANDARD WAGES
AND INFERIOR WORKING
CONDITIONS
LOCAL UNION NO. 3

ESTABLISHED 1891
INTERNATIONAL BROTHERHOOD OF
ELECTRICAL WORKERS

AFFILIATED WITH
A.F.L.—C.I.O.

Call GRamercy 5-3260
Union Label No. 194

Some of the pickets were stationed a part of the time at the rear and side delivery areas and, therefore, were not entirely confined to the front entrances where the general public went in and out. Early in January, 1962, a driver for a trucking firm attempted to make a delivery to Picoult at the job site. As he approached the picket line, he called for Picoult; but a picket advised him that they were on strike and offered to call the "picket captain." The picket left and then returned with another individual who indicated that the driver was not to cross the picket line. There was another incident on November 24, 1961 in which an employee of a secondary employer refused to cross the picket line.

The Respondent claimed that the objects of the picketing were "first, to induce the imployer to subcontract the electrical work to a contractor who would sign a collective-bargaining agreement with the Respondent, and failing that, to secure the cancellation of the employer's contract by the General Services Administration."

The Board made certain findings and conclusions and adopted those of the trial examiner not inconsistent with the Board's opinion. Its decision rested primarily, however, upon the following determinations:

" . . . we find that the Respondent picketed the Employer herein with an object of forcing or requiring it to recognize or bargain with the Respondent as the representative of its employees. The Respondent's efforts to gain recognition from the Employer and the picket sign initially used by it plainly show that the picketing began with a recognitional object.

"In the circumstances of this case, the mere change in the legend of the picket sign does not show a change in purpose of the uninterrupted picketing. It should be noted that the picket sign as changed did not reflect either of Respondent's purported objectives. This conflict between the asserted objectives and the picket sign strengthens our conclusion that the Respondent was at all times seeking recognition or bargaining from the Employer.

"We need not determine whether the Respondent's second picket sign would have satisfied the informational picketing proviso of Section 8(b) (7) (C) or, if so, whether the picketing had a prohibited effect, because we find that the picketing was not 'for the purpose of truthfully advising the public (including consumers) that an employer does not employ members of, or have a contract with a labor organization. ...' The picketing at delivery entrances of the post office and the truckdriver incident, related above, demonstrate that it did not have such an information purpose but, rather, was focused on the employees of secondary employees."

We decide that this case should be remanded for more adequate findings in the light of this opinion for two reasons: First, the Board improperly treated the wording on the two picket signs as evidence of an illegal purpose under Section 8(b) (7). Second, to the extent that the Board, in concluding that the picketing lacked an informational purpose, relied upon its previous finding that the union picketed the employer with the ultimate object of forcing or requiring it to recognize or bargain with the union, it misconstrued the import of subparagraph (C).

As to the first of these reasons, the Board appears to have disregarded or put aside the evidence of the wording of the two picket signs and a consideration of whether or not the language used was, on its face, within the permissive scope of the statute. Standing by itself the wording of both the first and second picket signs appears to come within the permissive terms of the second proviso. However, in its opinion the Board concluded that the first picket sign, together with the efforts to gain recognition from the employer, showed that the picketing began with a recognitional objective. It then went on to say, regarding the second picket sign, that it did not show a change in purpose nor, as changed, did it reflect either of respondent's purported objectives. The Board found that this was strongly corroborative of the conclusion it had previously reached that the respondent was at all times seeking recognition or bargaining.

There are doubtless cases where the wording of a picket sign may mean one thing standing alone and something quite different in the circumstances under which the sign is displayed or used, but the Board did not make any such finding about the second sign. It finds the second sign to be strong supporting evidence that the respondent was at all times seeking recognition or bargaining because the sign "did not reflect either of Respondent's purported objectives." The second proviso, however, does not require, for inclusion within its permissive scope, that the signs truthfully advise the public of the union's purported objectives. All that is required is wording which advises, in a truthful manner, "that an employer does not employ members of, or have a contract with, a labor organization. ..."

In treating the wording as it did, the Board failed to apply what this court said regarding the use of permissive wording on signs as proof of picketing directed to organized labor groups and employees of secondary employers to compel recognition.

> " . . . In considering this question, the fact that the union carried signs expressly allowed by the statute should not be a basis for concluding that the union had a recognitional objective."...

This does not mean that evidence that signs were being carried and that the subject matter of the signs concerned a labor-management dispute may not be considered in finding that the activity was in fact a picket line or in finding other facts relevant to issues under Section 8(b) (7) (C). Here, however, the Board clearly misused the *wording* of the signs as evidence that the union had from the first picketed and continued to picket for an illegal purpose.

The second reason for remanding this case is that the Board appears to have misconstrued the import of Section 8(b) (7) (C).

If the Board's opinion had centered upon the issue of absence of informational purpose in the picketing and had demonstrated a consideration of all of the relevant evidence bearing upon this, including the history of the picketing from its beginning, and a logical discussion of the factors which led to the Board's conclusion, its decision might well have stood. But as the opinion is written it is impossible to discover how much its finding of an absence of informational purpose was influenced or colored by its refusal to determine whether the wording of the signs was, as such, permissive under the second proviso, or by its declaration that the second picket sign "did not reflect either of Respondent's purported objectives" or by its threshold conclusion that the picketing was carried on "with an object of forcing or requiring the employer to recognize or bargain."

With regard to the last mentioned conclusion, the Board seems to have proceeded on the premise that Section 8(b) (7) (C) deals with organizational or recognitional picketing, except for the second proviso of subparagraph (C) which deals with an entirely separate kind or category of picketing, i. e., informational picketing, and that the two categories are somehow mutually exclusive. It seems, however, much more realistic to suppose that Congress framed a general rule covering the field of recognitional and organizational picketing, conducted under alternate sets of circumstances described in subparagraphs (A), (B), and (C), and then excepted from the operation of the rule, as it applied to the circumstances set forth in subparagraph (C), a comparatively innocuous species of picketing having the immediate purpose of informing or advising the public, even though its ultimate object was success in recognition and organization.

Looking at Section 8(b) (7) of the 1050 Act as a whole, it is apparent that it does not proscribe all recognitional picketing but only that which comes within the terms of the three "where" clauses, A., B., or C. For an unfair labor practice by the union to exist under 8(b) (7) (C) on the facts here alleged, the picketing must have been carried on under two conditions both of which must be operative at the time: (1) the picketing must have had as an object the forcing or requiring of an employer to recognize or bargain with a labor organization, etc.; and (2) such picketing must have been conducted without a petition under 9(c) having been filed within a reasonable period of time not to exceed thirty days, etc. (subsection C).

The Board has found that these two conditions exist here. But the second of these conditions is limited by two provisos, and this case is particularly concerned with the second of these provisos which says,

" . . . nothing in this subparagraph (C) shall be construed to prohibit any picketing or other publicity for the purpose of truthfully advising the public (including consumers) that an employer does not employ members of, or have a contract with, a labor organization, ..."

If, therefore, the union's picketing in this case came strictly within the "truthfully advising" provision of the second proviso and nothing more, the union would have no duty to file a petition under 9(c). In other words, the main provision of subparagraph (C) would be inoperative and the second of the two conditions, the existence of both of which are required for the finding of an unfair labor practive under Section 8(b) (7), would not apply.

Subparagraph (C) goes on in the "unless" clause to provide that if an effect of the informational picketing "is to induce any individual employed by any other person in the course of his employment, not to pick up, deliver or transport any goods or not to perform any services," the second of the main conditions remains in full force and the picketing is no longer permissive.

One of the principal difficulties in construing and applying subparagraph (C) is that Section 8(b) (7) contains the partially synonymous words, "object" and "purpose", used in two distinct contexts but to which much of the same evidence is relevant. These are: "where an object thereof is forcing or requiring an employer to recognize or bargain . . ." and "for the purpose of truthfully advising the public ... ." It does not necessarily follow that, where an object of the picketing is forcing or requiring an employer to recognize or bargain, the purpose of the picketing, in the context of the second proviso, is not truthfully to advise the public, etc. The union may legitimately have a long range or strategic objective of getting the employer to bargain with or recognize the union and still the picketing may be permissive. This proviso gives the union freedom to appeal to the unorganized public for spontaneous popular pressure upon an employer; it is intended, however, to exclude the invocation of pressure by organized labor groups or members of union, as such.

The permissible picketing is, therefore, that which through the dissemination of certain allowed representations, is designed to influence members of the unorganized public, as individuals, because the impact upon the employer by way of such individuals is weaker, more indirect, and less coercive.

In this connection what is meant by "advising the public," as used in the second proviso, is highly pertinent. Congress expressly provided that the word "public" should not be so narrowly construed as to exclude consumers, but the whole context of the phrase in which it appears makes it clear that it was not intended to be so broadly defined as to include organized labor groups which, at a word or signal from the picketeers, would impose economic sanctions upon the employer; otherwise Section 8(b) (7) would be, in effect, almost entirely emasculated. By this latest amendment to the Taft-Hartley Act Congress sought to circumscribe a kind of picketing which, by its nature, could in most cases bring an employer to his knees by threatening the destruction of his business and which, because of the attendant loss of employment, had a material tendency to coerce employees in their freedom to accept or reject union membership or freely select the union they wanted to represent them.

Professor Cox of Harvard, now Solicitor General, who worked with the Senate Labor Committee Chairman on the Section 8(b) (7) amendment to the Taft-Hartley Act, has said,

> "Picketing before a union election is divided by section 8(b) (7) into two categories: (1) picketing which halts pick-ups or deliveries by independent trucking concerns or the rendition of services by the employees of other employers, and (2) picketing which appeals only to employees in the establishment and members of the public. ... The theory is that the former class of picketing is essentially a signal to organized economic action backed by group discipline. Such economic pressure, if continued, causes heavy loss and increases the likelihood of the employer's coercing the employees to join the union. In the second type of picketing, the elements of communication predominate. If the employer loses patronage, it is chiefly because of the impact of the picket's message upon members of the public acting as individuals ... ." The Landrum-Griffin Amendments to the National Labor Relations Act, 44 Minnesota Law Review 257.

Although the two categories are described by him in terms of the *effect* of each, the express language of the second proviso uses the words "for the purpose of" and it is difficult to see how they can be ignored. Nevertheless, the description of the two categories is helpful in gaining insight to the second proviso. The concepts of "signal" picketing and "publicity" picketing should be used in characterizing the union's tactical purpose rather than in describing the picketing's effect. Yet purpose can be determined only through what is said and done under certain circumstances; and the effect of the picketing is one of the circumstances considered in determining in any case what the purpose was in so far as it is the natural and logical consequence of what the picketeers are saying and doing.

The effect might fall short of "inducing any individual employed by any other person in the course of his employment, not to pick up, deliver or transport any goods, or not to perform any services" and still be evidence of non-permissive purpose, such as display of qualifying signs accompanied by hostile gestures; or speech directed to persons unconnected with organized labor and not employees of secondary employers, such as a casual passer-by; or, for example, by forming a shoulder-to-shoulder picket line across an entrance which affected only members of the unorganized public who were not employees of a secondary employer.

Under the second proviso it is the difference in purpose which determines which is permissible picketing and which is not. In its context the second proviso means in terms of "signal" and "publicity" picketing that while most picketing with a "signaling" purpose is proscribed, most picketing for publicity is protected. The exceptions are that signal picketing is permissible when an object thereof is not forcing or requiring an employer to recognize or bargain, and publicity picketing is proscribed when it communicates more than the limited information expressly permitted by the second proviso or when it is apparently the purpose to advise organized labor groups or their members as shown by signal effects, unless there is persuasive proof that those effects are inspired by the employer who is seeking thereby to prevent legitimate second-proviso picketing by the union.

The Board must, therefore, approach its conclusion as to whether or not the picketing was "for the purpose of truthfully advising the public" by way of a finding of whether or not the union's tactical purpose was to signal economic action, backed by organized group discipline.

Accordingly the case is remanded.

• • •

CASE QUESTIONS

1. Local 3 stated its objectives in picketing as (1) to induce Picoult to subcontract its electrical work to the union, and failing this (2) to secure cancellation of the General Services Administration contract. Are these objectives sufficient to find an unfair labor practice?

2. Why did the court ignore the two instances where Local 3 pickets prevented employees of secondary employers from crossing the picket lines?

3. Why did the court remand the case and not reach a final conclusion on its own?

LOCAL 978, UNITED BROTHERHOOD OF CARPENTERS & JOINERS OF AMERICA, AFL—CIO v. MARKWELL
United States Court of Appeals, Eighth Circuit
305 F.2d 38 (8th Cir. 1962)

● ● ●

Before VOGEL, VAN OOSTERHOUT and MATTHES, Circuit Judges.

MATTHES, Circuit Judge.

This action for damages under § 303 of the Labor-Management Relations Act of 1947, as amended, (29 U.S.C.A. § 187), was instituted in the United States District Court for the Western District of Missouri by Kenneth Markwell and William Hartz, a co-partnership, doing business as Markwell and Hartz, Contractors.

The original defendants were five voluntary unincorporated labor organizations, namely: (1) Local 978, United Brotherhood of Carpenters and Joiners of America, AFL—CIO; (2) Local 676, International Hod Carriers, Building and Common Laborers Union of America, AFL—CIO; (3) Local 16—16—B, International Union of Operating Engineers; (4) Local 178, United Association of Journeyment & Apprentices of the Plumbing and Pipe Fitting Industry of the United States and Canada, AFL—CIO; and (5) Carpenters' District Council of Greater Kansas City and Vicinity.

The trial was before a jury, and at the close of all of the evidence the defendants made separate motions for directed verdict. The court sustained the motions of the Operating Engineers and the Plumbers but reserved ruling on the motions of the Laborers and the two Carpenter Associations. The jury found in favor of the plaintiffs and against the three defendants remaining in the case and assessed plaintiffs' damages at $50,000. None of these defendants filed after-trial motions under Rule 50(b) of the Federal Rules of Civil Procedure, 28 U.S.C.A., neither does the record disclose that the trial court expressly denied the motions for directed verdict upon which ruling had been reserved; however, formal judgment was entered on the verdict, thus implying a denial of the motions for directed verdict. The two Carpenter Associations are the only defendants who have appealed to this court.

Plaintiffs' cause of action was premised upon alleged unlawful picketing by defendant unions at the site of a construction project near Springfield, Missouri, where plaintiffs were engaged in constructing alterations and additions to the Northwest Sewage Treatment Plant, under contract with the City of Springfield. Plaintiffs' complaint alleged, and the cause was submitted under the theory of, violations of various subsections of § 303 of the Act, 29 U.S.C.A. § 187 (a) (1), (2), and (4), which in pertinent part provide:

"(a) It shall be unlawful . . . for any labor organization to engage in, or to induce or encourage the employees of any employer to engage in, a strike or a concerted refusal in the course of their employment to use, manufacture, process, transport, or otherwise handle or work on any goods, articles, materials, or commodities or to perform any services, *where an object thereof is—*

"(1) forcing or requiring . . . any employer or other person to cease using, selling, handling, transporting, or otherwise dealing in the products of any other producer, processor, or manufacturer, *or to cease doing business with any other person;*

"(2) forcing or requiring any other employer to recognize or bargain with a labor organization as the representative of his employees unless such labor organization has been certified as the representative of such employees under the provisions of section 159 of this title; . . .

"(4) *forcing or requiring any employer to assign particular work to employees in a particular labor organization* or in a particular trade, craft, or class rather than to employees in another labor organization or in another trade, craft, or class unless such employer is failing to conform to an order or certification of the National Labor Relations Board determining the bargaining representative for employees performing such work . . ." (Emphasis supplied).

The broad question presented by this appeal is whether the evidence was sufficient to present a question of fact for the jury to resolve. Appellants contend that the evidence established that the picketing activities complained of were, as a matter of law, legal, and not proscribed by § 303 of the Act, and that, therefore, their motions for directed verdict should have been sustained.

More precisely, appellants contend that § 303, and its counterpart covering unfair labor practices, § 8(b) (4), 29 U.S.C.A. § 158 (b) (4), were not designed to prohibit lawful primary activity; that the evidence conclusively establishes that all activities of defendant unions were directed at a primary dispute with plaintiffs; that all picketing was confined to the primary situs of the dispute, and at the *only* situs in Missouri where plaintiffs were doing business; and that there was no evidence of secondary picketing of neutral employers. In addition, as to § 187(a) (4), appellants contend that there was no "jurisdictional dispute" within the meaning of the Act.

With these contentions in mind, we briefly review the evidence.

Plaintiffs are Memphis, Tennessee contractors, and prior to the contract in question their construction projects were in the main confined to southern areas of the United States. In July, 1957, they were the successful bidders on the Northwest Sewage Plant project, and immediately thereafter an officer of the Operating Engineers Union and Secretary of the "Building Trades Council" of Springfield, contacted plaintiffs in reference to employment of local AFL—CIO union men on the job. In August, plaintiffs met with various representatives of the separate craft union, and although there is a dispute as to what transpired at this meeting, there is evidence from which the jury could have found that plaintiffs did agree to use the local AFL—CIO trade unions in filling requirements for construction men, apart from a few "key men" they wished to bring with them from Memphis.

On August 15, 1957, two of plaintiffs' employees, not members of the Carpenters' Union, began building a shed at the construction site, and this union offered to accept one of the men in the local AFL—CIO organization. Misunderstandings and disputes began, and negotiations broke down. Throughout the negotiations, the defendants "made it perfectly plain that they were seeking two things. First, that none but members of their organizations be employed. Second, that traditional jurisdictional lines be observed so that carpenters do only the work of carpenters and not the work of plumbers, etc." There is evidence that representatives of the interested labor organizations made statements to the effect that unless the job was AFL—CIO "we can starve you out; we can put a banner up out there, shut off your concrete and materials to where you can't operate this job" and that "You won't get any electricians or any other craftsmen to cross the picket line."

It appears that plaintiffs employed additional men who were not members of the unions affiliated with the "Building Trades Council," and that on August 23, 1957, plaintiffs signed a labor agreement with another organization known as the "United Construction Workers," an affiliate of the United Mine Workers.

Three days later and on August 26, defendants began picketing the only entrance to the construction site with a sign readings as follows:

"A. F. of L. Carpenters not employed, Markwell, Hartz Construction Company, Local Union 978, Kansas City District Council."

It is conceded that at all times the picketing was peaceful, that it was confined to the construction site, and that no neutral employers were picketed. Eleven of plaintiffs' employees were working at the site when picketing began, and all continued to work throughout the 42 days of picketing activity. However, the picketing was successful from the unions' standpoint, in that employees of various suppliers honored the picket line and refused to make deliveries or perform services for plaintiffs, and the picket line was maintained until October 22, when it was enjoined by an order of the United States District Court.

There was evidence of five different incidents at the picket line which successfully prevented plaintiffs from receiving needed services and supplies. They are briefly summarized as follows:

(A) On the first day of picketing, a crew of power line workers of the City of Springfield appeared to re-locate power lines within the construction area, but work was stopped by the foreman of the crew, who, according to the record, stated: "we were all union men; we wouldn't work behind a picket line."

(B) On the first day of picketing an employee-driver of the Southwest Plumbing & Heating Company, apparently carrying supplies, refused to drive through the picket line.

(C) Another truck driver, this time an employee of the Anton-Luce Electric Company, stopped short of the picket line and refused to continue on to the construction site.

(D) Again, on the first day of picketing, a driver for the Garrett Construction Company, carrying a load of ready-mixed concrete, was ultimately ordered by his employer to leave without making delivery of the concrete.

(E) Several weeks after picketing began, a driver for the Frisco Transportation Company honored the picket line, and his materials were unloaded and delivered by plaintiffs' own employees.

Apparently there was no picketing by defendants after normal working hours and plaintiffs in fact managed to proceed to some extent with the project by having their employees work at night, driving rented trucks in order to bring materials and supplies onto the job site.

It was admitted by appellants that they were not, at any time, the representatives of plaintiffs' employees or certified by the National Labor Relations Board as representatives of such employees under the provisions of § 9 [29 U.S.C.A. § 159] of the Act. See § 187 (a) (2). It was also admitted that plaintiffs were not "failing to conform to an order or certification of the National Labor Relations Board determining the bargaining representative" for their employees. See § 187(a) (4).

Under the evidence viewed in the light most favorable to plaintiffs, the legislative history of the Act, and decisional law which we consider as controlling, we must rule that there was no evidence to support a finding that the activities and conduct of the appellants constituted secondary boycott activities and that this issue should not have been submitted to the jury.

A literal reading of §§ 158 (b) (4) and 187(a) would seemingly impel the conclusion that all activities of labor organizations which induce or encourage the employees of any employer to cease doing business with any other person, regardless of the location of such activities, would be unlawful—in other words, that picketing at the primary employer's premises, otherwise lawful, would become illegal when employees of neutral employers honored the picket line. In neither of the above mentioned statutes is the situs of the picketing expressly mentioned or designated as a factor in determining whether the union's activity constitutes conduct proscribed therin, but we are satisfied that this is an element that must be read into §§ 158(b) (4) and 187(a). This conclusion finds support upon consideration of the Act in its entirety, its legislative history, and decisional law in a number of cases where the courts were dealing with alleged secondary boycott activities. It should be remembered that § 13 of the Act, 29 U.S.C.A. § 163, provides:

> "§ 163. Right to strike preserved
>
> "Nothing in this subchapter, except as specifically provided for herein, shall be construed so as either to interfere with or impede or diminish in any way the right to strike, or to affect the limitations or qualifications on that right."

A legitimate expectation of any labor organization which pickets an employer with whom it has a primary dispute is that all persons will honor the picket line, including employees of neutral employers making deliveries of supplies or performing services for the primary employer. The legislative history of § 158 (b) (4), frequently referred to as the "secondary boycott section," makes it compellingly clear that the evil sought to be eliminated by this legislation was not lawful primary activity, but those union activities which would embroil some neutral employer in a labor dispute not of his making, thus penalizing an unoffending employer to his damage. . . .

Obviously, the most blatant example of the forbidden secondary activity would be the actual picketing of a neutral employer's premises. That is not the situation here, for the evidence conclusively establishes, indeed plaintiffs concede, that the picketing activities were confined to the *primary* situs of the dispute, the *sole* situs available to defendants within the State of Missouri—this was the place plaintiffs were doing business—in fact the only place. Furthermore, and perhaps of distinguishing importance is the complete absence of evidence tending to prove that the construction project was a *common situs*. Apparently the picket line was set up before the employees of any subcontractor, if there were any, had actually begun work on the project. Appellants assert in their brief that "the record does not show that other employers or employees had their place of work within the situs area at any time here material." Plaintiffs have not attempted to refute that statement and our examination of the record attests to the accuracy thereof.

Plaintiffs rely principally upon National Labor Relations Board v. Denver Bldg. Council, supra, 341 U.S. 675, ... International Brotherhood of Electrical Workers, etc., v. National Labor Relations Board, 341 U.S. 694; ... and Local 74 United Broth. of Carpenters, etc. v. National Labor Relations Board, 341 U.S. 707, ... in support of their contention that the instant conduct constituted prohibited activities and that this issue was properly submitted to the jury. We refrain from a discussion of the factual situations presented in these cases or the basis for the court's ultimate conclusion that the conduct there complained of was proscribed by § 158(b) (4) (A). It is sufficient to observe that in each the presence of a neutral employer at the site of the picketing was a vital, if not the controlling, element which persuaded the Supreme Court to conclude that the activities fell within the proscription of the statute. It is this "common situs" element which, in our considered opinion, renders those cases inapposite and not controlling here.

In our view, National Labor Relations Board v. International Rice Milling Co., supra, 341 U.S. 665, ... is persuasive authority for the conclusion that defendants did not engage in secondary activities. We recognize that in Rice Milling the Supreme Court emphasized that the union did not engage in *concerted* activities; nevertheless, the situs of the picketing was not ignored. Thus, the Court stated, 341 U.S. at p. 671: ...

> "There was no attempt by the union to induce any action by the employees of the neutral customer which would be more widespread than that already described. There were no inducements or encouragements applied elsewhere than on the picket line. The limitation of the complaint to an incident in the geographically restricted area near the mill is significant, although not necessarily conclusive. The picketing was directed at the Kaplan employees and at their employer in a manner traditional in labor disputes."

Moreover, the Supreme Court in National Labor Relations Board v. Denver Bldg. Council, supra, ... recognized that Rice Milling was distinguishable, in part at least, because of the situs of the picketing, stating at pp. 687-688:

"The conduct which the Board here condemned is readily distinguishable from that which it declined to condemn in the Rice Milling case, ante, [341 U.S.] p. 665. ... There the accused union sought merely to obtain its own recognition by the operator of a mill, and the union's pickets near the mill sought to influence two employees of a customer of the mill not to cross the picket line. In that case we supported the Board in its conclusion that such conduct was no more than was traditional and permissible in a primary strike. The union did not engage in a strike against the customer. It did not encourage concerted action by the customer to boycott the mill. It did not commit any unfair labor practice proscribed by § 8(b) (4)."

In Local 618, etc. v. National Labor Relations Board, 8 Cir., 249 F.2d 332, this court was concerned with a factual situation bearing resemblance to that presented by this record. The basic question was whether the union's strike and subsequent picketing at the employer's Manchester service station was secondary and proscribed by § 158(b) (4) (A) of the Act. This determination turned on the question of whether the Board had properly followed the "an object" test applied in National Labor Relations Board v. Denver Bldg. Council, supra, 341 U.S. 675, 689, ... and International Brotherhood of Electrical Workers etc., v. National Labor Relations Board, supra, 341 U.S. 694, 700. ... The Court found that the picketing at the premises of the primary employer constituted lawful primary activity, and thus it was erroneous to apply the "an object" tests. During the course of the opinion the case of United Electrical, Radio and Machine Workers of America, 85 NLRB 417 (p. 418) was discussed and a portion of the Board's opinion was quoted at p. 335 of 249 F.2d. Pertinent here is—

" ' . . . Section 8(b) (4) (A) was not intended by Congress, as the legislative history makes abundantly clear, to curb primary picketing. It was intended only to outlaw certain *secondary* boycotts, whereby unions sought to enlarge the economic battleground beyond the premises of the primary Employer. When picketing is wholly at the premises of the employer with whom the union is engaged in a labor dispute, it cannot be called "secondary" even though, as is virtually always the case, an object of the picketing is to dissuade all persons from entering such premises for business reasons.' " (Emphasis supplied).

The cases which condemned as unlawful secondary activity at "common situs" projects are in no way applicable here. As we have seen, there was evidence tending to establish that appellants had a legitimate labor dispute with plaintiffs; and in the absence of any evidence whatsoever to support a finding of secondary activity, it was prejudicial error to submit this issue for jury determination.

Our ruling that appellants' activities did not fall within the proscriptions of § 187(a) (1) does not dispose of the case, for we reach a contrary conclusion with regard to the issue of liability under subsection (4) of § 187(a)—the so-called "jurisdictional strike" provisions. From legislative history, it is clear that §§ 187 and 158(b) (4) were designed to make unlawful secondary activities *and* jurisdictional strikes. In view of the stated purposes of the legislation, and when the object of the strike is found to be to force assignment of particular work to members of a labor organization, the situs of the picketing is not of determinative importance. It is our opinion that the provisions relating to jurisdictional strikes and other activities are designed to protect the *primary* employer as well as neutral employers from involvement in internal disputes between unions, not of his own making. For this reason, and regardless of the fact that appellants' activities were confined to the "primary situs," we find that the issue of unlawful activity on the part of appellants by reason of picketing for the purpose of "forcing any employer to assign particular work to employees in a particular labor organization," was properly submitted for jury determination.

Without going into detail, clearly there was substantial evidence to support a jury finding that appellants did "induce" or "encourage" other employees to refrain from doing business with plaintiffs and to find that the picket line was established for the purpose of forcing plaintiffs to assign jobs to AFL—CIO members which were already filled by workers affiliated with the United Construction Workers. The record indicates that plaintiffs were willing to hire appellants' members, but that plaintiffs maintained a neutral position as to the affiliation of certain "key men" required for the project. On the other hand, it is clear that appellants were seeking "100% AFL—CIO" affiliation, and the jury would be entitled to infer that appellants sought to force plaintiffs to replace these "key men" with members of appellants' organizations. The record would justify a conclusion that the picketing was maintained for no reason other than the dispute over the jobs already filled by members of the United Construction Workers. It was testified that one of appellants' agents, in addressing plaintiffs' employees, stated:

> "We understand you come from another part of the country where you have been working for the United Construction Workers. We are familiar with United Construction Workers and they have tried to come into this part of the country at another time, and the fact is we don't intend to let them light. We are, in the A.F. of L., have been, in this country for a long time and we intend for this job to be A. F. of L."

The record also establishes that plaintiffs took a "neutral position" in respect to the union affiliation of their employees. Thus, we find this testimony of Mr. Hartz concerning a meeting held August 23 at the construction site where representatives of the AFL—CIO unions were given an opportunity to address plaintiffs' employees and invite them to join with the A. F. of L.

> " . . . I addressed the people there, our men at that point, and I said, in effect, that they understood now what the A. F. of L. had to offer them; that if they wished to join the A. F. of L. we were behind them one hundred percent; if they wanted to join the U.C.W., or stay with the U.C.W. [United Construction Workers], we were still behind them one hundred percent. As far as Mr. Pauly's threat [agent of the Carpenters] was concerned, there might be a possibility he would be able to cut us off and shut us down, but if they wanted to work with the U.C.W., we would certainly be willing to try it.
> "The men then asked Mr. Pauly . . . several questions . . . [a]nd Mr. Pauly then asked the men if they were interested, and the men said they liked the way they were."

Appellants also contend that the facts here do not establish a true "jurisdictional dispute." While § 158(b) (4) (D) and its counterpart § 187 (a) (4) are of particular aid in disputes involving two rival unions within an employer organization, it is clear that these sections are also applicable when the dispute might be said to be solely between an employer and a union. . . .

Appellants also assert that the evidence relating to damages sustained by plaintiffs was insufficient to present a jury issue; that the evidence was too remote, speculative and uncertain to form the basis of a lawful judgment. This contention is without substance. We have examined the record and are satisfied that there was probative evidence from which the jury could legitimately find that as the direct and proximate result of the proscribed conduct of appellants, plaintiffs sustained actual damages, and appellants would not be entitled to a directed verdict solely upon the issue of damages.

We have ruled that while the issue of unlawful jurisdictional picketing was properly submitted to the jury, the issue of unlawful secondary activity was erroneously submitted. In looking to the trial court's instructions, we find that the two issues were submitted alternatively and in such a manner that we are compelled to hold that prejudicial error inhered in the verdict. After hypothesizing certain of the facts, the court instructed the jury as follows:

> " . . . but, even though one purpose of the picketing may be perfectly legal under primary picketing definition, *if one of the purposes is one of the three things I previously outlined* [the "three objects" being violations of §§ 187(a) (1), (2), *and* (4)] . . . that amounts to a secondary boycott within the definition of the law, *or* a jurisdictional dispute within that definition, it is illegal, and if you find that that sort of thing existed and that one or more of the defendants violated that statute *in any of the objects set forth,* as I have defined it here, then you will find for the plaintiff and against the defendants . . . ." (Emphasis supplied).

The principle is firmly established that where a case is submitted to the jury upon more than one theory, and the submission on one theory is erroneous and a general verdict is returned, the verdict cannot be upheld because it is impossible to determine with certainty the theory upon which the jury based its verdict. Under such circumstances a new trial should be granted. . . .

The verdict here is a general one. It is impossible for us to determine with certainty upon what theory the jury based its verdict. In this situation the cause must be remanded for a new trial.

By way of addendum—the failure of appellants to file an after-trial motion for judgment notwithstanding the verdict, as authorized by Rule 50(b) of the Federal Rules of Civil Procedure, limits the scope of relief we could grant. Even if the evidence were insufficient to present a question of fact for the jury on any issue, as appellants have contended, the maximum relief to which they would be entitled, in the absence of a motion n.o.v., is a new trial. . . .

The judgment is reversed and the cause remanded for a new trial.

• • •

CASE QUESTIONS

1. When does the situs of picketing determine an unfair labor practice?

2. Can picketing at the primary situs of a labor dispute be an unfair labor practice?

3. How does the existance of a common situs effect the presence of an unfair labor practice?

NLRB v. LOCAL 182, INTERNATIONAL BROTHERHOOD OF TEAMSTERS, CHAUFFEURS, WAREHOUSEMEN, & HELPERS OF AMERICA
United States Court of Appeals, Second Circuit
314 F.2d 53 (2d Cir. 1963)

• • •

Before LUMBARD, Chief Judge, and SWAN and FRIENDLY, Circuite Judges.

FRIENDLY, Circuit Judge.

The National Labor Relations Board seeks enforcement of an order, 135 NLRB No. 90, finding that Local 182, International Brotherhood of Teamsters, Chauffeurs, Warehousemen and Helpers of America, hereafter the Union or the respondent, violated § 8(b) (7) (B) of the National Labor Relations Act, 29 U.S.C. § 158(b) (7) (B), added by the Labor Management Reporting and Disclosure Act of 1959, ... which prohibits "recognitional" or "organizational" picketing within twelve months after a valid election. The order, entered February 5, 1962, required the Union to cease and desist from such picketing (a) "for a period of one year from March 1, 1961," and (b) "where within the preceding twelve months a valid election under 9(c) of the Act has been conducted which the Respondent did not win." We grant enforcement.

Woodward Motors, Inc. (hereafter Woodward, the Company or the employer) is engaged, in upstate New York, in the sale and servicing of automobiles procured from outside the state. On August 1, 1960, the Union informed Woodward that it represented a majority of the Company's employees and requested negotiations. After polling its 15 employees, Woodward, on August 8, recognized the Union as representative of the employees in a specified unit, agreed to enter into negotiations and to establish union shop conditions in the meantime, and further agreed to submit to arbitration the discharge of one Gorecki on August 2. Some seven bargaining sessions were held, without result. On September 21, Woodward received a petition signed by eight of the employees stating that they did "not want to become associated with the Local Teamsters Union" but did "want to form our independent shop union."

At the next scheduled bargaining session, Woodward informed the Union that, in the light of the petition, it could not continue to negotiate. On October 5 the Union filed charges alleging violation by the Company of § 8(a) (1), (2), (3) and (5)—because of a refusal to bargain, the discriminatory discharge of Gorecki, and unlawful assistance to the "independent" union. Woodward countered on October 7 with a petition for an election.

Beginning on October 10, 1960, representatives of the Union appeared at the entrance to the Company's property, carrying signs that read:

"WOODWARD MOTORS, INC.
UNFAIR LABOR PRACTICE AND
VIOLATION OF AGREEMENT
PICKET LINE
UNFAIR
TO ORGANIZED
LABOR
DO NOT PATRONIZE
TEAMSTERS-CHAUFFEURS
WAREHOUSEMEN & HELPERS
AFL LOCAL 182
UTICA & CENTRAL N.Y. STATE"

The Company, on October 28, filed charges that this picketing violated § 8(b) (7) (C) in that it was for recognitional and organizational purposes and was being conducted when a petition for an election had not been filed within a reasonable period after its commencement. On November 3 the Regional Director accepted a settlement of the Union's § 8(a) (1) and (3) charges with respect to the discriminatory discharge of Gorecki; he later notified the Union he was dismissing its other charges under § 8(a) (2) and (5). The Union appealed to the General Counsel from the dismissal of these charges; the appeal was denied on December 23. Next, on January 6, 1961, the Regional Director dismissed the Company's § 8(b) (7) (C) charge against the Union on the ground that a timely petition for election *had* been filed, to wit, the Company's own petition of October 7, "and a determination has been made that an expedited election should be conducted upon such petition in accordance with the provisions of sections 8(b) (7) (C) and 9(c)."

Picketing stopped on January 16, 1961. At the election on January 17, no labor organization achieved a majority of the valid ballots. About January 30 representatives of the Union reappeared near Woodward's premises and stationed themselves in autos parked on the shoulder of the adjacent highway, having previously planted two signs in a snowbank abutting the entrance. The first read:

"WE ARE NOT PICKETING FOR
ORGANIZATION OR RECOGNITION."

The second read:

"THE EMPLOYEES OF WOODWARD MOTORS, INC., ARE NOT PROTECTED BY A UNION CONTRACT."

The Union business representative testified that if people inquired of the sign watchers what this Janus-like display was supposed to mean, the watchers "would tell them we had a signed Union agreement with this Company and there are certain things that happened, we had lost the people, some were discharged for unjust cause, some were laid off. There was, in other words, a motive to break the Union I would tell these people." He conceded that if the Union had had a contract with Woodward at the time, "there would be no reason to place a sign out." Mr. Woodward testified that if a truck came along, the Union representatives "would run out, stop it, speak to the driver after which action the driver would always drive away", and that, in general, deliveries were thus interrupted. The Union continued this activity until March 1, 1961, when Judge Brennan granted a temporary injunction under § 10(*l*). Finding a violation of § 8(b) (7) (B) by the Union, the Board entered the order described above, which it asks us to enforce.

The Union challenges the order on five grounds. It (1) denies that there was picketing after the election, (2) says that if there was, this did not have the object defined in the introductory clause of § 8(b) (7), (3) claims that any picketing was within the second proviso to § 8(b) (7) (C), which, it asserts, applies also to § 8(b) (7) (B), (4) contends that the election was not "a valid election," and (5) urges finally that the order by its terms is "academic, useless, and illegal."

The Union's first objection, that the post-election activity was not "picketing", is without merit. Webster's New International Dictionary (2d ed.) says that the verb "picket" in the labor sense means "to walk or stand in front of a place of employment as a picket" and that the noun means "a person posted by a labor organization at an approach to the place of work. ..."

Movement is thus not requisite, although here there was some. The activity was none the less picketing because the Union chose to bisect it, placing the material elements in snowbanks but protecting the human elements from the rigors of an upstate New York winter by giving them the comfort of heated cars until a delivery truck approached. This was still "more than speech and establishes a locus in quo that has far more potential for inducing action or nonaction than the message the pickets convey." Building Service Employers' Int'l Union Local 262 v. Gazzam, 339 U.S. 532, 537. ... At the very least, the Board did not act unreasonably in construing "picket," a statutory term relating to a subject within its area of special competence, to include what the Union did here. ...

There is little more in the Union's second claim, that the post-election picketing did not have as "an object thereof . . . forcing or requiring an employer to recognize or bargain with a labor organization as the representative of his employees, or forcing or requiring the employees of an employer to accept or select such labor organization as their collective bargaining representative." The Union does not dispute that stopping deliveries would amount to "forcing or requiring" if the other conditions were met; but denies that they were. Professor Cox, who writes with peculiar authority on this subject, says, with respect to the phrases here at issue, "The very few men close to the drafting of the Conference Report who understood this problem had no common intention—perhaps 'had conflicting intentions' would be a better phrase"; he suggests that "The best solution would be to treat the union's objective as a question of fact." 44 Minn.L.Rev. at 266-67. So treating it, we cannot find unreasonable the Board's conclusion that the Union's protest "was directed to the Employer's withdrawal of recognition and discontinuance of bargaining negotiations" and that "Satisfaction of such protest required a renewal of recognition and resumption of negotiations." The Board was not bound to accept at face value the disclaimer on the sign first described; it was entitled to consider the totality of the Union's conduct. ... It is true that even the second sign did not contain specific reference to the picketing union, as did the signs in the Penello case, in Kennedy v. Los Angeles Joint Executive Board of Hotel & Restaurant Employees, 192 F. Supp. 339 (S.D. Calif. 1961), and in NLRB v. Local 239, IBT, 289 F.2d 41 (2 Cir.), cert. denied, 368 U.S. 833, ... but stated only that Woodward's employees "are not protected by a union contract." We assume in the Union's favor, without deciding, that in proscribing picketing whose object is to force or require the employer's recognition of a "a labor organization" or the employees' selection of "such labor organization," the statute refers only to the particular labor organization which is doing the picketing, so that § 8(b) (7) would not apply if the object of the picketing was merely to get *some* union into the shop—as, for example, if it were shown here that the Teamsters would have withdrawn their pickets if the Company made a suitable contract with the independent union. No such showing was made, and the Board was warranted—particularly in the light of the timing of the picketing and of the business representative's testimony quoted above—in concluding that recognition or organization of Local 182 as bargaining representative of Woodward's employees was at least "an" object of the post-election picketing.

Little need be said as to the Union's third objection, namely, that picketing of the sort described in the introductory clause may be conducted, as provided in § 8(b) (7) (C), "for the purpose of truthfully advising the public (including consumers) that an employer does not . . . have a contract with . . . a labor organization," even "where within the preceding twelve months a valid election under section 9(c) of this Act has been conducted," within the terms of § 8(b) (7) (B). The language and structure of § 8(b) (7), its legislative history, its manifest purpose, its administrative construction, and such judicial decisions as have been rendered, unite to negate this reading. ...

Congress intended, in Senator Kennedy's words, "to provide that for a certain period of time following a legitimate election, there could not be picketing" of the sort described in the introductory clause. It is thus unnecessary to consider whether the Board was warranted in finding, as it did, that the post-election picketing had the effect of inducing the stoppage of deliveries and services and hence in any event did not meet the standards of the second proviso to § 8(b) (7) (C).

This brings us to the fourth objection: that the election was not a "valid" one, primarily because, as the Union contends, the employer was guilty of unfair labor practices that had not been remedied. It has long been "customary Board policy not to proceed with a representation case while charges are pending against a company or the effects of prior unfair labor practices remain undissipated; employees cannot exercise true freedom of choice in the face of interference or coercion." Cox, Labor Law: Cases and Materials (1958) 341. Although § 8(b) (7) imposes no express conditions in this regard, the Board considers that "it strains credulity to believe, that Congress proposed to make the rights of unions and employees turn upon the results of an election which, because of the existence of unremedied unfair labor practices, is unlikely to reflect the true wishes of the employees." International Hod Carriers, Local 840, Supplemental Decision and Order, 135 NLRB No. 121, sheet 15 (1962). In view of the sense of the situation and Congressional acquiescence in the Board's long standing practice, cf. NLRB v. Gullett Gin Co., 340 U.S. 361, 365-366, ... (1951), this seems a sound view, at least if limited to practices of a sort that would be likely to prevent a fair election, which evidently is what the Board meant. The Trial Examiner, whose Intermediate Report was approved by the Board, overruled the Union's claim on the basis that here the General Counsel had dismissed the unfair labor practice charges against the employer under § 8(a) (2) and (5), and that the Examiner did "not believe it incumbent upon the trier of the facts in one case to re-examine an administrative determination reached in another case."

Although we appreciate the difficulties, which arise from the internal bifurcation of the Board and have led to a similar holding in another context, see Times Square Stores Corp., 79 NLRB 361 (1948), 2 Davis, Administrative Law Treatise (1958), § 13.05, ... we are not sure the issue can always be settled in such summary fashion. Section 8(b) (7) (B) applies only to picketing for the forbidden object within the twelve months after "a valid election". The Board's brief concedes, properly we think, that in an unfair labor practice proceeding under § 8(b) (7) (B), "all questions relating to the validity of the election, including the propriety of directing it, are open to Board and judicial review," citing Department & Specialty Stores Employees' Union, Local 1265 (Kinney Co.), 136 NLRB No. 29 (1962), and Department & Specialty Stores Employees' Union, Local 1265 v. Brown, 284 F.2d 619 (9 Cir., 1960), cert denied, 366 U.S. 934. .. (1961).

As the Board indicated in the Hod Carriers opinion, we cannot suppose that Congress was concerned only with validity in the formal sense; ... an election in which a union has in fact been strong-armed by tactics violating § 8(a) (7) (B)—even in the unlikely event that the General Counsel had refused to issue a complaint, and even though the Board could not make him issue one and his refusal would not be reviewable by a court of appeals under § 10(f), and only dubiously so by a district court ... However, a union wishing to argue that an election is invalid because of the employer's unremedied unfair labor practices, despite the General Counsel's refusal to act upon its charges, must do more than prove that it has filed charges which the General Counsel has dismissed; there must be something to indicate that he was wrong in doing so and that unfair labor practices in fact prevented a fair election. Here the Union neither proved nor offered to prove anything of the sort; indeed it did not even appeal from the Regional Director's settlement of its § 8(a) (3) and § 8 (a) (1) charges relating to the alleged discriminatory discharge, nor from his determination that an election should be conducted upon the Company's petition. . . .

Another possible flaw in the election is that it was held, purportedly under the authority of the first proviso of § 8(b) (7) (C), as an "expedited" one, "without regard to the provisions of section 9(c) (1)." Section 9(c) (1) directs that when a petition of a specified character has been filed, "the Board shall investigate such petition and if it has reasonable cause to believe that a question of representation affecting commerce exists shall provide for an appropriate hearing upon due notice"; "if the Board finds upon the record of such hearing that such a question of representation exists, it shall firect an election by secret ballot and shall certify the results thereof." Although determinations under § 9(c) (1) are made locally by the Regional Director, Regulations § 102.67(a), there are limited opportunities for review by the Board, § 102.67(b)—(j). All this may be dispensed with, however, if the conditions of the first proviso of § 8 (b) (7) (C) are met.

That they were met here might be questioned on two grounds. One arises from the fact that the Company's petition was filed before picketing began rather than "within a reasonable period of time not to exceed thirty days from the commencement of such picketing." This would appear to be at most a formal defect not impairing the validity of an election; we are unable to perceive how anyone's rights were adversely affected by the Board's pinning the election to a petition filed a few days before the start of picketing and allowed to remain on file thereafter, as against the one that could have been filed a few hours after the pickets appeared. The other question stems from the Board's view that "picketing which meets the requirements of the [second] proviso also renders the expedited procedure inapplicable." . . . Assuming in the Union's favor the propriety of this reading, which has some textual basis and derives support from the statement of Senator Kennedy in presenting the Conference Report to the Senate, the case is still one where the expedited procedure was proper. For there was ample evidence that the pre-election picketing was not within the second proviso since, as the Examiner found with respect to the post-election activity, "an effect of such picketing" was "to induce any individual employed by any other person in the course of his employment, not to pick up, deliver, or transport any goods or not to perform any services." Mr. Woodward testified that during the pre-election period the pickets "marched up and down and if a truck did enter they would stop the truck, stand in front of it, and engage the driver in conversation shortly after it came in," with the result that the picketing prevented deliveries of new vehicles, laundry, uniforms, undercoating materials, janitorial supplies, automotive parts—and Pepsi Cola.

We come finally to the respondent's challenge to the order as "academic, useless and illegal." The first two adjectives rest on the fact that the period of one year from March 1, 1961, during which respondent was ordered to cease and desist by subdivision (a) of the order, has expired, as it very nearly had when the order was made. Plainly the order is not academic or useless if we enforce subdivision (b), which forbids picketing for the proscribed object "where within the preceding twelve months a valid election under 9(c) of the Act has been conducted which the Respondent did not win." Respondent claims this to be "illegal," but we do not find it so. "It is a salutary principle that when one has been found to have committed acts in violation of a law he may be restrained from committing other related unlawful acts .... Having found the acts which constitute the unfair labor practice the Board is free to restrain the practice and other like or related unlawful acts. ..."

But even if subdivision (a) stood alone, the mere lapse of time would not render the proceeding moot. A direction to enforce the Board's order necessarily connotes judicial approval of its findings and conclusions that respondent's conduct violated § 8(b) (7), which are essential to its validity, and this might furnish "reasonable cause to believe" under § 10(*l*) with respect to subsequent picketing of the same general nature by the Union against the Company. ...

Enforcement granted.

• • •

CASE QUESTIONS

1. If the union's picketing had been in a form truthfully designed only to advise the public, including consumers, that Woodward did not have a contract with Local 182, would the court have enforced the National Labor Relations Board's order?

2. Who are the proper parties to determine the validity of an election?

3. How could Local 182 have had the election set aside?

NLRB v. TEXAS NATURAL GASOLINE CORPORATION
United States Court of Appeals, Fifth Circuit
253 F.2d 322 (5th Cir. 1958)

• • •

Before TUTTLE, JONES and BROWN, Circuit Judges.

JONES, Circuit Judge.

Since so much in this case is dependent upon the factual situation, it becomes necessary to relate the chain of events in some detail. The respondent, Texas Natural Gasoline Corporation, operated a number of natural gas processing plants. One of these was at Rankin, Texas, where fifty-eight persons were employed. Rex H. Snell was the plant superintendent. The plant operated twenty-four hours a day, seven days a week. Production employees worked three shifts, 7 a.m. to 3 p.m., 3 p.m. to 11 p.m., and 11 p.m. to 7 a.m. During the early part of July, 1955, Snell was on vacation. During his absence there was some discussion among the employees about the organization of a union. Some sort of a document was prepared by or under the guidance of a union representative. It was never shown to any representative of the Respondent, and there is no reason to suppose that the respondent heard of it until after the happening of the events from which the controversy before us arose. Some, we do not know how many, of the employees signed the paper. The petitioner presumes the document was for the purpose of designating a union as the employee bargaining representative. If such it was, it did not, during the sequence of events here pertinent, effect the intended design. On July 8th, Snell returned from his vacation. Snell was told that an employee named Henley had been lying on his desk when he should have been working at it. Snell directed that Henley be discharged, and Henley was discharged.

On the evening of July 8 a meeting of employees was held at the Court House in Rankin. Twenty or twenty-five of the employees were present. The union representative conducted the meeting and was the one who did the talking. The group decided, it seems, that unless Henley was reinstated they would strike at 3 o'clock the next day. At the meeting, a committee of four was selected and instructed to tell Mr. Snell that unless Henley was reinstated there would be a strike. The committee called on Snell on the following morning, July 9. They stated that they were speaking for other employees as well as for themselves, that there was dissatisfaction over Henley's discharge, and "some talk that they might walk out." Snell told the committee that several people had seen Henley lying on his desk, and that this was something that could not be tolerated. The committee members responded that they had not previously understood it that way, and that Snell's explanation put a different light on the matter. On this note the interview ended.

Bill Hood was an office clerk in the respondent's plant. As an office employee his work hours were from 8 a.m. until 4:30 p.m. six days a week. He had been a teacher in the Rankin School System until its summer vacation and then went to work for respondent. The School Board had designated him as a teacher for the following year. During the summer school vacation of 1954 he had worked for the Respondent. During the summer vacation of 1955 he lived in a teachery of the school system taking advantage of the reduced rental which teachers enjoyed. At the end of the summer vacation he resumed his activity in the teaching profession. He had attended the meeting on the evening of July 8. On the afternoon of July 9, about a quarter of three, Hood, who had apparently not been informed as to the result of the interview of the employees' committee with Snell, went to Snell and asked whether he could reconsider the discharge of Henley or did he want the employees to shut the plant down. He told Snell he was speaking as a representative of a majority of the employees. Obviously this was not so, and he made no effort to ascertain what had been done by the committee which had been selected to represent a group, but probably not a majority, of the employees. Snell gave Hood the same reason he had given the committee for Henley's discharge. Snell's explanation to Hood did not, as it had done with the committee, put a different light on the matter, but Hood did agree that Snell should have the right to fire a man for lying down on the job. Before the discussion ended, Snell warned Hood that if he left before the end of his workday, "his check would be made out for him," and that so far as Snell was concerned, his early leaving would be regarded as quitting. Hood told Kersten, the office manager, he was leaving and at Kersten's request turned in his key. At or about three o'clock Hood took his departure. At the same time the seven-to-three plant shift was going out and the three-to-eleven shift was coming in. On coming out of the plant, Hood inquired of the shift workers as to how many were striking with him. He had no response.

Henley, expecting that he would either be back at the desk from which he had been evicted or the participant in a strike staged in his honor, had spent a part of the morning having some picket signs made and painted. He was joined by Hood at the gate to the plant on the highway a half mile distant, and these two picketed for a while and then went to town. Hood did not then know of any other employees stopping work. So far as Hood then knew, it was Henley and himself. July 9 was Saturday. On the morning of Monday, July 11, Hood came to the plant and was told he had no job.

Shirley C. Little was a laboratory tester for the company. He was supposed to go to work at three in the afternoon. Instead, he went to the train rack and there, so he said, inquired of train engineers as to whether or not they would cross a picket line. No other employee was with Little. He was unaware of the activities of Henley and Hood. About four o'clock Snell came out, talked with Little, and suggested he go to work. Little refused and Snell told him he could either go back to work or "that was it." Later Little went to the office where he was paid off. At this meeting Snell suggested that Little tear up the check and go back to work. On the next day Little's replacement was hired. Little has not at any time sought re-employment.

On August 5, 1955, Henley filed a charge with the National Labor Relations Board that his employment had been terminated because of his activities on behalf of the union. On September 20, 1955, Henley filed an amended charge that the employment of Hood and Little had been terminated because of their union activities. A complaint was made against the respondent on the amended charge. A hearing was had before the Board. No contention was there made that Henley was not properly discharged, and none is made before us. At the hearing, Hood was asked whether he was then desirous of reinstatement. He replied that he would if he thought there was any security but "under the circumstances right now, no." The Board found, on the report of its Trial Examiner, that Hood and Little engaged in concerted activity, and the respondent violated Section 8(a) (1) of the National Labor Relations Act as amended, 29 U.S. C.A. § 151 et seq., by threatening and discharging them and in refusing to reinstate Hood at his request. The Examiner found that Henley was not an "employee" at the time he and Hood attempted to get a strike under way on the afternoon of July 9.

The Board took a different position and found that Henley was then an employee with whom Hood was acting in concert. The Board's order directed the Respondent to cease and desist from threatening to discharge or discharging employees or otherwise interfering with rights of employees under Section 7 of the Act, to offer Little, on request, re-employment, to offer Hood re-employment and to make Little and Hood whole for loss of pay; and to post a notice. We are asked to decree enforcement of the Board's order.

The complaint stated that Respondent discharged and refused to reinstate Hood and Little because of union activity or for engaging in other concerted activities for the purposes of collective bargaining or other mutual aid or protection. The Board's finding was only of a violation of Section 8(a) (1) of the Act, thus removing from the case any question of coercion for union activities or with respect to collective bargaining. The propriety of the discharge of Henley is not questioned. The Examiner found that Henley was not an employee on July 9 and hence Hood's activities in concert with Henley on the afternoon of that day were not within the protection of the Act. The Board held that Henley was an employee within the meaning of the Act and before us urges that the holding is correct. Both the Examiner and the Board reached the conclusion that Hood and Little were acting in concert. The Respondent contends that these determinations of the Board, as well as others, are erroneous. Henley had been discharged, and it is not now asserted that his discharge was by reason of any protected activity.

The status of Henley on July 9 was not within the commonly accepted meaning of the word "employee." We are reminded though that technical concepts of employment are to be rejected in determining whether at a specified time a particular person is an employee within the meaning of the Act. National Labor Relations Act, Sec. 2(3). ... We do not have here a case where it is claimed that an applicant for employment is an employee, nor is our case one involving a person wrongfully discharged. The statement that "employee" includes any member of the working class is too broad. No precedent is brought before us which holds that an employee who has been rightfully discharged for a cause wholly unrelated to any activity within the protection of the Act continues to be an employee within the intent and meaning of the Act. We conclude that Henley was not an employee at the time of his unsuccessful efforts to get a picket line set up and hence Hood's participation with him in that endeavor was not a "concerted activity" within Section 7 of the Act. ...

But, it is urged, there was a "concerted activity" between Hood and Little. Hood thought, when he walked off the job, that he was going to strike and when he got to the gate he talked to some of those whose workday had just ended for the purpose of finding out "whether we were supposed to be striking." Hood concluded, apparently, and we think correctly, that there was no strike. He was asked by some of those coming off shift to tell them "what the deal was" and his testimony was, "I couldn't—I would like to have been able to tell them we were striking, but I was unable to because there evidently wasn't much."

Little thought Henley had been given a raw deal. He had not been at the meeting held on the evening of July 8, and had not been at the plant on July 9 until three o'clock or thereabouts that afternoon. He talked to the engineers of the Santa Fe Railroad to see if they would cross a picket line, but Little had no picket line and did no picketing. All he did and all he set out to do was to talk to the engineers. There is no showing of any concert of plan between Hood and Little. There was no indication that Little knew that Hood was at the gate while he, Little, was at the train rack talking to the engineers; nor does it appear that

Hood knew of Little's absence from work while he, Hood, was wondering whether or not there was a strike.

While there should be no interpretation or application of the Act which would deny to employees the rights which the Act provides, or restrict the exercise of those rights, the language used should not be distorted so as to reach unintended results. We are unable to see any activity in which both Hood and Little were engaged, and we are unable to find any concert of activity between them. We reach the conclusion that they were not in any concerted activity.

It may not be amiss to observe that after Little was discharged, he was asked to tear up his check and go back to work. He declined doing so because of his anger at the other employees who "ran off and left" him "done hooked." Little was offered re-employment and rejected it. There is much that can be said in support of the contention that Hood, as a school teacher, was only a temporary employee of the Respondent. Since we have reached the conclusion that he was not discharged for any protected activity, we need not ascertain the nature of his employment.

For the reasons herein stated, the enforcement of the Board's order will be denied.

Enforcement denied.

• • •

CASE QUESTIONS

1. What persons must participate in picketing before it is a protected concerted activity?

2. Does the court's decision have the effect of denying protection which seems to be the spirit of the legislation?

3. Under what facts might the court have found a concerted activity?

PEOPLE ACTING THROUGH COMMUNITY EFFORT
v. DOORLEY
United States Court of Appeals, First Circuit
468 F.2d 1143 (1st Cir. 1972)

• • •

Before COFFIN, Chief Judge, McENTEE, Circuit Judge, and HAMLEY, Senior Circuit Judge.

McENTEE, Circuit Judge.

People Acting Through Community Effort (hereinafter PACE) initiated this action against certain officials of the City of Providence seeking declaratory and injunctive relief, pursuant to 28 U.S.C. §§ 2201 and 2202 (1970), from the enforcement of Section 2 of Providence Ordinance No. 461, chapter 1971-55, as amended. This ordinance, with certain exceptions, prohibits residential picketing. After issuing a preliminary order curtailing the enforcement of the ordinance, the trial court, 338 F.Supp. 574, upheld the constitutionality of the ordinance and denied the requested relief. PACE appeals. For the reasons set forth below, we reverse.

The underlying facts are not in dispute. The challenged ordinance was adopted by the City on October 21, 1971, and became effective immediately. It prohibited all residential picketing with the exception of labor picketing where a residence is the site of, or is in the same building as the site of, a labor dispute. On November 16, 1971, nine PACE members (eight demonstrators and one photographer) engaged in a peaceful demonstration at the residence of one Abraham Konoff, a Providence landlord. The pickets marched in single file, six to eight feet apart, on the public sidewalk in front of his home. Some PACE members carried signs reading, "Mr. Konoff, fix your propery on Dudley Street." Others distributed leaflets to neighboring houses. Approximately forty-five minutes after the demonstration began, Providence Police Sergeant Inglesby arrived on the scene. He informed the group that their conduct violated the anti-residential picketing ordinance and ordered them to disperse. He did not interfere with the leaflet distribution. Fearing arrest and prosecution, the PACE members abandoned the demonstration.

On these facts PACE alleged that the ordinance unconstitutionally abridged the rights of freedom of speech, freedom of assembly, equal protection, and due process guaranteed to its members by the first and fourteenth amendments. Specifically, PACE argued that the ordinance was impermissibly overbroad, unconstitutionally vague, and, in light of the exception for labor picketing, violative of equal protection.

The trial court held that the challenged ordinance was a reasonable regulation justified by the City's interest in protecting the privacy of its citizens. It thus found no violation of the first amendment. The court also held that the ordinance was not unconstitutionally vague since it employed words of common understanding. Further, it found no equal protection violation because it found the exception for labor picketing essential to insure to employees the right to picket at the situs of a labor dispute.

On appeal PACE asserts the arguments raised below. Since we find that this ordinance draws an impermissible distinction between labor picketing and other peaceful picketing, we reverse on equal protection grounds, and do not reach appellants' other contentions.

Ordinance No. 461 regulates expressive conduct which falls within the ambit of protected first amendment activity. ... We thus employ an active standard of review in scrutinizing the classifications which this statute creates. ... The crucial question is whether the classification is "necessary to promote a compelling state interest."

We note initially that the ordinance in question distinguishes between permissible and impermissible conduct on the basis of the content of the demonstrator's message. Information about labor disputes may be disseminated, but other information may not. In Police Department of Chicago v. Mosley, ... and Grayned v. City of Rockford, ... the Supreme Court considered two municipal ordinances which prohibited picketing within 150 feet of any school building during specified periods. Both ordinances excepted peaceful labor picketing when the school was the site of a labor dispute. In striking down these provisions on equal protection grounds, Mr. Justice Marshall analyzed the Chicago ordinance in the following terms:

"The central problem with Chicago's ordinance is that it describes permissible picketing in terms of its subject matter. Peaceful picketing on the subject of a school's labor-management dispute is permitted but all other peaceful picketing is prohibited. The operative distinction is the message on a picket sign. But, above all else, the First Amendement means that government has no power to restrict expression because of its message, its ideas, its subject matter, or its content. (Citations omitted.)....

" . . . Selective exclusions from a public forum may not be based on content alone, and may not be justified by reference to centent alone.". . .

We find this reasoning to be fully applicable to the provision in question in the instant case.

We also find that the ordinance in question draws an unwarranted distinction between labor picketing and other residential demonstrations. While we recognize the interest of the City of Providence in both promoting the privacy of its citizens and permitting laborers to demonstrate at the site of labor disputes, this interest cannot justify the City's preferred treatment of labor picketing. We again find the reasoning of *Mosley* to be persuasive.

"Chicago itself has determined that peaceful labor picketing during school hours is not an undue interference with school. Therefore, under the Equal Protection Clause, Chicago may not maintain that other picketing disrupts the school unless that picketing is clearly more disruptive than the picketing Chicago already permits. (Citations omitted.) If peaceful labor picketing is permitted, there is no justification for prohibiting all nonlabor picketing, both peaceful and nonpeaceful. 'Peaceful' nonlabor picketing, however the term 'peaceful' is defined, is obviously no more disruptive than 'peaceful' labor picketing. But Chicago's ordinance permits the latter and prohibits the former. Such unequal treatment is exactly what was condemned in Niemotko v. Maryland, 340 U.S. 268, at 272-273, . . . (1951). . . .

The Equal Protection Clause requires that statutes affecting First Amendment interests be narrowly tailored to their legitimate objectives. (Citations omitted.) Chicago may not vindicate its interest in preventing disruption by the wholesale exclusion of picketing on all but one preferred subject. Given what Chicago tolerates from labor picketing, the excesses of some nonlabor picketing may not be controlled by a broad ordinance prohibiting both peaceful and violent picketing." *Id.* at 100-102. . . .

In the instant case the ordinance authorizes lawful (and presumably peaceful) labor picketing at residential sites. Having chosen to open the residential forum to this extent, Providence may not, in a manner consistent with the command of the Equal Protection Clause, prohibit all other forms of residential picketing. Therefore, under the Equal Protection Clause, the ordinance may not stand.

Reversed.

•   •   •

CASE QUESTIONS

1. Under what conditions may a state regulate picketing?

2. Can a state qualify who has the right to picket?

3. Why was this case based upon a suit for a declaratory judgment?

BARGAINING 6

Although the National Labor Relations Act established the requirement that there is the duty for employers under Section 8(a) (5) and unions under Section 8(a) (3) to bargain in "good faith," the dimensions of this requirement are not specified; and a multitude of decisions and commentaries have not finalized the issue. In its 1947 decision in *Times Publishing Company,* the NLRB spoke of the measure of good faith as a changing one, "dependent in part upon how a reasonable man might be expected to react to the bargaining attitude displayed by those across the table."

GOOD-FAITH BARGAINING

The goal of the Taft-Hartley Amendments was to define the two-party good-faith bargaining duty. The proposed House bill did include a detailed objective measure for determining what constituted good faith in collective bargaining. However, the Senate version which did not detail a purely objective test was the primary basis for the final legislative form. The Senate bill used the subjective requirement of "concession" as a measure of whether the bargaining was in good or bad faith. It is noteworthy that the requirement in the amendments that the parties "confer in good faith" mirrored the language of the Supreme Court in its 1937 decision in *NLRB* v. *Jones & Laughlin Steel Corp.*

The Taft-Hartley Act mandates collective bargaining in the area of "rates of pay, wages, hours and other terms and conditions of employment." This terminology also identifies those areas in which the employer is barred from unilateral action, as well as those where an employee cannot make an individual agreement with his employer without a waiver by his union. "Wages, hours" offers minimal confusion when considering what conditions must be bargained. On the other hand, the phrase "other terms and conditions of employment" has been the subject of considerable litigation before the NLRB and the courts. In addition to the above issues, the bargaining parties must be aware of permissive and illegal subjects of negotiation under the Act and its interpretations.

INTRODUCTION TO THE CASES

The cases in this chapter cover the statutory authority for collective bargaining, the rights and duties of the parties, and those conditions subject to negotiation. The *Philamon Case* addresses a situation in which the employer refused to bargain. In *International Ladies' Garment Workers' Union* the Supreme Court examined the issue of employer recognition of a minority union.

The court in *Firch Baking Co.* was faced with a union's charges that the employer unilaterally changed wages and other conditions of employment during the pendency of collective bargaining negotiations. The *Connecticut Light & Power Co. Case* was concerned with the selection of the group insurance carrier as a condition of collective bargaining. Finally, in *United States Pipe & Foundry Co.,* the question presented was whether unions could insist upon common expiration date contracts.

NLRB v. PHILAMON LABORATORIES, INC.
United States Court of Appeals, Second Circuit
298 F.2d 176 (2d Cir. 1962)

• • •

MARSHALL, Circuit Judge.

The National Labor Relations Board found respondent violated § 8(a) (1), (2) and (5) of the National Labor Relations Act, as amended, and now petitions for enforcement of its order pursuant to § 10(e). Having reviewed the record, including that portion which "fairly detracts" from the findings of the Board, we hold the findings are supported by substantial evidence and conclusive upon us. § 10(e); Universal Camera Corp. NLRB, 340 U.S. 474, 488 . . . (1951). Because the remedy sought is appropriate, we grant the petition.

Respondent maintains a plant in Westbury, New York, and is engaged in the manufacture, sale, and distribution of electronic products. The parties have stipulated as to the appropriate bargaining unit. As a result of dissatisfaction arising primarily from Respondent's indifference to employee grievances, the operation of the existing profit-sharing plan, wages, and the lack of sick-leave provisions, some sixteen employees signed applications and bargaining authorizations for Local 868, International Brotherhood of Teamsters by August 5, 1959. There were then twenty-nine employees in the unit. On Thursday, August 6, respondent received a telegram from the union claiming to represent "the majority of your employees" and requesting an early appointment for purposes of negotiating a collective agreement. Respondent made no reply. On August 7, Bruckner, Local 868's business representative, telephone Respondent and asked to speak to its president, Grib. After being informed Grib could not be disturbed at that time, Bruckner left his name and requested that Grib call back. Grib failed to do so. On Monday, August 10, Bruckner and another representative of Local 868 went to the plant and asked to see Grib. They were informed that Grib had gone on vacation. Shinerer, the plant manager, told them Grib was expected back on Thursday or Friday. Shinerer said he would be in touch with Grib during the week and if they would call him, Shinerer, on Wednesday, the 12th, an appointment would be arranged for later in the week.

The same day, August 10, the union received two more authorizations, making a total of eighteen, and filed an election petition with the Board. Respondent received a letter from the Board's Regional Director concerning this before 3:00 p.m., on Thursday, August 13. On Wednesday, the 12th, Bruckner called Shinerer at the plant and was told he was gone for the day but would be in the next morning. Bruckner called the next morning, Thursday, and was told Shinerer was not in but was expected about 10:00 a.m. Bruckner asked that Shinerer return the call. Not having received a return call, Bruckner called the plant again at 4:00 p.m. He was told Shinerer was in conference and could not be disturbed, but would call Bruckner back. He did not.

Bruckner and the other representative went to the plant again the next morning, August 14, at 9:30 a.m. They asked to see Grib and, after being informed he was not in, talked to Shinerer. The latter told them to call back at noon. When asked what time he went to lunch, Shinerer replied, "I never go out." Bruckner expressed a desire for a negotiated recognition without an election and offered to show the authorization cards to an impartial person such as the neighborhood rabbi, priest, or minister. Shinerer stated the decision was for Grib to make. Between 1 and 1:30, Bruckner called the plant and was told everyone was in conference but that he should call back in an hour. Between 2:15 and 2:20 p.m., he called back, asking for Shinerer or Grib and was told they were out to lunch. Having been assured by the operator that they were receiving his messages, Bruckner asked that they call him back. They never did.

Although Grib had been indifferent to the employees' grievances for many months, he underwent a marked change of attitude upon his return to the plant on August 13. Anne Dee, a vigorously anti-union employee, requested that he call a meeting of all employees to discuss the union situation. Although Grib was wholly inaccessible to the union and doggedly avoided any contact with it, he immediately adopted Dee's suggestion. The meeting, which lasted an hour, was held that day on company time. Grib told the employees of the Teamsters' claims and of the election petition. He then asked for comments, and several employees spoke. As for the wage issue, Grib stated there had been a raise "in the fire" for a few months which would be granted whether or not there was a union. He made no comment upon the profit-sharing plan, but said he was against sick leave. He further stated that his lieutenants had let him down in not letting grievances get through to him.

The next day, Friday, August 14, a committee of employees, apparently led by Anne Dee and purporting to speak for those not present, asked to see Grib. They were admitted to his office within ten minutes. Grib repeated his earlier statement as to a pay raise and assured them they were going to get it. He also stated he was willing to do away with the profit-sharing plan and increase regular wages by a corresponding amount. The committee suggested a particular sick-leave plan, and Grib indicated he would look favorably upon it although he desired time to think it over. He also told the employees they "would get a better deal if [they] . . . passed the union by." At one or both of these meetings, Grib suggested the employees form their own committee to present such issues and indicated his willingness to deal with such a group. Immediately after this conference, the employees held a meeting of their own, and one Cotrufo related what had occurred in Grib's office and suggested the formation of a committee to negotiate with Grib. Ultimately this occurred, but the committee has since been inactive. At all times Grib assured the employees they could have the Teamsters if they so desired. After work that day two employees, representing the rest, went to Bruckner and asked the union to hold off for sixty days to see if Grib lived up to his promises.

On Monday, August 17, Shinerer polled the employees as to whether they wished to abolish the profit-sharing plan. A majority said they did. Beginning with the wages of that week, each employee received an increase of ten cents an hour as was told the additional amount represented the conversion of the profit-sharing plan to cash payments. Grib also questioned employee Trockel on the 17th. After describing what had occurred on Friday when Trockel was absent, Grib asked him what he thought about it. Trockel indicated he would go along with the majority, and Grib said he and another employee who had been union adherents did not have to worry about a "witch-hunt." On September 25, respondent instituted a sick-leave plan in accordance with the employees' proposal. On November 1, the general wage increase promised was instituted.

The union's charge was filed on August 21, and the regional director approved the withdrawal of the election petition on August 24. On the basis of the findings above, the Board concluded Respondent had violated §§ 8(a) (1), (2) and (5) of the Act. The order directs Respondent to recognize and bargain in good faith with Local 868, and to cease and desist from engaging in certain other unlawful conduct.

The § 8(a) (5) Violation

The act imposes a duty to bargain in good faith upon request whenever a labor organization has been designated by a majority of employees in an appropriate bargaining unit. The employer must recognize and bargain with such an organization whether or not it has been certified by the Labor Board. ... To be sure, an employer laboring under a good faith doubt as to a union's majority status need not extend recognition. Nevertheless, in the absence of such a doubt, the employer has no vested right to an election. ...

Respondent contends the union in fact did not have a majority because three designation cards were either invalid or not proven genuine. These contentions are baseless. Employee LaDisa testified he was told he would have no friends in the shop if he told his aunt, Anne Dee, that he had signed a card. This is hardly sufficient to indicate his bargaining authorization was coerced. Employee Manno was told on August 4 that a majority of the employees "wanted" a union, even though a majority had not signed designation cards by that date. Manno's testimony indicates he agreed with that estimate of the situation, and there is no evidence to show such was not the case. No representation was made that a majority had actually signed up. These circumstances distinguish the present case from NLRB v. H. Rohtstein & Co., 266 F.2d 407 (1 Cir., 1959) where a representation that a majority had signed up was shown to be false. The third card, allegedly signed by employee King, was admitted into evidence without testimony as to its authenticity. The trial examiner found, however, the signature matched a concededly genuine signature of King. In the absence of any showing to the contrary, this is sufficient to support a finding of authenticity. ...

Respondent asserts the union's request for bargaining was defective because it failed to specify a particular bargaining unit but referred only generally to "your employees." Respondent knew, however, of the unit involved by means of the Regional Director's letter which was received before the August 13 meeting. Moreover, Respondent's conduct was hardly prompted by uncertainty over the bargaining unit. It never sought to clarify this matter, or any other, with the union, and the nature and size of Respondent's operations are not such as to create complicated unit problems. In view of Grib's conduct in negotiating directly with the employees involved, the fairer inference would seem to be that he knew exactly what group the union was talking about.

Finally, Respondent contends it had a good faith doubt as to the union's majority status. The record shows, however, that Respondent in fact deliberately shut its eyes to the facts of its industrial life and assiduously avoided giving the union any opportunity to substantiate its claims. Such conduct is not indicative of good faith. Respondent in fact withheld recognition merely to gain time to dissipate the very majority which it now contends was in doubt. ... Nor is Respondent's alleged lack of an anti-union bias a defense. A refusal to bargain with a union designated by a majority and promises of benefit employed as inducements to leave the union violate the Act. ... The fact that such conduct is accompanied by assurances of free choice does not remove it from the ambit of the statute when the record as a whole demonstrates the unlawful purpose. ... The record before us convincingly demonstrates that purpose.

The 8(a) (1) Violation

The Board found that Grib's promises to the employees on August 13 and 14 (and to employee Trockel on August 17), and their subsequent fulfillment, were violations of § 8(a) (1). Promises of benefit designed to induce disaffection from a union violate that section. ... The context surrounding Grib's conduct indicates such a purpose. The employees were all aware of the union's demand for recognition, and Grib's sudden concern for their grievances, in contrast to his previous indifference, had an unmistakalbe meaning for them. While he assiduously avoided all contact with union representatives, he was more than willing to bargain directly with the employees. Indeed, he was quite anxious to discover why the employees wanted a union, or, to put it another way, how much it would cost him to get rid of the union. Having learned the price, he then met it. He assured the employees that better procedures for processing grievances would be worked out, that he would deal with an employee committee, that a pay raise which had been "in the fire" but was theretofore unannounced would be granted, that desired changes in the profit-sharing plan would be made, and that the sick-leave plan proposed by the employees would be given favorable consideration. Much of this was repeated in the individual interrogation of Trockel on Monday. Morcover, while he was making the promises in question, Grib told the employees they would get a "better deal" by forgetting the union. The clear implication of the timing and context of these events was that the employees would receive the promised benefits if they abandoned the union. The net result of Grib's conduct was a request to the union by the employees that it hold off for sixty days so they might see whether Grib lived up to his promises. The Board's conclusion that Grib intended and desired such a result is supported by substantial evidence and binding upon us.

The § 8(a) (2) Violation

On August 14, respondent openly negotiated with a hastily assembled committee of employees. This was done even though the union had bargaining authorizations from a majority of employees and had requested recognition. Grib further suggested to the employees the formation of a standing "grievance committee" to negotiate with him at future times over matters similar to those which had caused the dissatisfaction. The committee was designed to be a labor organization within the meaning of § 2(5) of the Act. ... Ultimately, it was formed but was inactive. There can be no question but that Respondent gave support and assistance to the August 14 committee. Grib negotiated with it even though he was bound by law to recognize Local 868. He also suggested the formation of the standing committee and assured the employees of his willingness to deal with it. When members were finally chosen, two supervisory employees were present at the selection. These activities constitute unlawful support within § 8(a)(2). . . .

The Remedy

The Board has ordered, *inter alia,* that respondent recognize and bargain in good faith with Local 868. Respondent asserts, however, that only six of the original eighteen union adherents remain in the bargaining unit. On this basis, it is argued, the appropriate remedy is not recognition but an election. Respondent relies in particular upon our decisions. ...

In *Adhesive Products* we directed an election because the employees' initial choice was made in an atmosphere which did not allow "opportunity of giving the matter due and proper reflection and consideration." In *Marcus Trucking,* the employer had recognized a majority union in violation of its obligations under the Board's contract bar rules. No element indicating employer interference with employee free choice was present, however, for the contract bar rules themselves are intended to allow considerations relating to stability to govern over employee choice in certain circumstances. In *Superior,* an election was directed because of an "inordinate delay" in the Board's proceedings and because the union had abandoned the employees for six months after certification and had not represented them for nearly four years.

The present case, however, does not involve such special considerations. The sole circumstance advanced by Respondent to support its contention is that in the process of normal personnel turnover many original union adherents have left its employ. While Respondent's argument is appealing in some aspects, we do not believe this is a case in which the Board has applied "a remedy it has worked out on the basis of its experience, without regard to circumstances which may make its application to a particular situation oppressive and therefore not calculated to effectuate a policy of the Act." . . .

In Franks Bros. Co. v. NLRB, 321 U.S. 702, ... (1944), the Supreme Court rejected the argument pressed here with the statement. "That the Board was within its statutory authority in adopting the remedy which it has adopted . . . seems too plain for anything but statement. . . . ," 321 U.S. at 705. Over seventeen years have passed since that decision, and the National Labor Relations Act has twice undergone searching Congressional revision in light of past experience. That decision, however, has not been upset, and the presumption of Congressional approval is strong indeed. . . . We followed Frank Bros. in *NLRB* v. *Stow Manufacturing Co.,* and enforced a Board order compelling recognition without an intervening election. The rationale was premised on the Board's expert conclusion that the employer's illegal conduct had turned the employees against the union even though there was not, in the language of Judge Learned Hand, "the proverbial scintilla to justify the . . . conclusion." We find the present case even stronger, however, for after the meetings on August 13 and 14, the employees asked the union to hold off for sixty days to see if Grib lived up to his promises. It is clear, therefore, the unfair labor practices here did in fact cause the union's loss of a majority.

Even without such established precedents, we would be hard pressed to reject this exercise of the Board's remedial powers. The union lost majority status because of respondent's violations of the law. The only effective remedy left in the present case is the requiring of recognition. And, indeed, as far as future cases are concerned, a denial of power to the Board here might well encourage employers to refuse to bargain, commit the ancillary violations, fight the unfair labor practice charges to the courts, and then rely upon the inevitable intervening turnover in personnel to ward off the only effective remedy remaining. In any case, we cannot say such a rationale may not be adopted and applied by the specialized agency entrusted by Congress with the principal enforcement duties under the Act.

Enforcement granted.

• • •

CASE QUESTIONS

1. Why was the employer required to recognize and bargain with the union?

2. Why did the court refuse to accept the employer's position that it had a good-faith doubt as to the union's majority status?

3. What specific acts by the employer constituted violations of the National Labor Relations Act?

INTERNATIONAL LADIES' GARMENT WORKERS' UNION, AFL—CIO v. NLRB
United States Supreme Court
366 U.S. 731 (1961)

• • •

Mr. Justice CLARK delivered the opinion of the Court.

We are asked to decide in this case whether it was an unfair labor practice for both an employer and a union to enter into an agreement under which the employer recognized the union as exclusive bargaining representative of certain of his employees, although in fact only a minority of those employees had authorized the union to represent their interests. The Board found that by extending such recognition, even though done in the good-faith belief that the union had the consent of a majority or employees in the appropriate bargaining unit, the employer interfered with the organizational rights of his employees in violation of § 8(a) (1) of the National Labor Relations Act and that such recognition also constituted unlawful support to a labor organization in violation of § 8(a) (2). In addition, the Board found that the union violated § 8(b) (1) (A) by its acceptance of exclusive bargaining authority at a time when in fact it did not have the support of a majority of the employees, and this in spite of its bona fide belief that it did. Accordingly, the Board ordered the unfair labor practices discontinued and directed the holding of a representation election. The Court of Appeals, by a divided vote, granted enforcement. ... We granted certiorari. ... We agree with the Board and the Court of Appeals that such extension and acceptance of recognition constitute unfair labor practices, and that the remedy provided was appropriate.

In October, 1956, the petitioner union initiated an organizational campaign at Bernhard-Altmann Texas Corporation's knitwear manufacturing plant in San Antonio, Texas. No other labor organization was similarly engaged at that time. During the course of that campaign, on July 29, 1957, certain of the company's Topping Department employees went on strike in protest against a wage reduction. That dispute was in no way related to the union campaign, however, and the organizational efforts were continued during the strike. Some of the striking employees had signed authorization cards solicited by the union during its drive, and, while the strike was in progress, the union entered upon a course of negotiations with the employer. As a result of those negotiations, held in New York City where the home offices of both were located, on August 30, 1957, the employer and union signed a "memorandum of understanding." In that memorandum the company recognized the union as exclusive bargaining representative of "all production and shipping employees." The union representative asserted that the union's comparison of the employee authorization cards in its possession with the number of eligible employees representatives of the company furnished it indicated that the union had in fact secured such cards from a majority of employees in the unit. Neither employer nor union made any effort at that time to check the cards in the union's possession against the employee roll, or otherwise, to ascertain with any degree of certainty that the union's assertion, later found by the Board to be erroneous, was founded on fact rather than upon good-faith assumption. The agreement, containing no union security provisions, called for the ending of the strike and for certain improved wages and conditions of employment. It also provided that a "formal agreement containing these terms" would "be promptly drafted . . . and signed by both parties within the next two weeks."

Thereafter, on October 10, 1957, a formal collective bargaining agreement, embodying the terms of the August 30 memorandum, was signed by the parties. The bargaining unit description set out in the formal contract, although more specific, conformed to that contained in the prior memorandum. It is not disputed that as of execution of the formal contract the union in fact represented a clear majority of employees in the appropriate unit. In upholding the complaints filed against the employer and union by the General Counsel, the Board decided that the employer's good-faith belief that the union in fact represented a majority of employees in the unit on the critical date of the memorandum of understanding was not a defense, "particularly where, as here, the Company made no effort to check the authorization cards against its payroll reocrds." ... Noting that the union was "actively seeking recognition at the time such recognition was granted," and that "the Union was [not] the passive recipient of an unsolicited gift bestowed by the Company," the Board found that the union's execution of the August 30 agreement was a "direct deprivation" of the nonconsenting majority employees' organizational and bargaining rights. ... Accordingly, the Board ordered the employer to withhold all recognition from the union and to cease giving effect to agreements entered into with the union; the union was ordered to cease acting as bargaining representative of any of the employees until such time as a Board-conducted election demonstrated its majority status, and to refrain from seeking to enforce the agreements previously entered.

The Court of Appeals found it difficult to "conceive of a clearer restraint on the employees' right of self-organization than for their employer to enter into a collective-bargaining agreement with a minority of the employees." ... The court distinguished our decision in National Labor Relations Board v. Drivers, Chauffeurs, Helpers, Local Union No. 639, 362 U.S. 274, on the ground that there was involved here neither recognitional nor organizational picketing. The court held that the bona fides of the parties was irrelevant except to the extent that it "was arrived at through an adequate effort to determine the true facts of the situation."

At the outset, we reject as without relevance to our decision the fact that, as of the execution date of the formal agreement on October 10, petitioner represented a majority of the employees. As the Court of Appeals indicated, the recognition of the minority union on August 30, 1957, was *"a fait accompli* depriving the majority of the employees of their guaranteed right to choose their own representative." ... It is, therefore, of no consequence that petitioner may have acquired by October 10 the necessary majority if, during the interim, it was acting unlawfully. Indeed, such acquisition of majority status itself might indicate that the recognition secured by the August 30 agreement afforded petitioner a deceptive cloak of authority with which to persuasively elicit additional employee support.

Nor does this case directly involve a strike. The strike which occurred was in protest against a wage reduction and had nothing to do with petitioner's quest for recognition. Likewise, no question of picketing is presented. Lastly, the violation which the Board found was the grant by the employer of exclusive representation status to a minority union, as distinguished from an employer's bargaining with a minority union for its members only. Therefore, the exclusive representation provision is the vice in the agreement, and discussion of "collective bargaining," as distinguished from "exclusive recognition," is pointless. Moreover, the insistence that we hold the agreement valid and enforceable as to those employees who consented to it must be rejected. On the facts shown, the agreement must fail in its entirety. It was obtained under the erroneous claim of majority representation. Perhaps the employer would not have entered into it if he had known the facts. Quite apart from other conceivable situations, the unlawful genesis of this agreement precludes its partial validity.

In their selection of a bargaining representative, § 9(a) of the Wagner Act guarantees employees freedom of choice and majority rule. J. I. Case Co. v. National Labor Relations Board, 321 U.S. 332, 339. . . . In short, as we said in Brooks v. National Labor Relations Board, 348 U.S. 96, 103, . . . the Act placed "a nonconsenting minority under the bargaining responsibility of an agency selected by a majority of the workers." Here, however, the reverse has been shown to be the case. Bernhard-Altmann granted exclusive bargaining status to an agency selected by a minority of its employees, thereby impressing that agent upon the nonconsenting majority. There could be no clearer abridgment of § 7 of the Act, assuring employees the right "to bargain collectively through representatives of their own choosing" or "to refrain from" such activity. It follows, without need of further demonstration, that the employer activity found present here violated § 8(a) (1) of the Act which prohibits employer interference with, and restraint of, employee exercise of § 7 rights. Section 8(a) (2) of the Act makes it an unfair labor practice for an employer to "contribute . . . support" to a labor organization. The law has long been settled that a grant of exclusive recognition to a minority union constitutes unlawful support in violation of that section, because the union so favored is given "a marked advantage over any other in securing the adherence of employees," National Labor Relations Board v. Pennsylvania Greyhound Lines, 303 U.S. 261, 267. . . . In the Taft-Hartley Law, Congress added § 8(b) (1) (A) to the Wagner Act, prohibiting, as the Court of Appeals held, "unions from invading the rights of employees under § 7 in a fashion comparable to the activities of employers prohibited under § 8(a) (1)." . . . It was the intent of Congress to impose upon unions the same restrictions which the Wagner Act imposed on employers with respect to violations of employee rights.

The petitioner, while taking no issue with the fact of its minority status on the critical date, maintains that both Bernhard-Altmann's and its own good-faith beliefs in petitioner's majority status are a complete defense. To countenance such an excuse would place in permissibly careless employer and union hands the power to completely frustrate employee realization of the premise of the Act—that its prohibitions will go far to assure freedom of choice and majority rule in employee selection of representatives. We find nothing in the statutory language prescribing *scienter* as an element of the unfair labor practices are involved. The act made unlawful by § 8(a) (2) is employer support of a minority union. Here that support is an accomplished fact. More need not be shown, for, even if mistakenly, the employees' rights have been invaded. It follows that prohibited conduct cannot be excused by a showing of good faith.

This conclusion, while giving the employee only the protection assured him by the Act, places no particular hardship on the employer or the union. It merely requires that recognition be withheld until the Board-conducted election results in majority selection of a representative. The Board's order here, as we might infer from the employer's failure to resist its enforcement, would apparently result in similarly slight hardship upon it. We do not share petitioner's apprehension that holding such conduct unlawful will somehow induce a breakdown, or seriously impede the progress of collective bargaining. If an employer takes reasonable steps to verify union claims, themselves advanced only after careful estimate—precisely what Bernhard-Altmann and petitioner failed to do here—he can readily ascertain their validity and obviate a Board election. We fail to see any onerous burden involved in requiring responsible negotiators to be careful, by cross-checking, for example, well-analyzed employer records with union listings or authorization cards. Individual and collective employee rights may not be tranpled upon merely because it is inconvenient to avoid doing so. Moreover, no penalty is attached to the violation. Assuming that an employer in good faith accepts or rejects a union claim of majority status, the validity of his decision may be tested in an unfair labor practice proceeding. If he is found to have erred in extending or withholding recognition, he is subject only to a remedial order requiring him to conform his conduct to the norms set out in the Act, as was the case here. No further penalty results. We believe the Board's remedial order is the proper one in such cases. . . .

Affirmed.

Mr. Justice DOUGLAS, with whom Mr. Justice BLACK concurs, dissenting in part.

I agree that, under the statutory scheme, a minority union does not have the standing to bargain for all employees. That principle of representative government extends only to the majority. But where there is no majority union, I see no reason why the minority union should be disabled from bargaining for the minority of the members who have joined it. Yet the order of the Board, now approved, enjoins petitioner union from acting as the exclusive bargaining representative "of any of the employees," and it enjoins the employer from recognizing the union as the representative of "any of its employees."

We have indicated over and again that, absent an exclusive agency for bargaining created by a majority of workers, a minority union has standing to bargain for its members. In Virginian R. Co. v. System Federation No. 40, 300 U.S. 515, 549, note 6, . . . , the Court quoted with approval a concession that "If the majority of a craft or class has not selected a representative, the carrier is free to make with anyone it pleases and for any group it pleases contracts establishing rates of pay, rules, or working conditions."

That case was under the Railway Labor Act. But it has been followed under the National Labor Relations Act. In Consolidated Edison Co. of New York v. National Labor Relations Board, 305 U.S. 197, . . . a union, the Brotherhood of Electrical Workers, was allowed to act as a bargaining representative for the employees who were its members, even though they were a minority. The Court said, ". . . in the absence of such an exclusive agency the employees represented by the Brotherhood, even if they were a minority, clearly had the right to make their own choice." . . . Maintenance of the status of a minority union, until an election was held, might well serve the purpose of protecting commerce "from interruptions and obstructions caused by industrial strife." . . . A decree requiring the employer to cease recognizing the Brotherhood as the exclusive representative of its members was modified:

> "The contracts do not claim for the Brotherhood exclusive representation of the companies' employees but only representation of those who are its members, and the continued operation of the contracts is necessarily subject to the provision of the law by which representatives of the employees for the purpose of collective bargaining can be ascertained in case any question of 'representation' should arise. . . . We construe [the order] as having no more effect than to provide that there shall be no interference with an exclusive bargaining agency if one other than the [union] should be established in accordance with . . . the Act."

It was in that tradition that we recently sustained the right of a minority union to picket peacefully to compel recognition. . . . There a minority union sought to compel exclusive representation rights. To be sure, this Court recognized in that case that "tension exists between . . . [the] right to form, join or assist labor organizations and [the] right to refrain from doing so." . . . But when a minority union seeks only to represent its own, what provision of the Act deprives it of its right to represent them, where a majority have not selected another union to represent them?

Judge Learned Hand in Douds v. Local 1250, . . . stated that "the right to bargain collectively and the right to strike and induce others to do so, are derived from the common-law; it is only insofar as something in the Act forbids their exercise that their exercise becomes unlawful." In that case a minority union was recognized as having standing in a grievance proceeding outside the collective bargaining agreement, even where a majority had chosen another union. . . .

Honoring a minority union—where no majority union exists or even where the activities of the minority union do not collide with a bargaining agreement—is being respectful of history. Long before the Wagner Act, employers and employees had the right to discuss their problems. In the early days the unions were representatives of a minority of workers. The aim—at least the hope—of the legislation was that majority unions would emerge and provide stabilizing influences. Yet I have found nothing in the history of the successive measures, starting with the Wagner Act, that indicates any purpose on the part of Congress to deny a minority union the right to bargain for its members when a majority have not in fact chosen a bargaining representative.

I think the Court is correct insofar as it sets aside the exclusive recognition clause in the contract. I think it is incorrect in setting aside the entire contract. *First,* that agreement secured valuable benefits for the union's members regarding wages and hours, work standards and distribution, discharge and discipline, holidays, vacations, health and welfare fund, and other matters. Since there was no duly selected representative for all the employees authorized in accordance with the Act, it certainly was the right of the employee union members to designate the union or any other appropriate person to make this contract they desired. To hold the contract void as to the union's voluntary members seems to me to go beyond the competency of the Board under the Act and to be unsupported by any principle of contract law. Certainly there is no principle of justice or fairness with which I am familiar that requires these employees to be stripped of the benefits they acquired by the good-faith bargaining of their designated agent. Such a deprivation gives no protection to the majority who were not members of the union and arbitrarily takes from the union members their contract rights.

Second, the result of today's decision is to enjoin the employer from dealing with the union as the representative of its own members in any manner, whether in relation to grievances or otherwise, until it is certified as a majority union. A case for complete disestablishment of the union cannot be sustained under our decisions. While the power of the Board is broad, it is "not limitless." ... Thus a distinction has been taken between remedies in situations where a union has been dominated by the employer and where unions have been assisted but not dominated. ...

The present case is unique. The findings are that both the employer and the union were in "good faith" in believing that the union represented a majority of the workers. Good-faith violations of the Act are nonetheless violations; and the present violation warrants disestablishment of the union as a majority representative. But this good-faith mistake hardly warrants full and complete disestablishment, heretofore reserved for flagrant violations of the Act. Its application here smacks more of a penalty than of a remedial measure.

I think this union is entitled to speak for its members until another union is certified as occupying the bargaining field. That is its common-law right in no way diluted or impaired by the Act.

• • •

CASE QUESTIONS

1. Why should an employer be guilty of an unfair labor practice where it in good faith recognizes a minority union?

2. Does the Supreme Court place a burden upon an employer to verify a union's claim of majority status?

3. Why is a grant of exclusive recognition to a minority union an unlawful support to a labor organization?

FIRCH BAKING COMPANY v. NLRB
United States Court of Appeals, Second Circuit
479 F.2d 732 (2d Cir. 1973)

• • •

TIMBERS, Circuit Judge:

The essential issue presented by the Company's petition to review, and the cross-petition by the National Labor Relations Board to enforce, an order of the Board, 199 NLRB No. 62 (1972), is whether there was substantial evidence to support the Board's conclusion that the Company violated Section 8(a) (5) and (1) of the National Labor Relations Act, 29 U.S.C. § 158(a) (5) and (1) (1970), by unilaterally instituting changes in wages and other conditions of employment without adequate bargaining with the Union. We hold that there was substantial evidence to support the Board's conclusion. We deny the Company's petition to review and we enforce the Board's order.

I.

A three-year collective bargaining agreement between Firch Baking Company of Jamestown, Inc. (the Company) and Local 15520, International Union of District 50, Allied and Technical Workers (the Union) by its terms would have been automatically renewed on January 1, 1972 unless timely notice of termination or desire to modify was given by either party. Such notice was given by the Union in October, 1971. Negotiations for a new contract followed. Ten collective bargaining sessions were held, six before and four after the contract expired on January 1, 1972.

In view of the essential issue presented by the petitions before us, we focus upon the critical events of the five day period—December 27—31—immediately preceding the expiration of the contract. Prior to December 27, negotiations had bogged down, chiefly over the Union's proposal that at least some of the negotiations take place "on-the-clock" (during working hours), a proposal which the Company flatly rejected.

On December 27, the Company delivered to the employee members of the Union bargaining committee a letter enclosing a summary of the Company's "fair, firm offer," including increases in wages, changed pension benefits, changed health coverage, and improved major medical benefits. This "offer" was in outline form, not in the form of proposed contractual provisions. On the same day, all bargaining unit employees received a copy of the Company's offer. The Union's chief negotiator received a copy of the offer two days later, on December 29, whereupon he immediately wired the Company that the Union was "willing and ready to meet immediately on mutually agreed time."

On December 30, the Company distributed to all bargaining unit employees another letter advising that if the Union did not accept the Company's "fair, firm offer" by the time the contract expired, the Company would have no alternative but to make the offer directly to the employees in the hope they would accept it and continue on the job. On the same day, at a bargaining session arranged by a federal mediator, the

Company's offer was discussed item by item. With the exception of agreement on two non-economic proposals, the Company's offer was rejected by the Union in its entirety. A further bargaining session was scheduled for the following day, December 31, at 6 p.m.

At the New Year's Eve bargaining session, the Company for the first time presented to the Union a document elaborating on and setting forth in contract form the Company's "fair, firm offer." Before the meeting was concluded at 11:45 p.m., the Company's offer had been fully discussed, and agreement had been reached on a number of economic as well as non-economic provisions. Since agreement had not been reached on the basic contract itself, however, the Union's chief negotiator announced that he intended to have a federal mediator present at the next bargaining session.

Upon expiration of the existing contract at midnight on January 1, 1972, the Company immediately put into effect all provisions of its "fair, firm offer," including wage increases and other economic benefits. On January 4, the Company announced to its employees that "our unilateral offer to all of you has been in effect since 12:01 a.m. Sunday, January 2. This pay increase will be in the pay check you will receive next week."

During January and after expiration of the contract, four additional bargaining sessions were held, with the employees remaining on the job. At the final session on January 26, the Union agreed to submit the Company's entire contract package, as modified during negotiations, to the employees to determine whether it was acceptable. The employees on February 1 voted to accept the Company's offer as submitted. On February 16, a new contract was signed covering the period through December 31, 1974.

Going back for a moment, on December 29, after the Union received a copy of the Company's first letter to its employees enclosing a copy of the Company's "fair, firm offer" and with the Union and Company still unable to agree upon the hours that negotiations should take place, the Union filed unfair labor practice charges against the Company, alleging that the Company had violated Section 8(a) (5) and (1) of the Act by refusing to meet at reasonable times for bargaining purposes and by attempting to by-pass the Union and deal directly with its employees. A complaint was issued on February 16, 1972, the same day the new contract was signed, limited to the charge based on the Company's conduct in instituting changes in wages and other conditions of employment during the pendency of collective bargaining negotiations. The Union continued to press this charge.

Following a hearing before a trial examiner on March 27 and 28 at Jamestown, New York, the examiner on June 2 filed his decision which in effect upheld the Union's position. His recommended order, adopted by the Board on September 29, required the Company to cease and desist from unilaterally instituting changes in wages and other conditions of employment without adequate bargaining with the Union, and required the Company to take certain affirmative action, including the posting of notices, to remedy the violations.

II.

After nearly four decades of life under the National Labor Relations

Act, few obligations are more firmly established than that of an employer pursuant to Section 8(a) (5) to bargain collectively with a union representing its employees, including its duty not to alter terms and conditions of employment without first giving notice to and conferring in good faith with the union. ... "Unilateral action by an employer without prior discussion with the union does amount to a refusal to negotiate about the affected conditions of employment under negotiation, and must of necessity obstruct bargaining, contrary to the congressional policy." ... And we have held that such unilateral action "at the end of the contract period" operates at a particularly sensitive point of labor-management relations, for "the Union's ability to function as a bargaining representative is seriously impaired. Indeed, such conduct amounts to a declaration on the part of the Company that not only the Union, but the process of collective bargaining itself may be dispensed with." ...

Viewed against these settled principles, the Company's conduct here in unilaterally instituting changes in wages and other conditions of employment during the pendency of collective bargaining negotiations, without affording an opportunity for good faith bargaining and agreement on its package offer, strikes us as a clear refusal to negotiate about affected conditions of employment under negotiation.

From the standpoint of timing alone, the extreme haste with which the Company put into effect its changes in wages and other conditions of employment is thoroughly convincing of bad faith in the negotiations, of disparagement of the union, and of obstruction of the congressionally mandated duty to bargain collectively. The formal contract proposals of the Company's so-called "fair, firm offer" were not presented to the Union until the evening of December 31, a few hours before the existing contract was due to expire and hardly a day before the Company put the proposals into effect. Even the preliminary summary of these proposals had been disclosed to the employee members of the Union bargaining committee and to all bargaining unit employees only four days before the formal contract proposals were submitted; and the Union's chief negotiator learned about them two days later. The Company's unilateral action in putting the proposals into effect came after only two bargaining sessions were held following preliminary announcement of the proposals.

The nature of the Company's proposals was such as to demand adequate time for study and discussion—item by item, not the entire program as a package. They involved wage increases for various categories of employees, entirely new pension benefits, changed health and life insurance plans, and other changes in benefits. The form of retirement plan referred to in the Company's preliminary summary was not furnished to the Union until the December 31 meeting. The Company never provided the Union with a copy of its proposed insurance plan—showing details of its new medical, surgical and term life insurance coverage—before it became effective.

Finally, if anything further were needed to dispel any vestige of good faith bargaining intent on the part of the Company in making its "fair, firm offer," that was surely provided by the manner in which the Company communicated the offer to its employees. All else aside, the Company's letter of December 30 to its employees, advising them "[i]n the event that the union does not accept our fair, firm offer by the time the contract expires, we have no alternative but to make our fair, firm offer to you directly," surely placed the Company in the position, as we observed in another case, of "having created a view of the bargaining process that admitted of no compromise, [and of being] trapped by its own creation," ... "The aim, in a word, was to deal with the Union through the employees, rather than with the employees through the Union." ...

Our careful examination of the record as a whole leaves us with the firm conviction that the Company became so enamored with its "fair, firm offer" technique that it ignored its basic duty of allowing adequate time and opportunity for reasonable discussion of the essential details of its offer. The Board, in its decision affirming the trial examiner in the instant case, stated:

> "Quite apart from [the Company's] argument that NLRB v. General Electric Company, 418 F.2d 736 (C.A. 2), sanctions its 'fair, firm offer' bargaining strategy, which argument we do not pass upon here, [the Company's] December 30 letter to the employees makes it clear that the 'fair, firm offer' was not so much an offer as it was a promise to [the Company's] employees that a specified wage increase would be granted. Inasmuch as the employees were promised the wage increase irrespective of its acceptance or rejection by the Union, before the increase had even been presented to the Union, therefore the wage increase was in fact a firm decision which removed the element of bargaining, and a fortiori, no good-faith bargaining impasse had resulted when the [Company] effectuated its 'fair, firm offer.'"

We agree. And despite the elaborate arguments which have been pressed upon us as to whether a company may unilaterally institute changes in wages and other conditions of employment without bargaining to impasse with the union about such changes, in our view this is not an "impasse case" at all. It more aptly might be called a "poisoned fountain case": the fountain was poisoned before it ever began to flow.

Petition to review denied; enforcement granted.

• • •

CASE QUESTIONS

1. Why are unilateral changes by the employer in employment conditions an unfair labor practice?

2. Is an employer prohibited from all communications with his employees during collective bargaining?

3. Why are the union's charges still valid after a contract of essentially the same terms of the employer's unilateral offer had been ratified?

CONNECTICUT LIGHT & POWER COMPANY v. NLRB
United States Court of Appeals, Second Circuit
476 F.2d 1079 (2d Cir. 1973)

• • •

TIMBERS, Circuit Judge:

The Connecticut Light & Power Company (the Company) has petitioned to review and set aside an order of the National Labor Relations Board issued May 8, 1972, 196 NLRB No. 149 (1972), which essentially required that the Company bargain in good faith with the Union as to the selection of an insurance carrier for the Company's employee medical-surgical benefits plan. The Board has cross-petitioned for enforcement of its order. We agree with the Company that the selection of an insurance carrier under the circumstances presented here is not a mandatory subject for bargaining within Section 8(d) of the National Labor Relations Act (the Act), 29 U.S.C. § 158(d) (1970). We therefore grant the petition to review and set aside the Board's order, and we deny the cross-petition to enforce the order.

I.

The Company is a Connecticut corporation. It is a public utility engaged in the production, distribution, and sale of electricity and gas. It is engaged in commerce within the meaning of the Act.

System Council U-24, International Brotherhood of Electrical Workers, AFL–CIO, and its Local Unions 420, 753, 1045, 1175, 1226, 1317 and 1817 (the Union), are labor organizations within the meaning of the Act. Together they serve as the exclusive representative for all the Company's employees within the relevant bargaining unit. For many years, the Company and the Union have had a collective bargaining relationship.

The Company has long provided its employees with a non-contributory, Company-paid, medical-surgical insurance plan. Since 1967 the carrier of this insurance plan, which includes major medical coverage, has been the Aetna Life Insurance Company (Aetna). For several years prior to 1967, the Company had contracted with Blue Cross-Connecticut Medical Service (Blue Cross) for the basic medical-surgical insurance, and with the Hartford Accident and Indemnity Company for major medical insurance.

In 1969, the Union informed the Company of its dissatisfaction with Aetna's administration of the insurance plan. As a result, the Company secured various changes from Aetna. Nevertheless, during the 1971 collective bargaining negotiations, the Union again expressed its dissatisfaction with Aetna and sought to include in those negotiations the reinstatement of Blue Cross as the carrier for the employee insurance plan. The Company did bargain during the 1971 negotiations with respect to coverage, benefits and administration of the plan; but it steadfastly refused to bargain as to the selection of the carrier, maintaining that it had the right unilaterally to choose the carrier.

On May 14, 1971, the Union filed a charge with the Board, alleging a refusal by the Company to bargain, in violation of Section 8(a) (1) and

(5) of the Act. . . . That charge resulted in the issuance of a complaint by the General Counsel on July 19, 1971. A hearing was held before a trial examiner on October 18, 1971. On February 2, 1972, the examiner filed a decision, in which he found that the Company had unlawfully refused to bargain as to the selection of an insurance carrier for the employee medical benefits plan. On May 8, 1972, the Board affirmed the trial examiner's decision and adopted his recommended order. It ordered the Company to cease and desist from refusing to bargain collectively as to the selection of an insurance carrier, to bargain in good faith on that subject upon request of the union, and to take certain other affirmative action to comply with the order.

The sole issue before us on the Company's petition to review and the Board's cross-petition to enforce is whether the Board correctly concluded that the selection of an insurance carrier under the circumstances presented here is a mandatory subject for bargaining within the meaning of Section 8(d) of the Act.

II.

The requirement that an employer bargain collectively with the representatives of its employees, pursuant to Section 8(a) (5) of the Act, is limited by Section 8(d) to an obligation to confer as to "wages, hours, and other terms and conditions of employment . . . ." 29 U.S.C. § 158(d) (1970). It is well established that included within that language are such "non-wage" benefits as the group health insurance here involved. . . . The Company here does not dispute the inclusion of the instant group insurance plan within the term "wages." Indeed, it has at all times freely negotiated with regard to the benefit levels and administration of the plan. Further, as noted above, it successfully obtained various changes from Aetna following notification from the Union of the latter's dissatisfaction with certain aspects of the plan.

In Chemical Workers, Local 1 v. Pittsburgh Plate Glass Co., 404 U.S. 157 (1971), the Court was asked to decide whether retirees' benefits—i.e., benefits for former employees already retired—is a mandatory subject for bargaining under Section 8(d). In holding that, because retirees are not "employees" under Section 2(3) of the Act, . . . the refusal to bargain was proper, the Court observed that it was required also to consider whether such benefits nevertheless were within the ambit of compulsory negotiation topics: "Section 8(d) of the Act, of course, does not immutably fix a list of subjects for mandatory bargaining. . . .But it does establish a limitation against which proposed topics must be measured. In general terms, the limitation includes only issues that settle an aspect of the relationship between the employer and employees." . . . This, as the Court observed, depends on whether the matter *"vitally affects the 'terms and conditions' of [the] employment."* . . . (emphasis added).

A recent Sixth Circuit decision examined the applicability of that standard to the selection of a carrier for an employee medical-surgical insurance plan. In Bastian-Blessing, Division of Golconda Corp. v. NLRB, . . . , the court held that under the specific facts of that case the naming of an insurance carrier for an employee group benefit plan was a mandatory subject for bargaining. We find *Bastian* distinguishable from the instant case in significant respects. There, Aetna had been the carrier of the group plan since World War II. The plan was contributory in nature, the employees paying approximately 40% of the cost. In 1970, the Company unilaterally cancelled the Aetna policy and began a self-insurance plan. The Board found that the change adversely affected the employees in important respects: (1) the new plan "omitted entirely two significant imployee benefits: a conversion privilege without evidence of insurability, and the certainty of coverage of new-born babies under the $20,000 major medical benefit"; (2) it deprived the employees of "enforceability of the prior master contract and of Aetna's administration of that contract"; and (3) a degree of uncertainty was created as to the funding of the new plan which the Board considered to have "an adverse impact on the employees' previously negotiated benefits." ...

The court's conclusion that the company had violated Section 8(a) (5) of the Act clearly was based on the unilateral *changes* in the *terms* of the insurance plan, referred to above. The court noted that it had found no case law which squarely supports "the proposition that the specific insurance carrier for a group health plan is a mandatory subject for bargaining." ... Instead, it chose to confine its ruling to the facts of the case before it, where it was impossible "to find a way to separate the carrier from the benefits." ... And it concluded that:

> "We emphasize that the conclusion reached herein is governed by the facts of this case and is not to be interpreted as a ruling by this Court that the naming of an insurance carrier for an employee group benefit plan, in the absence of other considerations, is a mandatory subject for bargaining." ...

Similarly, the other cases cited to us which required bargaining with regard to the carrier of the employees' insurance plans involved substantive changes in benefits which dictated the results. ... Here, there have been no specific allegations of any changes in coverage, levels or administration of the plan. All the Union has alleged is general "dissatisfaction" with Aetna. Equally important, the Company has responded to specific complaints with good faith negotiation; and, as the Board found, the Company has been able to obtain modifications from Aetna.

Consequently, we are unable to conclude that the Company has violated its obligation to bargain under *Pittsburgh Plate Glass*. The Company at no time has refused to negotiate with the employees as to any subject that "vitally affects the 'terms and conditions' of their employment." ... In Westinghouse Electric Corp. v. NLRB, 387 F.2d 542, 548 (4 Cir. 1967) (en banc), the court observed that:

> "[S]ince pratically every managerial decision has some impact on wages, hours, or other conditions of employment, the determination of which decisions are mandatory bargaining subjects must depend upon whether a given subject has a significant or material relationship to wages, hours, or other conditions of employment."

The benefits, coverage and administration of the plan in the instant case clearly are proper bargaining subjects.

We hold that the Company, having negotiated about those matters, was free to choose any carrier that would satisfy the Company's agreement with the Union.

III.

Our holding as stated above, however, should not be construed to mean that in all cases may the selection of a carrier be divorced from the elements of employee health insurance that traditionally have been held to be mandatory subjects of bargaining. As in *Bastian,* we are reluctant to attempt to formulate a test for determining in which cases the identity of the insurance carrier itself vitally affects the terms and conditions of the employment. In *Bastian,* the court found a sufficient interrelationship to require bargaining. Here, on the other hand, we find that all the matters within the bargaining requirement can be, and have been, the subject of negotiations between the Company and the Union *without* reference to the identity of the carrier. Moreover, should the Company's choice of a carrier produce a situation where the Company is unable to fulfill its agreement under the collective bargaining contract, the Union has a remedy under Section 301 of the Labor-Management Relations Act, 29 U.S.C. § 185 (1970). Thus, while a different result might be necessary where, as in *Bastian,* a change of carrier were found to affect the bargained-for terms of the employee insurance plan, or where, for example, the mal-administration of the plan by the company-selected carrier were found to be so pervasive and pernicious as to have the "Vital effect" contemplated in *Pittsburgh Plate Glass,* we do not pass on such matters here because they are not before us. All that the Union has alleged here is an undefined "dissatisfaction" with Aetna's administration.

We hold that the Board on the facts of this case erroneously concluded that the Company had violated its duty to bargain.

The petition to review and set aside the Board's order is granted; and the cross-petition for enforcement is denied.

• • •

CASE QUESTIONS

1. What aspects of an employee health insurance plan are subject to collective bargaining?

2. Why is the selection of the employee group insurance carrier not subject to collective bargaining?

UNITED STATES PIPE & FOUNDRY COMPANY v. NLRB
United States Court of Appeals, Fifth Circuit
298 F.2d 873 (5th Cir. 1962)

• • •

RIVES, Circuit Judge.

The difference between the parties is pointed up by their separate concepts of the question to be decided. The petitioner-employer submits that the issue is:

> "Whether a union, the certified representative of a plant bargaining unit may require of an employer as a condition to its agreement that its contract and all contracts under negotiation between the employer and other certified representatives of different bargaining units at other plants shall expire upon a common date."

The respondent-Board, on the other hand, argues that:

> ". . . where, as here, two or more unions are simultaneously negotiating separate contracts with the same employer, such unions have just as much right to insist that the contracts shall expire on the same date as the employer has to insist that they shall expire on different dates."

The original complaints were issued against the unions upon unfair labor practice charges filed by the employer to the effect that the unions refused to bargain in good faith with the employer in violation of Section 8(b) (3) of the National Labor Relations Act, 29 U.S.C.A. § 158(b) (3). The cases were consolidated for hearing. When the General Counsel rested his case in chief, each of the respondent unions moved to dismiss the complaint on the ground that the evidence failed to show a violation of Section 8(b) (3). The Trial Examiner took the motions to dismiss under advisement and recessed the hearing, commenting:

> "As an aid to me in determining whether I should grant the motions, as I am inclined to do, to grant it; I would welcome from all parties their legal analysis of the issue involved here; namely whether or not it is a violation of Section 8(b) (3) to require, *as the evidence indicates here respondents did require,* common termination dates of contracts to and beyond the point of impasse." (Emphasis supplied.)

Subsequently, the Trial Examiner dismissed the complaints holding squarely that the demand of each of the unions for common expiration dates of all contracts was, as a matter of law, within the realm of permissible bargaining.

The Board, in an extremely brief decision, affirmed; but, in so doing, refused to consider the ground upon which the Trial Examiner based his decision and, instead, held simply that, because contract duration is a bargainable issue, it is not an unfair labor practice for unions to insist upon specific expiration dates for their contracts.

The petitioner-employer urges that the Board's decision was based upon an erroneous conception of the facts, that this case does not involve a union demand for a specific expiration date of its contract, but, in each instance, a demand that its contract and contracts under separate negotiation with other unions expire on the same date common to all.

The two questions are not identical either legally or actually. Legally there can be no serious debate that each union may insist upon a specific expiration date for its contract whether or not that is the same date being insisted on by another union with respect to another contract. This case demonstrates, however, that strong legal objections can be raised to a union's demand that the employer agree with it and with another union or unions for a common expiration date as to two or more contracts.

Actually, in practical operation, an employer might accede to a union's request for a specific expiration date for its contract, but then adamantly, and perhaps successfully, resist the demand of another union for the same expiration date for its contract. In that event, the specific insistence of the first union would be met, but its real purpose and object would be defeated. Because we agree with the petitioner-employer that the Board did misconceive the issue to be decided, it becomes necessary to detail the facts and circumstances at some length.

Petitioner-employer, a manufacturer of a number of products, including cast iron pressure pipe, owns and operates several pipe plants, including one at Burlington, New Jersey, one at Bessemer, Alabama, and one at North Birmingham in Birmingham, Alabama.

Dating back to certifications issued by the Board in 1940, the Molders and its Local 256 have represented petitioner's employees at the North Birmingham plant, while the Steelworkers and its Local 2140 have represented a comparable unit consisting of the employees at the Bessemer plant, excluding, however, several craft groups which are represented by other unions. Acting through other locals, the Steelworkers also represents employees of petitioner at various other establishments, including a plant at Burlington, New Jersey, where the Steelworkers obtained a certification in 1942.

In 1959, the Steelworkers had contracts at the Burlington and Bessemer plants which were due to expire 70 days apart—August 20 at Burlington and October 31 at Bessemer. At the Burlington plant, the parties failed to reach agreement as to the terms of a new contract and the Steelworkers called a strike on or about August 20 when the old contract expired. A few days after that, the Steelworkers started negotiating with management representatives at Bessemer. Here, again, an impasse developed; and, as the old contract expired, the Union called a strike commencing October 31.

At North Birmingham, meanwhile, petitioner had been operating under a comparatively new contract with the Molders, which went into effect on June 1, 1959. That agreement was not due to expire until July 31, 1960, but it contained a "reopening" provision and, pursuant thereto, the Molders served notice on November 2 that its members designed to renegotiate certain matters. The parties accordingly started bargaining at that plant about mid-November, but failed to reach agreement, and the Molders called a strike beginning January 26, 1960.

We have carefully read and studied the record of negotiations at Bessemer between the petitioner and Steelworkers and those at North Birmingham between petitioner and the Molders. It would unduly prolong this opinion to set out those negotiations at length. Suffice it to say that we agree with the Trial Examiner on his characterization of the issue. The Steelworkers did suggest contract expiration dates of May 1 or June 1, but those suggestions were for adoption of a *common* date for *all* three contracts. The Molders' suggestion of a particular date was likewise conditioned upon acceptance by the employer of that date for all three contracts.

At the risk of repetition, we restate the question presented by the practically undisputed facts, viz.: whether by pre-arrangement among themselves, each of three unions, certified representatives of three separate plant bargaining units, simultaneously negotiating separate contracts with the same employer, may insist as a condition to its agreement that all three contracts under negotiation shall expire on some common date.

The scope of mandatory bargaining is limited to "wages, hours, and other terms and conditions of employment." Within that scope, the employer and the representative of the employees must bargain or be guilty of an unfair labor practice. Section 8(b) (3) of the Act. A further limitation of the scope of mandatory bargaining is implicit in the authority of the Board to decide upon the appropriate bargaining unit, and in each union's position as the exclusive representative of all employees in such unit:

> 29 U.S.C.A. § 159(a):
> " § 159. *Representatives and elections—(a) Exclusive representatives; employees' adjustment of grievances directly with employer*
> "Representatives designated or selected for the purposes of collective bargaining by the majority of the employees in a unit appropriate for such purposes, shall be the exclusive representatives of all the employees in such unit for the purposes of collective bargaining in respect to rates of pay, wages, hours of employment, or other conditions of employment. . . ."
> 29 U.S.C.A. § 159 (b):
> "The Board shall decide in each case whether, in order to assure to employees the fullest freedom in exercising the rights guaranteed by this subchapter, the unit appropriate for the purposes of collective bargaining shall be the employer unit, craft unit, plant unit, or subdivision thereof. . . ."

Under varying facts and circumstances, it has been often held that a proposal to expand the scope of the bargaining unit itself is not within the area of mandatory bargaining.

Under the facts of this case viewed realistically, a common expiration date of all three contracts had a vitally important connection with the "wages, hours, and other terms and conditions of employment" of the employees at each plant. Without a common expiration date, any union striking for a new contract on a different date might have to "bail with a sieve" while the employer shifted its production activities to the other plant or plants. With a common expiration date, it is obvious that each union might be able to negotiate a more advantageous new contract for the employees represented by that union.

None of the cases applying the provisions of the Act, which limit a union's representation to one particular unit, deal with the situation where the representatives of employees in several plant units of the same employer agree on a demand and are concurrently making the same demand in their several negotiations. Nor do any of those cases deal with the situation where the proposal seriously affects the ability of each union to bargain.

In such a situation, as presented by the facts and circumstances of this case, it seems to us that the importance of collective bargaining on questions affecting "wages, hours, and other terms and conditions of employment" overrides the *apparent* expansion of the scope of the bargaining unit. That expansion is more apparent than real, for the very real, hard problem faced by each of the three unions, acting as the exclusive representative of the employees in its unit, is that a common expiration date for all three contracts vitally affects the ability of each union separately to bargain.

Concededly, there is no legal obstacle to the right of the petitioner-employer to insist adamantly that the three contracts continue to expire on different dates. Correspondingly, we think, there is no valid legal reason why each union, with the consent of the other unions, cannot insist just as adamantly that all three contracts expire on some common date. In our opinion, the Board's order, as distinguished from its reasoning, is correct.

The petition for review is therefore denied.

CARSWELL, District Judge (dissenting).

Because I cannot agree that the action of the Union here was only *apparently* beyond the scope of bargaining units as set forth in 29 U.S.C.A. § 159(a), respectfully I must dissent.

The course of negotiations between the parties, concisely set forth in the Court's opinion, mean to me an unequivocal attempt by one bargaining unit to compel a contract expiration date for other and distinct bargaining units on other contracts as a *condition* of contract between this unit and this employer.

This, basically, is the position petitioner-employer has maintained throughout negotiation, hearing before the Board, and on this appeal. Its quest for answer has been once again without avail. I agree with the Court that the Board based its decision against petitioner-employer on the erroneous assumption that the issue before it could be met by simply reaffirming the unquestioned but irrelevant proposition that contract duration is a bargainable issue. Indeed, as the Court says, there can be no serious legal debate that each unit may insist upon a specific expiration date for *its own contract,* whether or not it be the same date insisted upon by another unit. But the emphasis supplied to this statement points up our basic disagreement. This does not mean to me that a distinct entity, here a bargaining unit deriving legal being from the enactment of the Taft-Hartley Act and having in 29 U.S.C.A. § 159(a) a plain limitation of scope, may inject as a *condition precedent* in the process of negotiation matters with reference to other units and involving other contracts.

As stated by the Supreme Court in National Labor Relations Board v. Wooster Division of Borg-Warner Corp., 356 U.S. 342 . . ..

"The company's good faith has met the requirements of the statute as to the subjects of mandatory bargaining. But that good faith does not license the employer to refuse to enter into agreements on the ground that they do not include some proposal which is not a mandatory subject of bargaining. We agree with the Board that such conduct is, in substance, a refusal to bargain about the subjects that are within the scope of mandatory bargaining. This does not mean that bargaining is to be confined to the statutory subjects. Each of the two controversial clauses is lawful in itself. Each would be enforceable if agreed to by the unions. But it does not follow that, because the company may propose these causes, it can lawfully insist upon them as a condition to any agreement."

Among the salutary purposes sought by the enactment of the Taft-Hartley amendments was a refinement of stated rules to delineate the employee-employer relationships, not the least of which was to make the compulsory negotiation process itslef subject to some standard of relevancy to the vital issues between conferees. In the first decision by the Supreme Court under the progenitor Wagner Act it was stated:

> "The theory of the act is that free opportunity for negotiation with accredited representatives of employees is likely to promote industrial peace and may bring about the adjustments and agreements which the act in itself does not attempt to compel." National Labor Relations Board v. Jones & Laughlin Steel Corp., 301 U.S. 1, 45. . . .

"Wages, hours, and other forms and conditions of employment" are made mandatory subjects of negotiation. 29 U.S.C.A. § 158(d). The area of permissive negotiation is much more broad and by *consent* of the parties may be expanded to include many things including common expiration dates on other contracts with other units as sought by the Union here. But such is not this case.

It is not a specific date, as such, which is the subject of controversy here, but a demand by separate bargaining units, having no authority to bargain for each other, as condition precedent to an agreement for all. The Court here finds that the common expiration date "vitally affects the ability of each union separately to bargain," stating that the separate unions face a "very real, hard problem" in this regard. Its preoccupation and concern with the respective difficulties of the parties at bargaining have fashioned, it seems to me, a new miscroscope of legal detection to see that which is and that which is not apparently visible in the Congressional language of 29 U.S.C.A. § 159(a). As I see it, this so extends and confuses the separability of unit duties and responsibilities as to enshroud the process with additional problems, which new problems themselves might just as logically be made the justification for even more expansion. Does not this mean, for example, that like demand can be made for industry-wide wages and hours by units of heretofore limited scope or that employer demand as condition to agreement same wages as paid to other units?

Industry-wide or plant-wide bargaining may well be desirable for one or the other party, or for both, but this determination can be made by the Board upon application under 29 U.S.C.A. § 159(b) for expansion of the certified bargaining unit, reference to which is made in the Court's opinion. The problems of negotiation asserted by the bargaining unit here are made by the Court the justification for an expansion of unit authority. These contentions are more properly for consideration of the Board under Section 159(b), supra, for plant-wide certification to remove the unit, or all of them, from an inequitable situation, if, indeed, the facts there developed require this result. Under the holding here the Court, in effect, is approving joint negotiation without consent of the parties and without plenary proceedings before the Board for determination of the need or desirability of such joint negotiation.

Moreover, the Union's claim that its demand for common expiration date was precipitated and made necessary by the action of the company in shifting its operations between (its three) plants should and could more properly have been the subject of a complaint for unfair labor practice under 29 U.S.C.A. § 158 (b) (3). . . .

Thus the Union was not without clear and appropriate recourse to seek directly joint bargaining by broadened certification or by bringing the petitioner-employer before the Board for a full hearing on the merits of its complaint that its shifting work must cease and desist as an unfair labor practice under Section 8(b) (3). Instead, the motivation of the Union in this case has been made the basis of the Court's opinion denying petitioner-employer hearing on either proposition, and this despite the fact that petitioner-employer's query as to whether or not each unit must bargain for itself has not been directly answered by the trial examiner, the Board, or the Court.

With great deference for the views of the majority, for the foregoing reasons I would answer petitioner-employer here by holding the action of the bargaining unit a refusal to bargain in good faith. I must, therefore, respectfully dissent.

• • •

CASE QUESTIONS

1. What issues are subject to mandatory bargaining between an employer and a union?

2. How is the subject of common expiration date contracts viewed in the context of bargaining?

The arbitration process was described by the Supreme Court in 1960 in *United Steelworkers v. Warrior & Gulf Navigation Co.* as a procedure:

> at the very heart of the system of industrial self-government. Arbitration is the means of solving the unforseeable by molding a system of private law for all the problems which may arise and to provide for their solution in a way which will generally accord with the variant needs and desires of the parties. The processing of disputes through the grievance machinery is actually a vehicle by which meaning and content is given to the collective bargaining agreement. . . . The grievance procedure is, in other words, a part of the continuous collective bargaining process. (363 U.S. 574, 581 (1960)).

The Supreme Court also said that "[i]n the absence of any express provision excluding a particular grievance from arbitration, we think only the most forceful evidence of a purpose to exclude [a] claim from arbitration can prevail, particularly where. . . . the exclusion clause is vague and the arbitration clause quite broad." (*Id.* at 583).

This case along with *United Steelworkers* v. *American Manufacturing Co.* and *United Steelworkers* v. *Enterprise Wheel & Car Corp.* are known as the *Steelworkers Triology* cases. The significance of the Supreme Court's holding in *American Manufacturing* is in its statement that:

> [t]he function of the court is very limited when the parties have agreed to submit all questions of contract interpretation to the arbitrator. It is then confined to ascertaining whether the party seeking arbitration is making a claim which on its facts is governed by the contract. Whether the moving party is right or wrong is a question of contract construction for the arbitrator. In these circumstances the moving party should not be deprived of the arbitrator's judgment, when it was his judgment and all that it connotes that was bargained for. (363 U.S. 564, 568 (1960)).

The importance of *Enterprise Wheel & Car Corp.* is the Supreme Court's ruling that:

> [i]nterpretation of the collective bargaining agreement is a question for the arbitrator. It is the arbitrator's construction which was bargained for; and so far as the arbitration decision concerns the construction of the contract, the courts have no business overruling him because their interpretation of the contract is different from his. (363 U.S. 593, 596 (1960)).

The *Steelworkers Trilogy* cases added significant prestige to the arbitration process. By these decisions the Supreme Court (1) limited the power of judicial review over arbitration awards, (2) determined that doubts as to the applicability of an arbitration clause should be resolved in favor of arbitration, and (3) required the courts to enforce an arbitrator's award based on the collective bargaining agreement even though a judicial interpretation would have been at variance with the arbitrator's ruling.

INTRODUCTION TO THE CASES

The cases in this chapter address the areas of the statutory basis for voluntary and compulsory arbitration, the arbitration proceeding, and review and enforcement of arbitration awards. The *Firestone Tire & Rubber Co. Case* deals with the arbitrability of breaches of no-strike clauses. The issue in *Howmet Corp.* was whether arbitration can be compelled on matters of job transfers and preferential hiring of former employees.

The court was faced with interpretation and application of a compulsory arbitration provision in the *Port Authority Case*. In *Heminger* the question presented was the burden of proof on a union seeking to compel arbitration. The court's power to interpret and to enforce an arbitration award was at issue in *General Dynamics Corp.*

FIRESTONE TIRE & RUBBER COMPANY v. LOCAL 887, INTERNATIONAL UNION OF THE UNITED RUBBER, CORK, LINOLEUM & PLASTIC WORKERS OF AMERICA, AFL—CIO
United States Court of Appeals, Fifth Circuit
476 F.2d 603 (5th Cir. 1973)

• • •

PER CURIAM:

This is an appeal from the entry of an order denying a stay pending arbitration and enjoining the defendant-union from pursuing any actions or proceedings arising out of the contract breach at issue in this lawsuit. We affirm.

This action was initiated by plaintiff-appelle, Firestone Tire & Rubber Company [Firestone] against defendants appellants, the International Union of the United Rubber, Cork, Linoleum and Plastic Workers of America, Local No. 887 of that Union, and several individuals. In the suit Firestone sought injunctive relief and damages for violation of the no-strike provision contained in the collective bargaining agreement. After considerable procedural jockeying, the Union filed a motion in the court below on March 29, 1972, seeking a stay of the court proceedings pending arbitration. After hearing argument on the motion, the district court found that the collective bargaining agreement did not contemplate arbitration of no-strike clause breaches. In an order dated April 11, 1972, the district court denied the stay pending arbitration and enjoined the Union:

from commencing or continuing, or causing the commencement or continuation, either directly or indirectly, of any action, suit, proceeding, case, controversy, or other form of litigation or dispute against the Plaintiff herein (including without in any way limiting the generality of the foregoing, the action presently pending as Civil Action No. C72—196 in the United States District Court for the Northern District of Ohio), which are based upon, arise out of or are related to the transactions or occurrences which are the subject matter of the Plaintiff's complaint herein; provided, however, that the foregoing shall not be deemed or construed as restricting, prejudicing or adversely affecting in any manner the rights of any or all of the Defendants herein to assert in this proceeding any defense or counterclaim that may be available to any or all of such Defendants to or against the claims asserted by the Plaintiff herein.

It is from the entry of the above order that the Union brings this appeal.

As a threshold matter, Firestone argues that (a) the order appealed from is non-appealable, and (b) the case is moot. It is true that an order denying a stay pending arbitration is non-appealable where the underlying suit seeks equitable relief. ... The order appealed from here, however, went beyond merely denying a stay. It enjoined any and all proceedings, including arbitration, that might have been pursued by the Union. An injunctive order of this type is clearly appealable, 28 U.S.C. § 1292(a)(1).

Firestone also challenges the justiciability of this appeal based upon the fact that subsequent to the submission of this appeal on February 6, 1973, the underlying suit went to trial and on March 9, 1973, the United States District Court for the Middle District of Georgia issued a memorandum opinion containing findings of fact and conclusions of law. The Union, seeking reversal, urges us to decide the case Firestone urges us to find in mootness a refuge from decision. If Judge Bottle's decision, in fact, left nothing of the order appealed from to pass upon, then our jurisdiction would be ousted. We do not sit to render advisory opinions as to the intrepretation of collective bargaining agreements. This is not, however, such a case. We are unable to say for a certainty that had we found the district court's injunction erroneously entered the Union would have been remediless. Inasmuch as we are affirming the injunction and thereby leaving the status quo undisturbed, it is unnecessary to catalogue the potential remedies had we reversed and decided the case should never have gone to trial. The justiciability of a controversy should not be dependent upon the result reached. It suffices to say that had we reversed, the possibility for some relief was present and we therefore conclude that the order appealed from is not moot ...

The Union challenges the district court's finding of non-arbitrability by contending that Art. XI, § 3(b) of the collective bargaining agreement evidences an intent of the parties to arbitrate the question of union fault prior to the commencement of a court suit for breach of the no-strike clause. The court below considered the contract as a whole, particularly the wholly employee-oriented grievance machinery, and concluded that the issue was non-arbitrable.

As the district court properly recognized,

> "First, there is a strong national policy favoring labor artitration and an order to arbitrate pursuant to an arbitration clause should not be denied unless it may be said with "positive assurance" that the arbitration clause does not reach the dispute in question. United Steelworkers of America v. Warrior & Gulf Nav. Co., 363 U.S. 574, ... (1960)."

The basis of arbitration is, however, contractual and unless the parties have provided for arbitration in the collective bargaining agreement, the court is powerless to compel arbitration. Numerous cases have held that breaches of a no-strike clause are not subject to arbitration where (1) the grievance provisions of the agreement neither explicitly nor implicitly provide for such arbitration, and (2) the contractual grievance machinery is wholly employee oriented. ... The district court correctly applied this principle to the instant contract, and we affirm its finding that the company was not obligated to seek arbitration of the no-strike breach.

Although the provisions of Art. XI, § 3(b), when viewed in isolation, might possibly raise an ambiguity as to arbitrability, when placed in the context of the whole contract, particularly the employee-oriented grievance procedures, there can be no question that the parties did not intend arbitration of no-strike breaches.

Affirmed.

• • •

CASE QUESTIONS

1. Does national labor philosophy favor arbitration or court resolution of conflicts?

2. In interpreting the arbitrability of violations of labor contract provisions, what rules are applied?

INTERNATIONAL ASSOCIATION OF MACHINISTS v. HOWMET CORPORATION
United States Court of Appeals, Ninth Circuit
466 F.2d 1249 (9th Cir. 1972)

• • •

DUNIWAY, Circuit Judge:

The International Association of Machinists, District Lodge 94, and its affiliated Local Lodge 1571 (the Union) filed this action under 29 U.S.C. § 185 to compel arbitration of several grievances against Howmet Corporation and Menasco Manufacturing Co. Summary judgment was entered by the district court in favor of the Union against Menasco, but against the Union with respect to Howmet. Menasco appeals. We remand to the district court for modification of the order.

I. FACTS.

Until 1970, Menasco and Howmet both manufactured aircraft landing gear. In 1970 Menasco, a corporation with manufacturing plants in Burbank, California, and Fort Worth, Texas, purchased two California plants from Howmet, in Montebello and Pomona, and took over Howmet's contracts and manufacturing operations for the production of aircraft landing gear. The Union represented the production and maintenance employees at the Montebello plant and was party to a collective bargaining agreement (the Agreement) with Howmet covering those employees at the time of the Menasco takeover. In the purchase contract, Menasco succeeded to the Agreement with the Union as soon as it began operating the Montebello plant.

Because the Montebello plant was operating at a substantial loss, Menasco decided to close the plant, and it so informed the Union. Negotiations followed concerning the details of the closure operation and its effect on the employees. After five meetings over a period of four months failed to result in agreement on the issues of severance and vacation pay, job transfer and preferential hiring of the Montebello employees at other Menasco plants, and payments to the Union pension plan, the Union demanded arbitration under the terms of the Agreement.   Menasco refused to arbitrate, and this action followed.

II. SCOPE OF COMPANY'S OBLIGATION
TO ARBITRATE

The Supreme Court has established a strong presumption in favor of arbitration as the preferred method of settlement of industrial disputes. When the standard form of arbitration clause is used in a collective bargaining agreement, as it was here, "an order to arbitrate the particular grievance should not be denied unless it may be said with positive assurance that the arbitration clause is not susceptible of an interpretation that covers the asserted dispute. Doubts should be resolved in favor of coverage." United Steelworkers of America v. Warrior & Gulf Co., 1960, 363 U.S. 574. ... See also United Steelworkers of America v. American Manufacturing Co., 1960, 363 U.S. 564, ... and United Steelworkers of America v. Enterprise Wheel & Car Co., 1960, 363 U.S. 593, ... (hereinafter referred to as the *Steelworkers Trilogy*).

Although arbitration is a matter of mutual agreement between the parties, and they may choose to exclude certain areas of contention from the arbitration process, the standard set by the Court for finding a dispute nonarbitrable is a strict one: There must be either an "express provision excluding a particular grievance from arbitration" or "the most forceful evidence of a purpose to exclude the claim from arbitration." *Id.* at 585, 80 S.Ct. at 1354. Here, there is no such "express provision." Whether or not a particular dispute is *prima facie* covered by the agreement's arbitration procedure is a question for the court to decide. ... The issue is therefore a simple one: is there forceful evidence of a purpose to exclude these grievances from arbitration so that the heavy presumption in favor of arbitration is overcome? We hold that there is not.

The "evidence" urged by Menasco as indicating that the claims involved were not to be subject to arbitration procedure is threefold: (1) the absence of a clause or reference in the Agreement dealing specifically with those issues; (2) the Union's attempt to negotiate with Menasco concerning the issues connected with the plant closure: and (3) the assertion that the arbitration clause involved here is more restrictive than the standard one because it specifically provided that the arbitrator "shall not have the power to add to, subtract from, or change any of the terms of this Agreement."

However, explicit language in collective bargaining agreements covering each specific claim alleged to be arbitrable is not required. We have held that the complete silence of an agreement on the issues sought to be arbitrated is not sufficient evidence to meet the rigorous standard set by the *Steelworkers Trilogy* for a finding of nonarbitrability. ... Like the Supreme Court . . . we are faced here with a situation created by an action (a merger in *Wiley,* a plant closure here) which was not, in all probability, expressly contemplated by the Union and Howmet when the Agreement was entered into. "Fairly taken, however, the Union's demands collectively raise the question which underlies the whole litigation: What is the effect of the merger [plant closure] on the rights of the covered employees? ... That question can be best answered by reference to and interpretation of the terms of the Agreement itself, a function of the arbitrator.

The second piece of "evidence" is likewise insufficient. It is true that the Union did not demand arbitration immediately upon learning of Menasco's refusal to accede to its claims, but evidenced a willingness to negotiate and compromise. Such behavior does not conclusively demonstrate that the claims were not covered by the Agreement. As we said ... "... to rule a controversy nonarbitrable on scant evidence falling short of a clear demonstration of that fact would set at naught the ... important policy enunciated in the Steelworkers trilogy to arbitrate all disputes not clearly outside the arbitration clause." ... Likewise, Menasco's third argument is without merit. We agree with the Fourth Circuit that a clause limiting the power of the arbitrator to add to, subtract from, or alter the provisions of the agreement does not affect the jurisdiction of the arbitrator, but merely limits his power to fashion an award. ...

We have rejected employers' contentions of nonarbitrability in situations where the evidence of a purpose to exclude the claims from the arbitration procedure was more forceful and substantial than that present in this case. ... In such cases, as in this one, the public policy favoring the resolution of industrial disputes in a nonjudicial forum, with its attendant advantages of economy, efficiency expertise, requires that we broadly construe arbitration clauses and uphold the arbitrability of issues which are even arguably covered by the collective bargaining agreement. From that perspective, we must affirm the district court's finding that the issues in question are arbitrable.

III. OTHER POINTS RAISED BY MENASCO

A. Inequity of compelling arbitration.

Menasco argues that arbitration should not be compelled because any award made by the arbitrator concerning some of the alleged grievances—job transfer and preferential hiring at other Menasco plants, as well as application of the Howmet Agreement to those Montebello employees who may be hired by Menasco at its other plants—would require conduct by Menasco which would be illegal as an unfair labor practice or would contravene Menasco's collective bargaining agreements with other unions at its other plants. The employees at Menasco's Burbank and Pomona plants are represented by other unions, and the Company argues that arbitration of the questions of job transfers and preferential hiring of Montebello employees and application of the Howmet Agreement to those hired at the plants involve matters which are within the exclusive purview of the unions representing Menasco employees at the other plants. Any effort on Menasco's part to comply with an arbitration award covering those matters would result in violation of its collective bargaining agreements with those other unions and the commission of unfair labor practices; and even the mere fact of arbitrating with one union issues which are committed to the exclusive bargaining purview of another union would create the very kind of industrial strife and unrest which it is the objective of national labor policy to avoid.

We think that Menasco's position has merit. The Supreme Court held in the *Steelworkers Trilogy* that the underlying objective of the policy favoring the resolution of disputes by arbitration is that of avoiding industrial strife and promoting industrial harmony through a fair, fast, and flexible system utilizing neutral but knowledgeable "peacemakers." That objective is served by a strong judicial policy, initiated by the *Trilogy,* of broadly construing the arbitration clauses of collective bargaining agreements and requiring the disputing parties to arbitrate whenever their agreement is possibly susceptible of an interpretation permitting such action. However, when situations arise, as here, in which the objective of avoiding industrial strife and disharmony would not be served by compelling arbitration, a court has the obligation to examine the potential consequences of compelling arbitration and to tailor its order accordingly.

We are faced with circumstances similar in many respects to that dealt with by the Second Circuit. . . . There, the Company had purchased a business and hired a few of the seller's former employees to continue working in the business. The seller and the buyer each had a collective bargaining agreement with a different union. Those new employees of the buyer who had formerly worked for the seller filed grievances with their new employer and demanded arbitration under their collective bargaining agreement with the seller. Meanwhile, the buyer obtained from the National Labor Relations Board a decision clarifying the bargaining unit: the union which had represented the buyer's employees was declared the sole bargaining agent for all current employees including those formerly working for the seller. Under those circumstances, the Second Circuit refused to compel arbitration with the seller's union, fearing that arbitration which might result in the seller's union continuing to represent former employees of the seller could lead to unrest and dissatisfaction among the majority of buyer's employees. Such arbitration would not serve the objective of avoiding industrial strife, but rather might foster it. The court also expressed concern that compelling the buyer to arbitrate with a union other than the one determined by the National Labor Relations Board to be the legitimate bargaining agent for all company employees might force the buyer to commit an unfair labor practice by "bargaining" with a minority union when a majority one was in existence. In a later case, the Second Circuit held that the absence of a specific National Labor Relations Board clarification order finding the buyer's union the official sole bargaining agent did not alter this result. . . .

Here, the buyer (Menasco) and the seller (Howmet) had collective bargaining agreements with different unions. Menasco is bound by Howmet's collective bargaining agreement with the Union at the Montebello plant. The Union, representing the employees at that plant, now seeks a judicial order compelling Menasco to arbitrate issues which directly involve Menasco's obligations under its collective bargaining agreements with other unions at its other plants: job transfers and preferential hiring of Montebello employees at Menasco's plants in Burbank and Pomona and continued application of the Montebello Agreement to former Montebello plant employees so hired. An award issued by the arbitrator which gave the Union any relief on these issues would, we believe, foster rather than alleviate industrial disharmony by forcing the employer to arbitrate with one union issues which touch the very heart of the employer's collective bargaining agreement with another union. We concur in remarks of the Fifth Circuit concerning an analogous situation:

> "Although we are mindful of the Supreme Court's belief in the flexibility of arbitration and actually share such a belief, we also share the apprehension felt by the Court in *McGuire*. . . . [T]he resolution of one employee grievance under one of the contracts might be the basis for another grievance under the other contract which would in turn produce a series of complaints. . . . Therefore, allowing the grievance machinery to remain in force would more likely produce industrial strife rather than prevent it.
>
> "We take cognizance of the fact that every grievance always gives rise to unrest in industrial relations and such grievances should be settled quickly and fairly in order to prevent the strife that usually accompanies them. But the resolution of such grievances should never give birth to additional unrest and dissatisfaction." . . .

It may well be true, as the Union urges, that Menasco will never be forced to comply with an arbitration award giving relief on issues covered by its collective bargaining agreements with other unions, because the remedy of an action to vacate or modify the award is always available. However, we do not consider that remedy adequate in the circumstances of this case. It is the arbitration itself—the fact of Menasco's dealing with one union on issues committed to the exclusive bargaining jurisdiction of another union—which gives rise to the unrest and dissatisfaction which national labor policy seeks to prevent. The realistic choice available here if these particular issues are submitted to arbitration is between an award denying all meaningful relief to the Union on those issues and one which could not be enforced without causing Menasco to violate its collective bargaining agreement with the Union representing all current employees at the other plants involved. Under these circumstances, we think the objectives of national labor policy dictate that arbitration not be compelled on those particular issues. Accordingly, we reverse that portion of the district court's order compelling arbitration on the questions of job transfers and preferential hiring of former Montebello employees at Menasco's Burbank and Pomona plants and the extent to which former Montebello employees who are hired at Burbank or Pomona are entitled to work under the terms of the Howmet collective bargaining agreement.

B. Laches.

Menasco argues that we should reverse the district court's granting of summary judgment in favor of the Union, so that Menasco will have an opportunity to present to the court a defense based upon the equitable doctrine of laches. We disagree.

Those circuit courts which have considered the question have disagreed on whether laches may be properly raised as a defense to an action to compel arbitration. The Fourth Circuit has held that the issue of laches, like the issue of compliance with procedural requirements of the collective bargaining agreement, should be considered by the arbitrator, not by the courts. ... The Sixth and Seventh Circuits, plus the Fifth Circuit by implication, have reached the opposite conclusion. ...

We have not yet had occasion to decide this issue, and we do not consider this case an appropriate vehicle for doing so. Like the employer before us in Lodge 1327, International Association of Machinists & Aerospace Workers v. Fraser & Johnston Co., ... , Menasco did not raise the laches issue in the district court, even though it had ample opportunity to do so. In its answer to the Union's petition to compel arbitration, Menasco raised a number of affirmative defenses; laches was not among them. Under such circumstances we follow the procedure established in Fraser & Johnston, ... , and decline to consider the Company's belated contention. ...

C. District Court's specification of the issues for arbitration.

Menasco objects to the form of the court's order compelling arbitration, insofar as it defined and framed the specific questions which the arbitrator is empowered to decide. Once the court has determined that the issues are arbitrable because covered by the collective bargaining agreement on its face, the Company contends, the judicial function is ended. The arbitrator must then be free to frame the issues in light of his interpretation of the collective bargaining agreement, and even to refuse to consider the merits of some of the issues found by the court to be arguably arbitrable. Those prerogatives of the arbitrator, it is argued, are circumscribed by the district court's detailed and specific delineation of the issues to be submitted to arbitration.

We doubt that the arbitrator will feel seriously limited by the district court's order in his ability to consider all aspects of the issues presented to him. However, we agree that the flexible nature of the arbitration process requires that the arbitrator be given as much freedom as possible—from the framing of the issues themselves to the fashioning of appropriate remedies. The district court's function in the process is essentially ended once it has found the collective bargaining agreement susceptible of an interpretation which would cover the dispute; it should not attempt in the usual case to frame the precise question which the arbitrator must decide. ... Likewise the arbitrator should not be foreclosed from passing on the question of arbitrability; the court has merely made the threshold decision that the collective bargaining agreement is susceptible of an interpretation making the dispute arbitrable, *i.e.,* the issue is *prima facie* arbitrable. The arbitrator should not be prevented from deciding whether or not he will so interpret the agreement.

The matter is remanded to the district court with directions to reframe its decree in a manner consistent with this opinion.

• • •

CASE QUESTIONS

1. What is the presumption under the standard form of arbitration clause?

2. What was the employer's evidence against arbitration of the grievance, and how did the court rule on each?

DIVISION 85, AMALGAMATED TRANSIT UNION v. PORT AUTHORITY OF ALLEGHENY COUNTY
Supreme Court of Pennsylvania
417 Pa. 299, 208 A.2d 271 (1965)

• • •

ROBERTS, Justice.

This appeal is from a decree of the Court of Common Pleas of Allegheny County directing appellant, the Port Authority of Allegheny County, to comply with arbitration provisions of the Second Class County Port Authority Act. The decree directs the Port Authority to submit to arbitration its labor dispute with appellee union, the recognized bargaining agent for appellant's employees.

Neither the complaint in mandamus nor the answer raise any factual issues and appellee's motion for judgment on the pleadings was granted by the court below.

The facts are not disputed. The Port Authority and the union are parties to a collective bargaining contract which provides that a party desiring any changes shall notify the other party in writing before a certain date. Both parties duly notified each other of their desire to make changes, but subsequent collective bargaining did not result in an agreement. Thereafter appellant refused to submit the dispute to arbitration and appellee sought mandamus.

The legal questions presented involve the interpretation and constitutionality of Section 13.2 of the Port Authority Act. This section provides: "In case of any labor dispute where collective bargaining does not result in agreement, the authority shall offer to submit such dispute to arbitration by a board composed of three person. ... "

Appellant's first contention is that the language of Section 13.2 leaves to the Port Authority sole discretion to decide whether a labor dispute shall be submitted to arbitration. The word *shall* is, however, generally regarded as imperative. ... We look to the intention and purpose of the statute in determining whether the word *shall* is to be given a permissive or imperative meaning. National Transit Co. v. Boardman, supra, and we see no evidence in Section 13.2 of any legislative intention to give this word a permissive meaning only. In fact, a study of the status indicates that an imperative meaning was clearly intended.

The first sentence of Section 13.2 states that the Port Authority "*shall* deal with and enter into written contracts with the employes of the authority through accredited representatives of such employes or representatives of any labor organization authorized to act for such employes concerning wages, salaries, hours, working conditions, and pension or retirement provisions." (Emphasis supplied.) The next sentence of the same section provides that where collective bargaining does not result in agreement with respect to any labor dispute the Authority "*shall* offer to submit such dispute to arbitration." (Emphasis supplied.) There follows a detailed procedure for the selection of arbitrators, a procedure carefully designed to insure that such selection will be handled expeditiously. Moreover, the Legislature manifested its intent to make the scope of arbitration as broad as possible by defining the term "labor dispute" in the widest possible manner.

Thus, from provisions contained in Section 13.2 there emerges an overriding legislative purpose to foster peaceful relations between the Port Authority and its employees and thereby to protect the public interest in transportation by preventing transit stoppages caused by labor disputes. As a further expression of legislative reliance on arbitration to resolve disputes, Section 13.2 provides that the "determination of the majority of the board of arbitration thus established shall be final and binding on all matters in dispute."

In such a setting, it is apparent from the provisions cited that the purpose of Section 13.2 is to utilize arbitration to prevent labor disputes from disrupting public service. We must agree with the court below that "in such a context . . . the word 'shall' is meant to be used in its true grammatical imperative form . . . and that this section requires the Authority to submit the issue to mandatory binding arbitration upon the failure of negotiations."

Similarly, we dismiss appellant's contention that it may refuse to submit to arbitration demands which it considers unreasonable. No such qualification appears in the statue nor is there any basis whatever for implying that the Authority is vested with such controlling power.

As an alternative argument, appellant contends that if Section 13.2 is construed to require compulsory arbitration by a private board of arbitrators, it is contrary to Article III, Section 20 of the Constitution of Pennsylvania, P.S. That section provides that "[t]he General Assembly

shall not delegate to any special commission, private corporation or association, any power to make, supervise or interfere with any municipal
improvement, money, property or effects, whether held in trust or
otherwise, or to levy taxes or perform any municipal function whatever."
This contention ignores the construction given this constitutional provision in Tranter v. Allegheny County Authority, 316 Pa. 65, 173 A.289
(1934).

The powers and limitations enacted with respect to the authority involved in Tranter are strikingly similar to the powers and limitations
enacted with respect to appellant. There the Legislature conferred upon
the authority, as a public corporation, essential governmental functions.
The authority was empowered to construct, maintain and operate bridges,
tunnels, streets, highways, traffic distribution centers, and traffic circles.
The authority was also authorized to collect fees, tolls, rentals and charges
in connection with the authority's property and projects. Here the Port
Authority is also a public body performing essential governmental functions. The Port Authority is entrusted with power to plan, acquire, hold
construct, improve, maintain, and operate port facilities and a transportation system in Allegheny County and outside the County to the extent
necessary for an integrated system. It has the additional power to fix
and collect fares and rentals for its facilities and operations.

The statute involved in Tranter authorized Allegheny County and the
City of Pittsburgh to grant and convey to the authority involved in
that case certain real peoperty which the county and city were already
devoting to public use, including a tunnel owned by the county and a
wharf owned by the city for which the city was receiving tolls. In the
present case, any municipality or owner is authorized to grant or convey
to the Port Authority any facility or any interest in real or personal
property which may be used by the Authority. There, as here, the authority was given no power to levy taxes and no power to pledge the
credit of the Commonwealth or of any political subdivision.

After discussing the powers and limitations of the authority, this
Court held in Tranter that any possible interference by private trustees
with the operation of the authority was immaterial since it did not deal
with municipal property, improvements, money or effects in the sense
contemplated by the constitutional provision. Following Tranter, we here
conclude that any interference by the board of arbitrators is constitutionally immaterial in the case before us. Nor could any action by the
board of arbitrators contravene the policy underlying Article III, Section
20 of the Constitution of Pennsylvania. This section was designed to
prevent the separation of the power to incur debts from the duty of
providing for their payment by taxation. Tranter v. Allegheny County
Authority, supra.

In a second alternative argument, appellant contends that arbitration
provided by the Port Authority Act constitutes an illegal delegation of
legislative power under Article II, Section 1 of the Constitution of Pennsylvania. The argument is founded on an assertion that the Act does
not contain appropriate standards for the board of artibtators to follow
in making its determinations.

The area of prohibited delegation has been carefully circumscribed
in Kelley v. Earle, 325 Pa. 337, 190 A. 140 (1937), where it was con-

tended there had been an unlawful delegation of legislative power to the State Authority. In rejecting that contention, this Court said:

> "The State Authority cannot make laws, nor can it levy or collect taxes, and it is specifically denied the power to create any indebtedness in the name of the State. Its broad functions are to arrange for the construction of designated types of public improvements, for their financing and for the retirement of the obligations thus incurred. These duties can hardly be termed purely legislative and to rest exclusively in the Legislature. [Citing cases.] There are many other governmental instrumentalities which have similar powers." ...

In the instant controversy neither the Port Authority nor the board of arbitrators can incur public debts, levy or collect taxes, or make laws. Furthermore, the Legislature may legitimately establish primary standards and impose upon others the duty to implement its policies in accordance with general provisions. ... It is clear that in the Port Authority Act the Legislature has announced its policies and that both the Authority and the board of arbitrators have standards sufficient to guide them in executing the legislative will.

Appellant also contends that the arbitration provisions of the Port Authority Act would deprive it of its procedural rights under the due process clause of the Fourteenth Amendment to the federal constitution. Although we need not consider this issue since it was evidently neither raised nor considered below, ..., we note in passing that it is totally lacking in merit.

We conclude that no constitutional provision has been invaded in this case.

Decree affirmed. Each party to pay own costs.

• • •

CASE QUESTIONS

1. How did the court determine the meaning to be applied to *shall* in the Port Authority Act?

2. What did the court conclude was the purpose of the arbitration provision in the Port Authority Act?

LOCAL 6, BRICKLAYERS, MASONS AND PLASTERERS INTERNATIONAL UNION OF AMERICA v. BOYD G. HEMINGER, INC.
United States Court of Appeals, Sixth Circuit
483 F.2d 129 (6th Cir. 1973)

• • •

PHILLIPS, Chief Judge.

This is a suit to compel arbitration. The District Court refused to order arbitration, rendering judgment in favor of the appellee employer,

Boyd G. Heminger, Inc. The tree labor unions appeal. Although Frank Fulton, Inc. also was a party to this litigation in the District Court, the unions, in this appeal, seek only a remand for direction of arbitration with Heminger. Jurisdiction is founded on § 301 of the Labor Management Relations Act, as amended. 29 U.S.C. § 185. We reverse and remand.

Each of the three unions is party to individual collective bargaining agreements with the Heminger corporation, which is in the construction industry. The bricklayers' agreement requires that seventy percent of all the employer's bricklayers must be union members, if they are available and competent. The carpenters' agreement requires that all unemployed carpenters in a four-county area in and around Canton, Ohio, be hired before any outside help is employed. The Ironworkers' agreement provides that other than a minimum of key employees, all of Heminger's ironworkers shall be furnished by the union.

The unions allege that Heminger violated each of these union security provisions by creating a sham corporation (appellee Frank Fulton, Inc.) to operate with non-union employees in the geographical areas covered by the agreements. A demand for arbitration for breach of the above provisions was made by each union on June 14, 1972. This suit was instituted after Heminger refused to arbitrate.

The bricklayers' arbitration agreement provides that the arbitration procedure will be used to settle "any disputes occurring during life of this Agreement in a peaceful manner . . ." The carpenters' arbitration agreement provides for arbitration "(I)n the event any . . . difference of opinion or dispute occurs, whether they concern the interpretation of the . . . Agreement or otherwise . . ." The Ironworkers' arbitration agreement provides "(t)he Board of Arbitration shall have jurisdiction over all questions involving the interpretation and application of any section of this Agreement."

The District Court, in its opinion, detailed the unions' allegations concerning the creation of the sham corporation and examined the evidence on the merits of the claim. The court concluded "this court can go no further than to determine whether or not plaintiffs have made out a prima facie case based on the alter ego or single employer theory." It refused to send the matter to arbitration because "the evidence and testimony indicate a lack of sufficient common factors to illustrate a single employer or alter ego theory."

Any inquiry into the applicable law in this area must begin with the *Steelworkers' Trilogy.* . . . The teaching of the *Trilogy* is that arbitration is preferred in the field of labor disputes. "An order to arbitrate . . . should not be denied unless it may be said with positive assurance that the arbitration clause is not susceptible of an interpretation that covers the asserted dispute. Doubts should be resolved in favor of coverage." . . . The role of the court in these cases "is confined to ascertaining whether the party seeking arbitration is making a claim which *on its face* is governed by the contract." . . . The Fifth Circuit has termed the standard to be applied the "arguably arbitrable" test. . . .

We hold that the District Court misconstrued its mandate. The duty of the courts is not to determine whether a prima facie case on the merits has been put forth by the party seeking arbitration. It is not the province of the court to look into the facts of the case. ... The arbitrator is not to be viewed as a special master who will be called in after a prima facie case on the merits has been made out.

In the context of this case, the burden of the unions was not to present a prima facie case on the creation of a sham or alter ego corporation by the employer. The burden was to show that, assuming there was a sham or alter ego corporation created by the Heminger Corp., there would then be a violation of the collective bargaining agreements. We have no doubt that such an asserted violation would be within the scope of the three arbitration agreements in question. In signing these arbitration agreements, the parties agreed to "submit all grievances to arbitration, not merely those that a court may deem to be meritorious." ...

Heminger has promised to arbitrate grievances concerning the application and interpretation of the collective bargaining agreement. This employer must be held to its promise.

We find inapposite two NLRB decisions relied on heavily by Heminger. ... Both of these unfair labor practice proceedings were concerned with the presence or absence of a single employer. There was no issue of arbitrability in either of those cases. We emphasize that this court is not faced with the question of whetherthere was a single employer. We simply decide the arbitrability of that claim.

Reversed and remanded with directions to the District Court to order arbitration between the unions and Boyd G. Heminger, Inc.

O'SULLIVAN, Senior Circuit Judge (dissenting).

I respectfully dissent. Whether a company may be ordered to submit any issue to arbitration depends upon whether it has contracted to do so. Resolution of such question "*is a matter to be determined by the Court* on the basis of the contract entered into by the parties." ... To hold that Fulton, Inc., is a party to a contract calling for arbitration requires, in the context of this case, a finding that it (Fulton, Inc.) is but an alter ego of Heminger, Inc., subject to whatever contracts Heminger, Inc., had made with appellant unions. Assertion that such was true and that defendants Heminger, Inc., and Fulton, Inc., together, constituted but a single employer, were the sole allegations of appellants' complaint whereby to invoke the jurisdiction of the District Court. The truth of such claims was put in issue by the answers of the defendants. It is my view that such issue presented a threshold question for resolution by the District Judge. He resolved it against plaintiffs-appellants. I would affirm.

The evidence before the District Judge showed that Boyd G. Heminger was the sole owner of defendant Boyd G. Heminger, Inc., a large commercial construction company doing business in the area of Canton, Ohio. He saw an opportunity to engage in the construction of residential housing, which work was then being done primarily by contractors who were not restricted by "closed shop" agreements with the plaintiff unions. His testimony was undisputed that no one could successfully compete in this activity and comply with the restrictive employment policies imposed by the building trades unions. The plaintiffs' brief to us asserts:

> "Frank Fulton, Inc., was created by Boyd G. Heminger to get into the housing construction market without the restrictions and burdens of Boyd G. Heminger, Inc.'s collective bragaining agreement with the plaintiff unions."

Appellants' argument is that what Heminger sought to do was forbidden by the "closed shop" contract. I disagree. I am not persuaded that the owners and employees of a corporate enterprise having such a "closed shop" contract are thereby denied the right to establish a separate and distinct legal entity by which to carry on a legitimate business.

Plaintiffs' complaint asked that the right of the separately formed corporation—Frank Fulton, Inc.—to carry on business free of the restraints imposed by the contract between Heminger, Inc., and the plaintiff unions, be submitted to arbitration; and that pending such arbitration, Frank Fulton, Inc., be restrained from carrying on work in which it was then engaged. The case came on for hearing upon plaintiffs' application for a preliminary and permanent injunction. District Judge Leroy J. Contie, Jr., of the United States District Court for the Northern District of Ohio, Eastern Division, elected as authorized by Rule 65(a) (2), to proceed with trial on the merits. He heard the testimony offered by the contesting parties to sustain their respective positions. He concluded:

> "This court cannot find sufficient evidence to send this matter to Arbitration, as the evidence and testimony indicate a lack of sufficient common factors to illustrate a single employer or alter ego theory. Therefore, this court finds for the defendants and against the plaintiffs."

While I believe that there is nothing in the law forbidding Boyd Heminger to enter upon a new and separate enterprise, such view is not essential to my conclusion. It is true that the creation of Frank Fulton, Inc., was initially the product of Heminger's desire to get into the residential construction market. However, the proofs taken before the District Judge showed, without dispute, that he did not realize this goal. He was instrumental in organizing Merit Shop, Inc., which, by change of name, became Frank Fulton, Inc. He and his wife were initially named as officers and directors of Merit Shop, Inc., but both had resigned from such positions prior to this litigation and before any operations were conducted by Frank Fulton, Inc. At the beginning, no stock was issued by Merit Shop, Inc., but Heminger did loan this skeletal corporation $5,000. This had been repaid to him before this litigation commenced. Heminger never acquired any shares of the stock ultimately issued by the new corporation. One Thomas McMahon, an employee of Heminger, Inc., subscribed and paid for the only shares issued by Frank Fulton, Inc. Shortly thereafter he resigned from his employment with the Heminger Corporation. It was undisputed that Heminger at no time had any ownership interest in the new corporation; likewise, it was undisputed that he took no part in its management or its labor relations. Frank Fulton, Inc., rented space in the office building maintained by Heminger, Inc., as well as some of Heminger's equipment. One or more supervisory employees of Heminger, Inc., did work for Fulton, Inc., at various job sites, but they did so without impairment of their duties to Heminger, Inc., and the latter billed Fulton for the services so rendered. At the time of the District Court hearing, Fulton, Inc., had some six employees; whereas, Heminger, Inc., had a payroll of 77 employees. Notwithstanding its thin capitalization, Fulton, Inc.'s initial contracts were on a cost-plus basis, and it was able to meet its payroll from progress payments received from the owners.

The relevant collective bargaining agreement requires that Heminger, Inc., hire only members of plaintiff unions if they were available, but no member of the plaintiff unions ever sought a job with Fulton, Inc. Fulton, Inc., did obtain one contract for the construction of a so-called Republic Steel building; Heminger, Inc., had an exclusive franchise to market such buildings in the Canton area; this construction job was subcontracted to Heminger, Inc. In proceeding, as a subcontractor, with the erection of such building Heminger, Inc., was required to and did observe its contract with plaintiff unions. The record is void of any evidence that Heminger, Inc., lost any business to Fulton, Inc.; the jobs of none of the employees of Heminger, Inc., were lost or impaired by the formation and activities of Fulton, Inc.

My brothers believe that the question of whether Fulton, Inc., is the alter ego of Heminger, Inc., should be decided by arbitration. They emphasize *the Trilogy* . . . the teaching of which "is that arbitration is preferred in the field of labor disputes." They then go on to say:

> "The role of the court in these cases 'is confined to ascertaining whether the party seeking arbitration is making a claim which *on its face* is governed by the contract.' . . . "

Respectfully, I urge that this sentence should be read in context with the one preceding it, found on page 567, 80 S.Ct. 1343, 1346 of the same decision:

> "The function of the court is very limited *when the parties have agreed* to submit all questions of contract interpretation to the arbitrator." . . . (Emphasis supplied).

Thus, whether the parties "have agreed to submit all questions of contract interpretation to the arbitrator" is a thresh-old question for the Court to decide. In Atkinson v. Sinclair Refining Co., . . . , the Supreme Court said:

> "Under our decisions, whether or not the company was bound to arbitrate, as well as what issues it must arbitrate, *is a matter to be determined by the Court* on the basis of the contract entered into by the parties. 'The Congress . . . has by § 301 of the Labor Management Relations Act, *assigned the courts the duty of determining whether the reluctant party has breached his promise to arbitrate. For arbitration is a matter of contract and a party cannot be required to submit to arbitration any dispute which he has not agreed so to submit.'* . . . (Emphasis supplied).

Thus, the only way that Fulton, Inc., could be made a party to a contract requiring arbitration was by a finding that it was but the alter ego of Heminger, Inc. This was a threshold question which was a "matter to be determined by the Court" under *Atkinson, supra.* I do not agree with my brothers' observation that the courts have no duty to determine "whether a *prima facie case* on the merits has been put forth by the party seeking arbitration." If such were the law, then a District Court would indeed have no function in such a case as this. Plaintiffs-appellants' complaint—as the sole basis for invoking District Court jurisdiction—charged that "defendant formed a sham-alter ego corporation, Frank Fulton, Inc." I cannot agree that plaintiffs had no duty to sustain this allegation, *even by a prima facie showing.* Here the District Judge resolved that the basic allegation of the complaint was not made out, even by a prima facie showing.

In Radio Union v. Broadcast Service, 380 U.S. 255, ... (1965), the Supreme Court set out the criteria whereby to determine whether one enterprise is but the alter ego of another, thus to create one integrated enterprise. The Court said:

> "The controlling criteria, set out and elaborated in Board decisions, are interrelation of operations, common management, centralized control of labor relations and common ownership." ... (Citing numerous Board decisions).

These criteria are missing in the case at bar. In Gerace Construction, Inc., 193 NLRB 645 (1971), the Board was dealing with the criteria needed to establish one enterprise as the alter ego of the other, thus to require both to conform to the same bargaining contract. In holding that the facts there involved did not justify a holding of an alter ego relationship, the Board said:

> "The record shows that Helger Construction is a separate legal entity with separate bank and payroll accounts. While Gerace Construction and Helger share a common bookkeeper, she keeps separate corporate records, and the two companies file separate tax returns. Francis Gerace initially controlled a majority of Helger's stock, and he and Wardin, who is an official of Gerace Construction, constituted two of Helger's three directors. However, in late November 1970, Francis Gerace resigned as a director of Helger and transferred his shares of stock to Lawrence E. Sweebe, who has been Helger's principal managerial official since its inception." ...

> "There is no showing that Gerace Construction has lost business to Helger or that any Gerace employee has lost work he otherwise would have had. Helger's contracts amount to less than $50,000 while Gerace's are seldom less than $250,000. Unlike Gerace, Helger operates an open shop without regard to craft lines and pays employees less than Gerace's contract rates." ...

> "Gerace has an average employee complement of 95; Helger has only 16. While some Helger employees previously worked for Gerace on occasion, there is no interchange of employees. It is undisputed that Helger uses Francis Gerace's trailer for its temporary office and some tools and

equipment of Gerace Construction. However, Helger pays rent for them. Moreover, the renting of tools and equipment appears to be common practice in the construction industry.

"We find the above facts show that Francis Gerace was the prime mover in organizing Helger Construction and that he and Wardin had potential control over its operations, but such control was gradually relinquished to Sweebe who in fact had actual control over Helger's operations and employees. In these circumstances and upon the entire record, as outlined above, we find that Gerace Construction and Helger Construction constitute separate employers under the Act and that the employees of each constitute separate bargaining units. Accordingly, we find that the Respondents had no obligation to recognize the Charging Parties as bargaining representatives of Helger's employees or extend the terms of the existing agreements to such employees. We shall therefore order that the complaint be dismissed." 193 NLRB at 645–46.

Substantially to the same effect is Carpenters District Council, et al. and Baxter Construction Company, Inc., 201 NLRB No. 16 (1973). The arbitration agreements here involved have to do with settlement of grievances and resolution of disagreements arising out of the contracts between the unions and the members of the Contractors Association [The Labor Relations Division, Building Section, of the Ohio Contractors Association, the General Contractors of America, Inc.]. Fulton, Inc., is a stranger to such Contractors Association and to the arbitration provisions contained in its contracts; but the relief here sought is to subject Fulton, Inc., to an arbitration clause to which it is not a party, and thus to have an arbitrator determine how it should conduct its future labor relations. Neither the majority opinion nor the plaintiff unions' address to us cite any authority to support such a rule. The fact that arbitration is asked does not, in my view, make Gerace Construction, Inc., *supra,* 193 NLRB 645, and Carpenters District Council, *supra,* 201 NLRB No. 16, without controlling analogy here. The District Judge correctly defined and discharged his function after hearing the relevant proofs:

"In other words, this court can go no further than to determine whether or not plaintiffs have made out a prima facie case based on the alter ego or single employer theory. It is the opinion of this court that plaintiffs have failed to do so, and that, therefore, judgment should be rendered for the defendants.

"This court heard evidence and took testimony on issues relating to the common ownership and the integrated relationship between the companies of Boyd Heminger, Inc. and Frank Fulton, Inc. The court is of the opinion that said evidence and testimony will not support a finding that the two defendants can be considered to be a single employer."

Whether the proofs made out even a prima facie case of alter ego or single employer theory, thus to make Fulton, Inc., a party to a contract containing an arbitration clause, was for resolution by the District Judge. I consider that his finding in this regard was correct.
I would affirm.   • • •

CASE QUESTIONS

1. What is the province of a court when presented with a question of whether a particular grievance is subject to arbitration?

2. How can a union satisfy its burden of proof in establishing that a sham corporation was created so that an employer might hire non-union men?

GENERAL DYNAMICS CORPORATION v.
LOCAL 5, INDUSTRIAL UNION OF MARINE
AND SHIPBUILDING WORKERS OF AMERICA, AFL—CIO
United States Court of Appeals, First Circuit
469 F.2d 848 (1st Cir. 1972)

● ● ●

COFFIN, Chief Judge.

These two appeals arise out of a dispute between the parties in the summer of 1969 over the interpretation of the seniority provisions in their collective bargaining agreement [the Agreement], signed in the spring of that year and effective until 1974. The dispute resulted in a work stoppage by members of the defendant Union and an arbitration award, pursuant to provisions of the Agreement, ordering the employees to return to work. Alleging non-compliance with the award, the plaintiff Corporation brought one suit for an order to enforce the award and another for damages resulting from the work stoppage. The district court, without opinion, granted the defendant's motion to dismiss in the first action and the motions for summary judgment in the second. The plaintiff appealed from both orders.

On July 25, 1969, the Corporation ordered the layoff of eleven machine shop employees, effective August 1. On July 31, approximately twenty-five machine shop employees did not return to work at the end of the lunch period, apparently in protest over the layoffs which the Union felt were not in accordance with the Agreement's seniority provisions. A meeting between the parties on August 1 resulted in the postponement of the layoffs and efforts to resolve the dispute. After the Union refused on August 19 to arbitrate the seniority issue, as the Corporation contends it had previously agreed to do, new notices of layoffs were sent out on August 22, to take effect the following Friday, the 29th. On August 25, a grievance was filed on behalf of three machine shop employees and a walkout began which by the next day included practically the entire work force. After telegrams to both the national and local unions requesting them to take all reasonable steps to end the walkout produced no results, the Corporation initiated the expedited arbitration proceedings provided for by the Agreement. On August 27, Arbitrator Fallon rendered his award, holding the work stoppage on July 31, August 25, and August 26 in violation of the Agreement and ordering the employees to cease and desist from that conduct, as provided in the Agreement. The work stoppage, however, continued, notwithstanding the arbitrator's award. The Corporation then brought these suits in the district court. A hearing on the plaintiff's request for a temporary restraining order to enforce the award took place on August 29, but during a recess the parties agreed to arbitrate the machine shop seniority dispute. On September 2, Arbitrator Santer issued his award agreeing with the Corporation's interpretation, after the announcement of which the employees began to return to work, full attendance being achieved within two days. Since then there has been apparently no work stoppage with regard to the machine shop seniority dispute, although there was allegedly one one-hour work stoppage in 1971 with regard to another matter.

We consider first our power to grant the relief requested in the first suit. In Boys Markets, Inc. v. Retail Clerk's Union, Local 770, 398 U.S. 235, ... (1970), the Supreme Court held that federal courts have the power to enjoin strikes over disputes subject to binding arbitration under a collective bargaining agreement. It reasoned that this narrow power was necessary to further the strong Congressional policy favoring peaceful arbitration of industrial disputes, and was not inconsistent with the Norris-LaGuardia Act which was designed to avoid the interjection of the federal judiciary into labor disputes on the behalf of management by means of sweeping, often *ex parte,* decrees. As courts both before and after *Boys Markets* have recognized, ... , an arbitrator's action, in accordance with the collective bargaining agreement, in issuing a cease and desist order against a work stoppage presents an even stronger case for federal power to issue injunctive relief. For here the court is not being asked to force a party to go to arbitration, which he agreed to undertake, ... , to restrain a party from violating its contractual promise to arbitrate, *Boys Markets, supra,* or to compel compliance with an arbitrator's award confined to interpreting a provision of the collective bargaining agreement. ... We are merely being asked to give judicial enforcement, specifically provided for by the Agreement, to an arbitrator's injunction, specifically provided for by the Agreement, issued after voluntary compliance with the expedited arbitration procedure established by the Agreement. Nothing could be closer to the core of the federal labor arbitration policy and further from the core of the Norris-LaGuardia policy.

Concluding that we have power to enforce an arbitrator's order, explicitly authorized by the contract, we turn to the order before us. The arbitrator's award reads as follows:

> "It is my finding that employees of General Dynamics, Quincy Division, engaged in a work stoppage on July 31, August 25, and August 26, 1969 in violation of Article XI, Section 1 of the collective Bargaining Agreement.
>
> Employees who have participated in this prohibited work stoppage are directed to refrain from such conduct forthwith and return to work immediately and cease and desist from any such further contract violations."

There is much controversy over the meaning of the final Delphic phrase. We see only two viable interpretations—either the arbitrator meant to bar any further work stoppage, like the one he found occurred on the three named dates, relating to the machine shop dispute, or he meant to bar any further work stoppage in violation of that section of the Agreement. We adopt the former view for two reasons. First, we note the very precise provisions of the collective agreement regarding cease and desist orders:

> "In such case, the arbitator shall make findings of fact concerning the alleged violation, and if a violation shall be found to have occurred, he shall prescribe appropriate relief, which shall include an order requiring any party . . . or group of employees to desist from any violations of Section 1 hereof. . . . In the event the arbitrator enters an order to desist from any violations of Section 1 above, it is agreed that he shall make as part of his order a provision in his award to the effect that if he finds there is thereafter a continuing or future violation of this Agreement it shall automatically be deemed to be subject to the desist order entered by the arbitrator in such proceeding."

Here the arbitrator did not include in his award the provision for applicability of the order, after subsequent findings, to continuing or future violations. Moreover, we cannot read the arbitrator's words as implying such applicability; he used the words "cease and desist" only in the final phrase, and the Agreement clearly indicates that future violations are to be made subject to that "desist order." We can understand plaintiff's disappointment in the award, but we are powerless to add words to an arbitrator's award.

Our limited reading of the award is bolstered not only by the specificity of the Agreement but also by the potential Norris-LaGuardia difficulties with an injunctive order susceptible of application to an indefinite number of yet uncommenced strike actions over an extended period in the future. . . . Certainly in an area where our power is grounded in the policy of enforcing the will of the parties we would not even entertain such a sweeping order unless it was perfectly clear that the parties so intended. Even then we would be most cautious in issuing an order which would in effect involve relinquishment of an equity court's obligation to weigh the circumstances and exercise its discretion in each instance. . . .

Since we intend to enforce the award, as interpreted to apply only to illegal work stoppages over the machine shop seniority dispute that arose in July 1969, we must consider both whether the issue is now moot and whether we can enforce this order directed at "employees" against their union. The Supreme Court has held that cease and desist orders of the National Labor Relations Board are not moot simply because the picketing at issue had ceased before its issuance, when one cannot say there is no danger of recurrent violation. . . . Here similarly we cannot say there is no danger of recurrent violation. The grievance filed by the Union on behalf of the three machinists was never processed, though apparently requests were made even after the strike ended. We cannot be absolutely certain even now that a work stoppage over the original dispute will not recur. . . . More significantly, we are far from sure that other work stoppages in violation of Article XI, Section 1 will not occur during the remaining term of this Agreement. Indeed, both parties admit that one brief stoppage did occur in 1971. Since the basic dispute here is over the enforceability of arbitrators' awards under Article XI, there is a real possibility that it will recur if not resolved. ... Indeed, if we were to hold it moot, the employees could forever prevent judicial resolution of the issue by returning to work each time just before a decision is issued. We note that at least one court has in an analogous circumstance, found the issue not moot even though the collective agreement under which the award was issued had expired. ...

Nor is there merit in the claim that the order which enjoins "employees" cannot be enforced against the Union. First, it is not at all clear whether a § 301 suit for injunctive relief lies against individual strikers. The cases raising the liability of individuals have involved money damages and found against such liability. ... Moreover, even if individuals could be directly sued, it would not necessarily follow that a suit against the Union would not lie. Section 301(b) specifically provides that a "labor organization may . . . be sued . . . in behalf of the employees whom it represents in the courts of the United States." 29 U.S.C. § 185(b). This Union's status as representative of the employees is also explicitly recognized in the Agreement. It would certainly frustrate the policies of the federal statute and the intention of the parties were relief against as many as 5000 employees for the same contract violation available only after service of and provision of an opportunity for defense to each and every individual.

We turn now to the damage suit. The two defendants [hereinafter the Union] claims that the suit was properly dismissed by summary judgment since the claim for damages as a result of the alleged breach of the no-strike clause was subject to arbitration under the Agreement. The Corporation, although admitting that the issue is arbitrable, claims it is no longer obliged to submit to arbitration because the Union's conduct amounted to repudiation of the Agreement's arbitration provision. The Corporation argues vigorously that the facts of this case are very different from those in the leading repudiation case of Drake Bakeries, Inc. v. Local 50, American Bakery & Confectionery Workers International, 370 U.S. 254 ... (1962), and that the   Union's conduct here, unlike there, constitutes repudiation of the arbitration provision as a matter of law. The Union similarly urges us to decide whether the conduct here constitutes repudiation. ...

We find, however, that in light of International Union of Operating Engineers, Local 150 v. Flair Builders, Inc., 406 U.S. 487 (1972), the issue of repudiation is for the arbitrator, not us. There the Supreme Court held that the equitable defense of laches even though "extrinsic" to the arbitral process was encompassed within an arbitration provision covering "any difference" and thus an issue for the arbitrator. The dissent noted the implications of that holding for "other affirmative defenses that go to the enforceability of a contract." ... We believe that if the equitable defense of laches, which is a general defense not limited to contract suits nor dependent on the provisions of the contract, can be subject to an arbitration provision, then certainly the legal defense of repudiation, which necessarily requires an interpretation of the meaning of the contract and the intent of the parties, can be subject to an arbitration provision, if covered by its terms. In this Agreement, the word "grievance," as to the employer, is defined in the opening definitional Article as:

> "dissatisfaction and complaint by the Employer with any act or failure to act by the Union on members or representatives of the Union."

Although awkwardly worded, we read this clause as applying to any action or failure to act by the Union to induce its members or representatives to do something. We think it therefore clearly covers the Union's failure to induce its representatives to abide by their alleged agreement to arbitrate the machine shop dispute, its failure to prevent its members from striking both before the grievance it filed could be processed and after the cease-and-desist order was issued, its encouragement of mass picketing and violence, and its failure to induce members to accept the arbitrator's award as to the machine shop dispute, which are essentially the five allegations of the Corporation as to repudiation. However, whatever doubts we may have as to the proper interpretation of the oddly-phrased grievance definition are dispelled by Section 7 of the Grievance Procedure Article, Article IV:

> "In the case of any question involving the interpretation or application of this Agreement, or affecting employes of more than one department, the first two (2) steps of the grievance procedure shall be omitted. . . ."

This sentence obviously intends to identify two subclasses of the general class of grievances subject to the procedure for special treatment. It is indisputable that the question of what conduct, if a breach, constitutes repudiation of the arbitration provision is a "question involving the interpretation or application of this Agreement" and thus an arbitrable grievance.

The Corporation has asked us, should we find arbitration necessary, to stay the action pending arbitration rather than affirm the dismissal. It cites language in *Drake Bakeries* to the effect that such a procedure is the only means of preserving both the no-strike and arbitration clauses. ... But that case was decided in the district court on a motion for a stay pending arbitration and thus the only alternatives before the Supreme Court were affirmance or reversal of the stay. Since we see no statute of limitations problem, Mass. Gen. Laws Ann. ch. 260, §§ 1, 2, and since several other issues could be presented to the arbitrator which might obviate the need for future litigation, we believe the district court properly denied the plaintiff's request and dismissed the action.

No. 72-1112 reversed and remanded for entry of an order enforcing the arbitrator's award; No. 72-1113 affirmed.

• • •

CASE QUESTIONS

1. What is the source of a court's power to enforce an arbitration award?

2. Why did the court interpret the breadth of the arbitrator's award, and what was its interpretation?

CIVIL RIGHTS   8

Many economic and social conditions influence the behavior of unions, minority employees, and company officials. During recession periods economic opportunities have restricted minority employment. This has happened repeatedly and the majority of the nation's citizens benefited from the resultant employment stratification which left the minorities with the least desirable and the lowest paying jobs. The passage of the 1964 Civil Rights Act was a culmination of much social upheaval and an economic willingness by the majority to share more of the American prosperity.

CIVIL RIGHTS ACT OF 1866

There was some statutory protection against racial discrimination in the Civil Rights Act of 1866. However, application of this Act has been uneven due to changing social conditions and widely different interpretations.

NATIONAL LABOR RELATIONS ACT

In the beginning unions were organized for self-protection. Employees were concerned about possible discrimination because of their union activities. The *1935 Wagner Act* covered employees or applicants who were engaged in protected activities. Protected activities include the right to join or not join a labor organization or to express feelings about a labor organization.

The National Labor Relations Board was created as the administrative agency to enforce the Act. The early cases which were handled by the National Labor Relations Board (NLRB) were violations of Sections 8(a) (1) based on interference, restraint, or coercion of individuals. These cases arose out of the unionization drives of 1935-1945. In these ten years the unions won many demands which strengthened the process of collective bargaining. The unions were assisted by the influence of World War II on public opinion. The country desparately wanted economic recovery, and unionism was accepted because it seemed to help improve social as well as economic working conditions.

As the union movement grew, the cases handled by the NLRB increased. The National Labor Relations Board was testing its jurisdiction, and one new area was racial discrimination. The discrimination may have been real or imagined, but the Board was moving to stop such discrimination. In a leading case, *Steele* v. *Louisville & Nashville Railroad,* 323 U.S. 192 (1944), the Court struck down a discriminatory hiring contract negotiated by an all-white railroad union. The court relied on the public policy embodied in the Railway Labor Act which required the union to represent the entire membership of the craft. The social and economic conditions supported unionism, but there was a need for a public policy to prevent discrimination in union practices.

STATE STATUTES

State laws were passed to protect minority groups in the areas of employment and political rights. Jurisdiction of the states was limited to *intrastate* activities of firms doing business in that state. The federal government also acted to preempt a jurisdictional area and thus remove it from state power. The 1866 Civil Rights Act allowed dual jurisdiction for state and federal government in the interest of promoting public policies of fairness in employment, housing, and political rights. Figure 8-1 shows the relationship between the federal and state laws and jurisdictional areas.

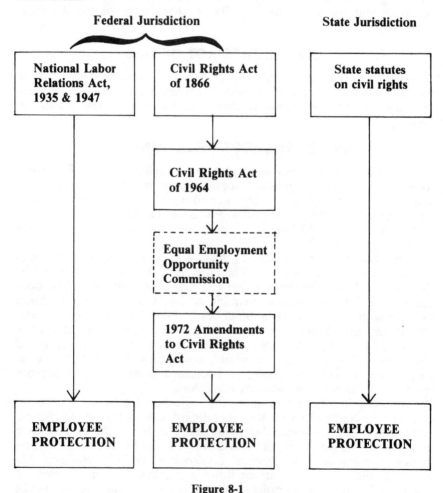

Figure 8-1

Civil Rights Legislation

The states were serious in their attempts to protect the civil rights of citizens. Strong feelings about protecting civil rights do not indicate a new trend thinking but have been an important part of labor law for many years.

An excellent example of this is seen in the *Railway Mail Association v. Corsi,* 326 U.S. 89 (1945). In the *Railway* case, the New York Court of Appeals upheld the constitutionality of Section 43 of the New York Civil Rights Law. The U.S. Supreme Court found no violation of the Fourteenth Amendment's due process clause, but rather said that such statutes represent the policy which is at the *heart* of the federal constitution. The U.S. Supreme Court affirmed the New York Court of Appeals ruling that the state prohibition against this out state corporation doing business in New York could include the provisions that there be no discrimination due to race, color, or creed.

A minority of other states had civil rights statutes. With the passage of the 1964 Civil Rights Act, the states were given the option of enforcing their own fair employment practices acts before the federal Equal Employment Opportunity Commission would take jurisdiction. Many states expanded their civil rights statutes at the same time to include housing, political, and voting rights. Dual jurisdiction now exists on most civil rights matters.

INTRODUCTION TO THE CASES

Civil rights cases are complex in fact and law. In the first case, *Steele* v. *Louisville & Nashville Railroad,* the U.S. Supreme Court explains its stand on the union duty to protect equally all craft members. In the second case, the court looks at the behavior of *Duke Power Company's* personnel practices. This important case started the serious review of employment tests in business. The third case, *Multi-Line Cans,* combines arbitration and civil rights issues. The Florida court is asked to examine what protection was given the grievant in the arbitration hearing before looking at the second hearing of the same facts.

The trend of the cases is toward a broader jurisdiction for civil rights cases and a more thorough hearing. There will be a constant stream of cases as the courts interpret the rights and obligations of public and private employers.

STEELE v. LOUISVILLE & NASHVILLE RAILROAD
United States Supreme Court
323 U.S. 192 (1944)

• • •

MR. CHIEF JUSTICE STONE delivered the opinion of the Court.

The question is whether the Railway Labor Act, 48 Stat. 1185, 45 U.S.C. §§ 151 *et seq.,* imposes on a labor organization, acting by authority of the statute as the exclusive bargaining representative of a craft or class of railway employees, the duty to represent all the employees in the craft without discrimination because of their race, and, if so, whether the courts have jurisdiction to protect the minority of the craft or class from the violation of such obligation. ...

The allegations of the bill of complaint, so far as now material, are as follows: Petitioner, a Negro, is a locomotive fireman in the employ of respondent Railroad, suing on his own behalf and that of his fellow employees who, like petitioner, are Negro firemen employed by the Railroad. Respondent Brotherhood, a labor organization, is, as provided under § 2, Fourth of the Railway Labor Act, the exclusive bargaining representative of the craft of firemen employed by the Railroad and is recognized as such by it and the members of the craft. The majority of the firemen employed by the Railroad are white and are members of the Brotherhood, but a substantial minority are Negroes who, by the constitution and ritual of the Brotherhood, are excluded from its membership. As the membership of the Brotherhood constitutes a majority of all firemen employed on respondent Railroad, and as under § 2, Fourth, the members because they are the majority have the right to choose and have chosen the Brotherhood to represent the craft, petitioner and other Negro firemen on the road have been required to accept the Brotherhood as their representative for the purposes of the Act.

On March 28, 1940, the Brotherhood, purporting to act as representative of the entire craft of firemen, without informing the Negro firemen or giving them opportunity to be heard, served a notice on respondent Railroad and on twenty other railroads operating principally in the southeastern part of the United States. The notice announced the Brotherhood's desire to amend the existing collective bargaining agreement in such manner as ultimately to exclude all Negro firemen from the service. By established practice on the several railroads so notified only white firemen can be promoted to serve as engineers, and the notice proposed that only "promotable," i.e. white, men should be employed as firemen or assigned to new runs or jobs or permanent vacancies in established runs or jobs.

On February 18, 1941, the railroads and the Brotherhood, as representative of the craft, entered into a new agreement which provided that not more than 50% of the firemen in each class of service in each seniority district of a carrier should be Negroes; that until such percentage should be reached, all new runs and all vacancies should be filled by white men; and that the agreement did not sanction the employment of Negroes in any seniority district in which they were not working. The agreement reserved the right of the Brotherhood to negotiate for further restrictions on the employment of Negro firemen on the individual railroads. On May 12, 1941, the Brotherhood entered into a supplemental agreement with respondent Railroad further controlling the seniority rights of Negro firemen and restricting their employment. The Negro firemen were not given notice or opportunity to be heard with respect to either of these agreements, which were put into effect before their existence was disclosed to the Negro firemen.

Until April 8, 1941, petitioner was in a "passenger pool," to which one white and five Negro firemen were assigned. These jobs were highly desirable in point of wages, hours, and other considerations. Petitioner had performed and was performing his work satisfactorily. Following a reduction in the mileage covered by the pool, all jobs in the pool were, about April 1, 1941, declared vacant. The Brotherhood and the Railroad, acting under the agreement, disqualified all the Negro firemen and replaced them with four white men, members of the Brotherhood, all junior in seniority to petitioner and no more competent or worthy. As a consequence petitioner was deprived of employment for sixteen days and then was assigned to more arduous, longer, and less remunerative work in local freight service. In conformity to the agreement, he was later replaced by a Brotherhood member junior to him, and assigned work on a switch engine, which was still harder and less remunerative, until January 3, 1942. On that date, after the bill of complaint in the present suit had been filed, he was reassigned to passenger service.

Protests and appeals of petitioner and his fellow Negro firemen, addressed to the Railroad and the Brotherhood, in an effort to secure relief and redress, have been ignored. Respondents have expressed their intention to enforce the agreement of February 18,1941 and its subsequent modifications. The Brotherhood has acted and asserts the right to act as exclusive bargaining representative of the firemen's craft. It is alleged that in that capacity it is under an obligation and duty imposed by the Act to represent the Negro firemen impartially and in good faith; but instead, in its notice to and contracts with the railroads, it has been hostile and disloyal to the Negro firemen, has deliberately discriminated against them, and has sought to deprive them of their seniority rights and to drive them out of employment in their craft, all in order to create a monopoly of employment for Brotherhood members. ... While the majority of the craft chooses the bargaining representative, when chosen it represents—as the Act by its terms makes plain—the craft or class and not the majority. The fair interpretation of the statutory language is that the organization chosen to represent a craft is to represent all its members, the majority as well as the minority, and it is to act for and not against those whom it represents. It is a principle of general application that the exercise of a granted power to act in behalf of others involves the assumption toward them of a duty to exercise the power in their interest and behalf, and that such a grant of power will not be deemed to dispense with all duty toward those for whom it is exercised unless so expressed.

We think that the Railway Labor Act imposes upon the statutory representative of a craft at least as exacting a duty to protect equally the interests of the members of the craft as the Constitution imposes upon a legislature to give equal protection to the interests of those for whom it legislates. Congress has seen fit to clothe the bargaining representative with powers comparable to those possessed by a legislative body both to create and restrict the rights of those whom it represents, cf. *J. I. Case Co.* v. *Labor Board, supra,* 335, but it has also imposed on the representative a corresponding duty. We hold that the language of the Act to which we have referred, read in the light of the purposes of the Act, expresses the aim of Congress to impose on the bargaining representative of a craft or class of employees the duty to exercise fairly the power conferred upon it in behalf of all those for whom it acts, without hostile discrimination against them.

This does not mean that the statutory representative of a craft is barred from making contracts which may have unfavorable effects on some of the members of the craft represented. Variations in the terms of the contract based on differences relevant to the authorized purposes of the contract in conditions to which they are to be applied, such as differences in seniority, the type of work performed, the competence and skill with which it is performed, are within the scope of the bargaining representation of a craft, all of whose members are not identical in their interest or merit.

Without attempting to mark the allowable limits of differences in the terms of contracts based on differences of conditions to which they apply, it is enough for present purposes to say that the statutory power to represent a craft and to make contracts as to wages, hours, and working conditions does not include the authority to make among members of the craft discriminations not based on such relevant differences. Here the discriminations based on race alone are obviously irrelevant and invidious. Congress plainly did not undertake to authorize the bargaining representative to make such discriminations.

The representative which thus discriminates may be enjoined from so doing, and its members may be enjoined from taking the benefit of such discriminatory action. No more is the Railroad bound by or entitled to take the benefit of a contract which the bargaining representative is prohibited by the statute from making. In both cases the right asserted, which is derived from the duty imposed by the statute on the bargaining representative, is a federal right implied from the statute and the policy which it has adopted. It is the federal statute which condemns as unlawful the Brotherhood's conduct. "The extent and nature of the legal consequences of this condemnation, though left by the statute to judicial determination, are nevertheless to be derived from it and the federal policy which it has adopted." ...

So long as a labor union assumes to act as the statutory representative of a craft, it cannot rightly refuse to perform the duty, which is inseparable from the power of representation conferred upon it, to represent the entire membership of the craft. While the statute does not deny to such a bargaining labor organization the right to determine eligibility to its membership, it does require the union, in collective bargaining and in making contracts with the carrier, to represent non-union or minority union members of the craft without hostile discrimination, fairly, impartially, and in good faith. Wherever necessary to that end, the union is required to consider requests of non-union members of the craft and expressions of their views with respect to collective bargaining with the employer and to give to them notice of and opportunity for hearing upon its proposed action. ...

The judgment is accordingly reversed and remanded for further proceedings not inconsistent with this opinion.

Reversed

• • •

CASE QUESTIONS

1. To what extent could the facts of the 1944 case pertain to current union-management problems?

2. What did the court say about the union making a contract which may have some unfavorable effects on some of the employees in the craft?

3. How did the court characterize the duty of representation due the minority employees in the craft?

GRIGGS v. DUKE POWER COMPANY
United States Supreme Court
401 U.S. 424 (1971)

● ● ●

MR. CHIEF JUSTICE BURGER delivered the opinion of the Court.

We granted the writ in this case to resolve the question whether an employer is prohibited by the Civil Rights Act of 1964, Title VII, from requiring a high school education or passing of a standardized general intelligence test as a condition of employment in or transfer to jobs when (a) neither standrad is shown to be significantly related to successful job performance, (b) both requirements operate to disqualify Negroes at a substantially higher rate than white applicants, and (c) the jobs in question formerly had been filled only by white employees as part of a long-standing practice of giving preference to whites.

Congress provided, in Title VII of the Civil Rights Act of 1964, for class actions for enforcement of provisions of the Act and this proceeding was brought by a group of incumbent Negro employees against Duke Power Company. All the petitioners are employed at the Company's Dan River Steam Station, a power generating facility located at Draper, North Carolina. At the time this action was instituted, the Company had 95 employees at the Dan River Station, 14 of whom were Negroes; 13 of these are petitioners here.

The District Court found that prior to July 2, 1965, the effective date of the Civil Rights Act of 1964, the Company openly discriminated on the basis of race in the hiring and assigning of employees at its Dan River plant. The plant was organized into five operating departments: (1) Labor, (2) Coal Handling, (3) Operations, (4) Maintenance, and (5) Laboratory and Test. Negroes were employed only in the Labor Department where the highest paying jobs paid less than the lowest paying jobs in the other four "operating" departments in which only whites were employed. Promotions were normally made within each department on the basis of job seniority. Transferees into a department usually began in the lowest position.

In 1955 the Company instituted a policy of requiring a high school education for initial assignment to any department except Labor, and for transfer from the Coal Handling to any "inside" department (Operations, Maintenance, or Laboratory). When the Company abandoned its policy of restricting Negroes to the Labor Department in 1965, completion of high school also was made a prerequisite to transfer from Labor to any other department. From the time the high school requirement was instituted to the time of trial, however, white employees hired before the time of the high school education requirement continued to perform satisfactorily and achieve promotions in the "operating" departments. Findings on this score are not challenged.

The Company added a further requirement for new employees on July 2, 1965, the date on which Title VII became effective. To qualify for placement in any but the Labor Department, it became necessary to register satisfactory scores on two professionally prepared aptitude tests, as well as to have a high school education. Completion of high school alone continued to render employees eligible for transfer to the four desirable departments from which Negroes had been excluded if the incumbent had been employed prior to the time of the new requirement. In September, 1965, the Company began to permit incumbent employees who lacked a high school education to qualify for transfer from Labor or Coal Handling to an "inside" job by passing two tests—the Wonderlic Personnel Test, which purports to measure general intelligence, and the Bennett Mechanical Comprehension Test. Neither was directed or intended to measure the ability to learn to perform a particular job or category of jobs. The requisite scores used for both initial hiring and transfer approximated the nation median for high school graduates.

The District Court had found that while the Company previously followed a policy of overt racial discrimination in a period prior to the Act, such conduct had ceased. The District Court also concluded that Title VII was intended to be prospective only and, consequently, the impact on prior inequities was beyond the reach of corrective action authorized by the Act.

The Court of Appeals was confronted with a question of first impression, as are we, concerning the meaning of Title VII. After careful analysis a majority of that court concluded that a subjective test of the employer's intent should govern, particularly in a close case, and that in this case there was no showing of a discriminatory purpose in the adoption of the diploma and test requirements. On this basis, the Court of Appeals concluded there was no violation of the Act.

The Court of Appeals reversed the District Court in part, rejecting the holding that residual discrimination arising from prior employment practices was insulated from remedial action. The Court of Appeals noted, however, that the District Court was correct in its conclusion that there was no showing of a racial purpose or invidious intent in the adoption of the high school dipolma requirement or general intelligence test and that these standards had been applied fairly to whites and Negroes alike. It held that, in the absence of a discriminatory purpose, use of such requirements was permitted by the Act. In so doing, the Court of Appeals rejected the claim that because these two requirements operated to render ineligible a markedly disproportionate number of Negroes, they were unlawful under Title VII unless shown to be job related. We granted the writ on these claims. 399 U.S. 926.

The objective of Congress in the enactment of Title VII is plain from the language of the statute. It was to achieve equality of employment opportunities and remove barriers that have operated in the past to favor an identifiable group of white employees over other employees. Under the Act, practices, procedures, or tests neutral on their face, and even neutral in terms of intent, cannot be maintained if they operate to "freeze" the status quo of prior discriminatory employment practices.

The Court of Appeals' opinion, and the partial dissent, agreed that, on the record in the present case, "whites register far better on the Company's alternative requirements" than Negroes. 420 F.2d 1225, 1239 n.6. This consequence would appear to be directly traceable to race. Basic intelligence must have the means of articulation to manifest itself fairly in a testing process. Because they are Negroes, petitioners have long received inferior education in segregated schools, and this Court expressly recognized these differences in Gaston County v. United States, 395 U.S. 285 (1969). There, because of the inferior education received by Negroes in North Carolina, this Court barred the institution of a literacy test for voter registration on the ground that the test would abridge the right to vote indirectly on account of race. Congress did not intend by Title VII, however, to guarantee a job to every person regardless of qualifications. In short, the Act does not command that any person be hired simply because he was formerly the subject of discrimination, or because he is a member of a minority group. Discriminatory preference for any group, minority or majority, is precisely and only what Congress has proscribed. What is required by Congress is the removal of artificial, arbitrary, and unneccessary barriers to employment when the barriers operate invidiously to discriminate on the basis of racial or other impermissible classification.

Congress has now provided that tests or criteria for employment or promotion may not provide equality of opportunity merely in the sense of the fabled offer of milk to the stork and the fox. On the contrary, Congress has now required that the posture and condition of the job-seeker be taken into account. It has—to resort again to the fable—provided that the vessel in which the milk is proffered be one all seekers can use. The Act proscribes not only overt discrimination but also practices that are fair in form, but discriminatory in operation. The touchstone is business necessity. If an employment practice which operates to exclude Negroes cannot be shown to be related to job performance, the practice is prohibited.

On the record before us, neither the high school completion requirement nor the general intelligence test is shown to bear a demonstrable relationship to successful performance of the jobs for which it was used. Both were adopted, as the Court of Appeals noted, without meaningful study or their relationship to job-performance ability. Rather, a vice president of the Company testified, the requirements were instituted on the Company's judgment that they generally would improve the overall quality of the work force.

The evidence, however, shows that employees who have not completed high school or taken the tests have continued to perform satisfactorily and make progress in departments for which the high school and test criteria are now used. The promotion record of present employees who would not be able to meet the criteria thus suggests the possibility that the requirements may not be needed even for the limited purpose of preserving the avowed policy of advancement within the Company. In the context of this case, it is unnecessary to reach the question whether testing requirements that take into account capability for the next succeeding position or related future promotion might be utilized upon a showing that such long-range requirements fulfill a genuine business need. In the present case the Company has made no such showing.

The Court of Appeals held that the Company had adopted the diploma and test requirements without any "intention to discriminate against Negro employees." 420 F. 2d, at 1232. We do not suggest that either the District Court or the Court of Appeals erred in examining the employer's intent; but good intent or absence of discriminatory intent does not redeem employment procedures or testing mechanisms that operate as "built-in headwinds" for minority groups and are unrelated to measuring job capability.

The Company's lack of discriminatory intent is suggested by special efforts to help the undereducated employees through Company financing two-thirds the cost of tuition for high school training. But Congress directed the thrust of the Act to the *consequences* of employment practices, not simply the motivation. More than that, Congress has placed on the employer the burden of showing that any given requirement must have a manifest relationship to the employment in question.

The facts of this case demonstrate the inadequacy of broad and general testing devices as well as the infirmity of using diplomas or degrees as fixed measures of capability. History is filled with examples of men and women who rendered highly effective performance without the conventional badges of accomplishment in terms of certificates, diplomas, or degrees. Diplomas and tests are useful servants, but Congress has mandated the commonsense proposition that they are not to become masters of reality.

The Company contends that its general intelligence tests are specifically permitted by § 703 (h) of the Act. That section authorizes the use of "any professionally developed ability test" that is not "designed, intended *or used* to discriminate because of race. ..." (Emphasis added.)

The Equal Employment Opportunity Commission, having enforcement responsibility, has issued guidelines interpreting § 703 (h) to permit only the use of job-related tests. The administrative interpretation of the Act by the enforcing agency is entitled to great deference. ... Since the Act and its legislative history support the Commission's construction, this affords good reason to treat the guidelines as expressing the will of Congress.

Section 703 (h) was not contained in the House version of the Civil Rights Act but was added in the Senate during extended debate. For a period, debate revolved around claims that the bill as proposed would prohibit all testing and force employers to hire unqualified persons simply to job discrimination. Proponents of Title VII sought throughout the debate to assure the critics that the Act would have no effect on job-related tests. Senators Case of New Jersey and Clark of Pennsylvanis, co-managers of the bill on the Senate floor, issued a memorandum explaining that the proposed Title VII "expressly protects the employer's right to insist that any prospective applicant, Negro or white, *must meet the applicable job qualifications*. Indeed, the very purpose of title VII is to promote hiring on the basis of job qualification, rather than on the basis of race or color." ... (Emphasis added.) Despite these assurances, Senator Tower of Texas introduced an amendment authorizing "professionally developed ability tests." Proponents of Title VII opposed the amendment because, as written, it would permit an employer to give any test, "whether it was a good test or not, so long as it was professionally designed. Discrimination could actually exist under the guise of compliance with statute." . . .

The amendment was defeated and two days later Senator Tower offered a substitute amendment which was adopted verbatim and is now the testing provision of § 703 (h). Speaking for the supporters of Title VII, Senator Humphrey, who had vigorously opposed the first amendment, endorsed the substitute amendment, stating: "Senators on both sides of the aisle who were deeply interested in title VII have examined the text of this amendment and have found it to be in accord with the intent and purpose of that title." 110 Cong. Rec. 13724. The amendment was then adopted. From the sum of the legislative history relevant in this case, the conclusion is inescapable that the EEOC's construction of § 703 (h) to require that employment tests be job related comports with congressional intent.

Nothing in the Act precludes the use of testing or measuring procedures; obviously they are useful. What Congress has forbidden is giving these devices and mechanisms controlling force unless they are demonstrably a reasonable measure of job performance. Congress has not commanded that the less qualified be preferred over the better qualified simply because of minority origins. Far from disparaging job qualifications as such, Congress has made such qualifications the controlling factor, so that rac-, religion, nationality, and sex become irrelevant. What Congress has commanded is that any tests used must measure the person for the job and not the person in the abstract.

The judgment of the Court of Appeals is, as to that portion of the judgment appealed from, reversed.

MR. JUSTICE BRENNAN took no part in the consideration or decision of this case.

• • •

CASE QUESTIONS

1. Did the court find that the company had intended to discriminate against minority employees?

2. What rule should be applied to employment tests given all applicants?

3. What was the problem in applying the high school graduation rule equally to all employees?

EQUAL EMPLOYMENT OPPORTUNITY COMMISSION v. MULTI-LINE CANS, INC.
United States District Court, Middle District of Florida, Tampa Division
No. 73-223 January 31, 1974

• • •

KRENTZMAN, D. J.

This case came on for hearing on plaintiff's motion to strike an affirmative defense and upon defendant's motion for summary judgment.

The motions pose the question whether this case, brought to redress violations of § 703(a) of Title VII of the Civil Rights Act of 1964, as amended, 42 U.S.C. 2000e, is effectively barred by an earlier arbitration decision rendered upon a grievance of the charging party herein pursuant to the terms of a collective bargaining agreement.

maintaining job classifications which are segregated on the basis of sex, promotions, job assignments, and in terms and conditions of employment.

Defendant asserted as an affirmative defense in its answer, the prior arbitration decision and award against grievant Shirley D. Duggan, whose charge of employment discrimination filed with the Commission provides the genesis for the present action. Plaintiff moved to strike the affirmative defense. Defendant moved for summary judgment on the grounds that the arbitration decision and award was a "complete defense to the action."

It is undisputed that on October 3, 1970, Shirley D. Duggan filed a grievance against the company alleging a violation of Article 23 of the collective bargaining agreement which dealt with promotions. Pursuant to the terms of that collective bargaining agreement her grievance was submitted to arbitration on the issue of "whether the company violated Article 23 of the Agreement when it refused to place the Grievant on the job of Lift Truck Operator."

Defendant asserts that the issues of employment discrimination based on sex alleged by Shirley D. Duggan in her charge to the Commission are factually identical to the issues determined by the arbitrator; hence, the action by the Commission would be merely a relitigation of matters previously fully determined by the arbitrator. Consequently, defendant maintains that the arbitration decision and award herein, is a complete bar to the instant action.

[EEOC's Arguments]

Essentially, two arguments are made by the plaintiff, first, that as an agency of the United States bringing an enforcement action under a law of the United States government, it is not barred by a private contractual arrangement, and secondly, that in any event, under the decisions of the United States Court of Appeals for the Fifth Circuit in *Hutchings* v. *U.S. Industries,* [2 EPD § 12,244] 428 F. 2d 303 (5th Cir. 1970) and *Rios* v. *Reynolds Metals,* [5 EPD § 7980] 467 F. 2d 54 (5th Cir. 1972) deference to an arbitration award is only proper where the contract and arbitral process involved adequately safeguard the public interest in Title VII to eliminate discrimination in employment; plaintiff argues that the contract and arbitral process herein, is insufficient to conclusively protect this public interest.

However, while the former argument has merit, it is not necessary for the court to consider this contention at this time. The second argument is based upon decided law in this Circuit. This court is bound to follow the decisions of the United States Court of Appeals for the Fifth Circuit and relies on these decisions for its ruling.

Law

The United States Court of Appeals for the Fifth Circuit in *Hutchings v. United States Industries Inc., supra,* held that the invocation of arbitration under a collective bargaining agreement does not bar an employee from seeking Title VII relief in federal district court. *Hutchings* specifically held that neither res judicata nor election of remedies applies in Title VII cases when an employee first seeks to enforce his rights under a contract grievance process.

In *Rios v. Reynolds Metals Co., supra,* the Fifth Circuit held, under a different set of facts than those encountered in *Hutchings,* that a federal district court may, under limited circumstances, defer to a prior arbitration award. Two factors not present in *Hutchings* were present in *Rios.* First, the arbitral process, under the collective bargaining agreement, placed upon the employer an obligation similar to that imposed by Title VII. Moreover, the district court in *Rios* held that the issue, decided by the arbitrator, was the same as that presented in the Title VII complaint in court. The Fifth Circuit in *Rios* enumerated the conditions required before a federal district court may defer to a prior arbitration award:

> First, there may be no deference to the decision of the arbitrator unless the contractual right coincides with the rights under Title VII. Second, it must be plain that the arbitrator's decision is in no way violative of the private rights guaranteed by Title VII, nor of the public policy which inheres in Title VII. In addition, before deferring, the district court must be satisfied that (1) the factual issues before it are identical to those decided by the arbitrator; (2) the arbitrator had power under the collective [bargaining] agreement to decide the ultimate issue of discrimination; (3) the evidence presented at the arbitral hearing dealt adequately with all factual issues; (4) the arbitrator actually decided the factual issues presented to the court; (5) the arbitration proceeding was fair and regular and free from procedural infirmities. . . . Id. at p. 55.

Turning to the facts before this court in the present action, and applying the guidelines set forth in *Rios,* the plaintiff's motion to strike has merit and should be granted. First, the collective bargaining agreement, which was in effect, (from Oct. 1, 1970 to Oct. 1, 1972) at the time of the arbitration of Ms. Duggan's grievance did not place upon the employer an obligation similar to that imposed by Title VII. Nowhere in the collective bargaining agreement was there any expressed prohibition against sexual discrimination in hiring, employment, promotion, discharge or other terms and conditions of employment. Section 16.5 of the collective bargaining agreement provides:

> "The arbitrator shall have jurisdiction and authority to apply, interpret, and determine compliance with the terms of this Agreement but may, in no case, add to, detract from or alter in any way any of the provisions of this Agreement."

Thus, the issue of sex discrimination raised in the Commission's suit before this court was beyond the arbitrator's power of decision. The arbitrator in his decision stated the issue to be: ". . . whether the company violated Article 23 of the Agreement when it refused to place the grievant on the job of Lift Truck Operator." Article 23 of said agreement involves promotions. The issue of sex discrimination was not decided by the arbitrator. The Court concludes that major aspects of this complaint were either not submitted to arbitration or were beyond the arbitrator's power of decision.

It is, therefore, Ordered that defendant's motion for summary judgment be denied and that plaintiff's motion to strike defendant's third affirmative defense be, and the same is hereby, granted.

● ● ●

CASE QUESTIONS

1. What was the issue in this case?

2. How does the judge view the arbitration process as a means of protecting the rights of the employees?

3. What was the issue in the arbitration case?

FAIR EMPLOYMENT PRACTICES

9

Fair Employment Practices is a term used to describe the body of laws, regulations, and executive orders which are designed to reduce discrimination in employment. Since there are many different sources of these regulatory laws, investigation becomes complicated. The basic federal law in this body is the Civil Rights Act of 1964, Title VII. Another regulatory law is the 1967 Age Discrimination in Employment Act which provides protection against discrimination to those in the forty-sixty age bracket. In an attempt to use the great purchasing power of the federal government, Executive Orders 11246 and 11141 prohibit employment discrimination by contractors or subcontractors on construction of federal projects. In a positive step to protect federal employees, Executive Order 11478 prohibits discrimination in hiring and awarding promotions on the basis of race, color, religion, sex, or national origin.

State laws also provide some protection for employees engaged in intrastate commerce. Since state legislators are often under great pressures from pro-business sources, state laws to protect employees frequently have been weak and/or not enforced vigorously. However, today's employees or job applicants may find that several possible avenues of protection open to them in their search for fair employment opportunities. The federal and the state governments have created join filing procedures for helping employees and applicants. Often this help is available without charge to the employee or applicant when there is reasonable cause to bring an action against an employer. Such help may come from civil rights commissions and fair employment practices agencies at either the state or local level.

THE EMPLOYMENT SETTING

Some selectivity on the basis of personal characteristics is lawful, and some is not. The main guideline throughout the fair employment cases is that the employer must establish a relationship between a job requirement and on-the-job performance. This is technically known as a *bona fide occupational qualification* or *bfoq*. The general concept is that employees should have the mental and physical skills to do the job. Employers must be allowed to manage their businesses and seek profits in the private sector. The difficulty lies in drawing the distinction between those skills which would *improve* performance beyond the minimum and those which are actually *required* to reach minimum performance.

For example, if a person is applying for a job as a salesman in a national food company, the job could be examined and those skills which are job related could be determined.

Job Performances	*Knowledge/Skills*
1. Explain technical engineering	1. Engineering or technical training.
2. Drive an automobile.	2. Manual/mental skills.
3. Sell to customers.	3. Psychological skills in listening or persuasion.

The first two job-performance requirements are more measureable. A familiarity with engineering terms may have been self-taught or acquired in other job experiences. Thus, an engineering degree is not required. Some measurement of the applicant's engineering knowledge is possible. Driving a car can be measured through the performance test required for a driver's license.

The ability to sell is the complicated issue. Selling is a general ability which is difficult to define. Selling is influenced by many intangibles, such as a sense of humor, dress, and style. There are different types of selling. Some require great technical skills; others involve merely taking orders for products which have been largely presold. If the position basically requires someone to take orders, then employers face possible discrimination charges if they have very high requirements for applicants in terms of education, training, and experience in sales.

PUBLIC EMPLOYEES

The concept of competitive examinations and fairness is a keystone in most civil service systems. The 1972 amendments to the 1964 Civil Rights Act take direct steps to include federal, state, and local government employees under the Title VII non-discrimination protection. Executive Order 11478 states that it is the government's policy to provide equal opportunity in federal employment regardless of race, color, religion, sex, or national origin. The U.S. Civil Service Commission is charged with enforcing the 1972 amendments as they apply in federal government. Executive Order 11141 states that the federal government will present equal employment opportunities to people of all ages. The Equal Pay Act excludes the federal government employee from its coverage.

At the state level government employees may find protection in state civil service commission regulations. Local goverment employees may be protected by ordinances, or in some cities by a separate municipal civil service commission which issues regulations. State employees may seek equal protection by using the Fourteenth Amendment to the U.S. Constitution which forbids states to act without due process. Suits may also come from state constitutional guarantees.

Many of the practical problems of obtaining equal opportunity for public employees are similar to those of private employees or applicants. There are financial problems of obtaining legal assistance and fears of reprisals on the job. Employee organizations are taking a stronger role now that third-parties may file on behalf of the person alleging employment discrimination.

ADMINISTRATIVE PROCEDURES

Administrative law is different from the normal statutory process. Administrative law treats agencies as a novel form of regulation. The people through their elected representatives place certain safeguards on the administrative law process. These safeguards include requiring a clear statement to the public of the jurisdiction of the agency, its internal procedure for accepting complaints, and its adjudiciation process. Often, an administrative agency is created which is staffed by a mixture of administrative and legal personnel. The administrative personnel usually do the field investigation, and the legal staff acts as administrative law judge or counsel in court actions.

A telephone call is usually the first contact between a fair employment practices agency and an employer. The call informs the employer that a complaint has been lodged against him and is now being investigated.

After the telephone contact, the field investigator requests a meeting with the employer's representative at the employer's office or some mutually acceptable place. At this first meeting the complaint is read to the employer's representative, and an answer is requested. The employer's representative may choose to answer or simply deny the allegations. Often there is some informal bargaining between the parties as well as a re-statement of the facts as both parties see them. This may end the investigation if there does not seem to be any merit to the complaint.

Administrative procedures in the area of fair employment practices are complex. They are designed to be fair to all parties. However, there is a gray area where the rights of the employer, the applicant or employee, and the public begin to overlap. The public has the right to have fair employment practice law enforced. The applicant/employee has the right to be considered for work on an equal basis other people—skills and ability to be the deciding factors. The employer has the right to avoid harrassment and wasted time.

ENFORCEMENT PROCEDURES

The enforcement procedures are complicated. The first complication comes from the application of administrative law by the Equal Employment Opportunity Commission. There are internal regulations which require that the agency act as both the investigative and the judicial branch in the complaint cases. There are internal safeguards, but problems of maintaining fairness arise since the two functions are not separate.

To begin an enforcement proceeding, a complaint must be filed in writing, signed, and sworn to before a notary public or some other authorized individual. The charge should contain basic information: the names and addresses of all parties, a clear statement of the allegation, and information about any other legal actions which may have been started against this employer. It is standard procedure for federal authorities to defer to the state agency, if there is one, for sixty days to allow them to settle the case or produce a compromise. Because of this deferrence, many states have adopted procedures which are similar to those of EEOC; these states are called *deferral states*. As of 1973 thirty-seven states had agencies to enforce fair employment practices legislation.

During the sixty-day period, the EEOC waits. If no state action is taken, then the EEOC begins the investigation phase. If reasonable cause is determined by the Commission, then a formal attempt at conciliation is made. If conciliation efforts are unsuccessful, the EOCC files suit in the federal district court.

INTRODUCTION TO THE CASES

The *Xerox* case provides an excellent example of the total proceedings in an Equal Employment Opportunity case. The plaintiff sues defendant, Xerox Corporation and some of its officers, for alleged acts of discrimination and finally termination of employment. *Daugherty* v. *Continental Can* discusses problems of back pay.

XEROX CASE COMMENT

The sequence of events in this case is especially important.
1. Plaintiff contacts the California Fair Employment Practices Commission for help.
2. The California Fair Employment Practices Commission, after a time, terminates its proceedings which allows the Equal Employment Opportunity Commission to enter the case.
3. The case can now come to the Federal District Court with the Equal Employment Opportunity Commission joining with plaintiff in the action against Xerox Corporation and some of its officers.

An interesting part of the case concerns the facts which the plaintiff added in his written charge against the corporation. The defendant corporation argues that the plaintiff did not follow proper procedures and, therefore, has missed his opportunity to sue. This is related to the practical matter of how well an employee can understand the legal requirements of making a discrimination charge and whether the federal court can allow any amendment of the complaint. Note that the court is concerned with allowing a plaintiff to add defendants to a lawsuit when they were *not* named in the earlier Fair Employment Practices case. The concern is with the principle that individuals have a right to know the circumstances so that they defend their reputation in this charge.

On the issue of damages, the plaintiff is asking for back pay, reinstatement of his job, special damages for pain and suffering, and punitive damages. The court looks at the history of the Civil Rights Act in Congress and the analogies to the National Labor Relations Act in answering the question of damages.

The plaintiff tries to make use of the 1866 Civil Rights Act, Section 1981. The problem with this argument is that the court finds that there was no discrimination against the plaintiff due to his race, which is Caucasian. The protection of that earlier statute would have expanded the possible remedies allowed to the plaintiff against Xerox Corporation.

The final issue before the court concerns a claim for emotional distress under a California law. The federal court has to decide whether joining a state and a federal claim will confuse the jury. If not, hearing all the issues at one time will constitue more efficient justice.

DAVE VAN HOOMISSEN, PLAINTIFF AND EQUAL EMPLOYMENT OPPORTUNITY COMMISSION v. XEROX CORPORATION ET AL.

United States District Court, Northern District of California
No. C-73-0423 December 19, 1973

• • •

[Statement of Case]

CARTER, Ch. J.: Defendant Xerox and the nine individual defendants in this case have moved the Court to dismiss plaintiff's complaint and to strike each of its counts.

Plaintiff Van Hoomissen is suing defendants for various alleged acts of retaliation, to wit: denial of job advancement opportunities with the accompanying salary increases, demotion, and finally, termination of employment. The alleged retaliation was in response to plaintiff's asserted attempts to change the hiring policy of Xerox, which he believes discriminates against Mexican Americans at its Mountain View, California, plant. Plaintiff is seeking compensatory and punitive damages, in addition to back pay and reinstatement in an appropriate job position. He has been joined in the suit by the Equal Employment Opportunity Commission (hereinafter EOCC) as plaintiff-intervenor.

Count One of plaintiff's complaint is based on § 704(a) of Title VII of the 1964 Civil Rights Act (42 U.S.C. 2000e-2 (a)). Count Two is based on 42 U.S.C. § 1981, while Count Three originally rested upon the Unruh Civil Rights Act of California (*Calif. Civil Code §§ 51 and 52*). Plaintiff has conceded that a cause of action under the Unruh Act cannot be maintained . . . but now prays leave to amend his complaint to state a cause of action for intentional infliction of emotional distress under California law as a pendant state claim. . . .

Count One

A. The Jurisdictional Issue

The Court will first examine defendants' contentions as to Count One, plaintiff's alleged cause of action under Title VII. Defendants first claim that the Court lacks jurisdiction over the subject matter since plaintiff did not properly allege in his complaint that the California Fair Employment Practices Commission (FEPC) ever had jurisdiction over plaintiff's charge as required under 42 U.S.C. 2000e-5(c). The statute also requires that the FEPC must terminate its proceedings on the complaint and refer the charge back to the EEOC before the EEOC can act on the charge.

It was agreed by counsel in oral argument that an amendment to the complaint alleging appropriate dismissal of the action by the FEPC would remedy this jurisdictional defect; such an amendment was made by plaintiff on November 10, 1973. Therefore, the Court now considers that it has jurisdiction of this count of plaintiff's complaint.

B. Discharge is Within the Scope of the EEOC Charge

Defendants' more important contention in regard to Count One is that the issue of Van Hoomissen's alleged discharge by Xerox is improperly before this Court. Defendants argue that, since the discharge itself was not mentioned in either charge lodged with the EEOC, it cannot be litigated here.

In his first charge to the EEOC dated August 3, 1971, plaintiff stated that he was being retaliated against for encouraging minority hiring at Xerox by the withholding of a sales bonus of $4794.00. Apparently this bonus was later paid, according to plaintiff's Complaint (XI(2)). Plaintiff also stated that he was attaching other papers to his charge outlining his allegations of retaliation by Xerox Corporation against him and the discrimination practiced by Xerox against Chicanos at the Mountain View plant.

Plaintiff did in fact attach to his charge part of a letter which he had sent to the President of the "BPG Division" of Xerox, a Mr. J. P. O'Neill, one of the named defendants herein. In that letter, plaintiff alleged that a Mr. Jim Noren, a branch manager, and also one of the individual defendants, "denied opportunities to me for personal growth" (i.e. promotional opportunities) because of plaintiff's efforts to boost minority hiring. Plaintiff also stated in that letter that he "was threatened with termination by management" because he attempted to seek "remedial action" in the matter of minority hiring (Charge of Discrimination and Attachments, Exhibits to Defendants' Motions to Dismiss and Strike, July 12, 1973).

On March 14, 1972, plaintiff filed another charge with the EEOC, stating simply:

> "I believe I was retaliated against and am still subject to retaliation because I have protested discrimination and have filed a charge of discrimination. This was done to me by depriving me of my full salary compensation." (*Id.*)

Plaintiff was then allegedly fired June 30, 1972.

Although the specific event of termination was not listed by plaintiff in either EEOC charge, plaintiff did state in his attached letter to the August 3 charge that he was "threatened with termination" and alleged continuing retaliation in the March 14 charge. The EEOC thus had notice of a potential continuing threat of termination.

Here, the Commission's investigation of plaintiff's claims of retaliation as outlined in his charges and attachments filed with the EEOC would have led it to examine an alleged potentially varied series of efforts by Xerox to retaliate against plaintiff caused by plaintiff's efforts to boost minority hiring. The retaliation charged by plaintiff was continuous; dismissal of plaintiff should be viewed as the final link in the chain of retaliation alleged by plaintiff.

Courts construing Title VII suits have been reluctant to allow procedural technicalities of pleading to ban potentially just claims. "Consequently, courts confronted with procedural ambiguities in the statutory framework have, with virtual unanimity, resolved them in favor of the complaint party." (*Sanchez* v. *Standard Brands, Inc., supra,* at 461).

Therefore, the subject of plaintiff's alleged discharge by Xerox is properly within the scope of his two EEOC charges, which claimed continuous retaliation by defendant Xerox and members of its management staff resulting in, among other things, loss of pay and loss of promotion.

C. The Individual Defendants

In plaintiff's complaint, in addition to defendant Xerox, plaintiff names nine individual defendants. All defendants have moved to dismiss the nine individuals from the suit on the ground that none were named by Van Hoomissen in the two charges he filed with the EEOC. The appropriate statute provides that, once a charge is made against an employer, the employer shall be served a notice of the charge by the EEOC and that the EEOC shall make an investigation thereof (42 U.S.C. 2000e-5(b)). 42 U.S.C. 2000e-5(f)(1) then provides that, within the appropriate time period and after the necessary administrative procedures have been followed, "a civil action may be brought against the respondent named in the charge . . . ." The question here is whether 42 U.S.C. 2000e-5(f)(1) should be narrowly interpreted or liberally construed, and if liberally construed the minimum boundaries that should be imposed.

As was described in the section above, two of the individual defendants, O'Neill and Noren, were named in *attachments* to the first EEOC charge filed by plaintiff. On the one-page charge form itself, in answer to the question: "Who discriminated against you?" plaintiff listed only "Xerox Corporation." However, under "Explain what unfair thing was done to you," plaintiff summarized the attachments, pages of a letter to O'Neill in which Noren's name prominently figured.

The courts, as noted above, have generally attempted to construe Title VII in a liberal fashion. In view of this trend, it seems to the Court that the charge and its attachments should be considered as a unit by the Court when determining the proper defendants in this matter.

Case law on the specific point here under discussion is scarce; neither plaintiff's nor defendants' citations are helpful. The court in *Bowe v. Colgate-Palmolive,* [2EPD § 10,090] 416 F. 2d 711 (7th Cir. 1969) constructed what is perhaps the most helpful, although admittedly sketchy, legal framework concerning the question of adding defendants not named in an EEOC charge to a Title VII suit: "It is a jurisdictional prerequisite to the filing of a suit under Title VII that a charge be filed with EEOC against the party sought to be sued. This provision serves two important purposes. First, it notifies the charged party of the asserted violation. Secondly, it brings the charged party before the EEOC. . . ." (at 719). The practical question left open by the *Bowe* court is how strictly form must be adhered to when filing an EEOC charge. Must the plaintiff, in order to properly file the charge against the party sought to be sued, place the appropriate answer after the correct question on the one page charge sheet, or is some deviation from form allowed as long as the charging party includes all necessary facts in a way that is intelligible and meaningful to the EEOC?

Here, once again, the *Sanchez* court is helpful in spotlighting the issue:

". . . the crucial element of a charge of discrimination is the *factual* statement contained therein. Everything else entered on the form is, in essence, a mere amplification of the factual allegations . . . In the context of a statute like Title VII it is inconceivable that a charging party's rights should be cut off merely because he fails to articulate correctly the legal conclusions emanating from his factual allegations" (431 F. 2d at 462).

The plaintiff in the case at bar, a layman, may have assumed that his answer to the question, "Who discriminated against you?"—"Xerox Corporation"—would encompass those employees of Xerox whom he mentions by name in his attachments to the charge. (Plaintiff should not have assumed, however, that the blanket accusation against Xerox would enable him subsequently to sue other employees of Xerox whom he had never named in those papers filed with the EEOC.) Plaintiff's factual allegations regarding O'Neill and Noren seem sufficiently complete to bring them to the EEOC's attention as possible Title VII violators upon its reading the charge and attachments. Thus, the two legal requirements set up by the *Bowe* court should, in theory, have been fulfilled in the instant case: (1) by his factual allegations contained in the Explanation and attachments, plaintiff notified the EEOC of his charges against O'Neill and Noren; (2) if the EEOC properly investigated the allegations made by plaintiff in his first charge, O'Neill and Noren should have been given notice of the investigation and of the alleged charges pertaining to them.

Whether in fact the EEOC did investigate the charges against both men and so notify them is an evidentiary question which can be resolved at the time of trial. If O'Neill and Noren are then able to demonstrate that no such investigation was made, and thus no notice was given prior to the serving of the court suit upon them, they may at that time move again for their dismissal from the case.

However, the Court agrees with defendants that the seven other individuals are not proper parties in this suit. According to plaintiff's complaint all hold posts with Xerox Corporation; Mr. McColough is Chairman of the Executive Committee; Mr. LaHue is Western Regional Manager; Mr. Hurley is a San Francisco Branch Manager; Mr. Judd is now a San Jose Branch Manager; Mr. Erickson and Mr. Sutter are Area Sales Managers, and Mr. Weinrich is an "employee." None of these people seem to be immediately connected with the Mountain View Branch; even if they are, the Court can find no reference to them individually anywhere in plaintiff's two charges or attachments. The Court does not feel that the liberality with which it may construe 42 U.S.C. 2000e-5(f)(1) stretches so far as to include as defendants in this suit seven persons whose only visible common denominator appears to be their employer—Xerox. Without any further indication by plaintiff as to some other connection between himself and the seven defendants in terms of this suit, it seems inappropriate in this instance to retain jurisdiction over the suit, as suggested by the parties, and to hold it in abeyance while plaintiff gives proper notice to the EEOC. Therefore, the seven defendants—McColough, La Hue, Hurley, Judd, Erickson, Sutter and Weinrich will be dismissed from the case with prejudice.

D. The Question of Damages

Defendants have challenged plaintiff's claim for compensatory and exemplary damages as inappropriate under Title VII. Plaintiff estimates his compensatory (or special) damages at $967,000 and his damages for pain and suffering at $100,000. He prays for relief in the sum of $926,516 compensatory damages and asks for $2,000,000 in punitive damages.

The relevant section of Title VII, 42 U.S.C. 2000e-5(g) (inclusive of the 1972 amendment), reads:

> "If the Court finds that respondent has intentionally engaged in or is intentionally engaging in an unlawful employment practice charged in the complaint, the court may enjoin the respondent from engaging in such unlawful employment practice, and order such affirmative action as may be appropriate, which may include, but is not limited to, reinstatement or hiring of employees, with or without back pay . . . *or any other equitable relief as the court deems appropriate. Back pay liability shall not accrue from a date more than two years prior to the filing of a charge with the Commission. Interim earnings . . . shall operate to reduce pay otherwise allowable."*

The question of the propriety of punitive and compensatory damages in Title VII cases has only recently arisen in the courts, and the results have been mixed.

Some courts have held that punitive damages are an appropriate form of relief in a Title VII cases, e.g., *Tooles v. Kellogg,* [4 EPD § 7661] 336 F. Supp. 142 (Neb. 1972) (court struck claim for compensatory relief but allowed claim for punitive damages to be retained).

Compensatory damages have also been allowed, e.g. *Tidwell v. American Oil Co.,* [4 EPD § 7544] 332 F. Supp. 424 (Utah 1971) (plaintiff allowed 6% interest on back wages and contributions defendant would have made to group life insurance plan and company savings); *Rosen v. Public Service Electric and Gas Co.,* [5 EPD § 8499] 477 F. 2d 90 (3rd Cir. 1973) (male employees who received reduced retirement benefits where women in the same position were awarded full benefits received the difference).

Other cases have refused to award any monetary damages other than back pay on the theory that the statute speaks of back pay only as an additional and limited remedy to equitable relief, e.g. *Johnson v. Georgia Highway Express, Inc.,* [2 EPD § 10,119] 417 F. 2d 1122 (5th Cir. 1969) ("The demand for back pay is not in the nature of a claim for damages but rather is an integral part of the statutory equitable relief," 417 F.2d at 1125).

After examining the lengthy legislative history of Title VII, in addition to the briefer history surrounding the 1972 amendments, this Court finds that Congress, when it drew up that part of the statue dealing with remedies for unlawful employment practices, had in mind a wide panorama of equitable tools that courts might use but did not intend that courts might use but did not intend that courts would punish defendants by imposing upon them large money awards in the form of compensatory or punitive damages.

Although the 1964 discussion in Congress regarding Section 2000e-5 (g) is not terribly illuminating, it does seem apparent from a reading of the Congressional debates and the legislative record that the main purpose of Title VII as seen by its proponents was to "seek to give people an opportunity to be hired on the basis of merit" (remarks by Senator

Humphrey in introducing the Civil Rights Bill for debate in the Senate on March 30, 1964, 110 *Cong. Rec.* 6549). According to the House Report *on the Bill,* "(t)he purpose of this title is to eliminate, through the utilization of formal and informal remedial procedures, discrimination in employment" (House Report No. 914, 1964 *U.S. Code Cong. and Admin. News* 2401). Additional members of the House Committee which wrote that Report referred to the Commission, the administrative body which would in large part carry out the purpose of the Title, as an agency which would work in a corrective, not a punitive, manner:

> "It must . . . be stressed that the Commission must confine its activities to correcting abuse, not promoting equality with mathematical certainty . . . Its primary task is to make certain that the channels of employment are open to persons regardless of their race" (*Id.* at 2516).

Again in 1972, when the amendment giving the Commission power to go into court on its own was being debated, the Title was again referred to primarily as a tool to ensure that opportunities for employment, were in fact equal: it was not described as a punitive measure against those who frustrated equal employment.

> "Most people just want to work. That is all . . . We are trying to see that all of us, no matter what race, sex, or religious or ethnic background, will have an equal opportunity in employment."
> (Representative Dent, 118 *Cong. Rec.* 1866-67, March 8, 1972).

In that 1972 debate, the concerns of Congress in amending 42 U.S.C. 2000e-5(g) revolved around the specific terms of the one money remedy allowed under the act—back pay. One Report makes note that, in debating the amendment to 2000e-5(g), the Senate had suggested that back pay be accruable not longer than two years prior to filing with the Commission; the House had argued for two years prior to filing with the court. The Senate prevailed (Joint Explanation Statement of Managers . . . , 1972 *U.S. Code Cong. and Admin. News 2183*).

The Senate analysis of the 1972 amendment to 2000e-5(g) accurately reflects the current sense of unease and uncertainty over the use of punitive damages in Title VII cases:

> "The provisions of this subsection are intended to give the courts wide discretion exercising their equitable powers to fashion the most complete relief possible. In dealing with the present section 706 (g) the courts have stressed that the scope of relief . . . is intended to make the victims of unlawful discrimination whole . . . (and restore them) to a position where they would have been were it not for the unlawful discrimination."
> (118 *Cong. Rec.* 3462.)

In one breath the Senators note that the equitable powers given to the courts are extremely broad; in the next they speak rather imprecisely of making a person "whole." What is intended by that second goal? The problem mirrored here has been a source of confusion among the district courts.

However, in addition to the general legislative history which indicates that the remedies intended were those provided for in 2000e-5(g), there are further factors which lead this Court to believe that Congress meant what it said in 2000e-5(g) and that it meant no more.

The provisions of 2000e-5(g) of Title VII are modeled closely upon the National Labor Relations Act, 28 U.S.C. 160(b) and 160(c). In 28 U.S.C. 160(c), the remedies provided for are "affirmative action including reinstatement of employees, with or without back pay." Punitive damages cannot, and have not been, awarded under this Act (*Consolidated Edison Co. v. NLRB,* [1 LC § 17,038] 305 U.S. 197, 235-236 (1938)). Neither have compensatory damages, aside from back pay, been allowed.

In explaining and introducing the Civil Rights Bill, Senator Humphrey in his address and Senators Clark and Case as Floor Managers refer to the fact that the relief under Title VII is similar to that available under the National Labor Relations Act (100 *Cong. Rec.* 6549, *and* 110 *Cong. Rec.* 7214). Although not conclusive, the similarity of the two statutes and the fact that Congress was aware that neither punitive nor compensatory damages were allowed under the National Labor Relations Act leads to the firm belief that Congress did not intend that any money damages other than back pay would be granted under the present statute.

Perhaps even more illuminating on the question of the scope of damages in Title VII is the fact that Title VIII, which deals with fair housing and is part of the same 1964 Civil Rights Act, now specifically provides for punitive damages (in the maximum amount of $1000) as the result of a 1968 amendment (82 Stat. 88, April 11, 1968, 42 U.S.C. 3612(c)). When the 1972 amendment was made to Title VII, the Title VIII amendment was already law, yet no such parallel provision for punitive damages was included, even though *other amendments* to the remedies section were made. No reference has been made in either the Title VII or the Title VIII statutes to compensatory damages.

Plaintiff argues that in several instances courts have awarded punitive damages where none were authorized by statute upon findings that such damages effectuate the purpose of the statute. ... Plaintiff suggests that Title VII is an appropriate statue to enforce by use of punitive damages.

However, in the majority of cases where such relief was given (usually in 42 U.S.C. 1982 and 1983 cases), the rationale has been that, where the statute speaks only in the most general of remedial terms, or in no terms at all, the federal common law allows the court to award punitive damages if such award carries forth the purpose of the statute. In the present case, however, we have a statute which is quite specific in the remedies it provides. This Court believes it would be beyond the scope of its power to find other remedies contained in that statute where none seemingly exists.

Therefore, the Court will strike from the complaint plaintiff's prayers for both compensatory and punitive damages on the ground that such relief is not provided for under Section 2000e-5(g) of Title VII.

Count Two

A. Can Plaintiff sue under 42 U.S.C. § 1981?

Count Two of the complaint is based upon Section 1981 of the 1866 Civil Rights Act, which states that "All persons within the jurisdiction of the United States shall have the same right in every State and Territory to make and enforce contracts, to sue, be parties, give evidence, and to the full and equal benefit of all the laws and proceedings for the security of persons and property as is enjoyed by white citizens . . ." Defendants move to strike this Count from the complaint.

Plaintiff and plaintiff-intervenor EEOC argue at length that plaintiff, a white male who is alleging retaliation by his employer because of plaintiff's attempts to encourage minority hiring by that employer, should be able to sue under Section 1981. This section has frequently been applied to acts of private racial discrimination in employment (*Macklin v. Spector Freight Systems, Inc.,* [5 EPD §8605] 478 F.2d 979 (D.C. Cir. 1973) and citations contained therein).

In the last few years, a goodly number of legal pages have been devoted to arguing the validity of a white person's standing to sue under Section 1981. Many cases hold that a white plaintiff cannot bring suit under Section 1981 because, in fact, he has not usually suffered any detriment *due to his race*. . . . Other cases have held further that a white person can *never* have standing to sue under Section 1981 since the section was designed to protect non-whites only. . . .

Only in a few cases have whites actually been permitted to bring an action under Section 1981; the two most frequently cited cases are *Central Presbyterian Church v. Black Liberation Front,* 303 F. Supp. 894 (E. D. Mo. 1969) and *Gannon v. Action,* 303 F. Supp. 1240 (E. D. Mo. 1969). In both these cases, however, the court allowed suit under Section 1981 because of the alleged infringement upon white plaintiffs' property rights; these were not employment discrimination cases.

The opinion of Judge Peckham in *N. O. W. v. Bank of California.—* F. Supp.—, 5 EPD § 8510 (N. D. Cal. 1973) provides a close parallel to this case and is helpful in resolving the issue. There plaintiff, a white male, was allegedly fired solely because he "sought to affect the participation of the Bank in the racially discriminatory practices of the Jonathan Club" (at 7442). Although attracted by what he termed the "better view"—to read Section 1981 as broadly as possible—Judge Peckham decided that he must adhere to the Ninth Circuit's unrepudiated holding in *Agnew v. City of Compton,* 239 F. 2d 226 (9th Cir. 1956) *cert. denied* 353 U.S. 959, that Section 1981 can only be sued upon when "appellant was deprived of any right which, under similar circumstances, would have been accorded a person of a different race" (*supra* at 230). Thus Judge Peckham held that the Court cannot allow a white plaintiff standing under Section 1981 when he has suffered a deprivation which was not the result of his race. This Court feels equally obliged to follow the reasoning put forth by Judge Peckham in this matter.

In the present suit, the "better view" referred to by Judge Peckham is vigorously asserted by plaintiff and plaintiff-intervenor as a basis for granting plaintiff standing in this suit. They argue that the line of cases which deal with Section 1982 of the 1866 Civil Rights Act and allow white plaintiffs standing to sue should be expanded to encompass Section 1981. In three leading cases, *Sullivan v. Little Hunting Park,* 396 U.S. 229 (1968), *Jones v. Alfred H. Mayer Co.,* [1 EPD §9832] 392 U.S. 409 (1968) and *Walker v. Pointer,* 304 F. Supp. 56 (1969), white persons who alleged interference with their *own* property rights as the result of discrimination against black persons were allowed standing under Section 1982.

The Ninth Circuit in *Trafficante v. Metropolitan Life Insurance Co.,* 446 F. 2d 1158 (9th Cir. 1971) approved this line of cases by positing a general thesis that, when a white person suffers some "racially motivated interference with his property rights," he has standing to sue under Section 1982. When the *Trafficante* decision was appealed to the Supreme Court, the Court in a footnote expressly reserved any ruling on the question of standing under Section 1982 (409 U.S. 205, at 209, n. 8, 34 L. Ed. 415 at 419, n. 8 (1973).

If a white person has standing to sue under Section 1982 when he suffers interference to his property rights due to racially motivated conduct (the *Trafficante* formula), should that right be expanded to include the companion statute, Section 1981, when a plaintiff suffers a direct injury to his *employment* as a result of racially motivated conduct? Most courts have refused to so expand the concept (see text and citations above at pages 16-17 [p. 67911]) and, as noted above, in the two cases which *have* allowed white persons standing under 1981, that standing was really predicated upon the interference by defendants with plaintiffs' *property* rights, not with their employment.

Therefore, as a result of the analysis *supra,* this Court does not believe it should expand the *Trafficante* formula to allow plaintiff standing under Section 1981. The Supreme Court's refusal to review the *Trafficante* holding on this point indicates to this Court that the matter should be left in *status quo* until further word from the Supreme Court is heard on this most difficult issue. Thus the Court holds that plaintiff, a white male, has no standing to sue under Section 1981, and that Count Two must be stricken from the complaint.

Count Three

Plaintiff has asked leave to amend Count Three to add a claim for intentional infliction of emotional distress under California law as a pendent claim, rather than alleging a cause of action under the Unruh Act. Although the Court has the power to hear a pendent state claim, it also has the discretion to refuse to hear it if it believes that sufficient reasons (such as possible jury confusion or variance in the scope of the issues) militate against joining a state claim to the federal cause of action *(United Mine Workers of America v. Gibbs,* [53 LC § 11,135] 383 U. S. 715 (1966)). Since the Court has stricken plaintiff's claims for punitive damages under Count One, the Court feels that it would be inconsistent with, and beyond the scope of, plaintiff's claim under Title VII to allow plaintiff to litigate the question of punitive damages by amending his complaint to bring in a state claim. Consequently, the Court will refuse to allow plaintiff to amend his third cause of action to add a pendent state claim for intentional infliction of emotional distress.

Accordingly, It Is Ordered that defendants' motion to strike the subject of plaintiff's discharge from the complaint be, and hereby is denied;

It Is Further Ordered that defendants' motions to dismiss defendants O'Neill and Noren are, and each of them is, hereby denied; while defendants' motions to dismiss defendants McColough, La Hue, Hurley, Judd, Erickson, Sutter, and Weinrich are, and each of them is, hereby granted with prejudice, and the action is hereby dismissed with prejudice as to each and all of the seven above-named defendants;

It Is Further Ordered that defendants' motion to strike plaintiff's claims for compensatory and punitive damages under Count One be, and hereby is, granted, and the allegations and claims set forth in paragraphs XVI, XVII, XVIII, and parts F and G of XXVI are hereby stricken from the complaint;

It Is Further Ordered that defendants' motions to strike Count Two, wherein plaintiff alleges a cause of action under 42 U.S.C. § 1981 be, and hereby is, granted, and Count Two is hereby stricken from the complaint;

It Is Further Ordered that leave to amend Count Three by plaintiff be, and hereby is, denied, and Count Three is hereby stricken from the complaint.

• • •

CASE QUESTIONS

1. Why was the chairman of Xerox Corporation sued as an individual? What did the court rule on suing the chairman?

2. How much in damages was the court willing to allow the plaintiff? Why?

DAUGHERTY CASE COMMENT

The problem of the Equal Pay Act in Pennsylvania, *Daugherty et al. v. Continental Can Company,* illustrates the mixed nature of the protection given individuals. This is a state court case where the plaintiffs are seeking back pay. The Pennsylvania court must examine its own line of case law and the rationale of the arguments.

The company's action in this case was held to be acceptable, probably to the surprise of many of the participants. It was an unexpected way of handling the problem of the men receiving more than the women for similar work. Note that while the court comments on the nature of the plaintiff's argument in a positive way, the decision hinged on the reading of the statute.

HAROLD DAUGHERTY ET AL.
v. CONTINENTAL CAN COMPANY, INC.
Pennsylvania State Superior Court, December 11, 1973
On Appeals from Pennsylvania Court of Common Pleas,
Allegheny County

• • •

[Statement of Case]

SPAETH, J.: This is an appeal from orders granting a compulsory nonsuit in two assumpsit actions. Appellant (plaintiffs below) are fifty-seven men and women who were employed by appellee, the Continental Can Co., Inc. (hereafter "Continental"), at its Hazel-Atlas Glass Division in Washington, Pennsylvania, from May, 1962, until February, 1964, when Continental sold its business. Appellants are seeking back wages, an equal amount in liquidated damages, and other sums allegedly due them under the Equal Pay Law, Act of Dec. 17, 1959, P. L. 1913, § 1, 43 P. S. § 336.1 *et seq.,* as amended by the Act of July 31, 1968, P. L. 869, No. 262, § 1, 43 P. S. § 336.3 *et seq.* (Supp. 1973), which in pertinent part read as follows:

> No employer shall discriminate in any place of employment between employees on the basis of sex by paying wages to any employe at a rate less than the rate at which he pays wages to employees of the opposite sex for work under comparable conditions on jobs the performance of which requires comparable skills, except where such payment is made pursuant to a seniority training or merit increase system which does not discriminate on the basis of sex. § 3, 43 P. S. § 336.3.

[*Background*]

If appellants' claims are to be understood, some background must be stated. Under the terms of a collective bargaining agreement between Continental and appellants' duly recognized bargaining agent, the Glass Bottle Blowers Association of the United States and Canada (hereinafter "the Union"), selector-packers were paid at a base hourly rate of $1.965 if they were men, but $1.77 an hour if they were women; the men also received more per hour in bonus pay than the women. Because of this disparity, in 1960 some of the female employees filed an action under the Equal Pay Law in the Court of Common Pleas of Washington County. The lower court sustained Continental's preliminary objection on the ground that, since the Union represented both male and female employees, the collective bargaining agreement constituted a waiver of the plaintiffs' rights under the Equal Pay Law. This court affirmed. ...

By memorandum dated March 13, 1962, effective May 1, 1962, the Union entered into an agreement providing for discontinuance of bonus plans and of all male classifications that duplicated female classifications. Thus, male selector-packers were classified the same, and received the same lower rate of pay, as female selector-packers. In addition, Continental offered to all employees whose bonus plans had been abolished an added 10½¢ per hour on the condition that the employee sign a waiver of any and all claims he or she might have under the Equal Pay Law. As a result, the maximum wage rate for selector-packers was a uniform $1.875 per hour.

[*Reduction of Wages*]

The actions now before this court were filed on March 4, 1963. Each proceeds on the theory that an employer who has been guilty of wage discrimination cannot bring himself into compliance with the Equal Pay

Law by reducing the wage rate of the group that he formerly favored or by paying both groups at some in between rate; rather he must increase the wage rate of the group that he has discriminated against, making it the same as the rate at which he paid the favored group. Because the statute provides that "[a]ny action pursuant to the provisions of this act must be brought within one year from the date upon which the violation complained of occurs," § 5(b), 43 P. S. § 336.5(b), the actions relate only to the period from March 5, 1962 through March 4, 1963. They were submitted together, on the pleadings and stipulated facts. The trial judge granted Continental's motions for compulsory non-suit and denied appellants' request to amend their complaints to include violations occurring after May 1, 1963. A court en banc affirmed.

Because we find that the lower court properly granted Continental's motions for compulsory non-suit, we do not reach the question whether appellants should have been permitted to amend their complaints.

[Equal Pay Goals]

Appellants place heavy emphasis on the goals that equal pay legislation might have. Among the possible goals the following four seem to be the most prominent: to end wage discrimination practiced against female employees performing tasks comparable to those performed by male employees; to improve the financial status of female employees by assuring them salaries equal to those paid male employees performing comparable tasks; to strengthen the job security of male employees who face the threat of replacement by lower paid female employees; and to improve the financial condition of male employees who, faced with competition from lower paid female employees, accept lower wages for themselves. With the identification of these goals, appellants reason as follows: To permit an employer to lower the wages paid to males as a means of ending a wage pattern that discriminated against females ends the discrimination by wiping out any disparity between the wages paid males and females, but it does not improve the economic lot of the females, and it puts the males in a worse financial position than before. Paying a sum somewhere between that formerly paid males and that formerly paid females is of some benefit to the females, but not to the males. If an employer were required to raise the salaries of the females, however, all four of the goals would be accomplished.

One difficulty with this argument is that it ignores the fact that there is no provision in the Equal Pay Law that to comply with the statute an employer must raise the wages paid female employees against whom he has discriminated, and we cannot add "a requirement which the legislature did not see fit to include." ...

Nor is there any ambiguous language in that statute that provides an excuse for reading into it a requirement such as appellants advance. The Equal Pay Law is violated when an employer "discriminate[s] . . . by paying wages to any employe at a rate less than the rate at which he pays wages to employes of the opposite sex" for comparable work. After Continental lowered the wages paid its male employees, it was no longer acting in violation of the statute. The words of the statute leave no doubt about that; they are free from obscurity and ambiguity and are incapable of two or more meanings. If it were otherwise, we would be required to rely on legislative intent in choosing among the possible meanings. See *Philadelphia v. Scholler,* 148 Pa. Superior Ct. 276, 281, 25 A. 2d 406, 409 (1942). In the absence of ambiguity, however, we have no occasion to be concerned with legislative intent. It is an established rule of statutory construction that "[w]hen the words of a statute are clear and free from all ambiguity, the letter of it is not to be disregarded under the pretext of pursuing its spirit." 1 Pa. S. § 1921 (1973).

In addition, in 1968, the following provision was added to the Equal Pay Law:

> Provided that any employer who is paying a wage rate differential in violation of this subsection shall not, in order to comply with the provisions of this subsection, reduce the wage rate of any employee. § 1, 43 P. S. § 336.3(a) (Supp. 1973).

As noted in *Funk v. Buckley & Co., Inc.,* 158 Pa. Superior Ct. 586, 593, 45 A. 2d 918, 921-22 (1946):

> A material change of the language of an original act always indicates a legislative intent to effect a change of legal rights. ... And a radical change in the phraseology of a statute . . . is a legislative declaration that the law so amended did not as originally framed embrace the amending provision. ...

Even if we were free to interpret the statue with reference to its possible goals, we would not be obliged to hold that an employer must increase the wages of employees against whom he has discriminated. It would be sufficient if we merely read the statute as barring wage discrimination based on sex. Perhaps the General Assembly intended only this narrow goal for the Equal Pay Law. This was in any event its "primary purpose." ... It must be remembered that the Equal Pay Law is not a minimum wage law. Pennsylvania has since 1937 had a minimum wage law covering women. ... The Minimum Wage Law fixes the wage rates of certain workers; nothing indicates that the Equal Pay Law was intended to duplicate this function. Viewing the Equal Pay Law merely as an antidiscrimination law leaves an employer with some flexibility in the event he cannot financially raise the wages of the group against whom he has discriminated. Consider the following statement made by Elizabeth S. Johnson, Director of the Bureau of Women and Children of the Pennsylvania Department of Labor and Industry, before the Select Subcommittee on Labor of the House Committee on Education and Labor, on the administration of the Equal Pay Law:

> In spite of our success in a few cases, we have not been able to move forward as effectively as the problem calls for. Where the size of the wage differential or the number of workers involved is small, adjustments to secure compliance are not usually difficult to arrange.
>
> The big problem comes when the number and proportion of workers affected is high and the size of the wage differential is large. The problem may be further compounded when a corporation's plants are operating in several States and management can shift production from one state to another.

The department of labor and industry has not yet succeeded in getting compliance in several cases of clear-cut violation for this reason. In one Pennsylvania plant of a corporation with plants in other States, 441 women are being paid approximately 20 cents per hour less than 239 men in the same occupation—a major one in the business.

To immediately raise the women's rates to the men's would increase the annual wage cost by $176,000 a year. The manufacturer threatened to move his Pennsylvania production to newer facilities in other States. The department consented to allow the company some time to come into compliance by transferring the men to other jobs.

However, the location of the plant and the relatively few openings for men in other occupations and the union security rights created problems that have made this approach to compliance impracticable.

I might add, also, that many people would question the propriety of considering any such adjustment a proper one, but we were in a difficult position because we did not want to see the men put out on the streets. *Hearings on H. R. 898 and H. R. 10266, supra* note 3, at 125.

There should be a clear indication that the legislature wanted to limit the options of employers, before the Equal Pay Law is read to require higher wages for some workers. There is none.

The orders of the court below are affirmed.

● ● ●

CASE QUESTIONS

1. How does Pennsylvania state law about equal pay compare to federal law?

2. What options does a company have in removing any pay bias in its compensation system?

WAGE AND HOUR LAWS 10

Wage and hour laws developed out of the constitutional jurisdiction of the Federal government to regulate interstate commerce. The passage of the Fair Labor Standards Act of 1938 [Public Law 718, 75th Congress] was a significant step in providing administrative machinery for the control of hours of work and wage rates. The actual determination of the coverage of the Act is a complex matter because the Act has been regularly amended, and it may apply to widely different factual situations. The statute is divided into basic parts covering eligibility for minimum wages, computation of overtime pay, protection of children, equal pay for equal work, and government contractors.

The trend since 1938 has been to expand the protection of the wage and hour laws. A 1966 amendment expanded the coverage to include hospitals and schools operated by the states or local governments. In 1974 the minimum wage rates were revised, and the jurisdiction expanded to include state, local, and municipal workers. Such changes are important not only for their immediate impact, but because they force management to re-evaluate their wage and salary systems.

Children have been exempted from the coverage of the law when working on a family-owned delivering newspapers, acting, working after school on a farm not owned by the family, and making evergreen wreaths. The ages partially exempted are the fourteen to sixteen and sixteen to eighteen year old groups. For those in the fourteen to sixteen bracket, the work must be retail, food service, or gasoline service stations. The intent of the regulations is to limit employment to low-risk jobs. In the sixteen to eighteen age bracket, the child may not be employed in work held to be hazardous by the Secretary of Labor. Examples of hazardous work are coal mining, working in a sawmill, or doing excavation work. At eighteen the worker is considered an adult.

ADMINISTRATIVE PROCEDURES

The Wage and Hour Administrator is subject to the control of the Secretary of Labor. Employees are assigned to field and headquarters locations to answer questions from the public, to investigate complaints, and to gather evidence for possible court determinations. The major offices follow the majority of the population so that the large cities have the larger offices. The office staff is made up of technical, clerical, and legal employees plus the local director. Coordination is through the Regional Office and the Washington, D.C. headquarters.

ROUTINE INVESTIGATIONS

The administrative staff is able to enter a business to check that records are being kept on the basic payroll data for the prior three years and that supplementary records are being kept two years. In addition to this routine checking, the investigations staff may talk with some employees to listen to possible complaints. Where possible, state officials are brought in and a joint check may be conducted. If the employer refuses entry, the administrator can request a subpoena to see the records.

EMPLOYEE COMPLAINTS

Complaints may be made orally or in writing. The person bringing the complaint will contact a member of the Division staff telling his name, employer's name, alleged errors such as mispayment, employment of youth, and dates. An investigative officer is assigned to the case. The employer will be requested to comply with the inspection and investigation on a voluntary basis. During the investigation the employee bringing the complaint may have to be present, but he is protected by the broad provisions of the act against any reprisal. The inspector may transcribe portions of the employer's records to support the claim or to close the case as not justified.

The regional office may request a subpoena from Washington if the employer refuses to cooperate. This written order allows access to the employer's records. The employer may challenge the subpoena by administrative and judicial means.

Most administrative agencies try for an informal settlement of the case. This saves time and effort for all the parties. If the employer agrees that a mistake was made, a consent judgment is entered and back pay is ordered. An employee action may be brought in federal or state courts to recover back wages. The employees have the burden of proof and must comply with the procedural requirements of whatever court they choose. In bringing suit, they are limited to recovering the amount of actual lost wages, reasonable attorney's fees, and the cost of the court actions. Only one suit is possible in the matter. Therefore, if the Secretary of Labor elects to bring suit on behalf of the employees, the employees may not bring any other actions. The presiding judge has the authority to reduce the monetary award if it is found that the defendent employer was acting in good faith and was relying on the advice of the Wage and Hour Administrator or agents of that office.

EQUAL PAY FOR EQUAL WORK

The general intent of the act is to reduce pay differentials unless the employer can show that they are related to productivity and not to any intent to discriminate. Most people covered under the Fair Labor Standards Act and the minimum wage standards are covered by the equal pay provisions. The 1972 amendments included white collar workers and outside salesmen in the equal protection against discrimination because of sex when work is performed under similar working conditions requiring equal skill, effort, and responsibility.

The employer still has the option to use pay systems with differentials so long as they do not rely on sex differences. The employer is allowed to use sensitory merit methods which measure earnings by quantity or quality or production, and other systems which do not use sex as a factor. The same procedures to enforce the Fair Labor Standards Act are applied to the equal pay questions.

INTRODUCTION TO THE CASES

The famous landmark case of *United States* v. *Darby* upheld the constitutionality of the Fair Labor Standards Act. The arguments present issues requiring a balancing of the rights and interests of the federal government and those of the several states. The *Jacksonville Paper Company* involves an application of the principles established in *Darby*. The court examines the facts of the case to see if the temporary shipment of the goods to a warehouse is enough to find that the goods are no longer in interstate commerce.

Maryland v. *Wirtz* (1968) involves an attempt to overturn the extension of the Fair Labor Standards Act to schools and hospitals. Arguments relating to the boundaries of the United States Constitution's commerce power clause are raised. Justice Douglas in his dissent argues that no more extensions of federal jurisdiction should be allowed. The 1966 amendments are upheld by the majority of the court. In *C & P Shoe Corporation* the U.S. Supreme Court applies the *Jacksonville* rule to a different set of facts.

The brief *Note Cases* at the end of this chapter illustrate some of the unusual turn of events which the law cannot change. The *Breitwieser* v. *KMS Industries, Inc.* case shows a void in legal coverage which produces a seemingly unjust result. The parents of a deceased minor employee killed in a forklift accident try to sue for civil money damages. It is an action for wrongful death because the boy was too young to operate that equipment, and such operation was in violation of a specific U.S. Department of Labor regulation about hazardous work. The case examines the limited protection of the State of Georgia's workmen's compensation laws.

Three employees and their boss are the participants in the *Hatton* case. The issues focus on defining what business Hatton is actually doing and if the business comes under the "enterprise coverage."

The *American Concrete Construction Co.* case illustrates the requirement that the payroll records be kept as a matter of law and good business practice. The *Griffin and Brand* case examines the technical issues of independent contractor status for crew leaders working on farms. The issues are important in determining who is the employer and whether the foreman or the farm owner is obligated to pay minimum wages for the farm workers.

UNITED STATES v. DARBY
United States Supreme Court
312 U.S. 100 (1940)

● ● ●

MR. JUSTICE STONE delivered the opinion of the Court.

The two principal questions raised by the record in this case are, *first,* whether Congress has constitutional power to prohibit the shipment in interstate commerce of lumber manufactured by employees whose wages are less than a prescribed minimum or whose weekly hours of labor at that wage are greater than a prescribed maximum; and, *second,* whether it has power to prohibit the employment of workmen in the production of goods "for interstate commerce" at other than prescribed wages and hours. A subsidiary question is whether in connection with such prohibitions Congress can require the employer subject to them to keep records showing the hours worked each day and week by each of his employees including those engaged "in the production and manufacture of goods to-wit, lumber, for 'interstate commerce.'"

Appellee demurred to an indictment found in the district court for southern Georgia charging him with violation of § 15(a) (1) (2) and (5) of the Fair Labor Standards Act of 1938; 52 Stat. 1060, 29 U.S.C. § 201, *et seq.* The district court sustained the demurrer and quashed the indictment, and the case comes here on direct appeal under § 238 of the Judicial Code as amended, 28 U.S.C. § 345, and § 682, Title 18 U.S.C., 34 Stat. 1246, which authorizes an appeal to this Court when the judgment sustaining the demurrer "is based upon the invalidity or construction of the statute upon which the indictment is founded."

The Fair Labor Standards Act set up a comprehensive legislative scheme for preventing the shipment in interstate commerce of certain products and commodities produced in the United States under labor conditions as respects wages and hours which fail to conform to standards set up by the Act. Its purpose, as we judicially know from the declaration of policy in § 2(a) of the Act, and the reports of Congressional committees proposing the legislation . . . is to exclude from interstate commerce goods produced for the commerce and to prevent their production for interstate commerce, under conditions detrimental to the maintenance of the minimum standards of living necessary for health and general well-being; and to prevent the use of interstate commerce as the means of competition in the distribution of goods so produced, and as the means of spreading and perpetuating such substandard labor conditions among the workers of the several states. The Act also sets up an administrative procedure whereby those standards may from time to time be modified generally as to industries subject to the Act or within an industry in accordance with specified standards, by an administrator acting in collaboration with "Industry Committees" appointed by him.

Section 15 of the statute prohibits certain specified acts and § 16(a) punishes willful violation of it by a fine of not more than $10,000 and punishes each conviction after the first by imprisonment of not more than six months or by the specified fine or both. Section 15 (1) makes unlawful the shipment in interstate commerce of any goods "in the production of which any employee was employed in violation of section 6 or section 7," which provide, among other things, that during the first year of operation of the Act a minimum wage of 25 cents per hour shall be paid to employees "engaged in [interstate] commerce or the production of goods for [interstate] commerce," § 6, and that the maximum hours of employment for employees "engaged in commerce or the production of goods for commerce" without increased compensation for overtime, shall be forty-four hours a week. § 7.

Section 15(a) (2) makes it unlawful to violate the provisions of § § 6 and 7 including the minimum wage and maximum hour requirements just mentioned for employees engaged in production of goods for commerce. Section 15(a) (5) makes it unlawful for an employer subject to the Act to violate § 11(c) which requires him to keep such records of the persons employed by him and of their wages and hours of employment as the administrator shall prescribe by regulation or order.

The indictment charges that appellee is engaged, in the State of Georgia, in the business of acquiring raw materials, which he manufactures into finished lumber with the intent, when manufactured, to ship it in interstate commerce to customers outside the state, and that he does in fact so ship a large part of the lumber so produced. There are numerous counts charging appellee with the shipment in interstate commerce from Georgia to points outside the state of lumber in the production of which, for interstate commerce, appellee has employed workmen at less than the prescribed minimum wage or more than the prescribed maximum hours without payment to them of any wage for overtime. Other counts charge the employment by appellee of workmen in the production of lumber for interstate commerce at wages at less than 25 cents an hour or for more than the maximum hours per week without payment to them of the prescribed overtime wage. Still another count charges appellee with failure to keep records showing the hours worked each day a week by each of his employees as required by § 11(c) and the regulation of the administrator, Title 29, Ch. 5, Code of Federal Regulations, Part 516, and also that appellee unlawfully failed to keep such records of employees engaged "in the production and manufacture of goods, to-wit lumber, for interstate commerce." . . .

The Act is sufficiently definite to meet constitutional demands. One who employs persons, without conforming to the prescribed wage and hour conditions, to work on goods which he ships or expects to ship across state lines, is warned that he may be subject to the criminal penalties of the Act. No more is required. *Nash* v. *United States,* 229 U.S. 373, 377.

We have considered, but find it unnecessary to discuss other contentions.

Reversed.

• • •

CASE QUESTIONS

1. What did the court indicate was the Congressional purpose of the minimum wage law?

2. The court says that there is now a definite change in its thinking. What was the previous position and what is the change?

3. The Georgia company argued that it cannot be forced to keep records about its payroll and its shipments. What did the court say in reply?

4. The defendant says that the law is too vague to be enforced against him. What did the court say?

WALLING, U.S. DEPARTMENT OF LABOR v.
JACKSONVILLE PAPER COMPANY
United States Supreme Court
317 U.S. 564 (1943)

• • •

MR. JUSTICE DOUGLAS delivered the opinion of the Court.

This is a suit brought by the Administrator to enjoin Respondent from violating provisions of the Fair Labor Standards Act. . . . Respondent is engaged in the wholesale business, distributing paper products and related articles. Its business covers a large area embraced within a number of states in the southeastern part of the country. The major portion of the products which it distributes comes from a large number of manufacturers and other suppliers located in other states and in foreign countries. Five of Respondent's twelve branch houses deliver goods to customers in other states, and it is not contended that the Act does not apply to delivery employees at those establishments. The sole issue here is whether the Act applies to employees at the seven other branch houses which, though constantly receiving merchandise on interstate shipments and distributing it to their customers, do not ship or deliver any of it across state lines.

Some of this merchandise is shipped direct from the mills to Respondent's customers. Some of it is purchased on special orders from customers, consigned to the branches, taken from the steamship or railroad terminal to the branches for checking, and then taken to the customer's place of business. The bulk of the merchandise, however, passes through the branch warehouses before delivery to customers. There is evidence that the customers constitute a fairly stable group and that their orders are recurrent as to the kind and amount of merchandise. Some of the items carried in stock are ordered only in anticipation of the needs of a particular customer as determined by a contract or understanding with Respondent. Frequently orders for stock items whose supply is exhausted are received. Respondent orders the merchandise and delivers it to the customer as soon as possible. Apparently many of these orders are treated as deliveries from stock in trade. Not all items listed in respondent's catalogue are carried in stock but are stocked at the mill. Orders for these are filled by respondent from the manufacturer or supplier. There is also some evidence to the general effect that the branch manager before placing his orders for stock items has a fair idea when and to whom the merchandise will be sold and is able to estimate with considerable precision the immediate needs of his customers even where they do not have contracts calling for future deliveries.

The District Court held that none of Respondent's employees in the seven branch houses in question was subject to the Act. The Circuit Court of Appeals reversed. 128 F.2d 395. (1) It held that employees who are engaged in the procurement or receipt of goods from other states are "engaged in commerce" within the meaning of § 6(a) and § 7(a) of the Act. (2) It also held that where Respondent "takes an order" from a customer and fills it outside the state and the goods are shipped interstate "with the definite intention that those goods be carried at once to that customer and they are so carried, the whole movement is interstate" and the entire work of delivery to their final destination is an employment "in commerce." Those were the only types of transactions which the court held to be covered by the Act.

The Administrator contends, in the first place, that under the decision below any pause at the warehouse is sufficient to deprive the remainder of the journey of its interstate status. In that connection it is pointed out that prior to this litigation Respondent's trucks would pick up at the terminals of the interstate carriers goods destined to specific customers, return to the warehouse for checking and proceed immediately to the customer's place of business without unloading. That practice was changed. The goods were unloaded from the trucks, brought into the warehouse, checked, reloaded, and sent on to the customer during the same day or as early as convenient. The opinion of the Circuit Court of Appeals is susceptible of the interpretation that such a pause at the warehouses is sufficient to make the Act inapplicable to the subsequent movement of the goods to their intended destination. We believe, however, that the adoption of that view would result in too narrow a construction of the Act. It is clear that the purpose of the Act was to extend federal control in this field throughout the farthest reaches of the channels of interstate commerce. There is no indication (apart from the exemptions contained in § 13) that, once the goods entered the channels of interstate commerce, Congress stopped short of control over the entire movement of them until their interstate journey was ended. No ritual of placing goods in a warehouse can be allowed to defeat that purpose. The entry of the goods into the warehouse interrupts but does not necessarily terminate their interstate journey. A temporary pause in their transit does not mean that they are no longer "in commerce" within the meaning of the Act. As in the case of an agency, ... if the halt in the movement of the goods is a convenient intermediate step in the process of getting them to their final destinations, they remain "in commerce" until they reach those points. Then there is a practical continuity of movement of the goods until they reach the customers for whom they are intended. That is sufficient. Any other test would allow formalities to conceal the continuous nature of the interstate transit which constitutes commerce.

The fact that all of Respondent's business is not shown to have an interstate character is not important. The applicability of the Act is dependent on the character of the employees' work. ...

If a substantial part of an employee's activities related to goods whose movement in the channels of interstate commerce was established by the test we have described, he is covered by the Act. ... The question of the Act's coverage depends on the special facts pertaining to the particular business. ... We merely hold that the decision of the Circuit Court of Appeals as construed and modified by this opinion states the correct view of the law. As so modified, the judgment below is

Affirmed.

• • •

CASE QUESTIONS

1. There are some important factual matters in this case relating to the issues. What was the movement of goods under discussion? What was important about the warehousing of the goods?

2. The facts seem to show that some of the company business was clearly intrastate. What did the Court say about that?

MARYLAND ET AL. v.
WIRTZ, SECRETARY OF LABOR, ET AL.
United States Supreme Court
392 U.S. 183 (1968)

• • •

MR. JUSTICE HARLAN delivered the opinion of the Court.

As originally enacted, the Fair Labor Standards Act of 1938 required every employer to pay each of his employees "engaged in commerce or in the production of goods for commerce" a certain minimum hourly wage, and to pay at a higher rate for work in excess of a certain maximum number of hours per week. The Act defined the term "employer" so as to exclude "the United States or any State or political subdivision of a State. ..." This case involves the constitutionality of two sets of amendments to the original enactment.

In 1961, Congress changed the basis of employee coverage: instead of extending protection to employees individually connected to interstate commerce, the Act now covers all employees of any "enterprise" engaged in commerce or production for commerce, provided the enterprise also falls within certain listed categories. In 1966, Congress added to the list of categories the following:

"(4) is engaged in the operation of a hospital, an institution primarily engaged in the care of the sick, the aged, the mentally ill or defective who reside on the premises of such institution, a school for the mentally or physically handicapped or gifted children, an elementary or secondary school, or an institution of higher education (regardless of whether or not such hospital, institution, or school is public or private or operated for profit or not for profit)."

At the same time, Congress modified the definition of "employer" so as to remove the exemption of the States and their political subdivisions with respect to employees of hospitals, institutions, and schools.

The State of Maryland, since joined by 27 other States and one school district, brought this action against the Secretary of Labor to enjoin enforcement of the Act insofar as it now applies to schools and hospitals operated by the States or their subdivisions. The plaintiffs made four contentions. They argued that the expansion of coverage through the "enterprise concept" was beyond the power of Congress under the Commerce Clause. They contended that coverage of state-operated hospitals and schools was also beyond the commerce power. They asserted that the remedial provisions of the Act, if applied to the States, would conflict with the Eleventh Amendment. Finally, they urged that even if their constitutional arguments were rejected, the court should declare that schools and hospitals, as enterprises, do not have the statutorily required relationship to interstate commerce. ...

We noted probable jurisdiction of the plaintiffs' appeal, 389 U.S. 1031. For reasons to follow, we affirm the judgment of the District Court.

I.

We turn first to the adoption in 1961 of the "enterprise concept." Whereas the Act originally extended to every employee "who is engaged in commerce or in the production of goods for commerce," it now protects every employee who "is employed in an enterprise engaged in commerce or in the production of goods for commerce," Such an enterprise is defined as one which, along with other qualifications, "has employees engaged in commerce or in the production of goods for commerce. ..." Thus the effect of the 1961 change was to extend protection to the fellow employees of any employee who would have been protected by the original Act, but not to enlarge the class of *employers* subject to the Act.

In *United States* v. *Darby,* 312 U.S. 100, this Court found the original Act a legitimate exercise of congressional power to regulate commerce among the States. Appellants accept the *Darby* decision, but contend that the extension of protection to fellow employees of those originally covered exceeds the commerce power. We conclude, to the contrary, that the constitutionality of the "enterprise concept" is settled by the reasoning of *Darby* itself and is independently established by principles stated in other cases.

The Fair Labor Standards Act, including the present "enterprise" definition of coverage, may also be supported by two propositions. One is identical with the first proposition supporting the NLRA: strife disrupting an enterprise involved in commerce may disrupt commerce. The other is parallel to the second proposition supporting the NLRA: there is a basis in logic and experience for the conclusion that substandard labor conditions among any group of employees, whether or not they are personally engaged in commerce or production, may lead to strife disrupting an entire enterprise.

It is clear that labor conditions in schools and hospitals can affect commerce. The facts stipulated in this case indicate that such institutions are major users of goods imported from other States. For example:

> "In the current fiscal year an estimated $38.3 billion will be spent by State and local public educational institutions in the United States. In the fiscal year 1965, these same authorities spent $3.9 billion operating public hospitals. ...

> "For Maryland, which was stipulated to be typical of the plaintiff States, 87% of the $8 million spent for supplies and equipment by its public school system during the fiscal year 1965 represented direct interstate purchases. Over 55% of the $576,000 spent for drugs, x-ray supplies and equipment, and hospital beds by the University of Maryland Hospital and seven other state hospitals were out-of-state purchases." ...

We think the District Court was correct in declining to decide, in the abstract and in general, whether schools and hospitals have employees engaged in commerce or production. Such institutions, as a whole, obviously purchase a vast range of out-of-state commodities. These are put to a wide variety of uses, presumably ranging from physical incorporation of building materials into hospital and school structures, to over-the-counter sale for cash to patients, visitors, students, and teachers. Whether particular institutions have employees handling goods in commerce, cf. *Walling* v. *Jacksonville Paper Co.,* 317 U.S. 564, may be considered as occasion requires.

The judgment of the District Court is
Affirmed.

MR. JUSTICE MARSHALL took no part in the consideration or decision of the case.

MR. JUSTICE DOUGLAS, with whom MR. JUSTICE STEWART concurs, dissenting.

The Court's opinion skillfully brings employees of state-owned enterprises within the reach of the Commerce Clause; and as an exercise in semantics it is unexceptionable if congressional federalism is the standard. But what is done here is nonetheless such a serious invasion of state sovereignty protected by the Tenth Amendment that it is in my view not consistent with our constitutional federalism. ...

If all this can be done, then the National Government could devour the essentials of state sovereignty, though that sovereignty is attested by the Tenth Amendment. ... As Mr. Chief Justice Stone said . . . the National Government may not "interfere unduly with the State's performance of its sovereign functions of government." 326 U.S., at 587. It may not "impair the State's functions of government," *id.,* at 594 (dissenting opinion of MR. JUSTICE DOUGLAS, joined by MR. JUSTICE BLACK). As Mr. Justice Frankfurter observed, "[t]here are, of course, State activities . . . that partake of uniqueness from the point of view of intergovernmental relations." *Id.,* at 582.

Whether, in a given case, a particular commerce power regulation by Congress of state activity is permissible depends on the facts. The Court must draw the "constitutional line between the State as government and the State as trader. ..." In this case the State as a sovereign power is being seriously tampered with, potentially crippled.

I would reverse the judgment below.

• • •

CASE QUESTIONS

1. What are the amendments at issue in this case?

2. What factual evidence was introduced about the extent to which the schools and hospitals deal in interstate commerce?

3. Consider the dissent of Justice Douglas in the 1968 case. Was it a prediction of future changes?

MITCHELL, SECRETARY OF LABOR v.
C & P SHOE CORPORATION
United States Court of Appeals, Fifth Circuit
286 F.2d 109 (1960)

• • •

RIVES, Circuit Judge.

One of these consolidated cases was brought by the Secretary of Labor under Section 17 of the Fair Labor Standards Act . . . to enjoin appellee from violating the minimum wage, overtime, record-keeping, and child labor provisions of the Act. The other five cases were brought under Section 16(c) of the Act . . . to recover unpaid minimum wages and unpaid overtime compensation claimed to be due and owing to 33 present and former employees. Defendant concedes that it has not complied with the minimum wage and overtime requirements of the Act. It contends, however, that the Act was inapplicable to the employees for whose benefit the action was brought. The trial court agreed, and entered judgment for the defendant.

Appellee, C & P Corporation, and its four subsidiary corporations own and operate twenty retail shoe stores within the State of Florida. C & P also owns and operates a central office and warehouse in Fort Lauderdale, Florida. The employees whose activities are involved in this case work in and about the Fort Lauderdale warehouse. Substantially all of the shoes which are sold at retail by the C & P chain are first received at the Fort Lauderdale warehouse from manufacturers and suppliers located outside the State of Florida. At the warehouse, the shoes are unloaded, and a receiving list is prepared, noting the types, sizes, and styles of shoes received. This list is sent to the office, where distribution sheets are then prepared designating those stores which will receive the shoes. The cartons in which the shoes arrive are then broken down and the shoes separated in accordance with the distribution sheet. The shoes are "tagged" with a price and code number and shipped on to the retail stores. About half the shoes are distributed immediately following their receipt at the warehouse. The remainder are stacked in the warehouse, where a 30-day inventory is maintained.

The determination of this case centers on an interpretation of Walling v. Jacksonville Paper Co., 1943, 317 U.S. 546, 568, 63 S.Ct. 332, 335, 87 L.Ed. 460, wherein the Supreme Court noted:

> "The entry of the goods into the warehouse interrupts but does not necessarily terminate their interstate journey. A temporary pause in their transit does not mean that they are no longer 'in commerce' within the meaning of the Act. ... if the halt in the movement of the goods is a convenient intermediate step in the process of getting them to their final destinations, they remain 'in commerce' until they reach those points. Then there is a practical continuity of movement of the goods until they reach the customers for whom they are intended. That is sufficient. Any other test would allow formalities to conceal the continuous nature of the interstate transit which constitutes commerce."

This is the test we must apply in determining whether the shoes came to rest when they were deposited on the receiving platform of the C & P warehouse by the interstate truckers or whether the shoes remained in commerce when the employees on whose behalf the Secretary here sues performed their services on, or in connection with, the shoes. ... The district court found: "No ordering is ever done by the retail stores. ... The decisions as to what shoes shall be sent to and sold in the retail stores are made in the defendant's central office and warehouse. ... No shoes are ever purchased on the basis of any prior order from . . . any customer or retail store in the chain."

Category two in the Jacksonville Paper case consisted of goods "obtained by the wholesaler from the manufacturer or supplier to meet the needs of specified customers pursuant to some understanding with the customer...." The court below found that "no shoes are ever purchased on the basis of . . . any contract with . . . any customer or retail store in the chain, or pursuant to any understanding with any customer, or with any individual retail store in the chain. ..."

Under such findings, the district court held that the Secretary has not brought C & P within the scope of the first two categories. As to the contention under the third category, that the shoes are "in commerce" in the C & P warehouse only because the shoes were brought into the warehouse "based on anticipation of the needs of specific customers," the district court found "while the needs of individual retail stores are never considered, except on an over-all chain basis, goods are ordered, received and stored in the warehouse in anticipation of the needs of the stores." Since the customers to whom the shoes would be shipped were identifiable when the shoes were ordered from the manufacturer, [The court below found that "one hundred per cent (100%) of the shoes which are handled [in the C & P warehouse] *are ordered* with the intention that they ultimately will be sold through the defendant's retail stores."], (Brackets added). It would appear that the Secretary has brought the activities at the C & P warehouse into the confines of the third category treated in the Jacksonville Paper case. The Sixth Circuit, 136 F.2d 75, 77, noted, (([g]oods in the third category are not necessarily in commerce after receipt by the wholesaler. They are said to remain in commerce only when the evidence with particularity shows them to be different from goods acquired and held by a local merchant for local disposition." We think it is evident that the "holding of the shoes at the C & P warehouse was unlike the "holding by a local merchant for local disposition." We believe that this latter class is composed largely of merchants who offer their wares to the public or trade at large, as the Jacksonville Paper Company did. Contrast that enterprise with the C & P warehouse. The C & P warehouse made no effort to sell to non-owned retailers. It was, instead, an agency of the C & P Shoe Company which existed for the sole purpose of storing and distributing shoes to its wholly-owned retail stores.

Nor need we base this judgment on such a narrow ground. To apply the categories established in *Jacksonville Paper, supra,* to a chain store warehouse would be to elevate form above substance. Where, as in *Jacksonville Paper,* we deal with a wholesaler and numerous independent retailers, it is reasonable to look for formal orders, contracts, and understandings between the parties. But, where retail units are owned by the wholesaler, as here, such formal dealings are usually absent. This is so because the same party or parties control both and set policy for both. In the case at bar, the General Manager supervised both the buying of the shoes and their distribution to the retail units. To expect the General Manager to send formal orders to himself, as manager of the warehouse, or to contract with himself where he represents both the management of the wholesaler and the retailers would be the ultimate in artificiality.

The defendant urges that the five actions seeking recovery of minimum wages and overtime compensation involve "an issue of law which has not been settled finally by the courts," and, hence, that the Secretary has no authority to sue. As has been aptly noted by the Fourth Circuit, an extreme application of that test "would virtually nullify the salutary provision for the recovery of unpaid compensation without expense to the claimant." We think that the issues of law in these cases were settled with reasonable finality in Walling v. Jacksonville Paper Co., supra, subject only to their application to ever-varying factual situations.

After the parties had presented their proof in this case, the court adjourned with an agreement to reconvene in two days for the purpose of receiving amendments to defendant's answers and stipulations as to the amounts which would be due certain employees if they were found covered by the Act. At this hearing the court relieved the defendant of its stipulation that four employees had filed claims with the Secretary of Labor for unpaid compensation. The effect of this action was to oust the Secretary of the authority to press their claims. The ground that the defendant advanced for this relief was that he had the impression that the four employees were present in the courtroom at the opening of the trial, when, in fact, as he learned later in the day, they were "far away." His position was that he only agreed to stipulate what the government was in a position readily to prove.

The court below had discretion to "relieve counsel of stipulations to prevent manifest injustice." What manifest injustice was prevented by the court's action in this case is not altogether clear. But, in view of the fact that the Secretary made no offer of proof that his representation of these employees was valid at the time the defendant was pressing for relief from the stipulation, we cannot say that the court below abused its discretion in taking such action.

Because of the view it took of the matter, the court below made no findings on the question of whether the individual plaintiffs devoted a "substantial" part of their work to the interstate operations of the C & P Shoe Corporation. Since it is the activities of the particular employee, rather than the employer, which determine coverage, we remand the case for such findings together with the determination of other issues left open by this appeal.

Reversed and remanded

• • •

CASE QUESTIONS

1. What was the major claim of the employees in this case?

2. What did the Court of Appeals have to say about the *Jacksonville Paper Company* case?

3. In what way was the present warehousing operation different from the *Jacksonville* case?

4. What did the Court decide in the case?

BREITWIESER v. KMS INDUSTRIES, INC.,
United States Court of Appeals, Fifth Circuit
467 F.2d 1391 (1972)

● ● ●

Diversity action to recover from employer, under Georgia wrongful death law and Fair Labor Standards Act, for death of plaintiffs' 16-year-old son, who dies when forklift truck he was allegedly driving in scope of his employment overturned. The United States District Court for the Northern District of Georgia, William C. O'Kelly, J., dismissed federal claim and rendered summary judgment for defendant on state law claim, and plaintiffs appealed. The Court of Appeals, Thornberry, Circuit Judge, held that child labor provisions of Fair Labor Standards Act and implementing administrative regulations did not create private cause of action for damages against employer for wrongful death of 16-year-old boy, who dies when forklift truck, which he was allegedly driving in course of his employment in violation of administrative regulation declaring operation of a high lift forklift truck to be an occupation particularly hazardous for employees under age of 18, overturned; fact that death award under state Workmen's Compensation Law amounted to only $750 did not justify creation of a new federal remedy in addition to substantial criminal penalties provided in Act.
Affirmed.

Wisdom, Circuit Judge, dissented and filed opinion.

● ● ●

BRENNAN, SECRETARY OF LABOR, v. HATTON, INDIVIDUALLY AND DOING BUSINESS AS AIR CONTROL ENGINEERING COMPANY
United States Court of Appeals, Fifth Circuit
No. 72-2703, February 27, 1973

● ● ●

Action was brought by Secretary of Labor to enjoin defendant, individually and as commercial employer, from violating minimum wage and overtime provisions, of Fair Labor Standards Act. The United States District Court for the Southern District of Texas, Owen D. Cox, J., found that defendant was not within coverage of Act, and denied requested relief, and plaintiff appealed. The Court of Appeals held that defendant was not exempt from Act's requirements solely because it was engaged in only one business. In addition, the court held that the business of installing, repairing and maintaining air-conditioning and heating system, including duct work, in residental properties is an enterprise engaged in business of construction or reconstruction or both within meaning of Act. Furthermore, the court held that employer meet other requirements necessary for "enterprise coverage."

Reversed and remanded.

• • •

HODGSON, SECRETARY OF LABOR, v.
AMERICAN CONCRETE CONSTRUCTION CO., INC.
United States Court of Appeals, Sixth Circuit
No. 72-1577, January 17, 1973

• • •

Civil suit was brought by Secretary of Labor to enjoin corporate construction contractor and its president from violating overtime pay provisions of Fair Labor Standards Act, and to require payment of earned but withheld overtime compensation to particular employees. The United States District Court for the Southern District of Ohio, Robert B. Krupansky, J., dismissed complaint except insofar as it charged maintenance of inadequate records and ordered future maintenance of such records as required by law, and the Secretary appealed. The Court of Appeals, Hastie, Senior Circuit Judge, held that there was abundant testimony of substantial overtime work and deliberate withholding of at least half of the earned overtime pay, so as to overcome motion to dismiss. In addition, the Court held that where employer's records were inaccurate or inadequate and employee could not offer convincing substitutes the solution was not to penalize the employee by denying him any recovery.

Judgment vacated and cause remanded.

• • •

HODGSON, SECRETARY OF LABOR, v.
GRIFFIN AND BRAND OF McALLEN, INC.
United States Court of Appeals, Fifth Circuit
No. 72-2441, January 4, 1973

• • •

Action to enjoin defendant from violating minimum wage, record-keeping, and child labor provisions of Fair Labor Standards Act. The United States District Court for the Southern District of Texas, at Brownsville, Reynaldo G. Garza, J., rendered judgment for plaintiffs and granted an injunction and defendant appealed. The Court of Appeals, Thornberry, Circuit Judge, held that evidence supported finding that fruit and vegetable company, which engaged field workers through "crew leaders," was a joint employer for Fair Labor Standards Act purposes.

Affirmed.

• • •

At first tort law was the only real cause of action that an employee had when working conditions were unsafe or detrimental to health. Then the adoption of workmen's compensation statutes and social security protection created a "no-fault" type of insurance-based system where payment for some losses was a matter of right. State governments funded safety and health programs with some states providing more funds than others. By 1970 there was an upward trend in the frequency and severity of rates for injury and illness in American industry. Through the joint efforts of labor union leaders, corporate officials, and public officials, the 1970 Occupational Safety and Health Act became law. The Act was a drastic change from the policy which allowed state control in safety and health matters. A new administrative unit was formed within the U.S. Department of Labor to help the states plan their own legislative efforts and to supply the necessary initial funding. The overall plan anticipated separate passage of state plans so that state compliance officers could enforce the law. The key phrase was that state plans must be "equal to or more effective than the federal law."

OCCUPATIONAL SAFETY AND HEALTH ACT

There was mixed feeling about the Occupational Safety and Health Act (OSHA). Some labor leaders spoke out against the proposed state plans calling them ineffective and weak. At the national level union officials publicly said that they would oppose the acceptance of weak state plans or poorly funded state efforts. Each state accepted planning grants to develop acceptable pieces of legislation. The problem was getting the legislation approved by the state legislatures. There was constant friction among management organizations, state officers, and union representatives. By 1974 about one-half of the states had passed some type of legislation, but most of the statutes did not meet the high expectations of the originators of OSHA. Funding has been less than expected and even the promise of shared federal funds has not increased the total expenditures to any great degree. A few states have increased their own jurisdiction following intense lobbying efforts by the AFL-CIO.

THE LAW BEFORE AND AFTER OSHA

In every state the common law provided for tort recovery of damages due to negligence of the employer. Proving negligence has always been difficult; employer defenses include: wilful misconduct, the fellow-servant rule, and contributory negligence. Under the wilful misconduct rule, recovery was denied if a company rule was broken. When the fellow-servant rule was applied to a case, recovery was denied because another employee injured the co-worker. Contributory negligence blocked recovery if the injured employee was himself negligent, even if only in a mior context. Circumstances such as these made recovery difficult and eventually led to the no-fault workmen's compensation statutes.

Under the workmen's compensation statutes each employer of a specified size was required to pay insurance premiums to a private carrier or to a state agency. Funds for medical care, disability benefits, survivor's insurance, and death benefits came from these funds according to a specified schedule. Some additional benefits were available if the employer could be shown to have violated some specific safety regulation in that state. A schedule of benefits due claimants was passed by the state legislature; it was drawn up according to a sliding scale based on average weekly earnings, number of dependents, and minimum amount authorized. Employer compliance with the workmen's compensation programs was good since there was a monetary incentive to keep the accident and illness rate as low as possible. A good safety record meant lower premiums.

OSHA PROCEDURES

Under OSHA the administrative investigating arm is separate from the judicial function. In practice, this means that the Federal Safety and Health Compliance Officer visits the worksite, may find a serious or a non-serious violation, and may issue a citation. An expedited citation can be delegated from the area director to the Compliance Officer. The citation is reviewed by the area director, who can amend the citation or dismiss it entirely.

If an appeal is made within fifteen days after receipt of the area director's decision, this "letter of contest" is referred to a hearing judge. The U.S. Department of Labor and the employer may present any evidence or testimony about the proposed citation or the proposed fine or the suggested abatement period. Either party may appeal such a hearing judge's finding to the Review Commission. Review by the Commission is a matter of discretion. The moving party should indicate the basis of the appeal and should file an additional brief and petition, within twenty-five days of the judge's decision. The Review Commission or any Commissioner may decide to direct a review. If no action is taken on the petition, it is considered to be denied.

A case may arise under OSHA when a inspector makes an unannounced visit to the employer and requests that he be allowed to have a "walk around." At that time the employer will usually permit the inspector to come on to the company premises. The inspector will follow a set procedure of checking fire, safety, noise level, air contamitants, and walking surfaces. Part of the inspection is made visually and part includes taking samples for the industrial hygiene staff to anaylze at the laboratory at a later time. The employer representative has a right to be present at all times and to note what the inspector is doing. An employee representative, a member of the union or just an appointed individual may be present.

At the meeting following the inspection the employer representative and his attorney have the right to a copy of the inspection report. If the inspector issues a proposed citation, the employer will receive a copy. The amount of the citation and the abatement period may be changed after consultation with the Area Director. The citation is a dollar penalty placed upon the business for this violation. It can be from $1 to $10,000 per violation. The abatement period, the amount of working time given to the employer to correct the violation, should be adequate to allow any machine modifications or the installation of new safety equipment.

INTRODUCTION TO THE CASES

After the U.S. Department of Labor through its compliance officers and the Area Directors issues citations and penalties, the employer has fifteen working days to contest. Such a contest (objection) must be in writing. The first case, *Selchow & Righter Company,* shows a complicated history of visits, letters, and finally a hearing before the Occupational Safety and Health Review Commission. The respondent company was asking for more time to analyze the problem and also complaining that the fine was too high. Among other questions, there was a concern for the lack of the federal government's response to the company attorneys.

In *Thorleif Larsen and Son, Inc.,* the Review Commission receives the case after one of the commissioners indicates that it should go beyond the administrative law judge's analysis. The problem centers on the extent of the Review Commission's discretionary power over company attorneys and the U.S. Department of Labor.

Judicial review of the Occupational Safety and Health Review Commission's authority is the focus of the *Interstate Glass Co.* case. Here the court of appeals examines a contested citation and penalty. The *Bill Echols Trucking* case illustrates the problem of incomplete legal work on the company's part after an OSHA citation. This case helps determine the scope and impact of the Secretary's rules and the Review Commission's ability to correct field problems.

The *Note Cases* in this chapter include the *American Shipbuilding Company* case, in which the employer appealed a citation and fine by filing a notice of contest. In another hearing before the Occupational Safety and Review Commission, the *Clements Paper Company* case, a citation and proposed penalty had been vacated when the case was appealed.

The Review Commission considers an extension of time in the *Walter A. Podpora* case. In *Osborn Contracting Company* a citation is contested. And finally, in *Arizona Public Service Company,* safety rules are considered.

SECRETARY OF LABOR v. SELCHOW & RIGHTER COMPANY
OSHRC Docket No. 1057, August 28, 1972
CCH § 15191, 1972

• • •

[Text of Judge's Decision]

Citation No. I:

On February 17, 1972, the Secretary of Labor (complainant) issued a citation to Selchow & Righter Company (respondent) alleging 16 non-serious violations of Occupational Safety and Health Standards, 29 CFR 1910. Abatement periods were fixed in that citation and, also on February 17, total penalties of $185.00 were assessed.

On March 8, 1972, the respondent advised the complainant that the citation was received on that date but indicated that the fixed abatement periods did not permit time for correction and requested an extended period to repair those alleged violations not already accomplished by the date of the letter. This letter did not question the allegations of violation nor the amount of the penalty which was paid on May 10, 1972.

During the period from March 8 to May 2, 1972, the abatement periods were extended several times at the request of the respondent.

Citation No. II:

Unrelated to Citation No. I, on April 26, 1972, the complainant again cited respondent on two non-serious counts involving a waste baler machine; fixed an abatement period to expire on May 26, 1972; and assessed a penalty of $105.00. The 15 working day period to contest this citation and penalty expired on May 24, 1972, and the following is an excerpt from some of the exchanges that occurred during the period from citation to June 1, 1972:

May 1, 1972: Respondent acknowledged receipt of Citation No. II and requested a 45-day abatement time, during which no fine be imposed instead of the proposed 15 days which was deemed to be too short.

May 2, 1972: Complainant extended the abatement time for one month.

May 8, 1972: Respondent informed complainant that both the $185.00 (Citation No. I) and the $105.00 (Citation No. II) were not in accord with the guidelines of the Act and not commensurate with his attempts to comply. (There does not appear any written response to this by complainant).

May 10, 1972: Respondent paid $185.00 concerning Citation No. I.

May 18, 1972: A "memo to file" by the complainant's compliance officer shows that he called respondent concerning the latter's letter of May 8, 1972. He explained how penalties are computed and, "after a lengthy discussion of his rights," the officer informed respondent of the May 24, 1972, date for filing a contest to violations or penalties or both.

May 24, 1972: Respondent contested the penalty assessed on Citation No. II. This was to supplement the letter of May 8, 1972.

June 1, 1972: Among other things, complainant explained method of assessing penalties; commended respondent on his abatement activity; and *made demand for payment of the $105.00 penalty.*

On June 5, 1972, respondent's attorney (his first appearance) asked for a hearing as to the reasonableness of the violation and penalty. There was no response to this request but the Complainant's Area Director asked the Regional Solicitor for advice on June 13, 1972. He was advised on June 20, 1972, to send the matter to this Commission since respondent's letter of May 24, 1972, "appears to be a timely notice of contest."

On June 26, 1972, Citation No. II was received at the Commission from the Area Director who explained in a covering letter that the delay in forwarding this case

". . . has been occasioned by our exchange of correspondence with the establishment owner defining the Law, Citations and the penalty assessment process. We now infer upon further examination of the establishment's comments that Contest is the intent in this case."

It appears that the Area Director's entire file including all worksheets, memos and correspondence on both citations were forwarded.

On June 26, 1972, the Commission received the proceeding and the matter was docketed on June 27. The complainant received a 10-day extension to file its complaint and the respondent duly answered. The pleading stage was thus completed on August 7, 1972, and the matter was assigned to me for disposition.

Discussion and Conclusion

In *Hodgson et al. v. Lennox Industries, Inc.,* OSHRC Docket No. 1106, the Commission vacated the citation and proposed penalty for the complainant's failure to file the notice of contest within three days of his receipt of it as required by rule 2200.7 (c) (2) [§ 7520.07] of the Commission's interim rules of procedure. It was transmitted two and a half months late.

The history of the present case underwrites the wisdom of the *Lennox* decision, *supra.* The policy of the Occupational Safety and Health Act of 1970, 29 U.S.C. 651, *et seq.,* is to separate the agency that cites from the agency that adjudicates, see 29 U.S.C. 651 (2) (b) (3).

The employer is given a forum for as speedy a disposition of its notice of contest as is practicable. And the complainant must "immediately" transmit that notice so that the hearing before this Commission, of which the contestant is statutorily assured, can be scheduled without delay, see 29 U.S.C. 659(c) and interim rule 2200.7 (c) (2). The use of the term *immediately* in the statute underscores the complainant's obligation to act and it severely restricts any discretion he might otherwise have had in the circumstances; cf., *Ex Parte Pennsylvania* 137 U.S. 451 at 454, 11 S. Ct. 141 at 142.

In the instant case, the respondent objected to the original abatement dates assigned to the alleged violations contained in Citation No. 1. Following that, there was an almost constant flow of similar requests for more time when—in law—the abatement period had been tolled upon the filing of the objection by the respondent with the complainant. At the same point in time, as to Citation No. I, the jurisdiction of this Commission vested. Hence, after that, the complainant could agree to an extension of time, but he could not have granted it. By then, it was a Commission matter.

As to Citation No. II, the frustration of the respondent is evident from its correspondence It knew not where to turn and the judicial machinery only began to turn when the complainant received (June 9) the respondent's attorney's demand for a hearing. Even after receipt of the May 24 penalty contest letter, demand for payment was made.

I find that the respondent properly contested Citation No. I (letter of March 8, 1972) as to the abatement period and Citation No. II, (letters of May 8 as supplemented May 24, 1972) as to abatement time and proposed penalty; that the complainant's delay in advising this Commission of these contests prejudiced the respondent by unnecessarily delaying the scheduling of a hearing to which the respondent was entitled and that this failure to abide by the mandate of the statute and Commission rule finds excuse nowhere. Additionally, prolonging this proceeding only increases respondent's hardship needlessly. That it is struggling to abate the alleged violations is clear from the correspondence of record and its employees' representative has come to its support by letter dated July 26, 1972, stating that —with regard to occupational safety—the respondent is careful, understanding and efficient. Therefore, this proceeding made up of Citations Nos. I and II should be vacated.

The question arises, however, whether all aspects of these citations may be acted upon or only those parts which have been contested. The Commission has consistently ruled upon the entire matter where the contest was directed to a single element. See, for example, *Hodgson v. Newman's, Inc.* OSHRC Docket No. 568, in which the citation and penalty were affirmed in all respects after a contest brought only abatement into issue.

But *Lance Roofing Co., et al. v. Hodgson, et al.,* No. 16012, May 23, 1972 [§ 15,079], U.S. District Court for the Northern District of Georgia, indicates that any noncontested issue is determined by the citation and penalty as prepared by the complainant. In that case, the court discussed the problem of when an abatement begins to run if only the penalty is contested. The court stated in footnote 4 of its decision that "it is true" that an abatement period will be considered to run retroactively from the date fixed in the citation if only the penalty is contested and decided. Query, then, does the Commission possess the jurisdiction to affect an aspect of a case not brought into issue. Stated differently, is the Commission's jurisdiction described and circumscribed by the extent of the notice of contest.

In section 10(a) [§ 2017] of the Occupational Safety and Health Act, a "citation *and* assessment, as proposed," are deemed a Commission final order if the employer fails to give notice that "he intends to contest the citation *or* proposed assessment of penalty". The necessary corollary to this is that, if the employer does contest either the citation or the assessment, no final order comes into being without further proceedings.

This is recognized in *Lance, supra,* for the court indicates that the non-contested abatement period would become retroactive to the citationally fixed date only upon entry of a final order by the Commission after deciding the issue that was raised by the contest and even this retroactivity may be stayed by the Commission pending judicial review. This rationale must be based on the assumption that the Commission could and did act on the whole matter by disposing of the issue raised by the contest and by affirming all other aspects of the citation and assessment. Otherwise, there would be no need to await the Commission's final order to enforce any non-contested aspect.

Thus, the Commission's jurisdiction attaches to the entire matter upon notice of contest directed to any element of the citation or assessment. The action which may be taken by the Commission under section 10(c) [§ 2021] again indicates that jurisdiction over entire matter is vested upon any contest. An order under that section may affirm, modify or vacate the citation or penalty, i. e., a ruling on the matter raised by the intention to contest; or it may direct other appropriate relief. This would indicate that the Commission is not bounded by only those matters raised in the contest or by the pleadings generally and it can direct a just result depending on the circumstances. *NLRB v. Merrill*, 388 F. 2d 514 at 519 (1968).

No injustice to the complainant results from this for it must stand ready to prove all of its allegations in any event or abandon them. But an impossible restriction is hoisted on any respondent if he is held to have—within the short 15 working day contest period—isolated finally the issue to be tried. This, too, is evident in this case for the initial reaction to Citation No. I by the respondent was that the abatement period was too short. Later, after expiration of the 15-day period, he raised the excessiveness of the penalty. So, too, with Citation No. II.

Thus, in *Lennox, supra,* although the notice of contest was directed solely to the penalty, the Commission vacated the cause in its entirety.

That result is equally appropriate here and it is ORDERED that the citation and proposed penalty issued February 17, 1972, and the citation and proposed penalty issued April 26, 1972, are vacated.

• • •

CASE QUESTIONS

1. Why did the administrative law judge refer to the *Lennox* case which had come before the Review Commission at an earlier date?

2. The administrative law judge said that there is great merit in separating the agency which cites companies in violation of the law and one which adjudicates. What does this mean?

3. What was held regarding the matter of the Review Commission looking at more issues than those initially raised?

**SECRETARY OF LABOR v.
THORLEIF LARSEN AND SON, INC.**
OSHRC Docket No. 370, January 17, 1973
CCH § 15090

• • •

Before MORAN, Chairman, VAN NAMEE and BURCH, Commissioners.

BURCH, Commissioner.

On May 19, 1972, Judge Joseph L. Chalk issued his recommended decision and order in the instant case, affirming the Secretary's citations for one serious and three non-serious violations and the notification of proposed penalties in a total amount of $688.

On May 26, 1972, I directed that the proposed decision and order be reviewed by the Commission pursuant to section 12(j) [§ 6154] of the Occupational Safety and Health Act of 1970 (29 U.S.C.A. 651 *et seq.,* 84 Stat. 1590, hereinafter referred to as "the Act").

The Commission has reviewed the briefs filed by the parties and has considered the entire record in this case. We adopt the Judge's recommended decision and order insofar as it comports with this decision.

On December 17, 1971, respondent was issued a citation for one alleged serious violation and a citation for three alleged other than serious violations of the Act together with a notification of proposed penalty in a total amount of $688. Respondent filed a timely notice of contest only as to the serious citation. Since no contest was filed within the statutory 15 day working period as to the citation for other than serious violations, that citation together with the notification of proposed penalty therefor became the final order of the Commission.

While there was some uncertainty in the pleading stage of this proceeding whether the parties considered the penalty proposed for the serious violation to be in issue, it was stipulated at the commencement of the hearing that said proposal was not in issue. Judge Chalk accepted that stipulation and, consequently, no evidence was adduced at the hearing with regard thereto.

In directing that this decision be reviewed by the Commission, submissions were invited from the parties on the appropriateness of the proposed penalty and the manner in which it was determined.

In responding to that invitation, the Secretary failed to provide the Commission with information relevant to the issue of penalty assessment, urging instead that since the proposed penalty was not contested, it is not in controversy and hence not reviewable.

We find complainant's argument with respect to the Commission's jurisdiction in this case to be without merit.

Sections 17(j) [§ 6172] and 10(a) [§ 6506] of the Act establish the Commission's authority to assess civil penalties once a citation has been contested, regardless of whether the amount of the penalty has been placed in issue by a party to the proceeding. Section 10(a) states, in relevant part, that "If . . . the Secretary issues a citation . . . he shall . . . notify the employer . . . of the penalty, if any, *proposed to be assessed* under section 17 [§ 6163] . . . ." [Emphasis added.] If not contested, it is specified that ". . . the citation and the assessment, as proposed, shall be deemed a final order of the Commission. . . ." Section 17(j) provides that: "The Commission shall have authority to *assess* all civil penalties provided in this section, giving due consideration to the appropriateness of the penalty with respect to *the size of the business* of the employer being charged, the *gravity of the violation, the good faith of the employer, and the history of previous violations"* [Emphasis added].

Thus, where a notice of contest is not filed, the proposed assessment is "deemed" a final order of the Commission. However, where there is a contest, the Commission must perform its statutory duty to determine what, if any, penalty is appropriate in a case before it, taking into consideration those criteria set forth in section 17(j). This responsibility, having been delegated to the Commission, cannot be derogated by a stipulation between the parties.

The Secretary has presented no evidence upon which the Commission may base an appropriate penalty assessment pursuant to its exclusive statutory responsibility. The case must be remanded for adducement of such evidence. In the event that this evidentiary void is not filled, a penalty of $0 is to be assessed.

Accordingly, it is Ordered that (1) the Judge's order is amended to provide that the citation for serious violation is affirmed and (2) the case is remanded so that evidence may be adduced on the appropriateness of the penalty.

[Dissenting Opinion]

MORAN, Chairman, dissenting:

There are six principal reasons why I dissent from this decision of the Commission.

First: By proclaiming that it must decide the amount of the penalty when there is no dispute between the parties on that issue, the Commission has come forth with a difficulty to be applied to a solution in lieu of its statutory role which is exactly the reverse.

This Commission was created to resolve contested issues. When issues are not in dispute, the law gives no authority to the Commission to act. Nor should it. Congress has never established a government agency with authority to create disputes where none exist. It didn't do so with this Act.

It is said that one cannot contest the fact of a violation without also thereby putting in issue the amount of penalty proposed for the alleged violation. Even assuming that to be true as a general rule, it has no applicability in a case such as this where the parties took care to specifically exclude any consideration of the penalty by the Commission. They disagreed only on one issue: Did respondent violate Section 5(a) (1) [§ 6610] of the Act as charged by complainant? No other question was before this Commission. The complainant determined that $550 was an appropriate penalty in this case and the respondent agreed that it was indeed a proper amount provided the Commission gave an affirmative answer to the question submitted. It has now given that answer. Nothing more need be done by this Commission.

The hopeless folly of the position taken in this case by the Commission is revealed in the very order it is forced to issue to the parties. In the decision, the Commission says it "must perform its statutory duty to determine what, if any, penalty is appropriate." But in the order, it confesses that it cannot perform that "duty" because no evidence was introduced on this matter. Consequently, in what may well be regarded as a bizarre fit of pique, coming from an adjudicatory body, the parties are told that if they don't introduce evidence so the Commission can decide what the penalty shall be, we won't allow any penalty at all. So there!

I submit that the helplessness reflected in the Commission's order is just cause for re-examination of the premise that caused it: The self-proclaimed "statutory duty to determine what, if any, penalty is appropriate." Such a re-examination would disclose that there is no such duty. The Commission simply has the "authority" to assess all civil penalties. It is not compelled to exercise that authority at any time.

Second: The decision in this case was rendered following a hearing. That hearing, like hearings conducted by other Federal adjudicatory bodies, was conducted in accordance with the Administrative Procedure Act. The Administrative Procedure Act sensibly limits the agency to the resolution of only those issues upon which the parties are unable to agree. Section 554(c) (1) requires that the agency give all interested parties the opportunity for "the submission and consideration of . . . *offers of settlement, or proposals of adjustment* when time, the nature of the proceeding, and the public interest permit." Section 554(c) (2) further requires the opportunity for a hearing in accordance with Section 556 and 557 of Title 5, U.S. Code, only *"to the extent that* the parties are unable . . . to determine a controversy by contest. . . . ,"* Section 556(c) (6) empowers an administrative agency to "hold conferences for the settlement or simplification of the issues *by consent of the parties."* Section 557(c) (3) (A) requires that administrative agencies make findings and conclusions "on all the material issues of fact, law or discretion *presented on the record."* (emphasis supplied)

Clearly, in this case, the Commission has failed to observe the statutory mandates for adjudicatory bodies indicated by the phrases underlined above.

Lest there be any doubt of the emphasis attached to settlements in the Administrative Procedure Act, the following is quoted to demonstrate the purpose of its framers.

> "Sec. 5 Adjudications.
>
> (b) Procedure—the agency is *required* first to afford parties an opportunity for the settlement or adjustment of issues, followed, to the extent that issues are not so settled, by hearing and decision under sections 7 and 8.
>
> The preliminary settlement-by-consent provision of this subsection is of greatest importance. *Such adjustments may go to the whole or any part of any case."* (emphasis supplied)

It has also been said that, "the settlement by consent provision is extremely important because agencies ought not to engage in formal proceedings where the parties are perfectly willing to consent to judgments or adjust situations informally."

There is no escape from the fact that this decision is in direct conflict with the Administrative Procedure Act.

Third: This decision will also mean additional and unnecessary costs in both time and money by extending the length of future proceedings before this Commission in order to obtain the additional evidence.

Fourth: A further result of this decision is to change the plain meaning of Sections 10(a) [§ 6506] and (c) of the Act. Those provisions clearly grant an unconditional option to an employer to contest *either* a citation *or* a proposed penalty. Under the terms of those sections, an employer may opt to accept or contest a proposed penalty. This decision, however, eliminates this unconditional option. The Commission has re-written the statute *de facto* so that it now reads, in effect, "an employer may elect to contest either a citation or a proposed penalty, provided, however, that if he elects to contest a citation he must contest the penalty and evidence must be introduced so that the Commission may decide the issue of appropriateness." We thus see that the misinterpretation of the word "authority" in Section 17(j) so that it will mean "duty" alters the meaning of other sections of the Act.

Fifth: This decision also runs contrary to the concept that disputes should be settled, to whatever extent possible, by consent of the litigants; a principle which appeared at one time to have been accepted by this Commission. This concept is part of the Commission's Rules of Procedure and has been recognized in many decisions involving the withdrawal by an employer of a notice of contest previously filed, the method by which nearly half of all cases entered in this Commission to date have been disposed. In such cases, the Commission has permitted full settlement of a case without exercising its "duty" to assess penalties whenever a respondent moves to withdraw a notice of contest.

In such cases, the Commission has, without exception, permitted a respondent to agree with the complainant on the amount of the penalty. The only difference between this case and the withdrawal cases is that the respondent did not concede that he violated the Act. It is a distinction without meaning to say that a pre-trial agreement between the respondent and the complainant on the latter's penalty proposal is acceptable if the respondent concedes the violation prior to a hearing, but unacceptable if the violation is proved at the hearing.

The stipulation of the parties that a proposed penalty is appropriate if a violation is found is a partial settlement fully consistent with Commission Rule 100(a) and with the Commission's prior decisions on the complete settlement of a case resulting from the withdrawal of a notice of contest.

Sixth: If this case is ultimately concluded, as I suspect it will be, with a finding that respondent violated the Act, but that he shall not be monetarily penalized because the parties wouldn't give the Commission the evidence it asked for, I submit that the final order should attempt to answer how such a disposition has enhanced the cause of occupational safety and health in any way order than to proclaim to all concerned that the Commission has the last word on penalties whenever an employer contests an enforcement action which goes to a hearing.

It is my opinion that this decision has not only added nothing to that worthy cause, but that it will prove to be a negative factor both to occupational safety and health in general and the Commission in particular.

The excellent brief filed by counsel for complainant had forebodings that the Commission would hold as it has in this case. It outlined the consequences which would result as follows:

> "Rather than passing on the merits of contested cases as advanced by the parties, the Commission would assume a larger role, combining its express adjudicative functions with assumed, general, and undefined powers approaching the prosecutorial level.

> "Employers and employees seeking a legitimate redress of one aspect (e.g. unreasonable abatement date) of the Secretary's series of enforcement actions (inspection, citation, abatement date, proposed penalty) would find themselves arguing uncontested matters. The chilling effect of such action on the part of the Commission would, at worst, raise questions of procedural fairness, and, at best, turn the Commission

into a forum with few parties or controversies. Employers or employees seeking partial redress of perhaps legitimate grievances regarding the Secretary's enforcement action might elect to suffer a partial injustice rather than engage the Secretary and the Commission in a broader adversary proceeding with the possibility of receiving an adverse ruling regarding an issue not raised."

The "chilling effect" which the complainant feared is especially pertinent in a case such as this where all parties have agreed upon the amount to be assessed as a penalty. If, for example, the Secretary proposed a monetary penalty in an amount with which a respondent is inclined to agree, the respondent should feel free to pursue the course of requesting a hearing on the violation only, and, if desired, a review by this Commission, without fear that the penalty may be increased even *after* the hearing. The ruling in this case subjects a respondent to that risk even though he chooses to litigate only the fact of a violation. The net effect is to deter a respondent from requesting either a hearing or a review by the Commission itself. By inhibiting the use of contest procedures, this decision interferes with a respondent's right to "appeal" what he considers to be an erroneous citation. Such a result circumscribes the very purposes for our existence.

The adverse consequences of this decision have been related at some length. They are among the reasons why Congress specifically excluded this Commission, and all other agencies with adjudicatory powers, from deciding matters not in issue among the parties.

• • •

CASE QUESTIONS

1. Why did the masonary owner and the Secretary of Labor's representative agree on the $550 penalty as opposed to having a hearing on the matter?

2. What factors should be considered in assessing penalties in contested cases?

3. What did the dissenting commissioner argue about this case?

BRENNAN, SECRETARY OF LABOR v. INTERSTATE GLASS CO.
United States Court of Appeals, Eighth Circuit
No. 73-1029, 487 F.2d 483 (1973)

• • •

WEBSTER, Circuit Judge.

In this petition the Secretary of Labor seeks judicial review of an order of the Occupational Safety and Health Review Commission in which the Commission, while upholding the Secretary's citations for violations of the Act, nonetheless vacated the proposed penalties for such citations. We affirm the order of the Commission.

The Occupational Safety and Health Act of 1970, now popularly known as "OSHA," is of recent origin and will have substantial impact upon American Industry. The Secretary of Labor is charged with its enforcement, and in this action he seeks to limit the power of the Commission to modify penalties proposed by him which are within lawful limits. Because this appears to be a case of first impression, and one which tests in part the respective roles of the Secretary and the Commission, some initial explication of OSHA is appropriate.

"OSHA"

The Act was adopted in 1970 and became effective on April 28, 1971. The bill as passed is a compromise between two competing bills that were submitted both to the House and to the Senate. One bill was administration-backed and the other was strongly supported by organized labor. Although the difference in the two bills primarily involved whether both rule-making and enforcement powers should be located in the same agency, it is clear that both sides favored a bill which would establish a comprehensive program that would substantially reduce the large number of job-related deaths, injuries and health hazards which have existed. It is estimated that 4.1 million businesses and 57 million employees are affected.

The Act provides for the development of a "laundry-list" of violations. Companies are subject to periodic compliance inspections which are carried out at random either upon complaint or upon the inspector's own initiative. Advance notice of an inspection is prohibited, and violators of this provision are subject to criminal sanctions. Violations may be either of standards promulgated by the Secretary or of the "general duty" provision, a catch-all provision intended to supplement the standards formulated by the Secretary.

A violation is "serious" if there is a possibility of an accident and a substantial probability that death or serious physical injury would result. Under the Act, a penalty may be imposed of up to $1,000 for a non-serious violation. Upon receiving notice from the Secretary of the citations and proposed penalties, the employer has 15 days to contest either the citation or the proposed penalty or both by notifying the Secretary who transmits the information to the Commission. The Commission is an independent adjudicatory agency established under the Act, 29 U.S.C. § 661. The Commission is authorized to conduct hearings under § 659(c), which hearings are conducted under § 5 of the Administrative Procedure Act, 5 U.S.C. § 554.

The Commission's hearing is presided over by a single Commission Judge who writes an opinion which is then subject to review by the entire three-man Commission at its discretion. After 30 days, if no other member requests a review, his order becomes final and the order of the Commission.

FACTS

On March 28, 1972, a compliance officer of the United States Department of Labor conducted a compliance investigation of respondent Interstate Glass Company, Lincoln, Nebraska. As a result of conditions uncovered during this investigation, Interstate was cited by the Secretary of

Labor on March 29, 1972, for seven "non-serious" violations.[1] The fines totalled $375.00. The Company was ordered to abate item #3 immediately and was given until April 7, 1972, to abate the remaining six. Thereafter, the Secretary withdrew items 6 and 7 and the penalty was reduced to $225.

On April 13, 1972, respondent advised the Secretary that all five remaining violations were abated and that it wished to contest the citations and proposed penalties. This notice of contest was properly transmitted to the Secretary, who thereupon transmitted it to the Commission. The Secretary then submitted to the Commission a complaint under 29 CFR § 2200.7(d) setting forth the substance and penalties of the five violations. The respondent company answered, admitting a violation as to items 3 and 4 but denying the remaining allegations (items 1, 2, 5).

The Commission Judge, after hearing, determined that all five proposed violations did exist as set forth in the citation and were supported by the evidence. However, he vacated all five proposed penalties on the grounds that employees had never complained of the conditions, the employer was either unaware that the conditions were violations or had no knowledge of them, and the employer exercised diligence and good faith in abating the hazards immediately after the citation. Consequently, he concluded, "it will serve no useful purpose of the Act to levy these small fines under the total circumstances involved in this case." It is the vacation of the proposed penalties from which the Secretary appeals.

I

SCOPE OF ADMINISTRATIVE REVIEW

The Commission is granted the power to review either the citation or the proposed penalty or both under 29 U.S.C. § 659(a) and (c). The scope of such review is set forth in § 659 (c):

> "The Commission shall thereafter [after hearing] issue an order, based on findings of fact, affirming, modifying, or vacating the Secretary's citation or proposed penalty or directing other appropriate relief, and such order shall become final thirty days after its issuance." (emphasis added)

---

1. The seven non-serious violations cited, authority for such citations and the fines proposed by the Secretary were as follows:

Violation	C F R Section	Amount of Fine
(1) Excessive play in forklift	[1910.178(p)(1)]	$ 25
(2) Inaccessible electrical panel controlling plant's heat and power tools	[1910.310(i)]	25
(3) Flammable liquid stored in open containers	[1910.106(e)(2)(ii)]	125
(4) Power saw with missing ground prong	[1910.314(d)(4)(iii)(c)]	25
(5) Defective ladder	[1910.29(d)(1)(x)]	25
(6) Loading area not protected with required guardrails	[1910.23(c)(1)]	75
(7) Insufficient fire extinguishers	[1910.157(c)(1)(iv)]	75

Some writers have interpreted this section of the Act as granting the Commission final authority to affirm, modify, or vacate penalties. The Commission has acted upon a similar view of its power. "As of May 16, 1972, penalties proposed by the Department of Labor had been modified in 58 percent of the cases appealed to the Review Commission. In 43 percent of the cases, the penalty was reduced; in 15 percent, it was increased." In other instances the Commission has vacated the penalties but not the violations.

It is the position of the Secretary-Petitioner that by vacating all five proposed penalties, the Commission abused its discretion and frustrated the purposes of the Act. This assertion is based on a well-reasoned argument that such action frustrates the purpose of OSHA, which relies primarily on voluntary compliance, by nullifying the employer's incentive in self-policing and self-enforcement. Notwithstanding the validity of this argument, the threshold question is whether the review by the Commission is *de novo*.

Prior to the Commission's review, the Secretary had already taken the "circumstances" into consideration in setting the proposed penalties. As each violation was categorized as "non-serious", a fine not exceeding $1,000.00 was authorized, although not required, for each violation. 29 U.S.C. § 666(c). After placing each violation in a particular category depending upon its gravity, the Secretary reduced the five unadjusted penalties (1) 20% for the good faith of employer, (2) 10% for having less than 20 employees and (3) 20% for having no history of past violations. The adjusted penalties were further reduced 50% because all violations were abated within the period specified. This method of calculating proposed penalties is the standard procedure prescribed by the Secretary's published *Compliance Operations Manual*. It must be assumed that the Secretary's complaint is the Commission's failure to uphold his procedures for imposing penalties when the Commission affirms the Secretary's findings of violations. Obviously, the Secretary does not want his imposed penalties continually contested with the hope or expectation of the employer that the Commission will reduce or vacate them.

The Secretary's argument, however, ignores the clear statutory language. His imposition of penalty is denominated a "proposed penalty." 29 U.S.C. § 659(a). This proposed penalty becomes final only if the employer accepts it or does not "contest" it, in which case it becomes a final order not subject to review by any court or agency. 29 U.S.C. § 659(a). If, on the other hand, the employer contests the order and proposed penalty, the Commission acts *de novo*. Moreover, 29 U.S.C. § 666(i) provides as follows:

> "The Commission shall have authority to assess all civil penalties provided in this section, giving due consideration to the appropriateness of the penalty with respect to the size of the business of the employer being charged, the gravity of the violation, the good faith of the employer, and the history of previous violations."

The Congressional intent is thus plainly manifested that the Commission shall be the final arbiter of penalties if the Secretary's proposals are contested and that, in such a case, the Secretary's proposals merely become advisory. We find no authority to the contrary. In one recent Fifth Circuit opinion, the court vacated an order of the Commission setting aside proposed penalties and reinstated the Secretary's proposed penalties. *Brennan* v. *Occupational Safety and Health Review Commission* and *Brent Towing Co., Inc.,* 481 F.2d 619 (5th Cir. 1973). The question presented there was whether a particular letter constituted a "notice of contest." The Commission determined that it did and vacated the proposed penalties because the Secretary had not forwarded the letter within the required time period. The respondent-employer conceded its liability and indicated a desire not to proceed further. The court refused to decide the issue presented by the Secretary and the Commission because the "chief party in interest has long since . . . declined to remain the focal center for an administrative whirlwind of such minor proportions."

SCOPE OF JUDICIAL REVIEW

29 U.S.C. § 660(a) authorizes review in the Court of Appeals for "any person adversely affected or aggrieved" and § 660(b) authorizes review for the Secretary. Section 660(a) provides in pertinent part:

> "Upon such filing, the court shall have jurisdiction of the proceeding and of the question determined therein, and shall have power to grant such temporary relief or restraining order as it deems just and proper, and to make and enter upon the pleadings, testimony, and proceedings set forth in such record a decree affirming, modifying, or setting aside in whole or in part, the order of the Commission and enforcing the same to the extent that such order is affirmed or modified. ... The findings of the Commission with respect to questions of fact, if supported by substantial evidence on the record considered as a whole, shall be conclusive."

The reviewing court is thus bound to apply the substantial evidence test to the Commission's findings of fact. The assessment of penalties is not a finding but the exercise of a discretionary grant of power. And while the court has jurisdiction to review and power to modify, the test of a penalty within the statutory range must be whether the Commission abused its discretion.

In this case, the Commission had discretion to impose a fine of up to $1,000 for each non-serious violation. Its order reflected its consideration of the statutory criteria for the appropriateness of penalties. We are unable to say from the record before us that the Commission abused its discretion in vacating the proposed penalties. In so doing, we do not adopt the position of the Commission that "[r]elatively minor monetary penalties do little" to "obtain compliance with [the Act's] requirements in order to insure a safe and healthful work place." 1 O.S.H.R. 1198 (May 18, 1972). Nor do we think that the self-compliance aspects of the Act can only be enforced by mandatory penalties, as implied by the Secretary. The Act calls for the exercise of discretion, and our review is not to be directed to what policy best furthers the objectives of the Act, but rather to whether the statutory discretion has in fact been exercised and has not been abused.

Affirmed.

• • •

CASE QUESTIONS

1. Why is the Secretary of Labor bringing an appeal against the Occupational Safety and Health Review Commission?

2. How did the company react to the citations proposed by the U.S. Department of Labor inspectors? What did the company do?

3. How did the Commission Judge react to the petition of the company to remove the citations and proposed penalties?

4. How does the court interpret the role of the Review Commission in such cases?

BRENNAN, SECRETARY OF LABOR v. OCCUPATIONAL SAFETY AND HEALTH REVIEW COMMISSION AND BILL ECHOLS TRUCKING CO.
United States Court of Appeals, Second Circuit
487 F.2d 230 (1973)

● ● ●

GOLDBERG, Circuit Judge:

In this case the Secretary of Labor (the Secretary) has invoked the jurisdiction of this Court under Section 11(b) of the Occupational Safety and Health Act of 1970 (the Act), and asked that we review a "Supplemental Order" of the Occupational Safety and Health Review Commission (the Commission) vacating a citation and proposed penalty issued by the Secretary to Bill Echols Trucking Co. (Echols).

We note that the difficulty of our task has been magnified by the paucity of the written argument presented to us. Whether out of utter frustration, battle fatigue, or neglect, neither the Commissioner nor Echols saw fit to file a responsive brief, although both had been solicited and importuned to do so. Nevertheless, on the basis of the petitioner's brief and the record before us, we must endeavor to decide the issues presented. ...

THE FACTS

The series of actions, inactions, and reactions that propelled this dispute into the Court of Appeals began on August 23, 1972, when the Secretary cited Echols for a serious violation of a safety regulation promulgated under the Act, and proposed a penalty of $600.00. The Secretary charged that Echols had violated 29 C.F.R. § 1926.601(b) (4) by its "failure to provide motor vehicles having an obstructed view to the rear with a reverse signal alarm or an observer to signal the vehicle it is safe to travel in reverse gear," and ordered Echols to abate this condition within three days after its receipt of the citation.

Section 10(a) of the Act, 29 U.S.C. § 659(a), and regulations promulgated thereunder, provide a means of appealing citations and penalties. Under 29 C.F.R. § 1903.17, Echols could have obtained Commission review by notifying the Occupational Safety and Health Administration Area Director of its intention to contest within 15 days of its receipt of the notification of proposed penalty. The regulation directs that "[e]very notice of intention to contest shall specify whether it is directed to the citation or to the proposed penalty, or both." On September 5, 1972, less than 15 days after receiving notice of the proposed penalty, Echols' attorney wrote to the Secretary's regional representative in Birmingham, stating:

> "This is to inform you that the signaling device has been installed within the three day period after the citation. We request that the penalty be abated since corrective action has been taken well within the time alloted. [sic].

> "If there is any further information you desire of [sic] if I can be of any further assistance to you kindly contact me."

The Secretary deferred forwarding this letter to the Commission until October 16, 1972, some 43 days later, at which time he filed a motion to strike Echols' letter as not constituting a notice of contest. After considerable procedural maneuvering, the Commission issued a Supplemental Order on January 26, 1973, holding that Echols' September 5 letter was a sufficient notice of contest, and therefore that the Secretary was required under 29 C.F.R. § 2200.32 to transmit the notice to the Commission within seven days of its receipt. The Commission vacated both the citation and proposed penalty because of the Secretary's failure to transmit the notice on time.

The Secretary filed a petition for reconsideration with the Commission on February 27, 1973. The record before us gives no indication of any response by the Commission. This petition for review followed.

The Secretary raises two issues for decision by this Court: (1) Did Echols' letter of September 5 constitute a notice of contest of the citation or of the proposed penalty, or both? (2) If the letter did constitute a notice of contest, did the Commission act improperly by vacating the citation and proposed penalty because of the Secretary's failure to transmit such notice in timely fashion?

I

Because the Commission's Supplemental Order of January 26, 1973 vacated both the citation and the proposed penalty against Echols, the question of whether Echols' September 5 letter was sufficient notice of contest actually becomes two issues: (a) whether the letter constituted a notice of contest of the citation; and (b) whether the letter constituted a notice of contest of the proposed penalty.

The first issue causes us little difficulty. Even construing the letter in the manner most favorable to Echols, we cannot conceive of any way it could be interpreted as a notice of contest of the citation. The September 5 letter, written by Echols' attorney, raised no objection whatsoever to the citation; to the contrary the letter noted that corrective action had been taken after receipt of the citation, and thus, in effect, conceded the existence of the violations at the time of issuance of the citation. Because

the letter requested that the *penalty* be abated, and because the regulation requires that a complainant specify whether it is contesting the citation or the penalty, 29 C.F.R. § 1903.17 *supra,* the inescapable conclusion
is that the letter could only have been a notice of contest of the penalty—
if it was a notice of contest at all.

The Act provides that a failure to notify the Secretary within 15 days
of intent to contest the citation or proposed penalty will render such
citation or penalty "a final order of the Commission and not subject to
review by any court or agency." 29 U.S.C. § 659(a). Thus, the citation had
become final and unreviewable, and the Commission had no authority
five months later to vacate the citation. As to the citation against Echols,
then, we vacate the Supplemental Order of the Commission and reinstate
the citation as issued by the Secretary on August 23, 1972.

The question of whether the September 5 letter constituted a notice of
contest of the proposed penalty is much more difficult to resolve. The
Commission has provided only the crudest of guidelines to aid the courts,
affected employers, or itself in making such a determination. Fortunately,
however, it is not the province of this Court to draw the fine lines separating letters that constitute notices of contest from those that do not.
The regulations stipulate that "[i]n its absolute discretion, and without
affirmative action by order or otherwise, the Commission or the Examiner
may permit the filing of pleadings or other documents which it deems to
comply substantially with" the regulations concerning form, filing, and
service. 29 C.F.R. § 2200.7(b) (4). Given such "absolute discretion" in the
Commission, we cannot and will not challenge its determination that the
September 5 letter constituted a notice of contest of the proposed penalty.
Particularly in view of the lack of guidance to be found in the regulations,
..., the Commission properly gave a liberal interpretation to the letter.
... The Secretary was, therefore, delinquent in failing to transmit the
letter to the Commission within seven days of its receipt.

II

Having found that the Commission did not abuse its discretion by
holding that the September 5 letter constituted a notice of contest of the
proposed penalty, we must now inquire whether the Commission acted
properly by vacating the proposed penalty because of the Secretary's delay in transmitting the letter to the Commission. An order vacating a
citation or proposed penalty is the most extreme sanction available to the
Commission. We can find no authorization in the Act or the regulations
for imposition of such a sanction without first providing an opportunity
for a hearing. We do not now decide whether any breach of the rules by
the Secretary could be serious enough to warrant dismissal of a penalty
without a prior hearing. We do hold, however, that in the case before us
the Commission acted improperly by vacating the proposed $600 penalty
against Echols. Our conclusion is supported by both the nature of the
Secretary's error and the underlying philosophy of the Act itself.

We have found that the Commission was within its discretionary
power in construing the September 5 letter as a notice of contest. Moreover, given the adjudicatory function of the Commission, the Secretary
should have resolved any doubts about the sufficiency of the letter in favor

of transmitting it to the Commission for its determination. Nevertheless, we cannot say that the Secretary's action was entirely without justification. The September 5 letter, written by an attorney, was phrased in terms of a "request" to the Secretary for an abatement of penalty. The letter contained no language to the effect that Echols wished to "contest" the penalty or had any reason to "object" to the penalty proposed. Echols gave no direct indication of any desire to incure the burdens of a proceeding before the Commission. Under the circumstances the Secretary was not unreasonable in construing the letter as a request for leniency rather than as a notice of contest. Dismissal of the penalty is a sanction much too harsh for such a reasonable, although ultimately unprevailing, interpretation.

Moreover, viewed in light of the purpose of the Act, the requirement that the Secretary promptly transmit notices of contest is obviously designed to protect employees rather than employers. Congress' statement of purpose at the beginning of the Act makes this abundantly clear:

> "The Congress declares it to be its purpose and policy, through the exercise of its powers to regulate commerce among the several States and with foreign nations and to provide for the general welfare, to assure so far as possible every working man and woman in the Nation safe and healthful working conditions and to preserve our human resources—"

29 U.S.C. § 651(b). Prompt transmittal is important for hastening abatement of health or safety hazards to employees because, if the employer contests in good faith, the period for correction permitted by the Secretary "shall not begin to run until the entry of a final order by the Commission . . . ." 29 U.S.C. § 659(b). We can find no justification for permitting an employer to reap the benefits of its own ambiguous correspondence and to go unpenalized for an admitted serious violation of a safety standard under the banner of a rule designed to protect employees. Congress could not have intended such a result, and it gave the Commission no authority to produce such a result.

By filing a notice of contest Echols was doing nothing more than requesting a hearing; the Commission should have provided exactly that. Commission decisions in subsequent cases apparently have recognized that at least a finding of prejudice to the employer must precede dismissal of a proposed penalty for violation of a procedural rule. ... The Secretary contends that Echols was not prejudiced by the delay in transmittal of his notice of contest to the Commission. The Secretary should be given an opportunity to make that argument to the Commission.

CONCLUSION

We therefore vacate that part of the Commission's January 26, 1973 Supplemental Order which vacated the proposed penalty against Echols, and remand to the Commission for a hearing on the merits. We do not limit the scope of the hearing in any way. In addition to all other factors normally considered in such a hearing, the Commission is free to inquire to what extent, if any, Echols was injured by the Secretary's delay in transmitting the notice of contest, and to modify the penalty accordingly upon an appropriate finding of fact. As previously indicated, the citation issued against Echols on August 23, 1972, was not contested and is hereby reinstated as a final order of the Commission.

Vacated and remanded.

• • •

CASE QUESTIONS

1. Why did the Secretary of Labor bring this appeals case?

2. How did the letter from the company's attorney cause problems in this case?

3. How did the Court of Appeals interpret the authority of the Review Commission?

SECRETARY OF LABOR v. AMERICAN SHIPBUILDING COMPANY
OSHRC Docket No. 70
May 8, 1972

• • •

The employer had appealed the citation and the fine by filing a notice of contest. This was dismissed by David J. Oringer, Judge. The $10,000 proposed penalities for the four willful and two serious violations were affirmed. The company made assurances that the conditions complained of had been corrected. The judge found that all parties had been properly served.

• • •

SECRETARY OF LABOR v. CLEMENTS PAPER COMPANY
OSHRC Docket No. 419
June 21, 1972

• • •

Judge James D. Burroughts vacated a citation and proposed $600 penalty when the case was appealed. The facts of the case relate to the long-term employee who was operating a forklife truck. In the course of his work, he tried to lift another vehicle, a roll-lift truck, with the fork-lift truck. The deceased employee then had crawled under the suspended truck only to have it fall upon him, causing his death. In the arguments, the employer said that they had tied the safety rules to the normal operating procedures of the plant. In this case, the employee committed an error which cost him his life. Section 5(b) places on the employees an obligation of compliance which cannot be evaded by the total shifting of the responsibility to the employer. The intent of the Act (OSHA) is not to make employers absolutely liable for every violation committed by their employees.

• • •

SECRETARY OF LABOR v. WALTER A. PODPORA
OSHRC Docket No. 721
May 18, 1972

• • •

[Text of Review Commission Decision]

This matter comes on upon petitioner's motion to dismiss the respondent's notice of contest as being untimely in that the mailing of notice of contest was not within the 15 working days of the receipt of the citation and proposed penalty by the respondent. Respondent in reply to said motion admits that the notice was one day untimely but in seeking a 30 day extension to answer and contest alleges the "newness and unfamiliarity of this respondent and his attorneys to the requisite published rules of the Commission" as grounds for the extension. Respondent further alleges the Commission has inherent power to extend the time of contest.

Section 10(a) of the Occupational Safety and Health Act of 1970, 29 U.S.C. 651, *et seq.,* provides in pertinent part that

> "If within fifteen working days from the receipt of notice of contest issued by the Secretary the employer fails to notify the Secretary that he intends to contest the citation or proposed assessment of penalty, and no notice is filed by any employee or representative of employees under subsection (c) within such time, the citation and the assessment, as proposed, shall be deemed a final order of the Commission and not subject to review by any court or agency."

The statutory language clearly forestalls the Commission from considering a notice of contest that is not timely filed by a respondent. There is therefore no inherent power, in view of the specific statutory time requirement, in the Commission to extend the time for filing under the facts of this case and no statutory provision for consideration of alleged mitigating circumstances as urged by Respondent.

It is therefore ORDERED that the notice of contest is dismissed and the Secretary's citation and proposed penalty are affirmed in all respects.

• • •

SECRETARY OF LABOR v. ARIZONA PUBLIC SERVICE COMPANY
OSHRC Docket No. 329
June 22, 1972

• • •

The company is appealing a proposed $600 penalty. Judge Robert N. Burchmore is hearing the case. The problem was in the company's assignment of men to work on the top of an electric transformer. The climbing route took the men within 24 inches of a high voltage conductor carrying 7800 volts. The company's own safety rules prohibited approaching within 24 inches of any equipment energized at between 2kv and 22kv and prohibited working within reach of energized conductors of 500 volts or more unless the conductors were completely covered with protective devices. The judge affirmed the penalty saying that this was a serious violation of the General Duty Clause of the Act.

• • •

SECRETARY OF LABOR v.
C. O. OSBORN CONTRACTING COMPANY
OSHRC Docket No. 549
June 20, 1972

• • •

Judge J. Marker Dern found that the company citation and proposed $700 penalty should be vacated. The company has contested the citation saying that there was no liability for the death of the employee. The facts of the case show that the employee was killed when the pipe and bucket fell from a backhoe digger as it was lowered into a trench. The rule in question referred to whether the employee was "under the load" which is a dangerous situation, as defined in Section 1926.650(h). The judge held that the common definition of "under the load" should be used. The judge did not accept the Secretary's argument that a boom, dipper stick, and bucket of the backhoe were all parts of the "load."

• • •

CASE QUESTIONS

1. How was the fine settled in the *American Shipbuilding Company* case?

2. How liable is the employer in an employee death, as in the *Clements Paper Company* case?

3. How did the Review Commission react in the *Walter A. Podpora* case to an extension of time?

4. How did the *Osborn Contracting Company* contest its citation?

5. What did the administrative law judge say about the company's safety rules in *Arizona Public Service Company?*

There is a greal deal of controversy over what rights exist for public employees and what rights remain with the sovereign state. Historically, sovereigns and governments have not readily recognized public employee's organizations. Even today some ambivalence still exists in the federal and state sectors about what public employee rights are "fair" and "appropriate." The job actions by nurses, sanitation workers, correctional officers, and social workers show that demands from public workers come from all wage levels. Employees in many agencies and organizations frequently want not only more benefits and compensation but also a grievance procedure with arbitration as the final step.

When governments were first organized, there were few legal restrictions in their dealings with their employees. Gradually as some rights were recognized on a negotiated basis, the courts began to balance and weigh employee rights and public risks of collective actions. In addition, public employees still have constitutional rights which prohibit harsh and unreasonable restrictions.

The National Labor Relations Act and its amendments specifically exclude public employees in Section 2. In spite of this exclusion employee organizations have been active in the state and federal government. These organizations, which operated on an informal recognition basis with the governmental units, have negotiated grievance procedures in some agreements which have benefited all parties.

FEDERAL POLICIES

Executive Order 10988 issued in 1962, gave formal recognition to a pre-existing official tolerance of public employee organizations. This order established some guidelines and administrative machinery for all parties. Executive Order 11491, effective January 1, 1970, revoked Executive Order 10988. This order set forth detailed administrative policies and procedures which resembled those used by the National Labor Relations Board. It also established a conflict-resolution system and generally showed more concern with the operation of day-to-day activities. Administrative policies and procedures included an exclusive recognition clause which was established because of the problems caused by splinter employees groups within an agency. A secret election process was developed for use by employees to choose whether to have a union.

In the conflict-resolution area a new organization, the Federal Service Impasse Panel, was established to consider negotiation impasses. Members of the panel were appointed by the President. The Panel operates after the Federal Mediation and Conciliation Service's efforts have failed in an attempt to avoid a strike or job action. Binding arbitration was authorized to settle the negotiations since strikes are illegal.

The growth of public employee unions showed that some procedures were not effective in management-union relations. Executive Order 11491 was amended to change the procedures.

Executive Order 11616, signed August 26, 1971, further refined the labor-relations policies of the federal government toward its employees. One of the important changes involved establishing the Federal Labor Relations Council, a body designed to act as an appeals body for disputes arising out of the collective-bargaining agreements or negotiations. The employee could grieve through the personnel process or the collective-bargaining grievance machinery. This restatement was necessary to preclude the problem of double appeals and also make sure that the employees did not lose any civil service rights of appeal. Arbitration clauses using private arbitrators were specifically allowed to settle disputes over the interpretation or application of the agreement. Dues were mentioned specifically so that employees could request dues' deductions from their paychecks. Such monies could then be transferred to the labor organization. Every six months employees have the opportunity to revoke this dues' deduction authorization by a written request.

In summary, the federal government through the use of the President's executive powers is moving voluntarily toward continuous collective bargaining with employee organizations. Executive Orders implement many of the procedures developed in the private sector and sanctioned by the National Labor Relations Board. Section 2 of the National Labor Relations Act, which excludes public employees, could be amended to include public employees, but so far the lobbying efforts by union officials have not been successful.

STATE POLICIES

State governments have mixed feelings about public employee labor organizations. In some states the public accepts the position that state employees should have the right to organize. In other states the public feels state and local employees are well compensated for very secure jobs. Feelings are strong and much of the common law *sovereign immunity theory* exists in state court rulings.

Sovereign immunity means the government cannot be sued for an error because the state represents unreachable higher authority. State and federal governments have used sovereign immunity as a protective device. Some states have voluntarily removed this restriction.

The historical pattern for developing bargaining rights is as follows: At first, the essential service groups may receive some limited right to organize. Recognition may come from the mayor, city council, department head, or other administrative officer. Interest in employee organizations then spreads. Authorization cards for an employee organization may be signed. If there is a state statute allowing for collective bargaining, then those processes for private collective bargaining may be made applicable to public employees.

An election may be held to determine if the employees in that agency or organization want union representation. A successful union may then enter into collective bargaining negotiations with the state officials. Even if the state does not have any collective bargaining legislation which permits organization, recognition, and negotiation these operations may occur. While some states have no-strike laws for public employees, recent job actions, such as strikes of sanitation workers, have been examples of the ineffectiveness of no-strike laws. Sometimes when employees feel that something must be done and if there is no settlement process, the strike weapon is used.

State statutes usually cover all public employees which means that employees in local, county, and city offices and in special-case areas such as state-operated hospitals and mental health facilities are treated similarly. In those states with permissive collective bargaining a state agency, sometimes called a *state industrial relations board* or a *mediation agency,* helps with the daily administrative duties of unfair labor practices. Without such legislation, the parties are often left to "self-help" which often means strikes and other pressure tactics.

POLITICAL CONSIDERATIONS IN NEGOTIATIONS

Public employee organizations have a great deal of power because of the many votes which can be influenced in state, local, and federal elections. These organizations know that political pressures can be brought at all levels and employees contribute time and money to help their friends in the legislature or the mayor's office.

ORGANIZATIONAL AND BARGAINING RIGHTS

Federal and state employees are still not sure about the rights they possess in the full extent of union activities. There are problems in securing recognition from different public employers, such as a city, or local school district. A challenge may be made to the validity of the employee organization and the need to bargain collectively. The courts have examined the issues in regard to constitutional rights. The Fourteenth Amendment rights extend to protect state citizens in the right of association. It is interesting to note that many of the cases are brought up under the Civil Rights Act of 1871, Section 1. This Act has been used to gain standing in the federal courts to examine many of the unionization issues.

Future developments will spell out the limits of protected collective bargaining activities between public employees and the employing unit. Specific legislation has been proposed by such groups as the American Federation of State, County, and Municipal Employees (AFSCME), the National Educational Association, the American Federation of Teachers, and other union groups. The courts have been examining the extent of the Constitutional rights of the parties. It seems easier for the courts to prevent restrictions of free speech and association than to proclaim that the employers have an obligation to recognize or bargain with the employee organizations. Specific legislation in many states has solved that problem by outlining what is required and establishing administrative rules for collective bargaining.

INTRODUCTION TO THE CASES

In this early case, *Norwalk Teachers* v. *Board of Education,* a new teacher union is seeking recognition and bargaining status from the employing Board of Education. The lower court has passed on to the Connecticut Supreme Court of Errors the broader issues of right to organize, strike, and bargain. The court then examines its own statutes, its case law, and the common law of the United States.

A case which is similar to *Norwalk Teachers* is *Postal Workers* v. *Bount Case.* Here the United Federation of Postal Clerks is asking for a declaratory judgment concerning an interpretation of the rights of the parties by the courts. It also requests an injunction to constrain the federal government from preventing any strike action by public employees. The court examines the basic right to strike and an Executive Order which restricts the rights of the postal clerks.

In *AFSCME* v. *Woodward* the court says that a person has the right to express attitudes or philosophies by membership in a group or by affiliation with it. In *Woodward* the teachers are asking that the Federal court restrain the City Commissioner in his efforts to restrict the union activities of the members of the State, County, and Municipal Employees union.

The right of associational freedom is crucial for a union to develop. This right is given constitutional protection in *Shelton* v. *Tucker.* The case is complicated by the civil rights questions, but the court strikes down the entire Arkansas statute saying that the state has violated the Due Process Clause of the Fourteenth Amendment.

NORWALK TEACHERS' ASSOCIATION v. BOARD OF EDUCATION
Supreme Court of Errors of Connecticut
83 A.2d 482

• • •

JENNINGS, Justice.

This is a suit between the Norwalk Teachers' Association as plaintiff and the Norwalk board of education as defendant for a declaratory judgment, reserved on the admitted allegations of the complaint for the advice of this court.

The complaint may be summarized as follows: The plaintiff is a voluntary association and an independent labor union to which all but two of the teaching personnel of approximately 300 in the Norwalk school system belong. In April, 1946, there was a dispute between the parties over salary rates. The board of estimate and taxation was also involved. After long negotiations, 230 members of the association rejected the individual contracts of employment tendered them and refused to return to their teaching duties. After further negotiations, in which the governor and the state board of education took part, a contract was entered into between the plaintiff and the defendant, and the teachers returned to their duties. The contracts, subject to conditions precedent therein set forth, recognized the plaintiff as the bargaining agent for all of its members, defined working conditions and set up a grievance procedure and salary schedule. Similar contracts were entered into for the succeeding school years, including 1950–1951.

From September, 1946, to the present and particularly with reference to the contract for 1950–1951, much doubt and uncertainty have arisen concerning the rights and duties of the respective parties, the interpretation of the contract and the construction of the state statutes relating to schools, education, and boards of education. "In addition," the complaint states, "there has been the possibility of strikes, work stoppage or collective refusals to return to work by the teachers through their organization and the possibility of discharges or suspensions by the defendant by reason of difficult personnel relations, all of which tends to disharmony in the operation of the school system and to the ever present possibility that either, or both, the parties may be unwittingly violating statutes by reason of mistaken or erroneous interpretation thereon." The parties agreed that the contract for the school year 1949–1950 would govern their relations for the school year 1950–1951, that they would join in this action, and "that whatever contractual obligations exist will be forthwith modified so soon as they shall have received from the Court judgments and orders declaring their respective rights, privileges, duties and immunities." ...

This court is not required to advise on abstract principles of law. ... In the case at bar, the admitted facts show that Norwalk has suffered from one disrupting teachers' strike. While the complaint is couched in diplomatic language, it is obvious that the city is likely to be faced with another in the fall. ...

Under our system, the government is established by and run for all of the people, not for the benefit of any person or group. The profit motive, inherent in the principle of free enterprise, is absent. It should be the aim of every employee of the government to do his or her part to make it function as efficiently and economically as possible. The drastic remedy of the organized strike to enforce the demands of unions of government employees is in direct contravention of this principle. It has been so regarded by the heads of the executive departments of the states and the nation. Most of the text writers refer to one or more of the following statements by three of our recent presidents. They are quoted, for example, in 1 Labor Law Journal 612 (May, 1950): "There is no right to strike against public safety by anybody anywhere at any time" (Calvin Coolidge on the Boston police strike). This same strike was characterized by President Wilson as "an intolerable crime against civilization." President Franklin D. Roosevelt said in a letter to the president of the National Federation of Federal Employees on August 16, 1937: "Particularly, I want to emphasize my conviction that militant tactics have no place in the functions of any organization of Government employees. ... [A] strike of public employees manifests nothing less than an intent on their part to prevent or obstruct the operations of Government until their demands are satisfied. Such action, looking toward the paralysis of Government by those who have sworn to support it, is unthinkable and intolerable." As the author of the article cited says, "The above statement by President Roosevelt, who certainly was no enemy of labor unions, epitomizes the answer to the problem. It seems to be axiomatic."

The commentators, generally, subscribe to this proposition. . . . Notwithstanding this fact, Ziskind was able to publish a well-documented book entitled "One Thousand Strikes of Government Employees," which contains an elaborate bibliography. See also Spero, Government as Employer. This would indicate that the law on the subject is still in the process of development.

Few cases involving the right of unions of government employees to strike to enforce their demands have reached courts of last resort. That right has usually been tested by an application for an injunction forbidding the strike. The right of the governmental body to this relief has been uniformly upheld. It has been put on various grounds: public policy; interference with governmental function; illegal discrimination against the right of any citizen to apply for government employment (where the union sought a closed shop). The following cases do not necessarily turn on the specific right to strike, but the reasoning indicates that, if faced with that question, the court would be compelled to deny that right to public employees. For example, Perez v. Board of Police Commissioners, . . . 178 P.2d 537, held that the board could, by rule, prevent police officers from joining a labor union. If it could do this, it would certainly be upheld in an attempt to enjoin a strike called by the union. . . . Other cases not published in the official reports are discussed in *National Institute of Municipal Law Officers Report No. 129* (1949) pp. 20-28. The court puts the matter succinctly in the Miami case, supra [157 Fla. 445, 26 So.2d 197]: "While strikes are recognized by the statute to be lawful under some circumstances, it would seem that a strike against the city would amount, in effect, to a strike against government itself—a situation difficult to reconcile with all notions of government."

The plaintiff, recognizing the unreasonableness of its claims in the case of such employees as the militia and the judiciary, seeks to place teachers in a class with employees employed by the municipality in its proprietary capacity. No authority is cited in support of this proposition. "A town board of education is an agency of the state in charge of education in the town . . ." In fulfilling its duties as such an agency, it is acting in a governmental, not a proprietary, capacity. Seymour v. Over-River School-District, 53 Conn. 502, 3 A. 552, cited by the plaintiff, does not hold to the contrary. It went no further than to hold that a teacher was not a "public officer" within the meaning of a statute authorizing the garnishment of wages.

In the American system, sovereignty is inherent in the people. They can delegate it to a government which they create and operate by law. They can give to that government the power and authority to perform certain duties and furnish certain services. The government so created and empowered must employ people to carry on its task. Those people are agents of the government. They exercise some part of the sovereignty entrusted to it. They occupy a status entirely different from those who carry on a private enterprise. They serve the public welfare and not a private purpose. To say that they can strike is the equivalent of saying that they can deny the authority of government and contravene the public welfare. The answer to question (c) is "No."

Questions (a) and (b) relate to the right of the plaintiff to organize itself as a labor union and to demand recognition and collective bargaining. The right to organize is sometimes accorded by statute or ordinance. See, for example, the Bridgeport ordinance adopted June 17, 1946 (Bridgeport Munic. Reg. [1947] p. 15), discussed in *National Institute of Municipal Law Officers Report No. 129,* p. 51. The right to organize has also been forbidden by statute or regulation. Perez v. Board of Police Commissioners, 78 Cal. App. 2d 638, 178 P.2d 537. In Connecticut the statutes are silent on the subject. Union organization in industry is now the rule rather than the exception. In the absence of prohibitory statute or regulation, no good reason appears why public employees should not organize as a labor union. Springfield v. Clouse, 356 Mo. 1239, 1246, 206 S.W.2d 539.

It is the second part of the question (a) that causes difficulty. The question reads: "Is it permitted to the plaintiff under our laws to organize itself as a labor union for the purpose of demanding and receiving recognition and collective bargaining?" The question is phrased in a very peremptory form. The common method of enforcing recognition and collective bargaining is the strike. It appears that this method has already been used by the plaintiff and that the threat of its use again is one of the reasons for the present suit. As has been said, the strike is not a permissible method of enforcing the plaintiff's demands. The answer to questions (a) and (b) is a qualified, "yes." There is no objection to the organization of the plaintiff as a labor union, but if its organization is for the purpose of "demanding" recognition and collective bargaining the demands must be kept within legal bounds. What we have said does not mean that the plaintiff has the right to organize for all of the purposes for which employees in private enterprise may unite, as those are defined in § 7391 of the General Statutes. Nor does it mean that, having organized, it is necessarily protected against unfair labor practices as specified in § 7392 or that it shall be the exclusive bargaining agent for all employees of the unit, as provided in § 7393. It means nothing more than that the plaintiff may organize and bargain collectively for the pay and working conditions which it may be in the power of the board of education to grant.

Questions (c) and (d) in effect ask whether collective bargaining between the plaintiff and the defendant is permissible. The statutes and private acts give broad powers to the defendant with reference to educational matters and school management in Norwalk. If it chooses to negotiate with the plaintiff with regard to the employment, salaries, grievance procedures, and working conditions of its members, there is no statute, public or private, which forbids such negotiations. It is a matter of common knowledge that this is the method pursued in most school systems large enough to support a teachers' association in some form. It would seem to make no difference theoretically whether the negotiations are with a committee of the whole association or with individuals or small related groups, so long as any agreement made with the committee is confined to members of the association. If the strike threat is absent and the defendant prefers to handle the matter through negotiation with the plaintiff, no reason exists why it should not do so. The claim of the defendant that this would be an illegal delegation of authority is without merit. The authority is and remains in the board. This statement is not to be construed as approval of the existing contracts attached to the complaint. Their validity is not in issue.

As in the case of questions (a) and (b), (c) and (d) are in too general a form to permit a categorical answer. The qualified "Yes" which we give to them should not be construed as authority to negotiate a contract which involves the surrender of the board's legal discretion, is contrary to law or is otherwise ultra vires. For example, an agreement by the board to hire only union members would clearly be an illegal discrimination. ... Any salary schedule must be subject to the powers of the board of estimate and taxation. "The salaries of all persons appointed by the board of education . . . shall be as fixed by said board, but the aggregate amount of such salaries . . . shall not exceed the amount determined by the board of estimate and taxation. . . ." One of the allegations of the complaint is that the solution of the parties' difficulties by the posing of specific issues is not satisfactory. Whether or not this is so, that course will be necessary if this discussion of general principles is an insufficient guide.

Question (f) reads, "Is arbitration a permissible method under Connectucut law to settle or adjust disputes between the plaintiff and the defendant?" The power of a town to enter into an agreement of arbitration was originally denied on the ground that it was an unlawful delegation of authority. ... It was later held that not only the amount of damages but liability could be submitted to arbitration. Hine v. Stephens, 33 Conn. 497, 504; Mallory v. Huntington, 64 Conn. 88, 96, 29 A. 245. The principle applies to the parties to the case at bar. If it is borne in mind that arbitration is the result of mutual agreement, there is no reason to deny the power of the defendant to enter voluntarily into a contract to arbitrate a specific dispute. On a proposal for a submission, the defendant would have the opportunity of deciding whether it would arbitrate as to any question within its power. Its power to submit to arbitration would not extend to questions of policy but might extend to question of liability. Arbitration as a method of settling disputes is growing in importance and, in a proper case, "deserves the enthusiastic support of the courts." International Brotherhood of Teamsters v. Shapiro, 138 Conn. 57, 69, 82 A.2d 345.

Agreements to submit all disputes to arbitration, commonly found in ordinary union contracts, are in a different category. If the defendant entered into a general agreement of that kind, it might find itself committed to surrender the broad discretion and responsibility reposed in it by law. For example, it could not commit to an arbitrator the decision of a proceeding to discharge a teacher for cause. So, the matter of certification of teachers is committed to the state board of education. General Statutes, §§ 1432, 1433, 1435. The best answer we can give to question (f) is, "yes, arbitration may be a permissible method as to certain specific, arbitrable disputes."

From what has been said, it is obvious that, within the same limitations, mediation to settle or adjust disputes is not only permissible but desirable. The answer to question (g) is "yes." The state board of mediation and arbitration and the state labor relations board, however, are set up to handle disputes in private industry and are not available to the plaintiff and defendant for reasons given in the opinion of the attorney general dated July 6, 1948. 25 Conn. Atty. Gen. Rep. 270. This was confirmed as to Norwalk teachers by an opinion dated June 12, 1950, not yet published. ... The answer to question (h) is "No."

General Statutes, Sup. 1949, § 160a, provides in part: "The contract of employment of a teacher shall be renewed for the following school year unless such teacher has been notified in writing prior to March first of that year that such contract will not be renewed." Question (i) asks whether this law creates "a status of employment within which the plaintiff may claim employment subject to the right to bargain salaries and working conditions?" The meaning of this is not clear and the briefs do not clarify it. It is the type of question that should be related to a specific state of facts. It cannot be answered in vacuo.

As to question (j), the plaintiff has no right to establish rules. As stated above, the right is and remains in the board.

Question (g) is answered, "yes, but not under chapter 369 of the General Statutes as amended." Questions (e), (h) and (j) are answered "no." Question (i) is not answered. No purpose would be served by answering the other questions categorically. Questions (a) and (b) are answered, "yes, with relation to the plaintiff's own members, provided its demands are kept within legal bounds." Questions (c) and (d) are answered, "yes, with relation to the plaintiff's own members, provided that this answer shall not be construed as approval of any specific contract which has been or may be entered into between the parties." Questions (f) is answered, "yes, arbitration may be a permissible method as to certain specific, arbitrable disputes." In answering some of these questions we have gone beyond the requirements of the specific questions asked in order to render such assistance as we properly may in helping to solve the difficulties of the parties.

No costs will be taxed in this court to either party.

In this opinion the other judges concurred.

• • •

CASE QUESTIONS

1. What did the court hold regarding the right to strike?

2. What was the court's feeling about the growth of unions among public employees?

3. How did the court answer the defendant Board of Education's argument that it did not have the power to make an agreement with the plaintiff organization?

UNITED FEDERATION OF POSTAL CLERKS v. BLOUNT, AS POSTMASTER GENERAL OF THE UNITED STATES
United States District Court, District of Columbia
325 F. Supp. 879 (1971)

● ● ●

PER CURIAM:

This action was brought by the United Federation of Postal Clerks (hereafter sometimes referred to as "Clerks"), an unincorporated public employee labor organization which consists primarily of employees of the Post Office Department, and which is the exclusive bargaining representative of approximately 305,000 members of the clerk craft employed by defendant. Defendant Blount is the Postmaster General of the United States. The Clerks seek declaratory and injunctive relief invalidating portions of 5 U.S.C. § 7311, 18 U.S.C. § § 1918, an affidavit required by 5 U.S.C. § 3333 to implement the above statutes, and Executive Order 11491, C.F.R., Chap. II, p. 191. The Government, in response, filed a motion to dismiss or in the alternative for summary judgment, and plaintiff filed its oppositon thereto and cross motion for summary judgment. A three judge court was convened pursuant to 28 U.S.C. § 2282 and § 2284 to consider this issue.

The Statutes Involved

5 U.S.C. § 7311(3) prohibits an individual from accepting or holding a position in the federal government or in the District of Columbia if he

"(3) participates in a strike . . . against the Government of the United States or the government of the District of Columbia. . . ."

Paragraph C of the appointment affidavit required by 5 U.S.C. § 3333, which all federal employees are required to execute under oath, states (POD Form 61):

"I am not participating in any strike against the Government of the United States or any agency thereof, and I will not so participate while an employee of the Government of the United States or any agency thereof."

18 U.S.C. § 1918, in making a violation of 5 U.S.C. § 7311 a crime, provides:

"Whoever violates the provision of section 7311 of title 5 that an individual may not accept or hold a position in the Government of the United States or the government of the District of Columbia if he . . .

"(3) participates in a strike, or asserts the rights to strike, against the Government of the United States or the District of Columbia . . .

"shall be fined not more than $1,000 or imprisoned not more than one year and a day, or both."

Section 2(e) (2) of Executive Order 11491 exempts from the definition of a labor organization any group which:

"asserts the right to strike against the Government of the United States or any agency thereof, or to assist or participate in such a strike, or imposes a duty or obligation to conduct, assist or participate in such a strike. ..."

Section 19(b) (4) of the same Executive Order makes it an unfair labor practice for a labor organization to:

"call or engage in a strike, work stoppage, or slowdown; picket an agency in a labor-management dispute; or condone any such activity by failing to take affirmative action to prevent or stop it; ..."

Plaintiff's Contentions

Plaintiff contends that the right to strike is a fundamental right protected by the Constitution, and that the absolute prohibition of such activity by 5 U.S.C. § 7311(3) and the other provisions set out above thus constitutes an infringement of the employees' First Amendment rights of association and free speech and operates to deny them equal protection of the law. Plaintiff also argues that the language to "strike" and "participates in a strike" is vague and overbroad and therefore violative of both the First Amendment and the due process clause of the Fifth Amendment. For the purposes of this opinion, we will direct our attention to the attack on the constitutionality of 5 U.S.C. § 7311(3), the key provision being challenged. To the extent that the present wording of 18 U.S.C. § 1918(3) and Executive Order 11491 does not reflect the actions of two statutory courts in Stewart v. Washington, 301 F.Supp. 610 (D.C.D.C. 1969) and N.A.L.C. v. Blount, 305 F.Supp. 546 (D.C.D.C.1969), said wording, insofar as it inhibits the *assertion* of the right to strike, is overbroad because it attempts to reach activities protected by the First Amendment and is therefore invalid. With this *caveat,* our treatment of the issue raised by plaintiffs with respect to the constitutionality of 5 U.S.C. § 7311(3) will also apply to 18 U.S.C. § 1918, the penal provision, and to Form 61, the affidavit required by 5 U.S.C. § 3333. For the reasons set forth below, we deny plaintiff's request for declaratory and injunctive relief and grant defendant's motion to dismiss.

I. PUBLIC EMPLOYEES HAVE NO CONSTITUTIONAL RIGHT TO STRIKE.

At common law no employee, whether public or private, had a constitutional right to strike in concert with his fellow workers. Indeed, such collective action on the part of employees was often held to be a conspiracy. When the right of private employees to strike finally received full protection, it was by statute, Section 7 of the National Labor Relations Act, which "took this conspiracy weapon away from the employer in employment relations which affect interstate commerce" and guaranteed to employees in the private sector the right to engage in concerted activities for the purpose of collective bargaining. See discussion in International

Union, U.A.W.A., A.F. of L. Local 232 v. Wisconsin Employment Relations Board, 336 U.S. 245,-257-259, 69 S.Ct. 516, 93 L.Ed. 651-(1948). It seems clear that public employees stand on no stronger footing in this regard than private employees and that in the absence of a statute, they too do not possess the right to strike. The Supreme Court has spoken approvingly of such a restriction, see Amell v. United States, 384 U.S. 158, 161, 86 S.Ct. 1384, 16 L.Ed.2d 445 (1965), and at least one federal district court has invoked the provisions of a predecessor statute, 5 U.S.C. § 118p–r, to enjoin a strike by government employees. Tennessee Valley Authority v. Local Union No. 110 of Sheet Metal Workers, 233 F.Supp. 997 (D.C.W.D.Ky.1962). Likewise, scores of state cases have held that state employees do not have a right to engage in concerted work stoppages, in the absence of legislative authorization. See, e. g. Los Angeles Metropolitan Transit Authority v. Brotherhood of R.R. Trainmen, 54 Cal. 684, 8 Cal.Rptr. 1, 355 P.2d 905 (1960); Board of Education, etc. v. Redding, 32 Ill.2d 567, 207 N.E.2d 427 (1965); Alcoa, City of v. International Brotherhood of Electrical Workers, 203 Tenn. 13, 308 S.W.2d 476 (1957). It is fair to conclude that, irrespective of the reasons given, there is a unanimity of opinion in the part of courts and legislatures that government employees do not have the right to strike. See Moberly, "The Strike and Its Alternative in Public Employment," *University of Wisconsin Law Review* (1966) pp. 549-550, 554.

Congress has consistently treated public employees as being in a different category than private employees. The National Labor Relations Act of 1937 and the Labor Management Relations Act of 1947, (Taft-Hartley) both defined "employer" as not including any governmental or political subdivisions, and thereby indirectly withheld the protections of § 7 from governmental employees. Congress originally enacted the no-strike provision separately from other restrictions on employee activity, i. e., such as those struck down in *Stewart* v. *Washington* and *N.A.L.C.* v. *Blount,* supra, by attaching riders to appropriations bills which prohibited strikes by government employees. See for example the Third Urgent Deficiency Appropriation Act of 1946, which provided that no part of the appropriation could be used to pay the salary of anyone who engaged in a strike against the Government. Section 305 of the Taft-Hartley Act made it unlawful for a federal employee to participate in a strike, providing immediate discharge and forfeiture of civil service status for infractions. Section 305 was repealed in 1955 by Public Law 330, and re-enacted in 5 U.S.C. § 118p–r, the predecessor to the present statute.

Given the fact that there is no constitutional right to strike, it is not irrational or arbitrary for the Government to condition employment on a promise not to withhold labor collectively, and to prohibit strikes by those in public employment, whether because of the prerogatives of the sovereign, some sense of higher obligation associated with public service, to assure the continuing functioning of the Government without interruption, to protect public health and safety or for other reasons. Although plaintiff argues that the provisions in question are unconstitutionally broad in covering all Government employees regardless of the type or importance of the work they do, we hold that it makes no difference whether the jobs performed by certain public employees are regarded as "essential" or "non-essential," or whether similar jobs are performed by workers in private industry who do have the right to strike protected by statute. Nor is it relevant that some positions in private industry are arguably more affected with a public interest than are some positions in the Government service. While the Fifth Amendment contains no Equal Protection Clause similar to the one found in the Fourteenth Amendment, concepts of Equal Protection do inhere in Fifth Amendment Principles of Due Process. Bolling v. Sharpe, 347 U.S. 497, 74 S.Ct. 693, 98 L.Ed. 884 (1954). The Equal Protection Clause, however, does not forbid all discrimination. Where fundamental rights are not involved, a particular classification does not violate the Equal Protection Clause if it is not "arbitrary" or "irrational," i. e., "if any state of facts reasonably may be conceived to justify it." ... Since the right to strike cannot be considered a "fundamental" right, it is the test enunciated in *McGowan* which must be employed in this case. Thus, there is latitude for distinctions rooted in reason and practice, especially where the difficulty of drafting a no-strike statute which distinguishes among types and classes of employees is obvious.

Furthermore, it should be pointed out that the fact that public employees may not strike does not interfere with their rights which are fundamental and constitutionally protected. The right to organize collectively and to select representatives for the purposes of engaging in collective bargaining is such a fundamental right. ... But, as the Supreme Court noted in *International Union, etc.,* Local 232 v. Wisconsin Employment Relations Board, supra,

> "The right to strike, because of its more serious impact upon the public interest, is more vulnerable to regulation than the right to organize and select representatives for lawful purposes of collective bargaining which this Court has characterized as a 'fundamental right' and which, as the Court has pointed out, was recognized as such in its decisions long before it was given protection by the National Labor Relations Act." 336 U.S. at 259, 69 S.Ct. at 524.

Executive Order 11491 recognizes the right of federal employees to join labor organizations for the purpose of dealing with grievances, but that Order clearly and expressly defines strikes, work stoppages and slow-downs as unfair labor practices. As discussed above, that Order is the culmination of a long-standing policy. There certainly is no compelling reason to imply the existence of the right to strike from the right to associate and bargain collectively. In the private sphere, the strike is used to equalize bargaining power, but this has universally been held not to be appropriate when its object and purpose can only be to influence the essentially political decisions of Government in the allocation of its resources. Congress has an obligation to ensure that the machinery of the Federal Government continues to function at all times without interference. Prohibition of strikes by its employees is a reasonable implementation of that obligation.

Accordingly, we hold that the provisions of the statute, the appointment affidavit and the Executive Order, as construed above, do not violate any constitutional rights of those employees who are members of plaintiff's union. *The Government's motion to dismiss the complaint is granted. Order to be presented.*

• • •

CASE QUESTIONS

1. What did the court say about the common law right to strike for public employees?

2. How did Section 7 of the National Labor Relations Act enter into the decision?

3. What interpretation was made of the Executive Order 11491?

AMERICAN FEDERATION OF STATE, COUNTY, AND MUNICIPAL EMPLOYEES, AFL—CIO, v. WOODWARD, AS CITY COMMISSIONER OF THE CITY OF NORTH PLATTE, NEBRASKA
United States Court of Appeals, Eighth Circuit
406 F.2d 137 (1969)

• • •

HEANEY, Circuit Judge.

The principal question raised on this appeal is whether public employees, discharged because they joined a labor union, have a right of action for damages and injunctive relief under Section 1 of the Civil Rights Act of 1871, 42 U.S.C. § 1983, against the public official who discharged them. The answer to this question turns on whether public employees have a constitutionally protected right to belong to a labor union.

The District Court dismissed the plaintiffs' complaint on the grounds that it failed to allege facts constituting a claim under 42 U.S.C. § 1983. We reverse.

The complaint alleged: that LeRoy Gage and John Engleman had been employed by the Street Department of the City of North Platte, Nebraska; that in May, 1967, the Union began an organizational campaign among the employees of the Street Department; that a number of employees, including Gage and Engleman, became members of the Union; that Defendant Woodward, the City Commissioner in charge of the Street Department, learned of the Union activities and of the fact that Gage and Engleman had become members of the Union; that Woodward "purposely and maliciously and solely for the purpose of discriminating against such employees of the Street Department . . . as joined or wanted to join a Union, threatened said employees with possible discharge; . . . [and] did in fact discharge . . . Gage and Engleman" solely because they joined the Union; and that Woodward reduced the salaries of other employees for the same reason.

Engleman and Gage claimed damages in the sum of $5,000 and, along with the plaintiff Union, sought an injunction prohibiting the defendant from discriminating against any employee of the Street Department because of membership or nonmembership in a union and interfering with the organization of the employees of the department.

To invoke the remedies provided by the Civil Rights Act of 1871, the plaintiffs must show that the Commissioner deprived them of rights, privileges or immunities secured by the United States Constitution or by the laws of the United States, and that the Commissioner acted under color of law. The plaintiffs argue that this was done here as the Commissioner deprived them of their right to freedom of association under the First Amendment made applicable to the states by the Fourteenth Amendment.

The First Amendment protects the right of one citizen to associate with other citizens for any lawful purpose free from government interference. The guarantee of the "right of assembly" protects more than "the right to attend a meeting; it includes the right to express one's attitudes or philosophies by membership in a group or by affiliation with it or by other lawful means. . . ."

Union membership is protected by the right of association under the First and Fourteenth Amendments. Thomas v. Collins, 323 U.S. 516, 65 S.Ct. 315, L.Ed. 430 (1945); McLaughlin v. Tilendis, 398 F.2d 287 (7th Cir. 1968).

The Court commented in *Thomas:*

". . . Great secular causes, with small ones, are guarded. The grievances for redress of which the right of petition was insured, and with it the right of assembly, are not solely religious or political ones. And the rights of free speech and a free press are not confined to any field of human interest.

"The idea is not sound therefore that the First Amendment's safeguards are wholly inapplicable to business or economic activity. . . ."

Id. 323 U.S. at 531, 65 S.Ct. at 323.

". . . This Court has recognized that 'in the circumstances of our times the dissemination of information concerning the facts of a labor dispute must be regarded as within that area of free discussion that is guaranteed by the Constitution. . . . Free discussion concerning the conditions in industry and the causes of labor disputes appears to us indispensable to the effective and intelligent use of the processes of popular government to shape the destiny of modern industrial society. Thornhill v. Alabama, 310 U.S. 88, 102, 103 [60 S.Ct. 736, 84 L.Ed. 1093,]. . . . The right . . . to discuss, and inform people concerning, the advantages and disadvantages of unions and joining them is protected not only as part of free speech, but as part of free assembly. . . ."

Id. at 532, 65 S.Ct. at 323.

In *Tilendis,* the Court held that a complaint alleging that a non-tenure teacher was dismissed because of his membership in a union stated a claim upon which relief could be granted under the Civil Rights Act of 1871. The Court stated:

"It is settled that teachers have the right of free association, and unjustified interference with teachers' associational freedom violates the Due Process clause of the Fourteenth Amendment. . . . Public employment may not be subjected to unreasonable conditions, and the assertion of First Amendment rights by teachers will usually not warrant their dismissal. ... Unless there is some illegal intent, an individual's right to form and join a union is protected by the First Amendment. ..."

The defendant argues that the plaintiffs have no federally protected right to be continued in public employment. The Supreme Court disposed of his argument in Wieman v. Updegraff, 344 U.S. 183, 191–192, 73 S.Ct. 215, 219, 97 L.Ed. 216 (1952):

". . . [T]he facile generalization that there is no constitutionally protected right to public employment is to obscure the issue. For, in United Public Workers, though we held that the Federal Government through the Hatch Act [18 U.S.C.A. §§ 118j, 118*l*] could properly bar its employees from certain political activity thought inimical to the interests of the Civil Service, we cast this holding into perspective by emphasizing that Congress could not 'enact a regulation providing that no Republican, Jew or Negro shall be appointed to federal office, or that no federal employee shall attend Mass or take any active part in missionary work.' ... We need not pause to consider whether an abstract right to public employment exists. It is sufficient to say that constitutional protection does extend to the public servant whose exclusion . . . is patently arbitrary or discriminatory."

This same theme has been repeated by the Supreme Court on a number of occasions. In Beilan v. Board of Public Ed. of Phila., 357 U.S. 399, 405, 78 S.Ct. 1317, 1321, 2 L.Ed.2d 1414 (1958), the Court stated that, "By engaging in teaching in the public schools, petitioner did not give up his right to freedom of belief, speech or association. ..." Again, in Keyishian v. Board of Regents of University of State of New York, 385 U.S. 589, 605, 87 S.Ct. 675, 685, 17 L.Ed. 2d 629 (1967), the Court specifically rejected the theory that public employment "may be conditioned upon surrender of constitutional rights which could not be abridged by direct government action."

No paramount public interest of the State of Nebraska or the City of North Platte warranted limiting the plaintiffs' right to freedom of association. To the contrary, it is the public policy of Nebraska that employment should not be denied on the basis of union membership. The Constitution of the State of Nebraska, Article XV, Section 13, and the laws of Nebraska, Reissue Revised Statutes of 1943, § 48–217, specifically provide that "no person shall be denied employment because of membership in or affiliation with . . . a labor organization." Neither the Constitution nor the statute is limited by its terms to private employment and, in our view, it is not so limited. ... We further note that Reissue Revised Statutes of 1943, § 48–224 provides that a municipal corporation may "check off" union dues if an employee so requests.

Reversed and remanded.

● ● ●

CASE QUESTIONS

1. What type of circumstances led up to the action by the commissioner against the employees?

2. The court is asked to comment on the protection given to the employees by the First and Fourteenth Amendments. What was said?

3. The City Commissioner argues that the employees did not have to work for the city if they did not want to obey its regulations. What did the court observe in this issue?

SHELTON v. TUCKER
United States Supreme Court
364 U.S. 479 (1960)

• • •

MR. JUSTICE STEWART delivered the opinion of the Court.

An Arkansas statute compels every teacher, as a condition of employment in a state-supported school or college, to file annually an affidavit listing without limitation every organization to which he has belonged or regularly contributed within the preceding five years. At issue in these two cases is the validity of that statute under the Fourteenth Amendment to the Constitution. No. 14 is an appeal from the judgment of a three-judge Federal District Court upholding the statute's validity, 174 F. Supp. 351. No. 83 is here on writ of certiorari to the Supreme Court of Arkansas, which also held the statute constitutionally valid. ...

The statute in question is Act 10 of the Second Extraordinary Session of the Arkansas General Assembly of 1958. The provisions of the Act are summarized in the opinion of the District Court as follows:

"Act 10 provides in substance that no person shall be employed or elected to employment as a superintendent, principal or teacher in any public school in Arkansas, or as an instructor, professor or teacher in any public institution of higher learning in that State until such person shall have submitted to the appropriate hiring authority an affidavit listing all organizations to which he at the time belongs and to which he has belonged during the past five years, and also listing all organizations to which he at the time is paying regular dues or is making regular contributions, or to which within the past five years he has paid such dues or made such contributions. The Act further provides, among other things, that any contract entered into with any person who has not filed the prescribed affidavit shall be void; that no public moneys shall be paid to such person as compensation for his services; and that any such funds so paid may be recovered back either from the person receiving such funds or from the board of trustees or other governing body making the payment. The filing of a false affidavit is denounced as perjury, punishable by a fine of not less than five hundred nor more than one thousand dollars, and, in addition, the person filing the false affidavit is to lose his teaching license." ...

These provisions must be considered against the existing system of teacher employment required by Arkansas law. Teachers there are hired on a year-to-year basis. They are not covered by a civil service system, and they have no job security beyond the end of each school year. The closest approach to tenure is a statutory provision for the automatic renewal of a teacher's contract if he is not notified within ten days after the end of a school year that the contract has not been renewed. Ark. 1947 Stat. Ann. § 80–1304(b)(1960); ...

The plaintiffs in the Federal District Court (appellants here) were B. T. Shelton, a teacher employed in the Little Rock Public School System, suing for himself and others similarly situated, together with the Arkansas Teachers Association and its Executive Secretary, suing for the benefit of members of the Association. Shelton had been employed in the Little Rock Special School District for twenty-five years. In the spring of 1959 he was notified that, before he could be employed for the 1959–1960 school year, he must file the affidavit required by Act 10, listing all his organizational connections over the previous five years. He declined to file the affidavit, and his contract for the ensuing school year was not renewed. At the trial the evidence showed that he was not a member of the Communist Party or of any organization advocating the overthrow of the Government by force, and that he was a member of the National Association for the Advancement of Colored People. The court upheld Act 10, finding the information it required was "relevant," and relying on several decisions of this Court. ...

The plaintiffs in the state court proceedings (petitioners here) were Max Carr, an associate professor at the University of Arkansas, and Ernest T. Gephardt, a teacher at Central High School in Little Rock, each suing for himself and others similarly situated. Each refused to execute and file the affidavit required by Act 10. Carr executed an affirmation in which he listed his membership in professional organizations, denied ever having been a member of any subversive organization, and offered to answer any questions which the University authorities might constitutionally ask touching upon his qualifications as a teacher. Gephardt filed an affidavit stating that he had never belonged to a subversive organization, disclosing his membership in the Arkansas Education Association and the American Legion, and also offering to answer any questions which the school authorities might constitutionally ask touching upon his qualifications as a teacher. Both were advised that their failure to comply with the requirements of Act 10 would make impossible their reemployment as teachers for the following school year. The Supreme Court of Arkansas upheld the constitutionality of Act 10, on its face and as applied to the petitioners. 231 Ark. 641, 331 S. W. 2d 701.

I.

It is urged here, as it was unsuccessfully urged throughout the proceedings in both the federal and state courts, that Act 10 deprives teachers in Arkansas of their rights to personal, associational, and academic liberty, protected by the Due Process Clause of the Fourteenth Amendment from invasion by state action. ...

The vigilant protection of constitutional freedoms is nowhere more vital than in the community of American schools. "By limiting the power of the States to interfere with freedom of speech and freedom of inquiry and freedom of association, the Fourteenth Amendment protects all persons, no matter what their calling. But, in view of the nature of the teacher's relation to the effective exercise of the rights which are safeguarded by the Bill of Rights and by the Fourteenth Amendment, inhibition of freedom of thought, and of action upon thought, in the case of teachers brings the safeguards of those amendments vividly into operation. Such unwarranted inhibition upon the free spirit of teachers . . . has an unmistakable tendency to chill that free play of the spirit which all teachers ought especially to cultivate and practice; it makes for caution and timidity in their associations by potential teachers." . . . "Scholarship cannot flourish in an atmosphere of suspicion and distrust. Teachers and students must always remain free to inquire, to study and to evaluate. . . ."

The unlimited and indiscriminate sweep of the statute now before us brings it within the ban of our prior cases. The statute's comprehensive interference with associational freedom goes far beyond what might be justified in the exercise of the State's legitimate inquiry into the fitness and competency of its teachers. The judgments in both cases must be reversed.

It is so ordered.

● ● ●

CASE QUESTIONS

1. What did the court say about the idea of checking on teachers beyond their ability to teach?

2. What did you get from the case concerning the possible union efforts of the teachers in question?

3. What protection did the U.S. Supreme Court say that the teachers had?

HOSPITALS AND HEALTH CARE INSTITUTIONS   13

Most health care institutions have been operated as nonprofit organizations either by a medical group or in conjunction with a city, state, or local political unit (although some hospitals are *proprietary, for profit*). This ownership characteristic has taken them out of the jurisdiction of traditional labor relations. Specifically, Section 2 of the National Labor Relations Act exempts nonprofit hospitals from the definition of an employer under the Act. This was changed, however, by the 1974 amendments to the Act which included nonprofit hospitals and health care institutions as employers under the Act and instituted some new procedural requirements. This change has had a profound effect on health care institutions and employer-employee relationships.

The economic structure of hospital and health care institutions is very complicated. At one end of the job scale are the professional physicians and specialists who receive high compensation for services. At the other end of the scale are the employees in the housekeeping, dietary, and maintenance departments who receive the minimum wage. Many of the basic functions of the health care system require tasks which are menial but nevertheless important.

As health care systems have become more mechanized, new job classifications have developed which include medical technicians, computer operators, communications specialists, and safety engineers. The total range of services in health care institutions has increased and forced a corresponding increase in the costs of medical care and services. The effect of technology on the employees has been mixed. While those at the middle and upper job levels have been rewarded with job satisfaction and reasonable wages, for the most part those at the bottom of the scale have received little job satisfaction and low wages.

UNIONIZATION DRIVES

Drives to organize unions have occurred in many hospitals and typically have started with the lower paid employees. Frequently these drives have been sponsored financially by the international unions. As a result of the drives at least a minority of the employees usually joins the union or signs representation cards. Such interest in the union ordinarily cannot be ignored by hospital administrators, and informal bargaining usually takes place during this period.

The National Labor Relations Board took jurisdiction over the nonprofit hospitals following the August 25, 1974 amendments. Most of the representation procedures are similar to those for other private employers. Investigations of employee support of the union petition are conducted following petitions for elections.

Some states have public employee bargaining laws. These were passed before the 1974 amendments and reflect an earlier felt need within the health care field for procedures to follow concerning elections and voting. A state labor relations board may assist the parties in counting representation cards, holding the election, and settling alleged unfair labor practices. Some overlapping jurisdiction is possible in those states which have public employee bargaining laws. The technical questions may be handled by informal negotiation or eventually by a formal state or federal hearing.

INTRODUCTION TO THE CASES

The National Relations Act has created jurisdiction for the National Labor Relations Board. The *Raymond Convalescent Hospital, Inc.* case involves a proprietary (for profit) hospital. The question is whether management has unlawfully refused to recognize the union and to bargain with it in good faith.

The *Butte Medical Properties* case is an excellent review of the background arguments which were brought before the NLRB. Background considerations include the economic impact of including proprietary hospitals versus the cost to NLRB. In this case the many parties are arguing *policy*. The individual case is important to the parties, but the policy is even more important.

In the *Walters Ambulance Service, Inc.* case the NLRB gives an advisory opinion. An *advisory opinion* is a service provided by the NLRB. After applying the given facts and current regulations, the Board gives the parties an advance decision, to advise the parties what will happen when a formal case is presented. This important function allows the parties to ask for guidance *before* the issues have become very involved. This is the preventive part of the law which attempts to teach the public what is acceptable and avoid conflicts.

RAYMOND CONVALESCENT HOSPITAL INC. v. LOCAL 399, SERVICE & HOSPITAL EMPLOYEES UNION, SEIU, AFL—CIO
Case 31-CA-4152, NLRB, July 16, 1974

● ● ●

DECISION
Statement of the Case

RICHARD D. TAPLITZ, Administrative Law Judge: This case was tried at Los Angeles, California, on March 26, 1974. The charge was filed on December 17, 1973, by Service & Hospital Employees Union, Local 399, SEIU, AFL–CIO, herein called the Union. The complaint issued on February 21, 1974, and alleges that Raymond Convalescent Hospital, Inc., herein called Respondent, violated Sections 8(a) (1) and (5) of the National Labor Relations Act as amended.

ISSUES

The primary issues are:

1. Whether Respondent through its agent, Mildred V. Ames, violated Section 8(a) (1) of the Act by: Interrogating an employee concerning his union sentiments; telling employees that Respondent could offer better benefits than the Union could; telling employees that they could come into her office to inform her if they did not want the Union; and telling employees that key employees would quit if the Union were designated as collective-bargaining representative.

2. Whether Respondent violated Section 8(a) (5) of the Act by refusing to recognize and bargain with the Union where Respondent was a successor to an employer having an outstanding contract with the Union and where Respondent did not have a good faith doubt that the Union continued to represent the employees. . . .

Findings of Fact

I.. The Business of Respondent

Respondent is a California corporation with its principal place of business in Pasadena, California, where it operates a nursing home. . . .

II. The Labor Organization Involved

The Union is a labor organization within the meaning of Section 2(5) of the Act.

III. The Alleged Unfair Labor Practices

A. *Background*

Through November 18, 1973, Park Raymond Convalescent Hospital, herein called Park Raymond, operated the nursing home now run by Respondent (Raymond Convalescent Hospital, Inc.). Respondent, as owner and lessor of the building housing Park Raymond, foreclosed on the lessee, Park Raymond, took possession and continued without interruption to operate a proprietary nursing home at the same location. Respondent used the same equipment, employed many of the same employees and supervisors and produced substantially the same services as Park Raymond previously had done. Park Raymond employed approximately 40 employees and of them 38 were employed by Respondent on November 19, 1973, with no interruption in their jobs. On December 1, 1973, four employees were hired, two of whom had previously worked for Park Raymond. Between December 3 and December 7, 1973, four additional employees were hired, none of whom had worked for Park Raymond. Respondent continued to perform services for substantially the same patients as had Park Raymond.

For many years Park Raymond had a collective-bargaining contract with the Union. The last contract, by its terms, is effective from April 17, 1972 through April 16, 1975.

Mildred V. Ames was administrator of the nursing home from November 19, 1973, when Respondent took over the nursing home, until February 11, 1974 when she left Respondent's employ. From September

1970 to October 3, 1973, Ames had been administrator for Park Raymond. During the approximately six weeks between October 3 and the commencement of her employment with Respondent on November 19, 1973, Ames had worked for another employer. During that period Myra Burman was administrator for Park Raymond. Burman was told by her employer at Park Raymond to contact Ames and tell her what had transpired at the facility in the time that Burman had been administrator. On November 14 or 15, 1973, Ames and Burman met and discussed some possible employee changes. Burman mentioned that the employees were strong union people. Ames replied, "I will have nothing to do with the Union," or, "I will kick the Union out as soon as I get back to Park Raymond."

On December 1, 1973, Respondent received a letter dated November 29 in which the Union stated that it had been informed that Respondent would give effect to the contract the Union had with Respondent's predecessor. The letter enclosed copies of the collective-bargaining agreement for Respondent to sign. Respondent neither signed the contract nor wrote a response to the letter. Instead, on December 7, 1973, Respondent filed with the Board a Petition for an Election. ... Respondent has not recognized or bargained with the Union, claiming that it has no legal obligation to do so. On December 10, 1973 Union Business Agent Booker Graham came to the nursing home and was told by Ames that as far as she was concerned, the place was not union.

By letter dated February 20, 1974, the Regional Director for Region 31 of the Board notified Respondent that a complaint was going to issue in the instant case and that Respondent's Petition for an Election was therefore dismissed.

B. *The Alleged Violations of Section 8(a)(1) of the Act*

1. The alleged interrogation of Brown

Theodore Brown, Jr., is an employee of Respondent in the housekeeping department. During the first week of December 1973, Brown had a conversation with Administrator Mildred V. Ames in Ames' office. No one else was present at the time. According to Brown: Ames asked him what his opinion was concerning the Union; Brown replied there were advantages and disadvantages but that he felt he didn't want to belong to the Union; Ames said that Leipzig, (the owner of Respondent) no longer had a contract with the Union; and Ames also said that she wanted to get everyone's opinion concerning how they felt about the Union.

Ames' testimony concerning this conversation was substantially different. According to Ames, Brown spoke to her in her office when he was doing maintenance work there. Ames averred that: Brown asked her about the Union; she replied that they didn't have a union contract. Brown asked, "Does that mean we don't have to belong to the Union?" She said, "Mr. Leipzig does not have a union contract." Brown said he didn't want to belong to the Union. Ames, in her testimony, denied that she asked Brown his opinion about the Union and further denied that she said she was going to ask other employees their opinions.

I credit Ames' version of the conversation. Ames was a direct and convincing witness. There is much testimony in the record concerning information volunteered by employees to Ames concerning the Union, but other than Brown's there is no testimony that Ames interrogated employees concerning the Union. Brown was not a convincing witness. At one point in his testimony he averred that he did not recall Ames saying that Leipzig had no contract with the Union. Later in his testimony, he acknowledged that Ames did mention something about Leipzig not having a contract with the Union.

My observation of Ames and Brown as they testified and the content of their testimony leads me to the conclusion that Ames was the more accurate witness of the two, and I therefore credit her denial that she interrogated Brown concerning his union sympathies. I shall therefore recommend that paragraph 12(a) of the complaint, which appears to allege that interrogation as a violation of the Act, be dismissed.

2. The December 7, 1973 meeting

On December 7, 1973, Ames called a meeting of Respondent's employees. About 20 or 25 employees attended the meeting at 2:45 p.m. that day. There is a substantial conflict in testimony as to what was said.

Ames testified as follows: Ames began the meeting by reading a statement that had been prepared by Harry Stang, Respondent's attorney. She read it word for word as follows:

> I want to take a few minutes of your time to discuss a subject which is of concern to all of us. I hope you will pardon me for reading this, but I do not want to be misquoted later on.
>
> Last Friday we received a letter from Local 399. The letter demanded that we sign a new contract with Local 399. Obviously, we will continue the wages and benefits which you now have. However, we are quite concerned about the clause in the contract which would require each and every one of you to join the Union and pay dues as a condition of keeping your jobs here. (At this point in her presentation, Ames read Article 2, paragraphs a, b, c and d of the contract Park Raymond had with the Union. Those paragraphs relate to union security.) In light of the fact that several of our employees have told me that they don't wish to be members of the union, we are worried about the effect this clause would have on our employees.
>
> It is my intention to review the situation with Mr. Leipzig before we make any decisions. However, I did want to let you know about the situation because it is so important to you.
>
> If you have any questions, I will try to answer them.

Ames then asked whether there were any questions. Employee Biggs told the group that he did not want the Union and he didn't think he received enough for his dues. Biggs added that Park Raymond had been fair in giving him merit increases and he preferred to go along with that system rather than joining the Union. Licensed Vocational Nurse, (L.V.N.) Evelyn Reser then said, "I will just tell you one thing. If we have to fool with that Union, I am quitting." Another employee, Mary Margo said that she did not receive any benefit from the Union and she did not want the Union. Margo then said, "Let's just vote on it now," and a number of people put up their hands. At that point Ames said, "Just wait a minute. We couldn't vote it in or out at this time as I understand it. I don't want you to make a hasty decision, please, think about it and you can let Mr. Leipzig or I know at a later time what you really feel about it." Employee Lee Thompson then asked Ames questions concerning the cost to join, how dues were collected, what benefits there were, and the starting rate under the contract. Ames answered Thompson and told her she was free to read the contract any time. Another employee asked if Leipzig was going to recognize vacation status or time that had been built up with Park Raymond, and Ames replied that she couldn't answer the question then but that any time the employee came to the office, they would discuss it. Ames went on to say that she was always willing to discuss any problem with the people, and her door was always open. Another employee asked what the benefits would be if they didn't join the Union. Ames picked up the paper she had read from and said, "Obviously, we will continue the wages and benefits which you have now."

Four witnesses in addition to Ames testified concerning what was said at the December 7 meeting. Nurses aides Frankie Wells (who was the shop steward) and Willie Minnifield, as well as supervisor Rose Triplett, testified on behalf of the General Counsel. Orderly William Biggs testified on behalf of Respondent. All five of the witnesses corroborated parts of each other's testimony and disagreed as to other parts. The pivotal differences are keyed to the matters alleged in paragraphs 12(b), (c) and (d) of the complaint.

Paragraph 12(b) of the complaint alleges that Ames told the employees that Respondent could offer the employees better benefits than the Union could. As noted above, Ames testified that her remark concerning benefits occurred during the time she was reading the speech prepared by her attorney and that she said, "Obviously, we will continue the wages and benefits which you now have." Biggs corroborated her testimony in this regard. Triplett testified that Ames did not say that Respondent could give the people better benefits than the Union. Minnifield in her initial testimony averred that Ames said that Leipzig would give them more benefits. However, on cross-examination Minnifield acknowledged that she could not remember if Ames said they would continue the benefits that they then had.

Wells testified that Ames said that Raymond Convalescent Hospital could give them better benefits than the Union. Wells' testimony in this regard is inconsistent with the witnesses of both Respondent and the General Counsel. I do not believe that Wells was accurate in her recollection of what happened at the meeting, and I do not credit her assertion that Ames promised better benefits than the Union. I shall, therefore, recommend that paragraph 12(b) of the complaint be dismissed.

Paragraph 12(c) of the complaint alleges that Ames told the employees that they could come into her office to inform her if they did not want the Union. As is set forth above, Ames acknowledged that she told the employees that they could let Leipzig or Ames know at a later time what they felt about it. However, she put the remark in the context of employee Margo's suggestion that the employees vote on the Union and the employees starting to put up their hands. She averred that she said, "Just wait a minute. We couldn't vote it in or out at this time as I understand it. I don't want you to make a hasty decision, please, think about it and you can let Mr. Leipzig or I know at a later time what you really feel about it." Biggs corroborated Ames in substantial part by testifying that after employee Margo spoke, Ames said that she didn't want a hasty decision and the employees could think it over in the next day or so and come to her office or let her know whether they wanted the Union.

Minnifield testified that Ames said that they could each come to her office to talk to her about the Union and whether they wanted it. Triplett testified that no one talked about a vote or a hasty decision. She also testified in substance that Ames told the employees that it was up to them whether they wanted to vote for or against the Union and that they could come to her office if they wanted to pursue the matter any further.

Wells testified that Ames said that she couldn't tell them how to vote but, if they wanted to, they could come to her office one at a time because her door was open to discuss if they wanted the Union or not. I believe that Ames was both a truthful and an accurate witness. Her testimony concerning what she said at the meeting was more detailed than that of the other witnesses and was fully credible. I do not believe that the recollection of the other witnesses was as accurate. In sum, I find that Ames was attempting to get the employees to refrain from conducting a poll of their union sentiment that might be considered unlawful, and was not soliciting them to come to her office and renounce the Union. In the context in which the statements were made, I find that Ames' remark did not violate the Act. I shall therefore recommend that paragraph 12(c) of the complaint be dismissed.

Paragraph 12(d) of the complaint alleges that Ames told the employees that licensed vocational nurses would quit if the Union were designated as collective-bargaining representative. Ames testified that she never said anything about LVN's quitting if the Union came in and that LVN Reser was the one who said that she (Reser) would quit if they had to "fool with that Union." Biggs in his testimony corroborated Ames' testimony to the effect that Ames did not say anything with respect to LVN's quitting. Minnifield testified as to the details of what was said at the meeting but she did not give any testimony concerning whether or not Ames made a statement concerning LVN's. Triplett testified that she did not hear anyone make a statement that the LVN's would quit if the Union got in.

In contrast to all the other witnesses, Wells testified that Ames told the employees that she had received a letter indicating the LVN's would quit if the Union got in. Wells also averred that LVN Reser did not threaten to quit if the Union came in. Ames' testimony is fully or partially corroborated by the testimony of the other witnesses while the testimony of Wells stands out in isolation. As indicated above, I believe that Ames was a more accurate witness than Wells and I credit Ames where her testimony conflicts with Wells'. I shall therefore recommend that paragraph 12(d) of the complaint be dismissed.

C. *The Refusal to Bargain*

1. The employee comments to Ames concerning union representation

Myra Burman, the administrator for Park Raymond from October 22,

1973 through November 17, 1973, credibly testified that during the time she was administrator there were no problems concerning the Union. However, Mildred Ames, the administrator who preceded Burman as Administrator for Park Raymond and who took over when Respondent began to operate the nursing home on November 19, 1973, credibly testified that from the first day she began working for Respondent employees told her that they did not want to be represented by the Union.

Respondent commenced its operations of the nursing home on November 19 with 38 employees, all of whom had immediately before been employed by Park Raymond in the bargaining unit represented by the Union. In the first 2 days of Respondent's operation, some 10 employees approached Ames and told her that they did not want the Union. Within the first 2 weeks of Respondent's operation (which began November 19, 1973) at least 23 of those 38 employees told Ames that they did not want the Union.

Respondent's records show that as of December 1, 1973, there were five additional employees. Two of the five had previously worked for Park Raymond while the others had not. Of these five, one, shortly after her hire, told Ames that she did not want the Union. Respondent's records also show that there were four more employees as of December 7, 1973. None of these had previously worked for Park Raymond. One, shortly after her hire, told Ames that she did not want the Union.

Summing up the above figures, it appears that of the 38 employees who started off with Respondent on November 19, 1973, at least 23, during the first two weeks of their employment, told Ames that they did not want the Union. In some circumstances it is proper to assume that new employees who are hired want union representation in the same proportion as the other employees. However, in the instant case, even if it is assumed that all of the new employees wanted the Union except those who specifically told Ames they did not, it appears that 25 employees out of a total complement of 47 told Respondent that they did not want the Union.

2. The checkoffs and union memberships

Ames credibly testified that she knew that only a small portion of the employees were on checkoff for the Union. Booker Graham, a business representative for the Union, testified concerning union records. He acknowledged that in the division of the Union in question it was the practice to have all union members on checkoff. Though Graham's analysis of the union records was at best confusing, he did admit that the Union only had eleven membership cards for the 38 employees listed on Respondent's records as being employed as of November 19, 1973. He also admitted that the Union had only 18 checkoffs for November.

3. Analysis and Conclusions

a. The Background principles

. . . Ordinarily, an employer may not question an incumbent union's majority status during the life of a contract. That risk, however, does not apply to successors because, under the principles established by the

Supreme Court. .. , a successor-employer is not bound by its predecessor's collective-bargaining contract in the absence of an undertaking to that effect. .... Respondent therefore stands in a similar position to a nonsuccessor employer at the end of a collective-bargaining contract. Respondent can rebut the presumption of continued majority either through proof that it predicated its refusal to bargain on a reasonably based doubt as to the continuing majority status of the Union or that the Union in fact no longer represented a majority of the unit employees. ...

b. *The lack of union membership and checkoff*

As is set forth above, Respondent has established through the testimony of Union Business Agent Booker that as of November 19, 1973 only a minority of its employees were members of or had checkoffs in favor of the Union. Respondent began operations with almost all of Park Raymond's employees, and on November 19, a representative employee complement had been hired. However, the Board has pointed out that majority support is not to be confused with majority union membership. The fact that a majority of employees are not members of a Union and do not pay dues is not equivalent to a lack of union support. *Orion Corp.,* 210 NLRB No. 71. As the Fourth Circuit Court of Appeals held in *Terrell Machine Co.* v. *N.L.R.B.,* 427 F.2d 1088 (C.A. 4, 1970): ". . . many employees are content neither to join the union nor to give it financial support but to enjoy the benefits of its representation. Nonetheless, the union may enjoy their support, and they may desire continued representation by it." Therefore, the evidence with regard to membership and checkoff, fails to establish that the Union did not continue to represent a majority of the employees.

c. *The good faith doubt*

Respondent has introduced substantial evidence with regard to its claim that its refusal to bargain was predicated on a good faith and reasonably grounded doubt of the Union's continued majority. As the Board held in *Terrell Machine Co.,* 173 NLRB 1480 enf. 427 F.2d 1088 (C.A. 4, 1970), there are two prerequisites for sustaining this defense. They are: "that the asserted doubt must be based on objective considerations and it must not have been advanced for the purpose of gaining time in which to undermine the Union. (footnotes omitted.)" In *Phil-Modes, Inc.,* 159 NLRB 944, 959, enf. 396 F.2d 131 (C.A. 5, 1968), the Board adopted the Administrative Law Judge's finding that: "And ordinarily evidence that employees reported or communicated to supervisors that they, the employees, wished to withdraw from the Union, absent any contemporaneous unfair labor practices, warrants a finding of good faith doubt as to majority. (Footnotes omitted.)"

As is set forth in detail above, some ten employees notified Respondent within the first day or two of its operation that they no longer wanted the Union to represent them, and within two weeks of the commencement of operations a majority of the employees had so informed Respondent. That two-week period ended December 3, 1973.

The Union's demand for recognition was received by Respondent on December 1, and on December 7, 1973 Respondent filed a petition for an election. As is set forth above, Respondent simply refrained from all action with regard to the Union prior to filing the petition for an election. The allegations of independent violations of Section 8(a) (1) of the Act have not been established by a preponderance of the evidence and there is no allegation nor proof that Respondent changed any wages, hours, or working conditions.

In determining whether Respondent had a good faith doubt as to the Union's majority, the remarks that Ames made to Burman (the administrator of Park Raymond from October 3 to November 18, 1973) must be considered. In the conversation which took place about November 14 or 15, 1973, which was four or five days before Respondent commenced operations, Ames referred to her anticipated employment with Respondent and said, "I will have nothing to do with the Union," or "I will kick the Union out as soon as I get back to Park Raymond." To some extent, this stated desire to be shed of the Union colors Respondent's assertion that it had a good faith doubt as to the Union's majority. There is no evidence in the record concerning Ames' prior relationship with the Union when she was administrator for Park Raymond or whether Ames had any reason to doubt the Union's majority status with regard to Park Raymond. Ames' remarks therefore give cause to view Respondent's defense with some skepticism. However, the remarks in themselves do not conclusively establish a lack of good faith with regard to Respondent's subsequent actions. The fact that Ames wanted to operate nonunion does not establish that at the time of the refusal to bargain with the Union Respondent did not have a good faith doubt that the Union represented a majority of the employees. As found above, by December 7, 1973, when Respondent filed a petition for an election, a majority of the employees in the bargaining unit had told Ames they didn't want the Union. Respondent had not engaged in any independent violation of Section 8(a) (1) of the Act which would have indicated that the employees were being coerced into expressing something other than their true desire. I therefore find that as of December 7, 1973, when it filed the petition for an election, Respondent did have a reasonably based good-faith doubt as to the Union's majority status and that doubt was based on objective considerations. I also find however, that Respondent has not proved that as of December 1, 1973, when it received the Union's demand for recognition, that it had such a good-faith doubt. Respondent has proved that some of the employees had indicated they did not want the Union by December 1 but has not proved that a majority had done so. The date upon which Respondent's obligation to bargain matured must therefore be considered.

A successor-employer is something of a hybrid creature. It does not have all the attributes of its predecessor, in whose shoes it partly stands, in that it is not bound by the predecessor's contract and it can raise a question concerning its good-faith doubt as to the Union's majority status at a time when the predecessor would have been barred from making such a claim because of an outstanding contract. In addition, a successor cannot withdraw recognition as can a predecessor, because a successor has never granted it in the first place. On the other hand, a successor is very unlike an employer who approaches a bargaining relationship for the first time, as the successor is bound by a presumption of continued majority from his predecessors relationship with the Union. In general, categorical analogies cannot always be properly drawn between the duties that a predecessor would have had and those that a successor in fact has.

An employer (where there is no successorship) can withhold further bargaining, after expiration of its contract, as of the date that it obtains a reasonably based doubt as to the Union's continuing majority. The date of the withholding of further bargaining or the withdrawal of recognition is decisive in determining whether there had been good faith. In the instant case, Respondent had hired a representative employee complement as of the moment it started operations. It had continued the predecessor's business with almost all of the predecessor's employees and had done so without interruption. Because it was a successor, Respondent had never bargained with or granted recognition to the Union and therefore did not cease bargaining or withdraw recognition. It did, however, refuse to bargain. It manifested its refusal by the filing of the RM petition on December 7, and by the statement of Ames to Union Business Agent Booker on December 10, that as far as Ames was concerned, the place was not union.

As a general rule, a successor's obligation to bargain with a union matures when the successor has hired a representative employee complement, a majority of whom had been represented by the Union. *Valley Nitrogen Producers, Inc.,* 207 NLRB No. 41; *NLRB* v. *Burns, etc, supra* at pg. 295. That rule presupposes that a demand for recognition and bargaining has been made by the Union. No Union demand is needed in a situation where there is a withdrawal of recognition or a cessation of bargaining by an employer. However, where an employer has not recognized the Union it can be found to have unlawfully refused to bargain only after the Union has demanded bargaining. Cf. *Spruce Up Corp.,* 209 NLRB No. 19, 85 LRRM 1426. The General Counsel therefore contends in his brief that the duty to bargain arose not on November 19 when Respondent had hired a representative employee complement but on December 1, 1973, when Respondent received the Union's demand. The date that a demand is received is ordinarily used as the refusal to bargain date in situations where an employer responds to the demand by engaging in unfair labor practices that are of such a nature as to prevent the possibility of a fair election. However, that is not the situation in the instant case. Here Respondent did not engage in any activities to undermine the Union. In the six days between the receipt of the demand and the filing by Respondent of the petition for an election, Respondent took no action with regard to the Union. Neither did it do anything to change wages, hours or conditions of employment. The first action of Respondent that could be construed as a refusal to bargain was the filing of the petition of December 7, 1973.

In the circumstances of this case, I see no compelling policy reason to require the legal conclusion that Respondent refused to bargain on the date the demand was received rather than on the date on which the Company responded to the demand. The demand was received in the context of a situation where there was ferment concerning the Union, and a number of the employees, though less than a majority, had told Respondent they did not want the Union. Respondent maintained the status quo for six days and did not use that time to attempt to undermine the Union or to unreasonably delay a response to the Union's demand. On the sixth day after the demand, and after a majority of the employees had indicated they did not want the Union, Respondent filed the RM petition and thereby indicated that it would not bargain with the Union unless the employees voted in a Board election in favor of the Union. Under these particular circumstances, I do not believe a finding that the Respondent violated Section 8(a) (5) of the Act is warranted.

In cases of this nature, two basic policy considerations must be weighed. The first is that the industrial stability that flows from the continuation of a collective-bargaining relationship, whether established through a history of bargaining or a successorship, should not be disturbed or subjected to question except for good cause. The second is that an employer's statutory obligation to bargain *only* with a majority union as well as the employees' right to affirm or deny their desire to be represented by an incumbent union, are meaningful only where the employees, at appropriate times, can make a definitive statement of their views. In this case such a statement was sought through the Board's election procedure. In the circumstances of this case, I believe that a proper balancing of these policies weighs in favor of the election procedure. ...

In sum, I find that, based on the particular circumstances set forth above, the General Counsel has not proved by a preponderance of the credible avidence that Respondent refused to bargain in violation of Section 8(a) (5) of the Act. *I shall therefore recommend that the complaint be dismissed in its entirety.*

• • •

CASE QUESTIONS

1. How did the administrative law judge establish that the convalescent home came under the jurisdiction of the NLRB?

2. Was was wrong with the administrator's talking with the employees in the convalescent hospital? Why did the union object?

3. What was the union argument about concerning the hospital's refusal to bargain in good faith? What action did the union want?

BUTTE MEDICAL PROPERTIES v. LOCAL 22, BUILDING SERVICE EMPLOYEES' UNION, AFL—CIO AND OTHER UNIONS
168 NLRB No. 52, 1967, Case 20-RC-6698

• • •

1. The Employer is a California corporation engaged in the operation of a private, or proprietary, 61-bed accredited short term general hospital located at Oroville, California. Its medical staff consists, *inter alia,* of 22 nonsalaried California-licensed physicians, 10 of whom are shareholders of the Employer and practice in Oroville, and 12 of whom maintain practices in various communities in the general Oroville area, which

includes communities located up to 25 miles distant from Oroville. Its patients are drawn exclusively from the Oroville area with the exception of occasional transients requiring emergency treatment.

The Employer's gross annual revenues during 1965 amounted to $1,000,000, 50 percent of which was obtained directly or indirectly from various health organizations, such as Blue Cross, and insurance companies, such as Metropolitan and Prudential. During this same period, the Employer expended a total of $191,000 for food, drugs, medical, and other supplies, part of which represents indirect out-of-State purchases of drugs, medicines, and hospital equipment valued in excess of $30,000.

While not disputing that its inflow of supplies and equipment from points outside the State of California suffciently establishes the Board's statutory jurisdiction, the Employer and those Intervenors supporting the Employer's position contend that the operation of the Employer in particular, and of proprietary hospitals in general, have an insufficient impact on commerce to warrant assertion of the Board's discretionary jurisdiction over such operations. Therefore, these parties argue, the Board should adhere to its past policy established in *Flatbush General Hospital,* 126 NLRB 144, of not asserting jurisdiction over this class of employers.

In *Flatbush,* the Board concluded, on facts before it at that time, that the operations of proprietary hospitals did not substantially affect commerce because such hospitals were essentially local operations subject to extensive state controls which would likely be extended to regulate such labor disputes as may arise involving such hospitals. A reevaluation of these factors compels us to reach a contrary conclusion.

There is no dispute that while all hospitals are primarily humanitarian facilities, some aspects of their operations are essentially business in character. Operationally, they are a multibillion dollar complex and, as such, comprise one of the largest industries in the United States. An effective part of this complex is composed of the approximately 970 proprietary hospitals which, as the record shows, influence and affect commerce beyond their immediate individual confines.

While it is generally true, as the Employer and its proponents argue, that hospitals such as the Employer's are "local" in that most of their medical staffs and patients come from nearby communities, that is not true with regard to difficult to secure personnel such as registered nurses, dieticians, and therapists. They often must be recruited from other areas. Nor are they local in the character of their operations since the present size and projected future growth of these hospitals indicate that their impact on commerce is already substantial and, in all likelihood, will become more so in the future. The facts show that despite a decrease in the number of proprietary hospitals in the last 20 years, these facilities are presently located in 44 states and, in fact, are an increasing part of the hospital industry in that, with fewer such hospitals, there has been a substantial increase in the number of beds, admissions, census, personnel, payroll, assets, and gross revenues which, in 1965, exceeded $551 million.

The operations of these facilities, moreover, necessarily include substantial purchases of food, beverages, china, silverware, linens, furniture, drugs, medication, supplies and equipment, utility services such as heat, light, and power, as well as various types of insurance. While the purchases made by a particular proprietary hospital may not directly involve interstate commerce, the aggregate purchases of all such facilities clearly have a substantial impact on the operations of the various supplying industries and involve substantial shipments of goods and supplies in interstate commerce. The Employer's operation alone, for example, discloses yearly out-of-state purchases in excess of $30,000.

Apart from the impact on commerce occasioned by the purchases of supplies and materials, there is also the financial interstate impact of billions of consumer dollars expended by millions of Americans for health protection and care, which dollars travel to and from national insurance companies and the Federal government which, in turn, make payments directly or indirectly to proprietary and other hospitals. The extent of national participation in health insurance benefits is indicated by a Department of Health, Education, and Welfare report showing that as of December 31, 1964, 79.2 percent of the United States civilian population were enrolled for health care benefits by private health insurance companies, viz, 62,429,000 in Blue Cross and Blue Shield, 104,230,000 in various insurance companies, and 6,960,000 in independent programs. An indication of the amounts received by proprietary hospitals for such health care is shown by the Employer's operation which obtained 50 percent of its $1,100,000 gross revenue from various national health insurance agencies.

Moreover, the material effect on commerce resulting from the nationwide individual expenditures for health care in which proprietary hospitals participate is further multiplied and augmented by the numerous public health and welfare enactments of Congress which are financed by the expenditure of public funds in which these facilities also participate, directly or indirectly. These concepts are manifest in the national Medicare program, which has a first year operating budget in excess of $2 billion and which provides for the payment of medical and hospital services to proprietary hospitals, including the Employer, as well as others, for the benefit of a large segment of our population. All of the foregoing unquestionably evinces a substantial national interest in, and a vital concern for, public health and welfare which, if affected by unregulated labor disputes in proprietary hospitals, would exert or tend to exert a wholly undesirable impact not only on the suppliers of these institutions, but also on the public, and, inevitably, on interstate commerce. We believe that these numerous private and public health care efforts have a very substantial effect on interstate commerce and that the public interest would be served by making available the orderly and peaceful procedures of this Act in the hospital industry. Indeed, concomitant with these particular efforts is the recognition in Sections 1(b), 201(a), and 206 of the National Labor Relations Act itself that the Act's policy of engendering stable industrial relations is based on advancing the health, safety, and general welfare of the Nation. Therefore, in view of the substantial interstate and national impact on commerce which is exerted by the Employer and by proprietary hospitals generally, it is apparent that these institutions are not insulated local enterprises.

Our reexamination has further revealed that although the Employer and other proprietary hospitals are subject to extensive state regulation, supervision, inspection, and licensing requirements, these controls generally do not pertain to labor matters which affect or tend to affect interstate commerce as contemplated by the Act. Thus, the state controls to which the Employer is subject pertain to matters such as building and construction, housing, fire protection, the use of drugs and medications, medical standards and similar matters, and to licensing requirements which relate to medical, nursing, and other hospital personnel. It is also subject to state wage and hour laws which detail working conditions for women and children. California has not legislated in the field of labor relations, however, except to the extent of providing a state conciliation service which becomes available to parties only upon mutual consent for the purposes of mediating disputes and conducting card checks and elections. The same situation prevails in greater or lesser degree in 45 other States. Such regulations, although germane to personal health and well being, are extremely limited in scope and application in the sphere of labor relations and, in reality, have little, if anything, to do with matters of union representation, collective bargaining, the effective settlement of labor disputes, or the stabilization and maintenance of industrial peace.

Therefore, inasmuch as the Employer's operation is representative of the operations of proprietary hospitals generally, and as the operations of proprietary hospitals affect commerce within the meaning of the Act, we find that the operations involved herein are within the Board's statutory jurisdiction. We further find, in view of all the foregoing, that the considerations bearing on our jurisdictional determination in this industry have markedly changed since the *Flatbush* decision and that it will effect the policies of the Act to assert our discretionary jurisdiction over the Employer as well as over proprietary hospitals generally. Accordingly, *Flatbush* is overruled. We are fully aware that our assertion of jurisdiction herein embraces those four States which have comprehensive labor law legislation affecting the hospital industry. However, the interests of orderly, effective, and uniform administration of our national policy require the assertion of jurisdiction over proprietary hospitals even in those few states which have legislated labor relations procedures and remedies in this industry.

Our action herein does not mean, however, that the Board must assert jurisdiction in all cases involving this class of employer. In the exercise of the Board's discretionary authority to decline to assert jurisdiction in those instances where it finds the policies of the Act will be effectuated by such action, we find that those policies will be effectuated by limiting assertion of jurisdiction to those cases involving proprietary hospitals which receive at least $250,000 in gross revenues per annum. The available evidence indicates that this standard will require the assertion of jurisdiction over that part of the class of employers involved herein which exerts a significant impact on commerce, and does so without burdening the Board's processes by involving the Board in the remainder of that class where the impact is relatively slight. The $250,000 standard imposed will accomplish this result while at the same time ensuring effective regulation of labor relations in this area.

Accordingly, as the Employer receives in excess of $250,000 gross revenues per annum, we find that it will effectuate the policies of the Act to assert jurisdiction herein.

2. The labor organization involved claims to represent certain employees of the Employer.

3. A question affecting commerce exists concerning the representation of certain employees of the Employer within the meaning of Sections 9(c) (1) and 2(6) and (7) of the Act.

Petitioner seeks to represent 74 of the Employer's 125 employees in a unit described as "all non-professional employees of the Employer at its Oroville location, including cooks, tray girls, maids, janitors, storekeepers, maintenance employees, grounds keepers, licensed vocational nurses, nurses aides, orderlies, surgical licensed vocational nurses, surgical technicians, surgical aides, and laboratory helpers, excluding physicians, registered nurses, medical technologists, and other professional employees, office clerical employees, head cook, chief housekeeper, chief engineer, and other supervisors as defined by the Act." The Employer agrees with the foregoing unit except that it would include the head cook, chief housekeeper, and chief engineer, and exclude surgical technicians; it takes no position with regard to nurses' aides, surgical aides (whom the Employer may consider to be part of the nurses' aides category), orderlies, and laboratory helpers.

With regard to the disputed classifications, the record shows that the head cook is in charge of the Employer's dietary department wherein she supervises general meal preparation, assigns and directs all kitchen work, and otherwise supervises two cooks and six tray girls, and effectively recommends the hiring and discharge of kitchen personnel. She is salaried and punches a time card—conditions apparently applicable to all of the Employer's employees—works 40 hours a week, and engages in cooking 4 days a week when the cooks are off duty. We find that the head cook is a supervisor within the meaning of the Act, and we shall exclude her from the unit.

The chief housekeeper assigns and supervises the work of nine maids and four janitors in the housekeeping department. She works 40 hours weekly on such shifts as she may be needed. In her absence, this department is not supervised. In addition to her supervisory duties, she spends a substantial part of her time performing the regular duties of a maid. She also may effectively recommend the hiring and discharge of employees in this department. We find that the chief housekeeper is also a supervisor, and we shall exclude her from the unit.

The chief engineer assigns and directs the work of four maintenance employees, two of whom work full time, and two of whom regularly work part time. He works a 40-hour week, primarily on the day shift, and also spends a considerable part of his time performing the same duties as other employees in this department. He also effectively recommends the hiring and discharge of maintenance department employees. Accordingly, we find that the chief engineer is a supervisor, and we shall exclude him from the unit.

As to the surgical technicians whom the Employer seeks to exclude from the unit, the record shows that the two employees in this classification perform certain work during surgery in the operating room where, *inter alia,* they handle surgical equipment and "actually help in surgery during the operation." They have had special training and are able to perform surgical techniques above the capabilities of surgical aides but below those of licensed vocational nurses. In the absence of affirmative evidence indicating that these employees lack a community of interest with other employees included in the unit, or are employees who otherwise should be excluded from the unit, and in view of the Employer's agreement to include therein the admittedly higher skilled licensed vocational nurses, we find that the surgical technicians are appropriately included in the unit sought by Petitioner.

We further find with respect to the nurses' aides, surgical aides, orderlies, and laboratory helper classifications on which the Employer takes no position, that these employees are also appropriately included in the unit. The record discloses that the Employer has 12 full-time and one regular part-time (16 hours weekly) nurses' aides, all of whom are women. These employees work 40 hours weekly on day and night shifts under the immediate supervision of licensed vocational nurses and the ultimate supervision of the director of nurses (a registered nurse). None of these employees has any supervisory responsibilities or any greater authority than any other employee in this classification. Their work is similar to that of orderlies in that they perform minimal care tasks for patients, such as aiding patients in bedpan use, bringing water to patients, taking temperatures and blood pressures, and sometimes handling transfusion and oxygen equipment. We shall include them in the unit.

The surgical aides, about whom the record is rather sparse in detail, appear to be basically nurses' aides attached to the surgery department. These employees, unlike the surgical technicians, perform no work in the operating room during surgery and are primarily responsible for the wrapping and sterilization of surgical packs (instruments) and the changing of blades on various instruments. We shall include them in the unit.

Orderlies perform minimal nursing care tasks, primarily for male patients, during a 40-hour week on both day and night shifts. They bathe male patients, transport patients by wheelchair, sometimes prepare patients for surgery, place patients on and remove them for the Guerney (a cart used to wheel patients to and from surgery), and handle some undisclosed types of equipment. These employees do not require a medical background and are not licensed. The Employer's four full-time and one regular part-time (32 hours weekly) orderlies have no supervisory responsibilities and perform their work under the supervision of the director of nurses. We shall include them in the unit.

As to the laboratory helpers, the record shows that the Employer's laboratory is composed of five employees, three of whom are admittedly professional employees (licensed medical technologists), and two laboratory helpers whose placement is here in issue. These helpers work on the day shift only, under the supervision of the chief laboratory technician. Fifty to seventy-five percent of their work is devoted to routine clerical duties in the laboratory, such as answering the telephone, running errands, filing EKG and other reports, and billing. The remainder of their time apparently is spent in routine laboratory duties such as washing test tubes, placing laboratory slips on patient's records, and attaching electrodes to patients for EKG tests. There are no educational requirements for these positions beyond the Employer's desire that these employees be high school graduates, and they are not required to be licensed. We shall include them in the unit.

Accordingly, we find that the following employees of the Employer constitute a unit appropriate for the purposes of collective bargaining within the meaning of Section 9(b) of the Act:

All nonprofessional employees of the Employer at its Oroville, California, location including cooks, tray girls, maids, janitors, storekeepers, maintenance employees, grounds keepers, orderlies, nurses' aides, surgical aides, surgical technicians, surgical licensed vocational nurses, licensed vocational nurses, and laboratory helpers, but excluding physicians, registered nurses, medical technologists, and other professional employees, office clerical employees, head cook, chief housekeeper, chief engineer, and other supervisors as defined in the Act.

• • •

CASE QUESTIONS

1. What is the medical center arguing about the jurisdiction of the National Labor Relations Board?

2. Why did all the other associations and organizations decide to offer their views in this case which involved one small hospital in California?

3. What was the issue in determing which employees are in the bargaining unit? Why does this make a difference to the Board?

WALTERS AMBULANCE SERVICE, INC. v.
ASSOCIATION OF UNITED AMBULANCE PERSONNEL
212 NLRB No. 60, 1974

• • •

ADVISORY OPINION

This is a petition filed on May 25, 1974, by Walters Ambulance Service, Inc., herein called the Employer, for an Advisory Opinion, in conformity with Sections 102.98 and 102.99 of the National Labor Relations Board's Rules and Regulations, Series 8, as amended, to determine whether the Board would assert jurisdiction over the Employer. On June 11, 1974, the Employer filed a brief in support of its petition.

In pertinent part, the petition and brief allege as follows:

1. There is pending before the New York State Labor Relations Board, herein called the State Board, a proceeding with docket numbers, Cases WE—1783, WU—1793, and WU—1794, involving the Employer and the Association of United Ambulance Personnel, herein called the Union.

2. The Employer operates an ambulance service in and about the Greater Rochester, New York, area. It purchases its own equipment and hires, schedules, and supervises its own employees. During the calendar year 1973, its gross annual revenues were $232,500, of which $85,575.07 represented payments for nonretail services rendered to institutional users in the State of New York, each of whom annually purchased goods and services outside the State of New York in excess of $50,000. During

the same period, the Employer made local purchases of materials, supplies, merchandise, or services in the amount of $60,083.40.

3. The State Board has not made any formal findings concerning the aforesaid commerce data and the Employer does not know whether the Union admits or denies the commerce data.

4. In its brief, the Employer contends that the assertion of jurisdiction over it is warranted by virtue of its more than $50,000 annual nonretail services in institutional users, albeit exempt employers under our Act, each of whom makes annual out-of-state purchases in excess of $50,000, and over whom the Board would assert jurisdiction if not exempt.

5. Although served with a copy of the petition, no reply as provided in the Board's Rules and Regulations has been filed by the State Board or the Union.

On the basis of the above, the Board is of the opinion that:

1. The Employer is a nonretail enterprise engaged in the operation of an ambulance service in and about the Greater Rochester, New York, area.

2. The Board's current standard for the assertion of jurisdiction over nonretail enterprise is an inflow or outflow, direct or indirect, across state lines of at least $50,000.

3. As indicated above, the Employer annually renders more than $50,000 worth of nonretail ambulance services to the institutional users . . . five of whom appear to be exempt from our jurisdiction under Section 2(2) of the Act as governmental bodies. These institutional users are nonretail enterprises each of whom makes annual out-of-state purchases in excess of $50,000. Such purchases constitute sufficient direct inflow across state lines to justify assertion of jurisdiction over each of the institutional users under the *Siemons* standards, if they were not otherwise exempt under Section 2(2) of the Act. In *Carroll-Naslund,* the Board treated as indirect outflow for jurisdictional purposes services rendered to a city whose operations were of a magnitude which would justify asserting jurisdiction over it, if it were not exempt under Section 2(2) of the Act. Similarly, the Employer's ambulance services to the exempt and nonexempt institutional users constitute indirect outflow for jurisdictional purposes herein, and, since such indirect outflow annually exceeds $50,000, it satisfies the current standard for the Board's assertion of jurisdiction over nonretail enterprises.

Accordingly, the parties are advised under Section 102.103 of the Board's Rules and Regulations, Series 8, as amended, that on the allegations submitted herein the Board would assert jurisdiction over the Employer's operations with respect to disputes cognizable under Sections 8, 9, and 10 of the Act.

● ● ●

CASE QUESTIONS

1. Why would an employer want an advisory opinion from the National Labor Relations Board?

2. Did the company ask for this hearing, without notifying the State of New York officials or contacting the union?

The 1960s saw rapid growth in teacher unions and professional bargaining organizations. This has continued into the 1970s with even greater speed. The reaction of the public, the government, and the courts to this phenomena has been mixed.

The traditional view has been that teachers should accept the sole authority of the school board in matters of teaching loads, curriculum, and compensation. However, in the past fifteen years teachers have gone through some dramatic changes of viewpoint and many now place job tenure and student welfare at least equally important with their concern for increased compensation and benefits.

When teacher organizations first began to form, the government (school board) used the sovereign immunity doctrine to avoid all bargaining. The sovereign immunity doctrine means that the "king is absolute" and, therefore, cannot be challenged or reviewed. The doctrine was well established, and many courts accepted this as the common law solution since there was no legislation to answer bargaining questions. Gradually, however, the courts have started to change their position by comparing teachers to other economic groups which have a right organize. Now many states have passed specific legislation authorizing collective bargaining between the boards of education and the local teacher organizations.

ISSUES

For the most part teachers organizations have developed along lines similar to those in industry. Teachers' organizations have started by trying to achieve recognition. Recognition is a procedural issue, but it grants the union the right to speak for the teachers. Once recognition is achieved, the substantive issues of pay, teaching load, and fringe benefits can be negotiated.

PROCEDURAL ISSUES

The first procedural issue is the right of teacher's groups to organize. The school may challenge this right entirely or just challenge some of the substeps used by the teacher organization in developing membership for the election. These substeps include the right to come on school property to distribute campaign literature or solicit signature cards from eligible teachers. Usually a state agency is involved in helping to settle these issues. A hearing is normally held to consider if there are enough teachers interested in the union to hold an election. The state agency also hears complaints about good-faith bargaining. Even after a contract is signed, many issues may develop about the interpretation of the contract. Using the grievance procedure can help resolve these problems.

SUBSTANTIVE ISSUES

The public, the teachers, and school boards have strong and often differing opinions about what is "fair." These opinions are at the heart of most controversies concerning teaching loads, professional services for students, and compensation. One important area of difference concerns policy toward teaching methods and what should be taught.

The teachers often feel that the school board members are interferring people who do not understand the psychological issues involved in learning theory or curriculum design. The school board members may lack this technical competence and become frustrated because they have been elected to approve or disapprove methodological issues.

Another controversial issue is teacher's pay which is related to the local economy, the past pay rates, and the tax base of that school district. Here again the conflict is real and deep. Other broad issues of disagreement may include definition of management's (the board's) rights, what areas are open for bargaining by the parties, and who shall decide the ground rules.

FUTURE DEVELOPMENTS

As teacher-school board bargaining increases, more and more states will pass legislation concerning individual school districts' responsibility to bargain. These state statutes will include schools of higher education which receive their support from private sources and the state legislature. The national teacher organizations will continue to grow stronger and become better organized. They will hire more experts to provide additional information for their bargaining teams. The school administrators will probably use their own experts more extensively. The conflict between teachers organizations and management will move into a period of expert negotiation.

INTRODUCTION TO THE CASES

The *Cornell University* case is important because it changed the policy of the National Labor Relations Board regarding nonprofit colleges and universities. The case explains the law, the arguments for and against extending jurisdiction, and the direct outcomes on Cornell University and Syracuse University.

The New Jersy case of *Burlington County College* illustrates the procedural problems in trying to determine what topics can and should be included in bargaining. This case came to the court because of the inability of the parties to determine whether the issues had to be negotiated or were only possible items for negotiation. More was at stake than just the specific calendar issue.

The *Board of Education, Huntington School District* illustrates the problems in living with a collective bargaining contract. The parties are unable to resolve the interpretation of the contract, so the case comes into the court system. The court rules on the specific issues and comments on the nature of the New York statutes as they relate to managing the school district. This shows the development of more technical issues and the complexity of mixing contracts and statutes.

CORNELL UNIVERSITY v. LOCAL 200, SERVICE EMPLOYEES INTERNATIONAL UNION, AFL—CIO
183 NLRB No. 41, June 12, 1970

● ● ●

DECISION, ORDER, AND DIRECTION OF ELECTION

By Members Fanning, McClulloch, Brown, and Jenkins

Upon petitions duly filed under Section 9(c) of the National Labor Relations Act, as amended, a consolidated hearing was held before Hearing Officer John W. Irving of the National Labor Relations Board.

Following the hearing and pursuant to Section 102.67 of the National Labor Relations Board Rules and Regulations and Statements of Procedures, Series 8, as amended, by direction of the Regional Director for Region 3, these cases were transferred to the Board for decision. Briefs were filed by the Employers, the Association of Cornell Employees— Libraries, Civil Service Employees Association, Inc., and Service Employees International Union, AFL–CIO, in behalf of Service Employees International Union, Local 200, AFL–CIO. The Hearing Officer's rulings made at the hearing are free from prejudicial error and are hereby affirmed.

On the entire record in this case, the Board finds:

1. Cornell University and Syracuse University, the Employers herein, have filed representation petitions seeking elections to determine the bargaining representatives of certain of their nonacademic employees. Association of Cornell Employees—Libraries (herein called ACE) has also filed a petition seeking to represent a group of library employees.

The threshold question is whether the Board has or should assert jurisdiction over nonprofit colleges and universities in view of the 1951 decision in the *Columbia University* case. In that case, the Board decided that it would not effectuate the policies of the Act "to assert its jurisdiction over a nonprofit, educational institution where the activities involved are noncommercial in nature and intimately connected with charitable and educational activities of the institution."

All the petitioners urge the Board to overrule the *Columbia University* case. Syracuse and Cornell argue that the operations and activities of educational institutions as a class, and of Cornell and Syracuse in particular, have an overwhelming impact and effect on interstate commerce, that the operations of universities and colleges have increasingly become matters of federal interest, and that this interest coupled with the failure of the states adequately to recognize and legislate for labor relations affecting these institutions and their employees now justifies the Board in asserting jurisdiction. In support of their contention as to the impact of the operations of Syracuse and Cornell, as well as of educational institutions as a class, upon interstate commerce, the Employers have presented extensive documentation of financial activities which are set forth hereinafter.

Syracuse University

Syracuse University is the largest employer in the city of Syracuse, New York. It has about 3,500 academic and nonacademic employees. The current student population is 21,000, of whom 4,000 to 5,000 are from out-of-state, and 900 from out-of-country. In addition to facilities in New York State, Syracuse has facilities in South America, Holland, Italy, and France.

The purchasing department of the University makes annual purchases approximating $8 million of which more than $5 million originate outside the State of New York. In addition, the University Book Store and Food Service annually make out-of-state purchases valued at more than $2 million. The University operates a theatre which annually makes out-of-state purchases valued at about $300,000. The University realizes $500,000 annually from the sale of tickets for football games, and $250,000 from the sale of television and radio rights.

Syracuse has an annual operating budget of $66 million. It has an investment portfolio valued at $36 million, which includes stockholdings in industrial firms, banks, and utilities. It also is the sole stockholder in a country club whose employees are represented by a union certified by the Board. Further, it has real estate investments outside New York State valued at $750,000.

Finally, Syracuse is a party to numerous sponsored research contracts with such Federal agencies as the Department of Defense, National Aeronautics and Space Administration, Institute of Health, and Department of Labor and such private sponsors as the Ford and Carnegie foundations. The annual value of these research contracts is in excess of $13 million.

Cornell University

Cornell University is the largest employer in Tompkins County, New York. It has more than 8,000 employees in New York State, of whom 2,700 are academic and 5,700 nonacademic. Cornell presently has an enrolled student body exceeding 14,000. Fifty percent of these students are from outside the State of New York. There are also in excess of 1,100 students from 87 foreign countries enrolled at the University.

The University has offices in Ohio, Massachusetts, Illinois, Florida, and Pennsylvania, and operates an observatory in Puerto Rico.

During 1968-69, the University's publishing department purchased goods valued at $16,400,000. Of this sum, $10,750,000 represented purchases of items manufactured outside the State of New York. During the same period, Cornell University Press made purchases of almost $1 million, of which more than half represented direct or indirect purchases of out-of-state manufactured products. During this same year, the Press made sales valued at $942,000 to purchasers outside the State. Cornell also owns a radio station, a CBS affiliate, which in 1968-69 received $296,000 from local and regional advertising, and $38,000 from national advertising.

Cornell's annual expenditures amount to $142,300,000. Its current assets are valued at $282,500,000. Included is an investment portfolio of over $250 million which consists, *inter alia,* of investments in industrial concerns, banks, insurance companies, and public utilities.

During 1968–69, Cornell had research contracts amounting to $26,600,000 sponsored by various agencies of the Federal Government, including National Science Foundation, Public Health Service, Atomic Energy Commission, Department of Defense, and National Aeronautics and Space Administration. In addition, the University received $6 million for research projects sponsored by such foundations as Ford, Carnegie, and Rockefeller.

Discussion

Section 2(2) of the Act defines an "employer" as follows:

> . . . any person acting as an agent of an employer, directly or indirectly, but shall not include the United States or any wholly owned Government corporation, or any Federal Reserve Bank, or any State or political subdivision thereof, or any corporation or association operating a hospital, if no part of the net earnings inures to the benefit of any private shareholder or individual . . . .

Although Section 2(2) specifically excludes nonprofit hospitals from the Act's coverage, it contains no such exclusion of private, nonprofit educational institutions. In the *Columbia University* case, the Board reviewed the then recently enacted Taft-Hartley amendments to the National Labor Relations Act and concluded that

> . . . the activities of Columbia University affect commerce sufficiently to satisfy the requirements of the statute and the standards established by the Board for the normal exercise of its jurisdiction. . . .

However, the Board, as a discretionary matter, declined to assert such jurisdiction because of statements in the House Conference Report which seemed to indicate approval of what the report believed to have been the Board's pre-1947 practice of declining in the exercise of its discretion to assert jurisdiction over certain nonprofit organizations. The Board concluded:

> Under all the circumstances, we do not believe that it would effectuate the policies of the Act for the Board to assert its jurisdiction over a nonprofit, educational institution where the activities involved are noncommercial in nature and intimately connected with the charitable purposes and educational activities of the institution.

It should be noted that, although the House Conference Report referred to the Board's pre-1947 practice with respect to exercising jurisdiction over nonprofit employers, the 1947 amendments themselves placed no curb on the Board's discretionary jurisdiction except as to nonprofit hospitals. The report did not say that, because the Board had decided before 1947 it would not effectuate the policies of the Act to assert jurisdiction over certain employers, it must continue to refuse to assert such jurisdiction indefinitely in the future despite change of circumstances. This hardly seems inadvertent. Congress was well aware that the Board's discretionary standards for asserting jurisdiction were not fixed, but had been changed from time to time. The very fact that Congress rejected the 1947 House proposals for the specific exemption from the Act of broad classes of charitable or nonprofit organizations seems to indicate that Congress was content to leave to the Board's informed discretion in the future as it had in the past, whether and when to assert jurisdiction over nonprofit organizations whose operations had a substantial impact upon interstate commerce.

We adhere to the view that the Board has statutory jurisdiction over nonprofit educational institutions whose operations affect commerce. But we shall no longer decline to assert jurisdiction over such institutions as a class.

In the intervening two decades since *Columbia University* was decided, the Board has declined to assert jurisdiction over nonprofit universities if the activity involved was noncommercial and intimately connected with the school's educational purpose. However, an analysis of the cases reveals that the dividing line separating purely commercial from noncommercial activity has not been easily defined.

Those who urge adherence to the *Columbia University* doctrine contend that the legislative history of the Taft-Hartley amendments establishes that Congress intended to exempt nonprofit educational institutions from the coverage of the Act. They further argue that Congress ratified its earlier position by amending the Act in 1959 without commenting on or altering the 1947 Conference Report relative to exclusion.

It is true that the legislative history of the 1959 Landrum-Griffin Act is completely silent on the matter of nonprofit employers. We are not persuaded, however, that congressional silence may be construed as history or Board reliance on it. The fact remains that Section 2(2) contains no express exemption for nonprofit employers. More to the point is that in 1959 Congress enacted Section 14(c) which for the first time both authorized and set limits on the Board's discretionary refusal to exercise jurisdiction.

Two years before the enactment of Section 14(c), the Supreme Court ruled in *Guss* v. *Utah Labor Relations Board* that the States were powerless to entertain cases which fell within the NLRB's statutory jurisdiction, even though the Board had declined to assert such jurisdiction. Thus, a "no-man's land" was created where employers and employees were denied a Federal forum for the resolution of labor disputes and yet were unable to turn to the States for alternative relief. Ample evidence in the legislative history reveals that Section 14(c) was the Congressional response designed to eliminate the "no-man's land." Toward this end, Section 14(c)(1) states that the Board in its discretion may "decline to assert jurisdiction over any labor dispute involving any class or category of employers, where, in the opinion of the Board, the effect of such labor dispute on commerce is not sufficiently substantial to warrant the exercise of its jurisdiction. . . ." Conversely, it impliedly confirms the Board's authority to expand its jurisdiction to any class of employers whose operations substantially affect commerce. Section 14(c)(2) further attempts to narrow the "no-man's land" gap by empowering the States to exercise jurisdiction when the Board declines to so assert.

While the language of Section 14(c) does not compel the Board to assert jurisdiction, it does manifest a congressional policy favoring such assertion where the Board finds that the operations of a   class of employers exercise a substantial effect on commerce.

In light of these statutory guidelines, Syracuse and Cornell have called upon the Board to re-examine the soundness of the *Columbia University* doctrine as it applies to colleges and universities today. Petitioners introduced extensive evidence at the hearing to document their claim that educational institutions as a class have not only a substantial, but massive, impact on interstate commerce. After carefully examining all the evidence submitted, we are compelled to conclude that, whatever guidance the 1947 Conference Report provided to the situation which existed in 1951 when *Columbia University* was decided, the underlying considerations no longer obtain two decades later.

No claim is made that education is not still the primary goal of such institutions. Indeed, more than 2 million students are enrolled in colleges today, almost double the number attending in 1951. Yet to carry out its educative functions, the university has become involved in a host of activities which are commercial in character.

Thus, the approximately 1,450 private 4- and 2-year colleges and universities in the United States have on their payrolls some 247,000 full-time professionals and 263,000 full- and part-time non-professional employees. Operating budgets of private educational facilities were an estimated $6 billion in 1969, an increase of $300 million over the previous fiscal year. Income is derived not only from the traditional sources, such as tuition and gifts, but from the purely commercial avenues of securities investments and real estate holdings. Revenues of private institutions of higher education for fiscal year 1966–67 totaled over $6 billion. More than $1.5 billion of that sum came from Government appropriations. Private colleges and universities also realized a commercial profit of $70,678,000 from furnishing housing and food services.

Expenditures to operate and maintain these academic communities necessarily include purchases of food, furniture, office equipment, supplies, utilities, and the like, much of which is obtained through the channels of interstate commerce. Merely to house its students the average private college budgeted $323,000 for fiscal 1969, and allotted another $360,000 for food services. Further, the expanding nature of higher education is reflected in the amount of new construction being planned. In 1969, over 1,000 institutions planned some 3,000 separate building projects with a total estimated value of $4.35 billion, one-half billion dollars more than was appropriated the preceding year.

Another phenomenon clearly distinguishing the current situation from the one which existed in 1951 is the expanded role of the Federal Government in higher education. In the last 12 years alone, three legislative acts have been passed which authorize allocations of millions of dollars of Federal aid for education. Total Federal funds for private and public education in 1969 amounted to $5 billion. This figure, moreover, does not include moneys expended for student loans, sponsored research, or Government-approved construction.

Increased Federal financial involvement in education is paralleled by an expanding congressional recognition that employees in the nonprofit sector are entitled to the same benefits which Federal statutes provide to employees in the profitmaking sphere. Of particular pertinence here is the amendment of the Fair Labor Standards Act in 1966 extending coverage to nonprofit private universities and hospitals. In 1968, the Supreme Court upheld the constitutionality of the amendments, holding that such institutions are engaged in commerce. In support of this conclusion, the Court stated, *inter alia:* "It is clear that labor conditions in schools and hospitals can affect commerc. Strikes and work stoppages involving employees of schools and hospitals, events which unfortunately are not infrequent, obviously interrupt and burden this flow of goods across state lines.

Given the congressional amendments to the FLSA and the Supreme Court decision upholding them, it is no longer sufficient to say that merely because employees are in a nonprofit sector of the economy, the operations of their employers do not substantially affect interstate commerce.

However, those who oppose Board jurisdiction contend that many private colleges, unlike Cornell and Syracuse, have remained relatively small and local in character and labor disputes involving their employees do not burden interstate commerce. They also allege that private colleges represent a declining proportion of higher educational institutions in the United States. Therefore, if the National Labor Relations Board were to take jurisdiction, it would be over only a fractional segment of the field. A more logical approach, they submit, is to have all such institutions subject to State control, thereby avoiding the conflict and instability that allegedly would result were both Federal and local agencies to function within a single State. We find no merit in these arguments.

It may be true that Cornell and Syracuse count among the largest of the private universities in the country. Nevertheless, within the class of employers, there are a number which, although smaller than these two universities, are sufficiently large so that their activities have a substantial impact on commerce.

It may also be true that, in certain respects, public colleges and universities tend to be larger than their private counterparts. Thus, only 29 percent of the student population is enrolled in private colleges and universities. Further, the rate of growth in terms of numbers of public institutions is more rapid than the growth rate for private schools.

This does not diminish the fact that 2,102,000 students are currently enrolled in private colleges, an increase of 21 and ½ percent in the past 5 years. Moreover, there are still 489 more private colleges in this country than public ones. Although the private sector has not grown to the same extent as has the public on a sheer percentage basis, it has grown substantially.

In any event, we note that in all cases where the Board applies a size criterion, expressed in dollar volume, in its assertion of jurisdiction, a portion of the industry is relegated to the State or other control. While complete uniformity in the application of Federal or state controls might be desirable in theory, in practice the resulting remission to state control of those enterprises falling below the Board's own jurisdictional standard has not in the past resulted in substantial instability or uncertainty in the application of the law.

The evidence clearly establishes that universities are enlarging both their facilities and their economic activities to meet the needs of mounting numbers of students. Greatly increased expenditures by the Federal Government also testify to an expanding national interest in higher education. Keeping pace with these developments is the surge of organizational activity taking place among employees on college campuses. With or without Federal regulation, union organization is already a *fait accompli* at many universities. Indeed, labor disputes have already erupted at a number of universities. As advancing waves of organizational swell among both nonprofessional and academic employees, it is unreasonable to assume that such disputes will not continue to occur in the future.

As noted previously, Section 14(c) was enacted primarily to provide forums to resolve labor disputes for those employers and employees who were denied Federal relief. Congress was aware that by 1959 only 12 States had any labor relations law. Presumably, Congress then expected that the other States would establish agencies to fill the void. If so, these expectations have been disappointed. To date, a total of 15 States have enacted labor-management legislation. In only eight of these States has the legislation been written or interpreted so as to expressly cover employees of private educational institutions. Moreover, even in those eight, the laws may be inadequate. For example, New York for years has had an equivalent of the Wagner Act, yet it contains no remedies for unfair labor practices which may be committed by unions. To put it another way, there are 35 States without labor codes under which matters such as union organization, collective bargaining, and labor disputes may be determined.

Consequently, we are convinced that assertion of jurisdiction is required over those private colleges and universities whose operations have a substantial effect on commerce to insure the orderly, effective, and uniform application of the national labor policy.

In view of all the foregoing considerations, we can no longer adhere to the position set forth in the *Columbia University* decision. Accordingly, that case is overruled. Charged with providing peaceful and orderly procedures to resolve labor controversy, we conclude that we can best effectuate the policies of the Act by asserting jurisdiction over nonprofit, private educational institutions where we find it to be appropriate.

At this time, the Board is not prepared to establish jurisdictional standards for nonprofit colleges and universities as a class, for the instant proceedings do not give us a sufficient basis for selecting an appropriate measure by which to determine whether the policies of the Act will be effectuated by the exercise of jurisdiction in a particular case. Therefore, we leave the development of an appropriate jurisdictional standard for subsequent adjudication.

Whatever dollar-volume standard we ultimately adopt for asserting jurisdiction over educational institutions can best be left to determination in future situations involving institutions which are far nearer the appropriate dividing line. In view of the foregoing facts disclosing the substantial involvement in operations in commerce and affecting commerce by Cornell and Syracuse Universities, there is no question that Cornell and Syracuse are engaged in commerce within the meaning of the Act. Accordingly, we find that it will effectuate the policies of the Act to assert jurisdiction herein.

2. The labor organizations involved claim to represent certain employees of the Employers.

3. Service Employees International Union, Local 200, AFL–CIO, was elected collective-bargaining representative for a unit of full-time and regular part-time service and maintenance employees at Syracuse University in an election conducted under the direction of the New York State Labor Relations Board.

At the hearing in the instant proceeding, the University and Local 200 virtually stipulated to the appropriateness of the above unit and were engaged at that time in collective bargaining. Both parties have urged the Board to honor the state certification of the Local in the event jurisdiction is asserted.

It is well established that the Board will recognize the validity of state-conducted elections and certifications where that election procedure was free of irregularities and reflected the true desires of the employees. Since neither party contends that the state-conducted election was attended by any irregularities, we shall accord the same effect to the results of the state election as we would attach to a determination of representatives based upon an election conducted by the Board. Accordingly, there is no question concerning representation of Syracuse University employees at this time. We shall, therefore, dismiss Syracuse University's petition.

4. A question affecting commerce does exist concerning the representation of certain employees of Cornell University within the meaning of Section 9(c)(1) and Section 2(6) and (7) of the Act.

Cornell has filed a petition seeking an election in a unit of all the University's nonacademic, nonsupervisory employees throughout the State of New York. Civil Service Employees Association agrees that a statewide unit is appropriate. Association of Cornell Employees—Libraries (ACE) requests a separate unit for approximately 270 nonprofessional, nonsupervisory employees of the Cornell libraries on the Ithaca campus. Staff Association of the Metropolitan District Office, School of Industrial Relations, Cornell University, United Federation of College Teachers, Local 1460 (UFCT), contends that a unit composed of 17 professionals and 20 nonprofessionals in the district office of the New York State School of Industrial Relations located in New York City is appropriate.

ACE Unit

In terms of the University's organizational structure, the libraries constitute a separate administrative unit. As such, this unit has established its own work rules and administers its own budget. There are 13 separate libraries on the Ithaca campus, with two-thirds of all proposed unit employees located in the main library. The ratio between library employees and others housed in the same building varies from 3 to 80 percent, depending on the size of the particular library.

There was conflicting testimony as to whether the nonprofessional employees' work in the libraries is distinct. On the other hand, there were assertions that, although much library work today is done by nonprofessionals, it is of semiprofessional character requiring a certain amount of training. Thus, new library employees now receive an 8- to

10-hour orientation as well as on-the-job training. Forty percent of the jobs allegedly require a college background. There are 9 job titles identifying positions which exist solely within the library system; 17 other classifications are used campuswide. However, while the nine job titles may be singular, apparently the job content is not. For example, "library assistants," "library searchers," and "proofreaders" perform duties comparable to many university clericals, research aides, and proofreaders throughout the campus.

With respect to employee interchange, 12 library positions were filled by employees transferring from other campus jobs during the 1967 academic year. During this time, 46 promotions and 11 transfers in the library system were of library employees. Over 60 percent of new hires were recruited from off campus.

ACE, formed as a labor organization approximately 2-½ years ago, has a constitution and a dues-paying membership and holds regular meetings. It has never been officially recognized by the University nor entered into collective-bargaining negotiations, but has represented library employees at a number of meetings held with University administrators and has handled numerous unitwide grievances as well as those of individual employees.

UFCT Unit

Because it is located some 280 miles from Ithaca, the New York City extension office of the Industrial and Labor Relations School (ILR) is accorded a great degree of autonomy. It controls its own hiring, establishes vacation and holiday schedules independently, and proposes its own programs and curricula tailored to the particular needs and demands of its New York City clientele. It location further requires that certain employment practices be followed in conformance with area standards. For example, employees are frequently hired above the minimum wage to compete with the higher wage market in the city. The workweek is 35 hours, whereas at the main campus it is 38-¾ hours. Holidays are in accord with those granted in the area.

However, there is testimony to the effect that the autonomy accorded to the ILR School's New York City office merely reflects Cornell's policy to grant relative independence to all its administrative departments. Thus, other department heads have considerable latitude in such matters as hiring and arranging work schedules and vacation leave. The three other ILR extension branches located in Ithaca, Albany, and Buffalo also gear their programs to meet specific local needs. Additionally, Cornell has other facilities in New York City which adapt employment practices to meet area standards.

Further, it does not appear that the functions of the nonprofessional employees at the New York City ILR office are distinct. Their job classifications and duties parallel similar titles and duties on the Ithaca campus.

Statewide Unit

There is considerable evidence that the operations of Cornell's facilities scattered throughout the State are integrated and centralized and that a community of interests is shared by all of its nonprofessional employees. Thus, the director of personnel testified that the personnel department establishes employment practices and labor relations policies for the entire University. This department conducts recruitment, interviews applicants, and refers them to job vacancies, although actual hiring is done by the respective department heads. It also determines the benefits to which employees are entitled and slots employees into various levels of the wage scale. Job titles of Cornell employees are identical throughout the State. Meetings are held occasionally for new employees, and there is some secretarial training offered. Job vacancies are posted throughout the University, and there is campuswide bidding and transfers. Although recruitment and hiring for installations remote from Ithaca are decided at the particular site, classification of positions is still done by a central office at the main campus. Financial records are maintained and checks are issued from the Ithaca campus.

Additionally, Cornell has developed uniform guidelines covering such matters as attendance, leaves of absence, vacations, holidays, tardiness, discipline, overtime, and seniority applicable to all its employees. With few exceptions, all Cornell employees participate in many of the same fringe benefit programs such as workmen's compensation, disability, life insurance, retirement, and a tuition scholarship plan for children.

In determining whether a particular group of employees constitutes an appropriate unit for bargaining where an employer operates a number of facilities, the Board considers such factors as prior bargaining history, centralization of management particularly in regard to labor relations, extent of employee interchange, degree of interdependence or autonomy of the plants, differences or similarities in skills and functions of the employees, and geographical location of the facilities in relation to each other. We are mindful that we are entering into a hitherto uncharted area. Nevertheless, we regard the above principles as reliable guides to organization in the educational context as they have been in the industrial, and will apply them to the circumstances of the instant case.

Although ACE has acted informally in behalf of the library employees in the handling of grievances, it has never negotiated a collective-bargaining contract for them, nor has it been recognized as their bargaining representative. Apart from the fact that these employees have organized themselves separately, there is little which justifies establishing a separate bargaining unit for them. Their work and skills are similar to those of many other employees on the Ithaca campus, and they enjoy the same working conditions and benefits as other Cornell employees. In view of the foregoing, we do not find that the library employees possess a sufficiently separate community of interest which would warrant establishing the separate unit sought by ACE.

We reach the same conclusion as to the employees of the Industrial Relations School. In the industrial context, our practice is to find a single plant of a multiplant employer presumptively appropriate where that facility is geographically separated from the others, where the operations of the single plant are not integrated with those of other plants, where there is a degree of local managerial autonomy, and where no other union is seeking a larger unit.

In the instant proceeding, a few of these factors are present. The

ILR School New York City branch is located at a considerable distance from the main campus and it is relatively autonomous in its operations. Were there no countervailing considerations involved, we might find justification for the bargaining unit claimed by the UFCT.

There are, however, other criteria which must be taken into account here. We find it significant that the nonprofessional employees of the ILR School perform the same duties as many other Cornell employees in the same job classifications, and they are equally subject to the uniform and centralized employment practices of the University. Further, there is no prior collective-bargaining history for these employees. Finally, there is a union which is seeking a broad inclusive unit coextensive with the Employer's administrative and geographic boundaries. In light of these circumstances, we find that a unit limited to the employees of the New York City ILR School is not appropriate. We find, instead, that the appropriate unit is one which is statewide in scope.

Accordingly, we shall dismiss the petitions in Cases 3–RC–4768, 3–RM–440, and 3–RM–441 and, in agreement with Cornell and CSEA, we find that the following employees constitute a unit appropriate for the purposes of collective bargaining within the meaning of Section 9(b) of the Act:

> All nonsupervisory, nonprofessional employees of Cornell University within the State of New York, excluding employees of the medical college and nursing school in New York City, skilled trades employees on the Ithaca campus who are currently represented, guards, confidential employees, professional employees and supervisors as defined in the Act.

ORDER

It is hereby ordered that the petitions filed in Cases 3–RM–433, 3–RC–4768, 3–RM–440, and 3–RM–441 be, and they hereby are, dismissed. [Direction of Election omitted from publication.]

• • •

CASE QUESTIONS

1. What was the decision in the important *Columbia University* case which the attorneys were arguing against in this case?

2. Syracuse University was trying to overturn the election held for its employees. What did the NLRB find in its argument?

3. What bargaining unit was Cornell University requesting in this case?

BURLINGTON COUNTY COLLEGE FACULTY ASSOCIATION v.
BOARD OF TRUSTEES
Superior Court of New Jersey
119 N.J. 276 (1972)

• • •

Martino, A. J. S. C. Plaintiff seeks a declaration as to the intent and interpretation of the New Jersey Employer-Employee Relations Act and particularly *N. J. S. A.* 34:13A–5.3, which among other matters provides:

> . . . representatives designated . . . shall be the exclusive representatives for collective negotiation concerning the terms and conditions of employment of the employees in such unit. . . . Proposed new rules or modifications of existing rules governing working conditions shall, be negotiated with the majority representative before they are established.

Plaintiff contends that the *college calendar* fits the category set forth in said statute when it refers to "proposed new rules or modifications of existing rules governing working conditions," and further, that the *college calendar* is a "terms and conditions of employment of the employees" which requires negotiation as a part of the contractual relationship between the faculty and its employer, defendant college.

A close reading *N. J. S. A.* 34:13A–5.3 indicates that it provides on the one hand that proposed new rules or modification of existing rules governing *working conditions* be negotiated, and on the other hand that *terms and conditions of employment* be negotiated in good faith.

Defendant institution contends that the college calendar is the establishment of educational policies which should remain within its control and is not mandatorily negotiable.

The matter being heard without a jury, the court makes the following findings of facts and conclusions of law pursuant to *R.* 1:7–4.

The president of plaintiff association, who was also the chief negotiator, testified that the first year negotiations were entered into was for 1970–71. Among the matters negotiated were salaries, faculty load, grievances, personnel files, sick and sabbatical leaves, parking privileges, offices for faculty members, and certain other minor items. The school board representatives refused to negotiate a calendar. A contract was nevertheless agreed upon for 1970–71. The following year another contract was entered into after negotiations, but again the school board refused to negotiate on the school calendar. A calendar controls the number of weeks in an academic year. The college offers evening courses and the college controls what members of the faculty shall work these courses. He stated that a calendar was important to a faculty member because a calendar could permit members of a faculty to arrange to attend other schools for the purpose of earning additional scholastic degrees, would permit teachers to plan to attend European countries which could add to their experiences in particular subjects which they taught, viz., England, the Shakespeare locale, Spain for the language and customs and so forth; that calendars sometimes are set up for a period of time which might affect the time allotted for the proper teaching of subjects to students who are eligible for admittance to a community college; that the efforts to have the school board consider suggestions for the calendar were refused. The suggestions which were typed and offered to the school board for the years and rejected for consideration were marked in evidence. One of these calendars was passed upon by a defendant witness, a qualified educator, who felt it was a favorable type of claendar.

A representative of the New Jersey Educational Association, of which organization plaintiff is an affiliate, testified as an expert in the field of school contract negotiations. He had experience in negotiations on calendars for other faculties. His organization assisted in the passage of *N. J. S. A.* 34:13A-1 *et seq.* He testified he had examined all the calendars of the county colleges in this State. He made up a chart, admitted in evidence, on which was diagramed the length of work time that was required under the various calendars he examined. He found that Bergen County worked 9 days less than Burlington under its calendar; Brookdale College (Monmouth County) worked 31 days less; Camden worked 39 days less; Cumberland worked 17 days less; Essex worked 41 days less; Gloucester worked 15 days less; Mercer worked 12 days less; Middlesex worked 16 days less; Ocean worked 21 days less; Somerset worked 28 days less and Union worked 8 days less. No effort was made to dispute these findings by testimony which had a basis in fact.

Defendant produced a witness who was the negotiator for the board of trustees. He said he refused to negotiate the calendar with plaintiff's representative because the board of trustees felt that the calendar was a management prerogative; that a calendar was prepared for all types of members of the college community, such as students, noninsturctional persons and others who were concerned with the college's welfare.

The president of the college testified that the calendar was prepared by studying other calendars for similar or like institutions; that the board of trustees felt that students and taxpayers also had to be taken into consideration in the preparation of the calendar; that a governance sturcture was created at the college, from which was established a calendar committee consisting of representatives of the studdents, the faculty, deans in the college and administrative personnel; that faculty members on the calendar committee were appointed by the faculty; that the new calendar has had some suggestions from that committee for adjustment of the 1972-73 calendar; that he has given some recommendations made by the calendar committee to the board of trustees. He feels that there is a relationship between the calendar and the budget, and that the board of trustees feels that the calendar is a management prerogative. He personally feels that the committees functioning in the college is a better way to prepare a calendar than direct negotiations with plaintiff's representatives. He had met with the calendar committee on three or four occasions. He stated there are many types of calendars, not only within the State but throughout the United States. He felt that he was to follow the dictates of the board of trustees, which felt that the calendar was a management prerogative. He conceded that the Board of Higher Education, Department of Higher Education, was not concerned with a school calendar and did not have to approve a calendar, and the only reason such a calendar was filed with that Board was to satisfy that Department a minimum of 30 weeks of instruction, exclusive of registration and final examination periods, would be provided for that year.

Another witness called by defendant, who was plaintiff's negotiator and who testified for it, was asked about the members of the faculty who were members of the calendar committee, and it was shown that of the sic faculty members who were on this committee, three were representative of management and three were members of plaintiff association but were not delegated to serve on that committee by the association.

The final witness called by defnedant was a professor of higher education at the University of Florida. For 12 years he was Director of Community Colleges in the State of Florida, which office he left in 1968. He has been consulted on community colleges in various parts of the United States. He has been working with the officials at the Burlington County College since it was first conceived. He has had many conversations with the college president and members of the faculty of Burlington College. He has had no experience with labor negotiations because Florida has never had an employer-employee relations act. He defined a calendar as the way a year is divided up. He stated there is a wide divergence of calendar types in the United States in institutions of higher learning. He was never consulted about the Burlington County College calendar. He agreed that there is quite a distinction between a calendar and a curriculum. He cannot conceive of any calendar that could be developed which would serve all colleges. He admitted that one of the calendars proposed by plaintiff organization in earlier negotiations and rejected was a good one.

He was not asked what in his expert opinion would be the interpretation of "terms and conditions of employment" or the expression "working conditions," as outlined in the Employer-Employees Relations Act of this State.

The jurisdiction of the court to pass upon this question arises from the failure of the Legislature to clearly define another course for plaintiff to pursue in order to afford it a remedy under these circumstances. The court's jurisdiction is not in dispute. See *Burlington County Evergreen Mental Hosp. v. Cooper,* 56 *N. J. 579* (1970).

[1—] Bargaining demands are divided into three categories. They are either mandatory, voluntary or illegal subjects of negotiations. *NLRB Wooster Division, v. BorgWarner Corp.,* 356 *U. S.* 342, 78 *S. Ct.* 718, 2 *L. Ed.* 2d 823 (1958). There is an obligation on the part of the employer and the representatives of the employees to bargain with each other with respect to the terms and conditions of employment and working conditions. The duty is limited to those subjects and that area. Neither party is legally obligated to yield. As to other matters, however, each party is free to bargain or not to bargain, and to agree or not to agree.

A supplement to the New Jersey Employer-Employee Relations Act, *N. J. S. A.* 34:13A–8.1, effective July 1, 1968, reads:

Nothing in this act shall be construed to annul or modify, or to preclude the renewal or continuation of any agreement heretofore entered into between any *public* employer and any *employee* organization, *nor shall any provision hereof annul or modify any statute or statutes of this State.* [Emphasis added]

County colleges are a creature of statute. Their maintenance, control and operation rests with the law responsible for their existence, *N. J. S. A.* 18A:64A-1 *et seq.* Among other provisions, a board of trustees shall be responsible for their management and control. *N. J. S. A.* 18A:64A-11. The general powers of the board of trustees is to determine the *educational curriculum and program* of the college. *N. J. S. A.* 18A:64A-12(d). The board of trustees appoints and fixes the compensation and term of office of the president of a college, who shall be the executive officer of the college and an *ex officio* member of the board of trustees, *N. J. S. A.* 18A:64A-12(e); makes and promulgates rules and regulations not inconsistent with the provisions of the statute or with the rules and regulations of the Board of Higher Education that are necessary and proper for the administration and operation of a county college and implements the provisions of the statute, and exercises all other powers, not inconsistent with the provisions of the statute or with the rules and regulations of the Board of Higher Education which may be reasonably necessary or incidental to the establishment, maintenance and operation of a county college. *N. J. S. A.* 18A:64A-12(*o*), (*p*).

A "calendar" is defined as a system by which the beginning, length and division of the civil year are fixed and by which days and longer divisions of time (as weeks, months and years) are arranged in a definite order. A "curriculum" is defined as the whole body of courses by an educational institution or one of its branches, while a "program" is defined as a plan determining the offerings of an educational institution. See *Webster's Third International Dictionary* (1967). The words "educational curriculum and program" referred to in the Statute apparently are meant to refer to the same subject matter.

A calendar which determines when an employee shall commence work and the period he shall continue in the performance of his work would certainly seem to be within the term and conditions of employment. It is conceded by all parties that hours and wages are compulsory items for bargaining, and certainly hours and wages must be determined by the period of time such work must be performed. A curriculum which would appear to rest entirely with the board of trustees should not be confused with a calendar.

An argument broached by defendant institution is that to permit the calendar to be negotiated on a strict employer-employee relationship will result, in great measure, in a disregard of the best interests of those the college exists to serve, *i. e.* the students. There is no reason to conclude that the negotiation of the parties would eliminate any permissive participation by students. Similarly, there appears no logical reason to eliminate qualified faculty members from that discussion. Blocker, Plummer and Richardson in *The Two Year College: A Social Synthesis* (1965), wrote:

> It must be pointed out that there are many individual faculty members who are interested and active in educational innovations and who develop — with or without encouragement from the administration — new concepts and procedures which improve and enrich the educational processes in their classrooms. Although these efforts may not be apparent to any other than those intimately related to the college, the significance of such work should not be underestimated. The impact

of these finite changes might, in the long run, stimulate major educational policy changes affecting the entire college. [at 109]

In *Joint School District No. 8, City of Madison v. Wisconsin Employment Relations Board, etc.,* 37 *Wis.* 2d 483, 155 *N. W.* 2d 78 (1967), the Wisconsin Supreme Court held that a school calendar was the subject of compulsory negotiations. The Wisconsin statute refers to the right to confer and to negotiate on the question of "wages, hours and conditions of employment." Our statute refers to "terms and conditions of employment of the employee"—hardly a distinction with a difference. The Wisconsin court went on to add that many items and restrictions in a school calendar required to be met by statute cannot be changed by negotiations. That court said:

> The contents of the curriculum would be a different matter. Subjects of study are within the scope of basic educational policy and additionally are not related to wages, hours and conditions of employment.

As previously indicated, under the provisions of *N. J. S. A.* 18A:64A–12(*o*) and (*p*) the rules of the board of trustees are not to be inconsistent with the provisions of the statute or with the rules and regulations of the Board of Higher Education, and the board of trustees may exercise all other powers not inconsistent with the powers of this statute or with the rules of the Board of Higher Education which may be reasonably necessary or incidental to the establishment, maintenance and operation of a county college.

Nothing in the aforementioned statute refers to a calendar, while it does provide that the board of trustees has the power "to determine the educational curriculum and program of the college." It is conceded that the Board of Higher Education does not by its rules need to approve a calendar.

In *Libby, McNeill & Libby v. Wisconsin Employment Relations Comm'n,* 48 *Wis.* 2d 272, 279 *N. W.* 2d 805 (1970), the Wisconsin Supreme Court held that while the management decision in that case was not a mandatory subject of collective bargaining, the decision and its "effects" were distinct issues, and concluded:

> It is well established that where the employment relationship is threatened by a unilateral economic move by the employer, the Federal Courts and the National Labor Realtions Board have found an enforceable duty to bargain over the *impact* of that decision on the employees. [Cited cases omitted; emphasis added]

The phrase "terms and conditions of employment" is no doubt susceptible of diverse interpretations. In common parlance the conditions of a person's employment are most obviously the various physical dimensions of his working environment. What one's hours are to be, what amount of work is expected during those hours, what periods of relief are available, would all seem "conditions" of one's employment. *Fibreboard Paper Products Corp. v. NLRB,* 379 *U. S.* 203, 85 *S. Ct.* 398, 13 *L. Ed.* 2d 233 (1964).

The board of trustees need not surrender its discretion in determining calendar policy nor come to an agreement in the collective bargaining sense. The board must, however, confer and negotiate, and this includes a consideration of the suggestions and reasons of the faculty representatives. There is no duty upon the board to agree against its judgment with the suggestions, and it is not a forbidden practice for the school board to determine in its own judgment what the school calendar should be even though such course of action rejects the faculty's wishes. The refusal may place the board in a position where, under the rule of the New Jersey Public Employment Relations Commission, it will result in the appointment of a mediator and, upon his failure to resolve the impasse, a fact-finding board. However, the fact-finders, if adverse to the board, are not binding upon it. The force of the fact-finding procedure is public opinion, and the legislative process thrives on such enlightment in a democracy. *Joint School District No. 8, City of Madison v. Wisconsin Employment Relations Board, etc., supra;* see also *N. J. A. C. 19:12-1 to 19:12-15.*

It is, therefore, concluded that an analysis of the facts and their application to N. J. S. A. 34:13A-1 et seq. and 18A:64A-1 et seq. requires that defendant board of trustees of the Burlington County College negotiate the format of the college calendar with plaintiff's representatives.

• • •

CASE QUESTIONS

1. What was the main concern of the teachers' organization?

2. How does the concern over "wages, hours, and conditions of employment" in New Jersey compare to the National Labor Relations Act language?

BOARD OF EDUCATION, HUNTINGTON v. ASSOCIATED TEACHERS
30 New York 2d 122, (1972)

• • •

APPEAL, by permission of the Appellate Division of the Supreme Court in the Second Judicial Department, from an order of said court, entered March 22, 1971, which modified, on the law, as modified, affirmed a judgment of the Supreme Court (THOMAS M. STARK, J.; opn. 62 Misc 2d 906), entered in Suffolk County, granting summary judgment to plaintiff in part and defendant in part and declaring the legal rights and relations of the parties with respect to a certain agreement. By the modification the Appellate Division struck the provisions from the judgment declaring section A of article XI of the agreement to be illegal and substituted therefor a provision adjudging that that portion of the agreement was legal. The appeal was from so much of the Appellate Division as modified the judgment of the Supreme Court and also that part which affirmed the judgment in Supreme Court insofar as it adjudicated that article VIII, sections E and F, and article XXI of the agreement were valid.

... I. Boards of education are solely creatures of statute and must look to the statute for all their powers and duties. ... The retirement award article of the agreement between the parties is unlawful. *(Matter of Boyd* v. *Collins,* 11 N Y 2d 228.) III. The provision of the agreement for reimbursement for lost or damaged property between the parties is unlawful. IV. The provision of the agreement between the parties for reimbursement of the cost of graduate courses is unlawful. V. The provision of the agreement between the parties for arbitration following dismissal of a tenure teacher is unlawful. ...

Robert H. Chanin, Richard R. Rowley and *Jeffrey G. Plant* for respondent-appellant. I. In the absence of an express legislative restriction against providing for a particular term or condition of employment, a school board may provide for such term or condition under the board powers bestowed upon it by the Taylor law, the Education Law and other statutes. *(Matter of Teachers Assn., Cent. High School Dist. N. 3 [Bd. of Educ., Cent. High School Dist. No. 3, Nassau County],* 34 A D 2d 351.) II. The contractual provision for a salary increment in the final year before retirement is lawful. ... III. The contractual provision for reimbursement of job related personal property damage is lawful. ... IV. The contractual provision for reimbursement of tuition for certian approved graduate courses is lawful. ... V. The arbitration provision is in no way inconsistent with the Tenure Law. ... VI. It is contrary to both the purpose and structure of the Taylor Law to incorporate into it the definition of a "grievance" contained in article 16 of the General Municipal Law. *(City of Auburn* v. *Nash,* 34 A D 2d 345.)* VII. School board members are not more qualified than arbitrators to rule in teacher dismissal cases nor is it contrary to public policy to refer such cases to arbitrators.

Chief Judge FULD. We are called upon to decide (1) whether a school board has the authority to enter into a collective bargaining agreement granting economic benefits to schoolteachers, absent specific statutory authorization to do so and (2) whether such a board lacks the power to enter into a collective bargaining agreement containing a clause which provides for the arbitration of disputes concerning disciplinary action taken against tenure teachers.

The facts are undisputed. The plaintiff (hereafter called the "Board"), as a public employer under the Taylor Law (Civil Service Law, art. 14), recognized the defendant (hereafter referred to as the "Association") as the employee organization representing the school district teachers. The parties—following recommendations by a fact-finding panel appointed by the New York State Public Employment Relations Board—entered into a collective bargaining agreement for the 1969-70 school year. Included in this agreement are five provisions which gave rise to this litigation. Four of them relate to the payment of economic benefits in the form of either salary increases or reimbursement for certain expenses incurred, and the fifth provides for arbitration in cases in which tenure teachers have been disciplined.

The first two challenged provisions deal with the reimbursement of teachers for job related personal property damage (the damage reimbursement provision). The next provides partial reimbursement to teachers for graduate courses taken with the approval of the school administration (the tuition reimbursement provision). The fourth questioned clause (art. XXI) provides for a salary increment for teachers during their last year of service before retirement (the retirement award provision) and reads as follows:

> "Each teacher who hereafter indicates his intention to retire one year prior to such retirement under the New York State Teachers Retirement System or whose retirement is mandatory under such system shall receive at the start of the last school year of service a salary increase for that year equal to 5/10 of 1% (0.5%) of his current salary multiplied by the number of years of service in this school district, such salary increase not to exceed $1500."

The remaining disputed provision (art. XVIII, § C) relates to the arbitration of disputes regarding disciplinary action taken against tenure teachers (the grievance provision):

> "No tenure teacher shall be disciplined, reprimanded, reduced in rank or compensation, suspended. demoted, transferred, terminated or otherwise deprived of any professional advantage without just cause. ... Any such action, including adverse evaluation of teacher performance or a violation of professional ethics asserted by the Board or any agent thereof, shall be subject to the grievance procedure set forth in this Agreement."

The Board, questioning its own power to agree and bind itself to the provisions set out above, raised the issue of their legality in September, 1969, during the negotiations leading up to the execution of the collective bargaining agreement, and shortly thereafter it brought this action for a judgment (1) declaring those provisions illegal and of no effect and (2) staying arbitration proceedings which had been commenced by the Association under the grievance provision. The court at Special Term held that the provisions relating to tuition reimbursement and to the grievance procedure were illegal but sustained the validity of the remaining provisions. On appeal, the Appellate Division agreed with Special Term in all respects except one; it concluded that the tuition reimbursement provision was also valid (36 A D 2d 753). Two of the justices, dissenting in part, believed that the retirement award provision was illegal.

In our view, all of the challenged provisions are valid.

The basic question posed by this appeal is whether there is any fundamental conflict between the provisions of the Taylor Law and the provisions of any other statute dealing with the powers and duties of school boards. Under the Taylor Law, a public employer, in order "to promote harmonious and cooperative relationships between government and its employees" (§ 200), is empowered to recognize an employee organization for the purpose of collective bargaining negotiations (§ 204, subd. 1). When such an organization is recognized, the public employer "is required to negotiate collectively with such employee organization in the determination of, and administration of grievances arising under, *the terms and conditions of employment of the public employees as provided in this article,* and to negotiate and enter into written agreements with such employee organizations in determining such terms and conditions of employment" (§ 204, subd. 2; italics supplied).

In other words, the validity of a provision found in a collective agreement negotiated by a public employer turns upon whether it constitutes a term or condition of employment. If it does, then, the public employer must negotiate as to such term or condition and, upon reaching an understanding, must incorporate it into the collective agreement unless some statutory provision circumscribes its power to do so.

It is manifest that each of the provisions here challenged constitutes a term or condition of employment. It is certainly not uncommon for collective agreements in the public sector, as well as in the private sector, to contain "damage reimbursement" provisions similar to the one before us. If, during the course of performing his duties, an employee has his clothing, eyeglasses or other personal effects damaged or destroyed, it is certainly reasonable to reimburse him for the cost of repairing or replacing them.

The tuition reimbursement provision, as well, clearly relates to a term and condition of employment. School boards throughout the State pay teachers a salary differential for completing a specified number of credit hours above the baccalaureate degree. Since graduate work tends to increase teacher skills and is beneficial to the school district, there is no reason why the Board should not encourage such work by absorbing one half of the tuition expense.

The so-called retirement award provision also involves a term and condition of employment. Employers, both in the public and private sectors, have traditionally paid higher salaries based upon length of service and training. In addition to the fact that the payment was to be for services actually rendered during their last year of employment, the benefit provided for served the legitimate purpose of inducing experienced teachers to remain in the employ of the school district. It is not, therefore, a constitutionally prohibited "gift" of public moneys (N. Y. Const., art. VII, § 8, subd. 1; art. VIII, § 1), since the retiring teachers who benefit from this provision have furnished a "corresponding benefit or consideration to the State." *(Matter of Teachers Assn. [Bd. of Educ.],* 34 A D 2d 251, 353.) Nor may the provision be regarded as creating a retirement plan since the additional compensation was made payable only upon completion of the required services during the year prior to retirement. If this were to be deemed a retirement benefit, then, it would be equally logical to argue that increases in compensation in the years immediately prior to retirement were part and parcel of the retirement plan.

This brings us to the grievance provision. It assures teachers with tenure that no disciplinary action will be taken against them without just cause and that any dispute as to the existence of such cause may be submitted to arbitration. It is a provision commonly found in collective bargaining agreements in the private and public sectors and carries out Federal and State policy favoring arbitration as a means of resolving labor disputes. (See *Steelworkers* v. *Warrior & Guld Co.,* 363 U. S. 574, 583–585; *Matter of Associated Teachers [Bd. of Educ.],* 60 Misc 2d 443, 447; Klaus, The Evolution of a Collective Bargaining Relationship in Public Education, 67 Mich. L. Rev. 1033, 1040–1041; Krislov & Peters,

Arbitration of Grievances in Educational Units, 23 Lab. L. J. 25.)

In sum, each of the provisions under attack relates to a term or condition of employment and, accordingly, the Board was, in light of the Taylor Law, required to negoitate—unless it contentions, to which we turn, compel a different conclusion.

Although the Board raises specific objections that are peculiar to each of the challenged items, its basic premises is the same—that, absent a statutory provision *expressly* authorizing a school board to provide for a particular term or condition of employment, it is legally prohibited from doing so. Proceeding from that premise, the Board would have us hold that school boards possess only those powers granted by a single provision, section 1709, of the Education Law. Quite apart from the fact that that section contains a broad grant of powers, the Board's premise is fallacious. Under the Taylor Law, the obligation to bargain as to all terms and conditions of employment is a broad and unqualified one, and there is no reason why the mandatory provision of that act should be limited, in any way, except in cases where some other applicable statutory provision explicitly and definitively prohibits the public employer from making an agreement as to a particular term or condition of employment.

Were it otherwise, a school board would have a hard time bargaining effectively with its teachers concerning terms of employment, since it would frequently be difficult, if not impossible, to find an express grant of power with respect to any particular subject. To adhere to the restrictive view advanced by the Board "would," the Appellate Division recently wrote in *Matter of Teachers Assn. (Bd. of Educ.)* (34 A D 2d, *supra,* at p. 356), "virtually destroy the bargaining powers which public policy has installed in the field of public employment and throttle the ability of a Board of Education to meet the changing needs of employer-employee relations within its district."

Public employers must, therefore, be presumed to possess the broad powers needed to negotiate with employees as to all terms and conditions of employment. The presumption may, of course, be rebutted by showing statutory provisions which expressly prohibit collective bargaining as to a particular term or condition but, "[i]n the absence of an express legislative restriction against bargaining for that term of an employment contract between a public employer and its employees, the authority to provide for such [term] resides in the [school board] under the broad powers and duties delegated by the statutes." *(Matter of Teachers Assn. [Bd. of Educ.],* 34 A D 2d 351, 355, *supra;* ... It is hardly necessary to say that, if the Board asserts a lack of power to agree to any particular term or condition of employment, it has the burden of demonstrating the existence of a specific statutory provision which circumscribes the exercise of such power. It has failed to meet this burden in the present case.

The Board cites no legislation which expressly or even impliedly prevented it from including the tuition and damage reimbursement provisions. Nor does section 113 (subd. a) of the Retirement and Social Security Law—to which the Board points—prohibit inclusion of the retirement award provision; that provision merely provided for the payment of a salary increment based upon length of service. We also find without substance the Board's claim that the grievance provision violates section 3020-a of the Education Law, generally known as the Tenure Law. That statute provides that, prior to any disciplinary action being taken against a teacher, the latter must be afforded a hearing before an impartial panel, which then submits recommendations to the school board (Education Law, § 3020-a, subds, 2, 3, 4). The Board is not bound by these recommendations and may disregard them in making its decision. Since a decision by the Board itself to impose discipline is a prerequisite to arbitration, the grievance provision in no way supplants this aspect of the Tenure Law. In addition, section 3020-a (subd. 5) declares that any employee "feeling himself aggrieved" may either appeal to the Commissioner of Education or commence an article 78 proceeding. The procedure thus set up is not mandatory, its implementation resting entirely in the teacher's discretion. Thus, the Legislature has given a tenure teacher a choice of two methods of statutory appeal if he desires to challenge an adverse decision of the school board. But it does not follow from this that the Board is inhibited from agreeing that the teacher may choose arbitration as a third method of reviewing its determination.

It is of more than passing significance that the Taylor Law explicitly vests employee organizations with the right to represent public employees not only in connection with negotiations as to the terms and conditions of employment but also as to *"the administration of grievances arising thereunder"* (Civil Service Law, § 203; italics supplied). Indeed, it is the declared policy of this State to encourage "public employers and . . . employee organizations to agree upon procedures for resolving disputes" (§ 200, subd. [c]). And arbitration is, of course, part and parcel of the administration of grievances. (See *Steelworkers* v. *Warrior & Gulf Co.,* 363 U. S. 574, 578, *supra; McGuire* v. *Humble Oil & Refining Co.,* 355 F. 2d 352, 358; ... There is, therefore, no reason to infer that the Legislature intended that the provisions of the Tenure Law should, by implication, deprive employee organizations of a right to represent employees in the administration of disciplinary grievances.

Nor can we agree that a board of education is better qualified than an arbitrator to decide whether a teacher in its employ should be dismissed for incompetency or misconduct. It may not be gainsaid that arbitrators, selected because of their impartiality and their intimate knowledge of school board matters are fully qualified to decide issues such as those under consideration. Moreover, if the school board's contentions were sustained, it would be the Supreme Court, not the board of education, which would pass upon the correctness of the determination in an article 78 proceeding. In any event, though, we cannot subscribe to the view that the legality of an arbitration provision turns on the relative competency of arbitrator and judge.

We would but add that there is no basis for the fear expressed that to permit the grievance to go to arbitration will enable the employee to appeal—pursuant to section 3020-a, subdivision 5, of the Education Law—to the arbitrator *after* he has lost before the commissioner or the court or, conversely, to the Commissioner of Education or the Supreme Court *after* he has submitted to arbitration and lost before the arbitrator. Once the controversy is heard and a decision arrived at *either* by the arbitrator *or* by the commissioner *or* by the judge, that is the end of the matter. As already indicated, the collective bargaining agreement does no more than give the employee a possible third means of reviewing a Board determination.

The order appealed from should be modified, without costs, by reversing so much thereof as holds illegal the provision permitting arbitration with respect to the disciplining of tenure teachers and, except as so modified, affirmed.

BREITEL, J. (dissenting in part). I quite agree with all but one feature of the majority determination, that dealing with the retirement award. While that feature may seem a small part of the collective bargaining agreement negotiated and executed, it has, as a precedent, marked significance in the relations between public employers and employees and critical impact on public retirement systems. Moreover, the retirement feature is one that falls in an area where government has been especially concerned because of accumulating economic burdens on retirement systems and the public fisc out of which some or all retirement reserves come. Indeed, the condition has become so critical that the Legislature in recent sessions has, as is publicly known, invoked a "freeze" on the general increase of retirement benefits.

As did two dissenting Justices at the Appellate Division, I conclude that the collective bargaining provision granting to retiring teachers a salary increase for their terminal year is invalid. Unlike the dissenting Justices, however, I do not find that the provision violates constitutional limitations on making gifts (N. Y. Const., art. VII, § 8, subd. 1); but do find in agreement with the dissenters that it is invalid because it violates applicable statute law.

Article XXI of the collective agreement reads:

> "Each teacher who hereafter indicates his intention to retire one year prior to such retirement under the New York State Teachers Retirement System or whose retirement is mandatory under such system shall receive at the start of the last school year of service a salary increase for that year equal to 5/10 of 1% (0.5%) of his current salary multiplied by the number of years of service in this school district, such salary increase not to exceed $1500."

Preliminarily, the provision is entitled as a "retirement award," and, therefore, the parties so regarded it. Moreover, it reads as a retirement formula would with a fraction determined by years of service as a numerator and the current salary as a base.

Section 113 of the Retirement and Social Security Law forbids any municipality from creating any retirement system for its officers or employees (subd. a). Section 526 of the Education Law provided since the merger of school retirement systems into the State system in 1923 for the abolition and discontinuance of local school retirement systems.

The "retirement award" provided by the collective agreement violates both statutes. Nor may the provision be regarded simply as a salary increase payable out of funds available to the school district. Its pivotal effect, by increasing final average salary in determining retirement allowances, is to increase the allowances payable by the State teachers' retirement system out of its reserves contributed by employers and employees (see, e.g., Education Law, §§ 510, 511, 511-a).

There may be a further consequential effect. Because the agreement, if valid, affects retirement system benefits it may be prospectively binding under the constitutional provision prohibiting the diminishment or impairment of retirement benefits. ... All this under a locally-negotiated agreement and, of course, subject to arbitration in the event of disputes.

If there were any doubt, and there should be none, that the provision, or its like, has direct bearing on retirement systems, and that "increases" in benefits of precisely this kind have been a matter of deep current concern, the recent enactment of chapter 503 of the Laws of 1971 resolves the doubt. Chapter 503 enacts, among others, a new section 431 to the Retirement and Social Security Law, which reads:

> "In any retirement or pension plan to which the state or municipality thereof contributes, the salary base for the computation of retirement benefits shall in no event include any of the following earned received, on or after April first, nineteen hundred seventy-two: . . .
> "2. any form of termination pay,
> "3. any additional compensation paid in anticipation of retirement, or
> "4. that portion of compensation earned during any twelve months included in such salary base period which exceeds that of the preceding twelve months by more than twenty per centum."

It is difficult to avoid the conclusion that everyone, including the Legislature, and even the parties to the collective agreement, regard a final year's salary in anticipation of retirement, as a retirement benefit under a retirement system. That tinkering locally or administratively with such benefits may invoke constitutional limitations on impairment. ...

To further point the analysis, the State Comptroller in opinions rendered in 1967 and 1968 held invalid, because beyond the statutory power of local boards of education, salary increases for final years in anticipation of retirement. ...

Obviously, the Taylor Law (Civil Service Law, art. 14) was not intended, and should not have the effect, of overriding the statutes discussed, simply because it authorizes collective bargaining between public employers and employees over the terms and conditions of employment (Civil Service Law, § 204). Otherwise, the whole body of statute and decisional law affecting public employment, penal and civil, would be subject to repeal or revision in public collective agreements so long as there is any effect on "the terms and conditions of employment."

Nor do the strictures apply to any increases in compensation which happen to occur in the final years of employment. The strictures do apply to increases in anticipation of and conditioned on retirement. Which also suggest that the provision is hardly an inducement to continued employment. On the contrary, it is an inducement to retire. To say that the purpose is to induce "experienced teachers to remain in the employ of the school district" is to state the contrary of the provision's effect. Of course, it is irrelevant whether the retirement award promotes or deters earlier retirement, so long as there is no power by local agreement to vary the retirement system's balanced incentives for encouraging continued employment and at certain points to encourage retirement.

Accordingly, I dissent in part and vote to modify except as to the provision for a retirement award which should be held invalid for the reasons indicated.

Judges BURKE, BERGAN and GIBSON concur with Chief Judge FULD; Judge BREITEL dissents in part and votes to further modify in a separate opinion in which Judges SCILEPPI and JASEN concur.

Ordered accordingly.

• • •

CASE QUESTIONS

1. What is the main argument the Board of Education when it says that it cannot agree to the teachers' demands?

2. The Board is challenging the three provisions of the contract it signed. What is the decision of the court?

3. The Board says that it is worried that a tenured teacher who is disciplined may have two or more hearings in trying to win his case. What does the court say?

4. What is the dissenting judge concerned about in this case?

APPENDIX A

THE NATIONAL LABOR RELATIONS ACT AS AMENDED, MANAGEMENT RELATIONS ACT, 1947, AS AMENDED BY THE REPORTING AND DISCLOSURE ACT OF 1959*

[PUBLIC LAW 101—80th CONGRESS]

AN ACT to amend the National Labor Relations Act, to provide additional facilities for the mediation of labor disputes affecting commerce, to equalize legal responsibilities of labor organizations and employers, and for other purposes.

Be it enacted by the Senate and House of Representatives of the United States of America in Congress assembled.

Short Title and Declaration of Policy

Sec. 1. (a) This Act may be cited as the "Labor Management Relations Act, 1947."

(b) Industrial strife which interferes with the normal flow of commerce and with the full production of articles and commodities for commerce, can be avoided or substantially minimized if employers, employees, and labor organizations each recognize under law one another's legitimate rights in their relations with each other, and above all recognize under law that neither party has any right in its relations with any other to engage in acts or practices which jeopardize the public health, safety, or interest.

It is the purpose and policy of this Act, in order to promote the full flow of commerce, to prescribe the legitimate rights of both employees and employers in their relations affecting commerce, to provide orderly and peaceful procedures for preventing the interference by either with the legitimate rights of the other, to protect the rights of individual employees in their relations with labor organizations whose activities affect commerce, to define and proscribe practices on the part of labor and management which affect commerce and are inimical to the general welfare, and to protect the rights of the public in connection with labor disputes affecting commerce.

---

* Section 201(d) and (e) of the Labor-Management Report and Disclosure Act of 1959 which repealed Section 9(f), (g), and (h) of the Labor Management Relations Act, 1947, and Section 505 amending Section 302(a), (b), and (c) of the Labor Management Relations Act, 1947, took effect upon enactment of Public Law 86–257, September 14, 1959. As to the other amendments of the Labor Management Relations Act, 1947, Section 707 of the Labor-Management Reporting and Disclosure Act provides:

The amendments made by this title shall take effect sixty days after the date of the enactment of this Act and no provision of this title shall be deemed to make an unfair labor practice, any act which is performed prior to such effective date which did not constitute an unfair labor practice prior thereto.

TITLE I
Amendment of National Labor Relations Act

Sec. 101. The National Labor Relations Act is hereby amended to read as follows:

Findings and Policies

Sec. 1. The denial by some employers of the right of employees to organize and the refusal by some employers to accept the procedure of collective bargaining lead to strikes and other forms of industrial strife or unrest, which have the intent or the necessary effect of burdening or obstructing commerce by (a) impairing the efficiency, safety, or operation of the instrumentalities of commerce; (b) occurring in the current of commerce; (c) materially affecting, restraining, or controlling the flow of raw materials or manufactured or processed goods from or into the channels of commerce, or the prices of such materials or goods in commerce; or (d) causing diminution of employment and wages in such volume as substantially to impair or disrupt the market for goods flowing from or into the channels of commerce.

The inequality of bargaining power between employees who do not possess full freedom of association or actual liberty of contract, and employers who are organized in the corporate or other forms of ownership association substantially burdens and affects the flow of commerce, and tends to aggravate recurrent business depressions, by depressing wage rates and the purchasing power of wage earners in industry and by preventing the stabilization of competitive wage rates and working conditions within and between industries.

Experience has proved that protection by law of the right of employees to organize and bargain collectively safeguards commerce from injury, impairment, or interruption, and promotes the flow of commerce by removing certain recognized sources of industrial strife and unrest, by encouraging practices fundamental to the friendly adjustment of industrial disputes arising out of differences as to wages, hours, or other working conditions, and by restoring equality of bargaining power between employers and employees.

Experience has further demonstrated that certain practices by some labor organizations, their officers, and members have the intent or the necessary effect of burdening or obstructing commerce by preventing the free flow of goods in such commerce through strikes and other forms of industrial unrest or through concerted activities which impair the interest of the public in the free flow of such commerce. The elimination of such practices is a necessary condition to the assurance of the rights herein guaranteed.

It is hereby declared to be the policy of the United States to eliminate the causes of certain substantial obstructions to the free flow of commerce and to mitigate and eliminate these obstructions when they have occurred by encouraging the practice and procedure of collective bargaining and by protecting the exercise by workers of full freedom of association, self-organization, and designation of representatives of their own choosing, for the purpose of negotiating the terms and conditions of their employment or other mutual aid or protection.

Definitions

Sec. 2. When used in this Act—

(1) The term "person" includes one or more individuals, labor organizations, partnerships, associations, corporations, legal representatives, trustees, trustees in bankruptcy, or receivers.

(2) The term "employer" includes any person acting as an agent of an employer, directly or indirectly, but shall not include the United States or any wholly owned Government corporation, or any Federal Reserve Bank, or any State or political subdivision thereof, or any corporation or association operating a hospital, if no part of the net earnings inures to the benefit of any private shareholder or individual, or any person subject to the Railway Labor Act, as amended from time to time, or any labor organization (other than when acting as an employer), or anyone acting in the capacity of officer or agent of such labor organization.

(3) The term "employee" shall include any employee, and shall not be limited to the employees of a particular employer, unless the Act explicitly states otherwise, and shall include any individual whose work has ceased as a consequence of, or in connection with, any current labor dispute or because of any unfair labor practice, and who has not obtained any other regular and substantially equivalent employment, but shall not include any individual employed as an agricultural laborer, or in the domestic service of any family or person at his home, or any individual employed by his parent or spouse, or any individual having the status of an independent contractor, or any individual employed as a supervisor, or any individual employed by an employer subject to the Railway Labor Act, as amended from time to time, or by any other person who is not an employer as herein defined.

(4) The term "representatives" includes any individual or labor organization.

(5) The term "labor organization" means any organization of any kind, or any agency or employee representation committee or plan, in which employees participate and which exists for the purpose, in whole or in part, of dealing with employers concerning grievances, labor disputes, wages, rates of pay, hours of employment, or conditions of work.

(6) The term "commerce" means trade, traffic, commerce, transportation, or communication among the several States, or between the District of Columbia or any Territory of the United States and any State or other Territory, or between any foreign country and any State, Territory, or the District of Columbia, or within the District of Columbia or any Territory, or between points in the same State but through any other State or any Territory or the District of Columbia or any foreign country.

(7) The term "affecting commerce" means in commerce, or burdening or obstructing commerce or the free flow of commerce, or having led or tending to lead to a labor dispute burdening or obstructing commerce or the free flow of commerce.

(8) The term "unfair labor practice" means any unfair labor practice listed in section 8.

(9) The term "labor dispute" includes any controversy concerning terms, tenure or conditions of employment, or concerning the association or representation of persons in negotiating, fixing, maintaining, changing,

or seeking to arrange terms or conditions of employment, regardless of whether the disputants stand in the proximate relation of employer and employee.

(10) The term "National Labor Relations Board" means the National Labor Relations Board provided for in section 3 of this Act.

(11) The term "supervisor" means any individual having authority, in the interest of the employer, to hire, transfer, suspend, lay off, recall, promote, discharge, assign, reward, or discipline other employees, or responsibly to direct them, or to adjust their grievances, or effectively to recommend such action, if in connection with the foregoing the exercise of such authority is not of a merely routine or clerical nature, but requires the use of independent judgment.

(12) The term "professional employee" means—

(a) any employee engaged in work (i) predominantly intellectual and varied in character as opposed to routine mental, manual, mechanical, or physical work; (ii) involving the consistent exercise of discretion and judgment in its performance; (iii) of such a character that the output produced or the result accomplished cannot be standardized in relation to a given period of time; (iv) requiring knowledge of an advanced type in a field of science or learning customarily acquired by a prolonged course of specialized intellectual instruction and study in an institution of higher learning or a hospital, as distinguished from a general academic education or from an apprenticeship or from training in the performance of routine mental, manual, or physical processes; or

(b) any employee, who (i) has completed the courses of specialized intellectual instruction and study described in clause (iv) of paragraph (a), and (ii) is performing related work under the supervision of a professional person to qualify himself to become a professional employee as defined in paragraph (a).

(13) In determining whether any person is acting as an "agent" of another person so as to make such other person responsible for his acts, the question of whether the specific acts performed were actually authorized or subsequently ratified shall not be controlling.

National Labor Relations Board

Sec. 3. (a) The National Labor Relations Board (hereinafter called the "Board") created by this Act prior to its amendment by the Labor Management Relations Act, 1947, is hereby continued as an agency of the United States, except that the Board shall consist of five instead of three members, appointed by the President by and with the advice and consent of the Senate. Of the two additional members so provided for, one shall be appointed for a term of five years and the other for a term of two years. Their successors, and the successors of the other members, shall be appointed for terms of five years each, excepting that any individual chosen to fill a vacancy shall be appointed only for the unexpired term of the member whom he shall succeed. The President shall designate one member to serve as Chairman of the Board. Any member of the Board may be removed by the President, upon notice and hearing, for neglect of duty or malfeasance in office, but for no other cause.

(b) The Board is authorized to delegate to any group of three or more members any or all of the powers which it may itself exercise. The Board is also authorized to delegate to its regional directors its powers under section 9 to determine the unit appropriate for the purpose of collective bargaining, to investigate and provide for hearings, and determine whether a question of representation exists, and to direct an election or take a secret ballot under subsection (c) or (e) of Section 9 and certify the results thereof, except that upon the filing of a request therefor with the Board by any interested person, the Board may review any action of a regional director delegated to him under this paragraph, but such a review shall not, unless specifically ordered by the Board, operate as a stay of any action taken by the regional director. A vacancy in the Board shall not impair the right of the remaining members to exercise all of the powers of the Board, and three members of the Board shall, at all times, constitute a quorum of the Board, except that two members shall constitute a quorum of any group designated pursuant to the first sentence hereof. The Board shall have an official seal which shall be judicially noticed.

(c) The Board shall at the close of each fiscal year make a report in writing to Congress and to the President stating in detail the cases it has heard, the decisions it has rendered, the names, salaries, and duties of all employees and officers in the employ or under the supervision of the Board, and an account of all moneys it has disbursed.

(d) There shall be a General Counsel of the Board who shall be appointed by the President, by and with the advice and consent of the Senate, for a term of four years. The General Counsel of the Board shall exercise general supervision over all attorneys employed by the Board (other than trial examiners and legal assistants to Board members) and over the officers and employees in the regional offices. He shall have final authority, on behalf of the Board, in respect of the investigation of charges and issuance of complaints under section 10, and in respect of the prosecution of such complaints before the Board, and shall have such other duties as the Board may prescribe or as may be provided by law. In case of a vacancy in the office of the General Counsel the President is authorized to designate the officer or employee who shall act as General Counsel during such vacancy, but no person or persons so designated shall so act (1) for more than forty days when the Congress is in session unless a nomination to fill such vacancy shall have been submitted to the Senate, or (2) after the adjournment *sine die* of the session of the Senate in which such nomination was submitted.

Sec. 4. (a) Each member of the Board and the General Counsel of the Board shall receive a salary of $12,000* a year, shall be eligible for reappointment, and shall not engage in any other business, vocation, or employment. The Board shall appoint an executive secretary, and such attorneys, examiners, and regional directors, and such other employees as it may from time to time find necessary for the proper performance of its duties. The Board may not employ any attorneys for the purpose of

---

* Pursuant to Public Law 90–206, 90th Congress, 81 Stat. 644, approved December 16, 1967, and in accordance with Section 225(f)(ii) thereof, effective in 1969, the salary of the Chairman of the Board shall be $40,000 per year and the salaries of the General Counsel and each Board member shall be $38,000 per year.

reviewing transcripts of hearings or preparing drafts of opinions except that any attorney employed for assignment as a legal assistant to any Board member may for such Board member review such transcripts and prepare such drafts. No trial examiner's report shall be reviewed, either before or after its publication, by any person other than a member of the Board or his legal assistant, and no trial examiner shall advise or consult with the Board with respect to exceptions taken to his findings, rulings, or recommendations. The Board may establish or utilize such regional, local, or other agencies, and utilize such voluntary and uncompensated services, as may from time to time be needed. Attorneys appointed under this section may, at the direction of the Board, appear for and represent the Board in any case in court. Nothing in this Act shall be construed to authorize the Board to appoint individuals for the purpose of conciliation or mediation, or for economic analysis.

(b) All of the expenses of the Board, including all necessary traveling and subsistence expenses outside the District of Columbia incurred by the members or employees of the Board under its orders, shall be allowed and paid on the presentation of itemized vouchers therefor approved by the Board or by any individual it designates for that purpose.

Sec. 5. The principal office of the Board shall be in the District of Columbia, but it may meet and exercise any or all of its powers at any other place. The Board may, by one or more of its members or by such agents or agencies as it may designate, prosecute any inquiry necessary to its functions in any part of the United States. A member who participates in such an inquiry shall not be disqualified from subsequently participating in a decision of the Board in the same case.

Sec. 6. The Board shall have authority from time to time to make, amend, and rescind, in the manner prescribed by the Administrative Procedure Act, such rules and regulations as may be necessary to carry out the provisions of this Act.

Rights of Employees

Sec. 7. Employees shall have the right to self-organization, to form, join, or assist labor organizations, to bargain collectively through representatives of their own choosing, and to engage in other concerted activities for the purpose of collective bargaining or other mutual aid or protection, and shall also have the right to refrain from any or all of such activities except to the extent that such right may be affected by an agreement requiring membership in a labor organization as a condition of employment as authorized in section 8(a)(3).

Unfair Labor Practices

Sec. 8. (a) It shall be an unfair labor practice for an employer—

(1) to interfere with, restrain, or coerce employees in the exercise of the rights guaranteed in section 7;

(2) to dominate or interfere with the formation or administration of any labor organization or contribute financial or other support to it: *Provided,* That subject to rules and regulations made and published by the Board pursuant to section 6, an employer shall not be prohibited from permitting

employees to confer with him during working hours without loss of time or pay;

(3) by discrimination in regard to hire or tenure of employment or any term or condition of employment to encourage or discourage membership in any labor organization: *Provided,* That nothing in this Act, or in any other statute of the United States, shall preclude an employer from making an agreement with a labor organization (not established, maintained, or assisted by any action defined in section 8(a) of this Act as an unfair labor practice) to require as a condition of employment membership therein on or after the thirtieth day following the beginning of such employment or the effective date of such agreement, whichever is the later, (i) if such labor organization is the representative of the employees as provided in section 9(a), in the appropriate collective-bargaining unit covered by such agreement when made; and (ii) unless following an election held as provided in section 9(e) within one year preceding the effective date of such agreement, the Board shall have certified that at least a majority of the employees eligible to vote in such election have voted to rescind the authority of such labor organization to make such an agreement: *Provided further,* That no employer shall justify any discrimination against an employee for nonmembership in a labor organization (A) if he has reasonable grounds for believing that such membership was not available to the employee on the same terms and conditions generally applicable to other members, or (B) if he has reasonable grounds for believing that membership was denied or terminated for reasons other than the failure of the employee to tender the periodic dues and the initiation fees uniformly required as a condition of acquiring or retaining membership;

(4) to discharge or otherwise discriminate against an employee because he has filed charges or given testimony under this Act;

(5) to refuse to bargain collectively with the representatives of his employees, subject to the provisions of section 9(a).

(b) It shall be an unfair labor practice for a labor organization or its agents—

(1) to restrain or coerce (A) employees in the exercise of the rights guaranteed in section 7; *Provided,* That this paragraph shall not impair the right of a labor organization to prescribe its own rules with respect to the acquisition or retention of membership therein; or (B) an employer in the selection of his representatives for the purposes of collective bargaining or the adjustment of grievances;

(2) to cause or attempt to cause an employer to discriminate against an employee in violation of subsection (a)(3) or to discriminate against an employee with respect to whom membership in such organization has been denied or terminated on some ground other than his failure to tender the periodic dues and the initiation fees uniformly required as a condition of acquiring or retaining membership;

(3) to refuse to bargain collectively with an employer, provided it is the representative of his employees subject to the provisions of section 9(a);

(4) (i) to engage in, or to induce or encourage any individual employed by any person engaged in commerce or in an industry affecting commerce to engage in, a strike or a refusal in the course of his employment to use, manufacture, process, transport, or otherwise handle or work on any goods, articles, materials, or commodities or to perform any services; or (ii) to threaten, coerce, or restrain any person engaged in commerce or

in an industry affecting commerce, where in either case an object thereof is:

(A) forcing or requiring any employer or self-employed person to join any labor or employer organization or to enter into any agreement which is prohibited by section 8(e);

(B) forcing or requiring any person to cease using, selling, handling, transporting, or otherwise dealing in the products of any other producer, processor, or manufacturer, or to cease doing business with any other person, or forcing or requiring any other employer to recognize or bargain with a labor organization as the representative of his employees unless such labor organization has been certified as the representative of such employees under the provisions of section 9: *Provided,* That nothing contained in this clause (B) shall be construed to make unlawful, where not otherwise unlawful, any primary strike or primary picketing;

(C) forcing or requiring any employer to recognize or bargain with a particular labor organization as the representative of his employees if another labor organization has been certified as the representative of such employees under the provisions of section 9;

(D) forcing or requiring any employer to assign particular work to employees in a particular labor organization or in a particular trade, craft, or class rather than to employees in another labor organization or in another trade, craft, or class, unless such employer is failing to conform to an order or certification of the Board determining the bargaining representative for employees performing such work:

Provided, That nothing contained in this subsection (b) shall be construed to make unlawful a refusal by any person to enter upon the premises of any employer (other than his own employer), if the employees of such employer are engaged in a strike ratified or approved by a representative of such employees whom such employer is required to recognize under this Act: *Provided further,* That for the purposes of this paragraph (4) only, nothing contained in such paragraph shall be construed to prohibit publicity, other than picketing, for the purpose of truthfully advising the public, including consumers and members of a labor organization, that a product or products are produced by an employer with whom the labor organization has a primary dispute and are distributed by another employer, as long as such publicity does not have an effect of inducing any individual employed by any person other than the primary employer in the course of his employment to refuse to pick up, deliver, or transport any goods, or not to perform any services, at the establishment of the employer engaged in such distribution;

(5) to require of employees covered by an agreement authorized under subsection (a)(3) the payment, as a condition precedent to becoming a member of such organization, of a fee in an amount which the Board finds excessive or discriminatory under all the circumstances. In making such a finding, the Board shall consider, among other relevant factors, the practices and customs of labor organizations in the particular industry, and the wages currently paid to the employees affected;

(6) to cause or attempt to cause an employer to pay or deliver or agree to pay or deliver any money or other thing of value, in the nature of an exaction, for services which are not performed or not to be performed; and

(7) to picket or cause to be picketed, or threaten to picket or cause to be picketed, any employer where an object thereof is forcing or requiring an employer to recognize or bargain with a labor organization as the representative of his employees, or forcing or requiring the employees of an employer to accept or select such labor organization as their collective

bargaining representative, unless such labor organization is currently certified as the representative of such employees:

> (A) where the employer has lawfully recognized in accordance with this
> Act any other labor organization and a question concerning representation
> may not appropriately be raised under section 9(c) of this Act,
> (B) where within the preceding twelve months a valid election under
> section 9(c) of this Act has been conducted, or
> (C) where such picketing has been conducted without a petition under
> section 9(c) being filed within a reasonable period of time not to exceed
> thirty days from the commencement of such picketing: *Provided,* That when
> such a petition has been filed the Board shall forthwith, without regard to
> the provisions of section 9(c)(1) or the absence of a showing of a sub-
> stantial interest on the part of the labor organization, direct an election
> in such unit as the Board finds to be appropriate and shall certify the
> results thereof: *Provided further,* That nothing in this subparagraph (C)
> shall be construed to prohibit any picketing or other publicity for the
> purpose of truthfully advising the public (including consumers) that an
> employer does not employ members of, or have a contract with, a labor
> organization, unless an effect of such picketing is to induce any individual
> employed by any other person in the course of his employment, not to pick
> up, deliver or transport any goods or not to perform any services.

Nothing in this paragraph (7) shall be construed to permit any act which
would otherwise be an unfair labor practice under this section 8(b).

(c) The expressing of any views, argument, or opinion, or the dissemination thereof, whether in written, printed, graphic, or visual form,
shall not constitute or be evidence of an unfair labor practice under any
of the provisions of this Act, if such expression contains no threat of
reprisal or force or promise of benefit.

(d) For the purposes of this section, to bargain collectively is the
performance of the mutual obligation of the employer and the representative of the employees to meet at reasonable times and confer in good
faith with respect to wages, hours, and other terms and conditions of
employment, or the negotiation of an agreement, or any question arising
thereunder, and the execution of a written contract incorporating any
agreement reached if requested by either party, but such obligation does
not compel either party to agree to a proposal or require the making of a
concession: *Provided,* That where there is in effect a collective-bargaining
contract covering employees in an industry affecting commerce, the duty
to bargain collectively shall also mean that no party to such contract
shall terminate or modify such contract, unless the party desiring such
termination or modification—

> (1) serves a written notice upon the other party to the contract of the
> proposed termination or modification sixty days prior to the expiration
> date thereof, or in the event such contract contains no expiration date,
> sixty days prior to the time it is proposed to make such termination or
> modification;
> (2) offers to meet and confer with the other party for the purpose of
> negotiating a new contract or a contract containing the proposed
> modifications;
> (3) notifies the Federal Mediation and Conciliation Service within
> thirty days after such notice of the existence of a dispute, and simul-
> taneously therewith notifies any State or Territorial agency established

to mediate and conciliate disputes within the State or Territory where the dispute occurred, provided no agreement has been reached by that time; and

(4) continues in full force and effect, without resorting to strike or lockout, all the terms and conditions of the existing contract for a period of sixty days after such notice is given or until the expiration date of such contract, whichever occurs later:

The duties imposed upon employers, employees, and labor organizations by paragraphs (2), (3), and (4) shall become inapplicable upon an intervening certification of the Board, under which the labor organization or individual, which is a party to the contract, has been superseded as or ceased to be the representative of the employees subject to the provisions of section 9(a), and the duties so imposed shall not be construed as requiring either party to discuss or agree to any modification of the terms and conditions contained in a contract for a fixed period, if such modification is to become effective before such terms and conditions can be reopened under the provisions of the contract. Any employee who engages in a strike within the sixty-day period specified in this subsection shall lose his status as an employee of the employer engaged in the particular labor dispute, for the purposes of sections 8, 9, and 10 of this Act, as amended, but such loss of status for such employee shall terminate if and when he is reemployed by such employer.

(e) It shall be an unfair labor practice for any labor organization and any employer to enter into any contract or agreement, express or implied, whereby such employer ceases or refrains or agrees to cease or refrain from handling, using, selling, transporting or otherwise dealing in any of the products of any other employer, or to cease doing business with any other person, and any contract or agreement entered into heretofore or hereafter containing such an agreement shall be to such extent unenforcible and void: *Provided,* That nothing in this subsection (e) shall apply to an agreement between a labor organization and an employer in the construction industry relating to the contracting or subcontracting of work to be done at the site of the construction, alteration, painting, or repair of a building, structure, or other work: *Provided further,* That for the purposes of this subsection (e) and section 8(b)(4)(B) the terms "any employer," "any person engaged in commerce or an industry affecting commerce," and "any person" when used in relation to the terms "any other producer, processor, or manufacturer," "any other employer," or "any other person" shall not include persons in the relation of a jobber, manufacturer, contractor, or subcontractor working on the goods or premises of the jobber or manufacturer or performing parts of an integrated process of production in the apparel and clothing industry: *Provided further,* That nothing in this Act shall prohibit the enforcement of any agreement which is within the foregoing exception.

(f) It shall not be unfair labor practice under subsections (a) and (b) of this section for an employer engaged primarily in the building and construction industry to make an agreement covering employees engaged (or who, upon their employment, will be engaged) in the building and construction industry with a labor organization of which building and construction employees are members (not established, maintained, or assisted by any action defined in section 8(a) of this Act as an unfair labor practice) because (1) the majority status of such labor organization has not been established under the provisions of section 9 of this Act prior to the making of such agreement, or (2) such agreement requires as a condition of employment, membership in such labor organization after the seventh day following the beginning of such employment or the effective date of the agreement, whichever is later, or (3) such agreement requires the employer to notify such labor organization of opportunities for employment with such employer, or gives such labor organization an opportunity to refer qualified applicants for such employment, or (4) such agreement specifies minimum training or experience qualifications for employment or provides for priority in opportunities for employment based upon length of service with such employer, in the industry or in the particular geographical area: *Provided,* That nothing in this subsection shall set aside the final proviso to section 8(a)(3) of this Act: *Provided further,* That any agreement which would be invalid, but for clause (1) of this subsection, shall not be a bar to a petition filed pursuant to section 9(c) or 9(e).*

Representatives and Elections

Sec. 9. (a) Representatives designated or selected for the purposes of collective bargaining by the majority of the employees in a unit appropriate for such purposes, shall be the exclusive representatives of all the employees in such unit for the purposes of collective bargaining in respect to rates of pay, wages, hours of employment, or other conditions of employment: *Provided,* That any individual employee or a group of employees shall have the right at any time to present grievances to their employer and to have such grievances adjusted, without the intervention of the bargaining representative, as long as the adjustment is not inconsistent with the terms of a collective-bargaining contract or agreement then in effect: *Provided further,* That the bargaining representative has been given opportunity to be present at such adjustment.

(b) The Board shall decide in each case whether, in order to assure to employees the fullest freedom in exercising the rights guaranteed by this Act, the unit appropriate for the purposes of collective bargaining shall be the employer unit, craft unit, plant unit, or subdivision thereof: *Provided,* That the Board shall not (1) decide that any unit is appropriate for such purposes if such unit includes both professional employees and employees who are not professional employees unless a majority of such professional employees vote for inclusion in such unit; or (2) decide that any craft unit is inappropriate for such purposes on the ground that a different unit has been established by a prior Board determination, unless a majority of the employees in the proposed craft unit vote against separate representation or (3) decide that any unit is appropriate for such purposes if it includes, together with other employees, any individual

---

* Section 8(f) is inserted in the Act by subsection (a) of Section 705 of Public Law 86–257. Section 705(b) provides:

Nothing contained in the amendment made by subsection (a) shall be construed as authorizing the execution or application of agreements requiring membership in a labor organization as a condition of employment in any State or Territory in which such execution or application is prohibited by State or Territorial law.

employed as a guard to enforce against employees and other persons rules to protect property of the employer or to protect the safety of persons on the employer's premises; but no labor organization shall be certified as the representative of employees in a bargaining unit of guards if such organization admits to membership, or is affiliated directly or indirectly with an organization which admits to membership, employees other than guards.

(c) (1) Whenever a petition shall have been filed, in accordance with such regulations as may be prescribed by the Board—

> (A) by an employee or group of employees or any individual or labor organization acting in their behalf alleging that a substantial number of employees (i) wish to be represented for collective bargaining and that their employer declines to recognize their representative as the representative defined in section 9(a), or (ii) assert that the individual or labor organization, which has been certified or is being currently recognized by their employer as the bargaining representative, is no longer a representative as defined in section 9(a); or
>
> (B) by an employer, alleging that one or more individuals or labor organizations have presented to him a claim to be recognized as the representative defined in section 9(a);

the Board shall investigate such petition and if it has reasonable cause to believe that a question of representation affecting commerce exists shall provide for an appropriate hearing upon due notice. Such hearing may be conducted by an officer or employee of the regional office, who shall not make any recommendations with respect thereto. If the Board finds upon the record of such hearing that such a question of representation exists, it shall direct an election by secret ballot and shall certify the results thereof.

(2) In determining whether or not a question of representation affecting commerce exists, the same regulations and rules of decision shall apply irrespective of the identity of the persons filing the petition or the kind of relief sought and in no case shall the Board deny a labor organization a place on the ballot by reason of an order with respect to such labor organization or its predecessor not issued in conformity with section 10(c).

(3) No election shall be directed in any bargaining unit or any subdivision within which, in the preceding twelve-month period, a valid election shall have been held. Employees engaged in an economic strike who are not entitled to reinstatement shall be eligible to vote under such regulations as the Board shall find are consistent with the purposes and provisions of this Act in any election conducted within twelve months after the commencement of the strike. In any election where none of the choices on the ballot receives a majority, a run-off shall be conducted, the ballot providing for a selection between the two choices receiving the largest and second largest number of valid votes cast in the election.

(4) Nothing in this section shall be construed to prohibit the waiving of hearings by stipulation for the purpose of a consent election in conformity with regulations and rules of decision of the Board.

(5) In determining whether a unit is appropriate for the purposes specified in subsection (b) the extent to which the employees have organized shall not be controlling.

(d) Whenever an order of the Board made pursuant to section 10(c) is based in whole or in part upon facts certified following an investigation pursuant to subsection (c) of this section there is a petition for the enforcement or review of such order, such certification and the record of such investigation shall be included in the transcript of the entire record required to be filed under section 10(e) or 10(f), and thereupon the decree of the court enforcing, modifying, or setting aside in whole or in part the order of the Board shall be made and entered upon the pleadings, testimony, and proceedings set forth in such transcript.

(3) (1) Upon the filing with the Board, by 30 per centum or more of the employees in a bargaining unit covered by an agreement between their employer and a labor organization made pursuant to section 8(a)(3), of a petition alleging they desire that such authority be rescinded, the Board shall take a secret ballot of the employees in such unit, and shall certify the results thereof to such labor organization and to the employer.

(2) No election shall be conducted pursuant to this subsection in any bargaining unit or any subdivision within which, in the preceding twelve-month period, a valid election shall have been held.

Prevention of Unfair Labor Practices

Sec. 10. (a) The Board is empowered, as hereinafter provided, to prevent any person from engaging in any unfair labor practice (listed in section 8) affecting commerce. This power shall not be affected by any other means of adjustment or prevention that has been or may be established by agreement, law, or otherwise: *Provided,* That the Board is empowered by agreement with any agency of any State or Territory to cede to such agency jurisdiction over any cases in any industry (other than mining, manufacturing, communications, and transportation except where predominantly local in character) even though such cases may involve labor disputes affecting commerce, unless the provision of the State or Territorial statute applicable to the determination of such cases by such agency is inconsistent with the corresponding provision of this Act or has received a construction inconsistent therewith.

(b) Whenever it is charged that any person has engaged in or is engaging in any unfair labor practice, the Board, or any agent or agency designated by the Board for such purposes, shall have power to issue and cause to be served upon such person a complaint stating the charges in that respect, and containing a notice of hearing before the Board or a member thereof, or before a designated agent or agency, at a place therein fixed, not less than five days after the serving of said complaint: *Provided,* That no complaint shall issue based upon any unfair labor practice occurring more than six months prior to the filing of the charge with the Board and the service of a copy thereof upon the person against whom such charge is made, unless the person aggrieved thereby was prevented from filing such charge by reason of service in the armed forces, in which event the six-month period shall be computed from the day of his discharge. Any such complaint may be amended by the member, agent, or agency conducting the hearing or the Board in its discretion at any time prior to the issuance of an order based thereon. The person so complained of shall have the right to file an answer to the original or amended complaint and to appear in person or otherwise and give testimony at the place and time fixed in the complaint. In the discretion of the member, agent, or agency conducting the hearing or the Board, any other person may be allowed to intervene in the said proceeding and to present testimony. Any such proceeding shall, so far as practicable, be conducted in accordance with the rules of evidence applicable in the district courts of the United States under the rules of civil procedure for the district courts of the United States, adopted by the Supreme Court of the United States pursuant to the Act of June 19, 1934 (U.S.C., title 28, secs. 723-B, 723-C).

(c) The testimony taken by such member, agent, or agency or the Board shall be reduced to writing and filed with the Board. Thereafter, in its discretion, the Board upon notice may take further testimony or hear argument. If upon the preponderance of the testimony taken the Board shall be of the opinion that any person named in the complaint has engaged in or is engaging in any such unfair labor practice, then the Board shall state its findings of fact and shall issue and cause to be served on such person an order requiring such person to cease and desist from such unfair labor practice, and to take such affirmative action including reinstatement of employees with or without back pay, as will effectuate the policies of this Act: *Provided,* That where an order directs reinstatement of an employee, back pay may be required of the employer or labor organization, as the case may be, responsible for the discrimination suffered by him: *And provided further,* That in determining whether a complaint shall issue alleging a violation of section 8(a)(1) or section 8(a)(2), and in deciding such cases, the same regulations and rules of decision shall apply irrespective of whether or not the labor organization affected is affiliated with a labor organization national or international in scope. Such order may further require such person to make reports from time to time showing the extent to which it has complied with the order. If upon the preponderance of the testimony taken the Board shall not be of the opinion that a person named in the complaint has engaged in or is engaging in any such unfair labor practice, then the Board shall state its findings of fact and shall issue an order dismissing the said complaint. No order of the Board shall require the reinstatement of any individual as an employee who has been suspended or discharged, or the payment to him of any back pay, if such individual was suspended or discharged for cause. In case the evidence is presented before a member of the Board, or before an examiner or examiners thereof, such member, or such examiner or examiners, as the case may be, shall issue and cause to be served on the parties to the proceeding a proposed report, together with a recommended order, which shall be filed with the Board, and if no exceptions are filed within twenty days after service thereof upon such parties, or within such further period as the Board may authorize, such recommended order shall become the order of the Board and become effective as therein prescribed.

(d) Until the record in a case shall have been filed in a court, as hereinafter provided, the Board may at any time, upon reasonable notice and in such manner as it shall deem proper, modify or set aside, in whole or in part, any finding or order made or issued by it.

(e) The Board shall have power to petition any court of appeals of the United States, or if all the courts of appeals to which application may be made are in vacation, any district court of the United States, within any circuit or district, respectively, wherein the unfair labor pactice in question occurred or wherein such person resides or transacts business, for the enforcement of such order and for appropriate temporary relief or restraining order, and shall file in the court the record in the proceedings, as provided in section 2112 of title 28, United States Code. Upon the filing of such petition, the court shall cause notice thereof to be served upon such person, and thereupon shall have jurisdiction of the proceeding and of the question determined therein, and shall have power to grant such temporary relief or restraining order as it deems just and proper, and to make and enter a decree enforcing, modifying, and enforcing as so modified, or setting aside in whole or in part the order of the Board. No objection that has not been urged before the Board, its member, agent, or agency, shall be considered by the court, unless the failure or neglect to urge such objection shall be excused because of extraordinary circumstances. The findings of the Board with respect to questions of fact if supported by substantial evidence on the record considered as a whole shall be conclusive. If either party shall apply to the court for leave to adduce additional evidence and shall show to the satisfaction of the court that such additional evidence is material and that there were reasonable grounds for the failure to adduce such evidence in the hearing before the Board, its member, agent, or agency, the court may order such additional evidence to be taken before the Board, its member, agent, or agency, and to be made a part of the record. The Board may modify its findings as to the facts, or make new findings, by reason of additonal evidence so taken and filed, and it shall file such modified or new findings, which findings with respect to questions of fact if supported by substantial evidence on the record considered as a whole shall be conclusive, and shall file its recommendations, if any, for the modification or setting aside of its original order. Upon the filing of the record with it the jurisdiction of the court shall be exclusive and its judgment and decree shall be final, except that the same shall be subject to review by the appropriate United States court of appeals if application was made to the district court as hereinabove provided, and by the Supreme Court of the United States upon writ of certiorari or certification as provided in section 1254 of title 28.

(f) Any person aggrieved by a final order of the Board granting or denying in whole or in part the relief sought may obtain a review of such order in any circuit court of appeals of the United States in the circuit wherein the unfair labor practice in question was alledged to have been engaged in or wherein such person resides or transacts business, or in the United States Court of Appeals for the District of Columbia, by filing in such court a written petition praying that the order of the Board be modified or set aside. A copy of such petition shall be forthwith transmitted by the clerk of the court to the Board, and thereupon the aggrieved party shall file in the court the record in the proceeding, certified by the Board, as provided in section 2112 of title 28, United States Code. Upon the filing of such petition, the court shall proceed in the same manner as in the case of an application by the Board under subsection (e) of this section, and shall have the same jurisdiction to grant to the Board such temporary relief or restraining order as it deems just and proper, and in like manner to make and enter a decree enforcing, modifying, and enforcing as so modified, or setting aside in whole or in part the order of the Board; the findings of the Board with respect to questions of fact if supported by substantial evidence on the record considered as a whole shall in like manner be conclusive.

(g) The commencement of proceedings under subsection (e) or (f) of this section shall not, unless specifically ordered by the court, operate as a stay of the Board's order.

(h) When granting appropriate temporary relief or a restraining order, or making and entering a decree enforcing, modifying, and enforcing as so modified, or setting aside in whole or in part an order of the Board, as provided in this section, the jurisdiction of courts sitting in equity shall not be limited by the Act entitled "An Act to amend the Judicial Code and to define and limit the jurisdiction of courts sitting in equity, and for other purposes," approved March 23, 1932 (U.S.C., Supp. VII, title 29, secs. 101-115).

(i) Petitions filed under this Act shall be heard expeditiously, and if possible within ten days after they have been docketed.

(j) The Board shall have power, upon issuance of a complaint as provided in subsection (b) charging that any person has engaged in or is engaging in an unfair labor practice, to petition any district court of the United States (including the District Court of the United States for the District of Columbia), within any district wherein the unfair labor practice in question is alleged to have occurred or wherein such person resides or transacts business, for appropriate temporary relief or restraining order. Upon the filing of any such petition the court shall cause notice thereof to be served upon such person, and thereupon shall have jurisdiction to grant to the Board such temporary relief or restraining order as it deems just and proper.

(k) Whenever it is charged that any person has engaged in an unfair labor practice within the meaning of paragraph (4)(D) of section 8(b), the Board is empowered and directed to hear and determine the dispute out of which such unfair labor practice shall have arisen, unless, within ten days after notice that such charge has been filed, the parties to such dispute submit to the Board satisfactory evidence that they have adjusted, or agreed upon methods for the voluntary adjustment of, the dispute. Upon compliance by the parties to the dispute with the decision of the Board or upon such voluntary adjustment of the dispute, such charge shall be dismissed.

(l) Whenever it is charged that any person has engaged in an unfair labor practice within the meaning of paragraph (4)(A), (B), or (C) of section 8(b), or section 8(e) or section 8(b)(7), the preliminary investigation of such charge shall be made forthwith and given priority over all other cases except cases of like character in the office where it is filed or to which it is referred. If, after such investigation, the officer or regional attorney to whom the matter may be referred has reasonable cause to believe such charge is true and that a complaint should issue, he shall, on behalf of the Board, petition any district court of the United States (including the District Court of the United States for the District of Columbia) within any district where the unfair labor practice in question has occurred, is alleged to have occurred, or wherein such person resides or transacts business, for appropriate injunctive relief pending the final adjudication of the Board with respect to such matter. Upon the filing of any such petition the district court shall have jurisdiction to grant such injunctive relief or temporary restraining order as it deems just and proper, notwithstanding any other provision of law: *Provided further,* That no temporary restraining order shall be issued without notice unless a petition alleges that substantial and irreparable injury to the charging party will be unavoidable and such temporary restraining order shall be effective for no longer than five days and will become void at the expiration of such period. *Provided further,* That such officer or regional attorney shall not apply for any restraining order under section 8(b)(7) if a charge against the employer under section 8(a)(2) has been filed and after the preliminary investigation, he has reasonable cause to believe that such charge is true and that a complaint should issue. Upon filing of any such peition the courts shall cause notice thereof to be served upon any person involved in the charge and such person, including the charging party, shall be given an opportunity to appear by counsel and present any relevant testimony: *Provided further,* That for the purposes of this subsection district courts shall be deemed to have jurisdiction of a labor organization (1) in the district in which such organization maintains its principal office, or (2) in any district in which its duly authorized officers or agents are engaged in promoting or protecting the interests of employee members. The service of legal process upon such officer or agent shall constitute service upon the labor organization and make such organization a party to the suit. In situations where such relief is appropriate the procedure specified herein shall apply to charges with respect to section 8(b)(4)(D).

(m) Whenever it is charged that any person has engaged in an unfair labor practice within the meaning of subsection (a)(3) or (b)(2) of section 8, such charge shall be given priority over all other cases except cases of like character in the office where it is filed or to which it is referred and cases given priority under subsection (1).

Investigatory Powers

Sec. 11. For the purpose of all hearings and investigations, which, in the opinion of the Board, are necessary and proper for the exercise of the powers vested in it by section 9 and section 10—

(1) The Board, or its duly authorized agents or agencies, shall at all reasonable times have access to, for the purpose of examination, and the right to copy and evidence of any person being investigated or proceeded against that relates to any matter under investigation or in question. The Board, or any member thereof, shall upon application of any party to such proceedings, forthwith issue to such party subpenas requiring the attendance and testimony of witnesses or the production of any evidence in such proceeding or investigation requested in such application. Within five days after the service of a subpena on any person requiring the production of any evidence in his possession or under his control, such person may petition the Board to revoke, and the Board shall revoke, such subpena if in its opinion the evidence whose production is required does not relate to any matter under investigation, or any matter in question in such proceedings, or if in its opinion such subpena does not describe with sufficient particularity the evidence whose production is required. Any member of the Board, or any agent or agency designated by the Board for such purposes, may administer oaths and affirmations, examine witnesses, and

receive evidence. Such attendance of witnesses and the production of such evidence may be required from any place in the United States or any Territory or possession thereof, at any designated place of hearing.

(2) In case of contumacy or refusal to obey a subpena issued to any person, any district court of the United States or the United States courts of any Territory or possession, or the District Court of the United States for the District of Columbia, within the jurisdiction of which the inquiry is carried on or within the jurisdiction of which said person guilty of contumacy or refusal to obey is found or resides or transacts business, upon application by the Board shall have jurisdiction to issue to such person an order requiring such person to appear before the Board, its member, agent, or agency, there to produce evidence if so ordered, or there to give testimony touching the matter under investigation or in question; and any failure to obey such order of the court may be punished by said court as a contempt thereof.

(3) [*]

(4) Complaints, orders, and other process and papers of the Board, its member, agent, and agency, may be served either personally or by registered mail or by telegraph or by leaving a copy thereof at the principal office or place of business of the person required to be served. The verified return by the individual so serving the same setting forth the manner of such service shall be proof of the same, and the return post office receipt or telegraph receipt therefor when registered and mailed or tele-graphed as aforesaid shall be proof of service of the same. Witnesses summoned before the Board, its member, agent, or agency, shall be paid the same fees and mileage that are paid witnesses in the courts of the United States, and witnesses whose depositions are taken and the persons taking the same shall severally be entitled to the same fees as are paid for like services in the courts of the United States.

(5) All process of any court to which application may be made under this Act may be served in the judicial district wherein the defendant or other person required to be served resides or may be found.

(6) The several departments and agencies of the Government, when directed by the President, shall furnish the Board, upon its request, all records, papers, and information in their possession relating to any matter before the Board.

Sec. 12. Any person who shall willfully resist, prevent, impede, or interfere with any member of the Board or any of its agents or agencies in the performance of duties pursuant to this Act shall be punished by a fine of not more than $5,000 or by imprisonment for not more than one year, or both.

Limitations

Sec. 13. Nothing in this Act, except as specifically provided for herein, shall be construed so as either to interfere with or impede or diminish in any way the right to strike, or to affect the limitations or qualifications on that right.

[* Section 11(3) is repealed by Sec. 234, Public Law 91-452, 91st Congress, S. 30, 84 Stat. 926, October 15, 1970. See Title 18, U.S.C. Sec. 6001, et seq.]

Sec. 14. (a) Nothing herein shall prohibit any individual employed as a supervisor from becoming or remaining a member of a labor organization, but no employer subject to this Act shall be compelled to deem individuals defined herein as supervisors as employees for the purpose of any law, either national or local, relating to collective bargaining.

(b) Nothing in this Act shall be construed as authorizing the execution or application of agreements requiring membership in a labor organization as a condition of employment in any State or Territory in which such execution or application is prohibited by State or Territorial law.

(c) (1) The Board, in its discretion, may, by rule of decision or by published rules adopted pursuant to the Administrative Procedure Act, decline to assert jurisdiction over any labor dispute involving any class or category of employers, where, in the opinion of the Board, the effect of such labor dispute on commerce is not sufficiently substantial to warrant the exercise of its jurisdiction: *Provided,* That the Board shall not decline to assert jurisdiction over any labor dispute over which it would assert jurisdiction under the standards prevailing upon August 1, 1959.

(2) Nothing in this Act shall be deemed to prevent or bar any agency or the courts of any State or Territory (including the Commonwealth of Puerto Rico, Guam, and the Virgin Islands), from assuming and asserting jurisdiction over labor disputes over which the Board declines, pursuant to paragraph (1) of this subsection, to assert jurisdiction.

Sec. 15. Wherever the application of the provisions of section 272 of chapter 10 of the Act entitled "An Act to establish a uniform system of bankruptcy throughout the United States," approved July 1, 1898, and Acts amendatory thereof and supplementary thereto (U.S.C., title 11, sec. 672), conflicts with the application of the provisions of this Act, this Act shall prevail: *Provided,* That in any situation where the provisions of this Act cannot be validly enforced, the provisions of such other Acts shall remain in full force and effect.

Sec. 16. If any provision of this Act, or the application of such provision to any person or circumstances, shall be held invalid, the remainder of this Act, or the application of such provision to persons or circumstances other than those as to which it is held invalid, shall not be affected thereby.

Sec. 17. This Act may be cited as the "National Labor Relations Act."

Sec. 18. No petition entertained, no investigation made, no election held, and no certification issued by the National Labor Relations Board, under any of the provisions of section 9 of the National Labor Relations Act, as amended, shall be invalid by reason of the failure of the Congress of Industrial Organizations to have complied with the requirements of section 9(f), (g), or (h) of the aforesaid Act prior to December 22, 1949, or by reason of the failure of the American Federation of Labor to have complied with the provisions of section 9(f), (g), or (h) of the aforesaid Act prior to November 7, 1947: *Provided,* That no liability shall be imposed under any provision of this Act upon any person for failure to honor any election or certificate referred to above, prior to the effective date of this amendment: *Provided, however,* That this proviso shall not have the effect of setting aside or in any way affecting judgments or decrees heretofore entered under section 10(e) or (f) and which have become final.

Effective Date of Certain Changes[*]

Sec. 102. No provision of this title shall be deemed to make an unfair labor practice any act which was performed prior to the date of the enactment of this Act which did not constitute an unfair labor practice prior thereto, and the provisions of section 8(a)(3) and section 8(b)(2) of the National Labor Relations Act as amended by this title shall not make an unfair labor practice the performance of any obligation under a collective-bargaining agreement entered into prior to the date of the enactment of this Act, or (in the case of an agreement for a period of not more than one year) entered into on or after such date of enactment, but prior to the effective date of this title, if the performance of such obligation would not have constituted an unfair labor practice under section 8(3) of the National Labor Relations Act prior to the effective date of this title, unless such agreement was renewed or extended subsequent thereto.

Sec. 103. No provisions of this title shall affect any certification or representatives or any determination as to the appropriate collective-bargaining unit, which was made under section 9 of the National Labor Relations Act prior to the effective date of this title until one year after the date of such certification or if, in respect of any such certification, a collective-bargaining contract was entered into prior to the effective date of this title, until the end of the contract period or until one year after such date, whichever first occurs.

Sec. 104. The amendments made by this title shall take effect sixty days after the date of the enactment of this Act, except that the authority of the President to appoint certain officers conferred upon him by section 3 of the National Labor Relations Act as amended by this title may be exercised forthwith.

TITLE II
Conciliation of Labor Disputes in Industries Affecting Commerce; National Emergencies

Sec. 201. That it is the policy of the United States that—

(a) sound and stable industrial peace and the advancement of the general welfare, health, and safety of the Nation and of the best interests of employers and employees can most satisfactorily be secured by the settlement of issues between employers and employees through the processes of conference and collective bargaining between employers and the representatives of their employees;

(b) the settlement of issues between employers and employees through collective bargaining may be advanced by making available full and adequate governmental facilities for conciliation, mediation, and voluntary arbitration to aid and encourage employers and the representatives of their employees to reach and maintain agreements concerning rates of pay, hours, and working conditions, and to make all reasonable efforts to settle their differences by mutual agreement reached through conferences and collective bargaining or by such methods as may be pro-

---

*[The effective date referred to in Sections 102, 103, and 104 is August 22, 1947.]

vided for in any applicable agreement for the settlement of disputes; and

(c) certain controversies which arise between parties to collective-bargaining agreements may be avoided or minimized by making available full and adequate governmental facilities for furnishing assistance to employers and the representatives of their employees in formulating for inclusion with such agreements provision for adequate notice of any proposed changes in the terms of such agreements, for the final adjustment of grievances or questions regarding the application or interpretation of such agreements, and other provisions designed to prevent the subsequent arising of such controversies.

Sec. 202. (a) There is hereby created an independent agency to be known as the Federal Mediation and Conciliation Service (herein referred to as the "Service," except that for sixty days after the date of the enactment of this Act such term shall refer to the Conciliation Service of the Department of Labor). The Service shall be under the direction of a Federal Mediation and Conciliation Director (hereinafter referred to as the "Director"), who shall be appointed by the President by and with the advice and consent of the Senate. The Director shall receive compensation at the rate of 12,000 * per annum. The Director shall not engage in any other business, vocation, or employment.

(b) The Director is authorized, subject to the civil-service laws, to appoint such clerical and other personnel as may be necessary for the execution of the functions of the Service, and shall fix their compensation in accordance with the Classification Act of 1923, as amended, and may, without regard to the provisions of the civil-service laws and the Classification Act of 1923, as amended, appoint and fix the compensation of such conciliators and mediators as may be necessary to carry out the functions of the Service. The Director is authorized to make such expenditures for supplies, facilities, and services as he deems necessary. Such expenditures shall be allowed and paid upon presentation of itemized vouchers therefor approved by the Director or by any employee designated by him for that purpose.

(c) The principal office of the Service shall be in the District of Columbia, but the Director may establish regional offices convenient to localities in which labor controversies are likely to arise. The Director may by order, subject to revocation at any time, delegate any authority and discretion conferred upon him by this Act to any regional director, or other officer or employee of the Service. The Director may establish suitable procedures for cooperation with State and local mediation agencies. The Director shall make an annual report in writing to Congress at the end of the fiscal year.

(d) All mediation and conciliation functions of the Secretary of Labor or the United States Conciliation Service under section 8 of the Act entitled "An Act to create a Department of Labor," approved March 4, 1913 (U.S.C., title 29, sec. 51), and all functions of the United States Conciliation Service under any other law are hereby transferred to the Federal Mediation and Conciliation Service, together with the personnel and

---

* Pursuant to Public Law 90–206, 90th Congress, 81 Stat. 644, approved December 16, 1967, in accordance with Sec. 225(f)(ii) thereof, effective in 1969, the salary of the Director shall be $40,000 per year.

records of the United States Conciliation Service. Such transfer shall take effect upon the sixtieth day after the date of enactment of this Act. Such transfer shall not affect any proceedings pending before the United States Conciliation Service or any certification, order, rule, or regulation theretofore made by it or the Secretary of Labor. The Director and the Service shall not be subject in any way to the jurisdiction or authority of the Secretary of Labor or any official or division of the Department of Labor.

Functions of the Service

Sec. 203. (a) It shall be the duty of the Service, in order to prevent or minimize interruptions of the free flow of commerce growing out of labor disputes, to assist parties to labor disputes in industries affecting commerce to settle such disputes through conciliation and mediation.

(b) The Service may proffer its services in any labor dispute in any industry affecting commerce, either upon its own motion or upon the request of one or more of the parties to the dispute, whenever in its judgment such dispute threatens to cause a substantial interruption of commerce. The Director and the Service are directed to avoid attempting to mediate disputes which would have only a minor effect on interstate commerce if State or other conciliation services are available to the parties. Whenever the Service does proffer its services in any dispute, it shall be the duty of the Service promptly to put itself in communication with the parties and to use its best efforts, by mediation and conciliation, to bring them to agreement.

(c) If the Director is not able to bring the parties to agreement by conciliation within a reasonable time, he shall seek to induce the parties voluntarily to seek other means of settling the dispute without resort to strike, lock-out, or other coercion, including submission to the employees in the bargaining unit of the employer's last offer of settlement for approval or rejection in a secret ballot. The failure or refusal of either party to agree to any procedure suggested by the Director shall not be deemed a violation of any duty or obligation imposed by this Act.

(d) Final adjustment by a method agreed upon by the parties is hereby declared to be the desirable method for settlement of grievance disputes arising over the application or interpretation of an existing collective-bargaining agreement. The Service is directed to make its conciliation and mediation services available in the settlement of such grievance disputes only as a last resort and in exceptional cases.

Sec. 204. (a) In order to prevent or minimize interruptions of the free flow of commerce growing out of labor disputes, employers and employees and their representatives, in any industry affecting commerce, shall—

(1) exert every reasonable effort to make and maintain agreements concerning rates of pay, hours, and working conditions, including provision for adequate notice of any proposed change in the terms of such agreements;

(2) whenever a dispute arises over the terms or application of a collective-bargaining agreement and a conference is requested by a party or prospective party thereto, arrange promptly for such a conference to be held and endeavor in such conference to settle such dispute expeditiously; and

(3) in case such dispute is not settled by conference, participate fully and promptly in such meetings as may be undertaken by the Service under this Act for the purpose of aiding in a settlement of the dispute.

Sec. 205. (a) There is hereby created a National Labor-Management Panel which shall be composed of twelve members appointed by the President, six of whom shall be selected from among persons outstanding in the field of management and six of whom shall be selected from among persons outstanding in the field of labor. . . .

(b) It shall be the duty of the panel, at the request of the Director, to advise in the avoidance of industrial controversies and the manner in which mediation and voluntary adjustment shall be administered, particularly with reference to controversies affecting the general welfare of the country.

National Emergencies

Sec. 206. Whenever in the opinion of the President of the United States, a threatened or actual strike or lock-out affecting an entire industry or a substantial part thereof engaged in trade, commerce, transportation, transmission, or communication among the several States or with foreign nations, or engaged in the production of goods for commerce, will, if permitted to occur or to continue, imperil the national health or safety, he may appoint a board of inquiry to inquire into the issues involved in the dispute and to make a written report to him within such time as he shall prescribe. Such report shall include a statement of the facts with respect to the dispute, including each party's statement of its position but shall not contain any recommendations. The President shall file a copy of such report with the Service and shall make its contents available to the public.

Sec. 207. (a) A board of inquiry shall be composed of a chairman and such other members as the President shall determine, and shall have power to sit and act in any place within the United States and to conduct such hearings either in public or in private, as it may deem necessary or proper, to ascertain the facts with respect to the causes and circumstances of the dispute.

(b) Members of a board of inquiry shall receive compensation at the rate of $50 for each day actually spent by them in the work of the board, together with necessary travel and subsistence expenses.

(c) For the purpose of any hearing or inquiry conducted by any board appointed under this title, the provisions of sections 9 and 10 (relating to the attendance of witnesses and the production of books, papers, and documents) of the Federal Trade Commission Act of September 16, 1914, as amended (U.S.C. 19, title 15, secs. 49 and 50, as amended), are hereby made applicable to the powers and duties of such board.

Sec. 208. (a) Upon receiving a report from a board of inquiry the President may direct the Attorney General to petition any district court of the United States having jurisdiction of the parties to enjoin such strike or lock-out or the continuing thereof, and if the court finds that such threatened or actual strike or lock-out—

(i) affects an entire industry or a substantial part thereof engaged in trade, commerce, transportation, transmission, or communication among the several States or with foreign nations, or engaged in the production of goods for commerce; and

(ii) if permitted to occur or to continue, will imperil the national health or safety, it shall have jurisdiction to enjoin any such strike or lock-out, or the continuing thereof, and to make such other orders as may be appropriate.

(b) In any case, the provisions of the Act of March 23, 1932, entitled "An Act to amend the Judicial Code and to define and limit the jurisdiction of courts sitting in equity, and for other purposes," shall not be applicable.

(c) The order or orders of the court shall be subject to review by the appropriate circuit court of appeals and by the Supreme Court upon writ of certiorari or certification as provided in sections 239 and 240 of the Judicial Code, as amended (U.S.C., title 29, secs. 346 and 347).

Sec. 209. (a) Whenever a district court has issued an order under section 208 enjoining acts or practices which imperil or threaten to imperil the national health or safety, it shall be the duty of the parties to the labor dispute giving rise to such order to make every effort to adjust and settle their differences, with the assistance of the Service created by this Act. Neither party shall be under any duty to accept, in whole or in part, any proposal of settlement made by the Service.

(b) Upon the issuance of such order, the President shall reconvene the board of inquiry which has previously reported with respect to the dispute. At the end of a sixty-day period (unless the dispute has been settled by that time), the board of inquiry shall report to the President the current position of the parties and the efforts which have been made for settlement, and shall include a statement by each party of its position and a statement of the employer's last offer of settlement. The President shall make such report available to the public. The National Labor Relations Board, within the succeeding fifteen days, shall take a secret ballot of the employees of each employer involved in the dispute on the question of whether they wish to accept the final offer of settlement made by their employer as stated by him and shall certify the results thereof to the Attorney General within five days thereafter.

Sec. 210. Upon the certification of the results of such ballot or upon a settlement being reached, whichever happens sooner, the Attorney General shall move the court to discharge the injunction, which motion shall then be granted and the injunction discharged. When such motion is granted, the President shall submit to the Congress a full and comprehensive report of the proceedings, including the findings of the board of inquiry and the ballot taken by the National Labor Relations Board, together with such recommendations as he may see fit to make for consideration and appropriate action.

Compilation of Collective Bargaining Agreements, etc.

Sec. 211. (a) For the guidance and information of interested representatives of employers, employees, and the general public, the Bureau of Labor Statistics of the Department of Labor shall maintain a file of copies of all available collective bargaining agreements and other available agreements and actions thereunder settling or adjusting labor disputes. Such file shall be open to inspection under appropriate conditions prescribed by the Secretary of Labor, except that no specific information submitted in confidence shall be disclosed.

(b) The Bureau of Labor Statistics in the Department of Labor is authorized to furnish upon request of the Service, or employers, employees, or their representatives, all available data and factual information which may aid in the settlement of any labor dispute, except that no specific information submitted in confidence shall be disclosed.

Exemption of Railway Labor Act

Sec. 212. The provisions of this title shall not be applicable with respect to any matter which is subject to the provisions of the Railway Labor Act, as amended from time to time.

TITLE III
Suits by and against Labor Organizations

Sec. 301. (a) Suits for violation of contracts between an employer and a labor organization representing employees in an industry affecting commerce as defined in this Act, or between any such labor organizations, may be brought in any district court of the United States having jurisdiction of the parties, without respect to the amount in controversy or without regard to the citizenship of the parties.

(b) Any labor organization which represents employees in an industry affecting commerce as defined in this Act and any employer whose activities affect commerce as defined in this Act shall be bound by the acts of its agents. Any such labor organization may sue or be sued as an entity and in behalf of the employees whom it represents in the courts of the United States. Any money judgment against a labor organization in a district court of the United States shall be enforceable only against the organization as an entity and against its assets, and shall not be enforceable against any individual member or his assets.

(c) For the purposes of actions and proceedings by or against labor organizations in the district courts of the United States, district courts shall be deemed to have jurisdiction of a labor organization (1) in the district in which such organization maintains its principal office, or (2) in any district in which its duly authorized officers or agents are engaged in representing or acting for employee members.

(d) The service of summons, subpena, or other legal process of any court of the United States upon an officer or agent of a labor organization, in his capacity as such, shall constitute service upon the labor organization.

(e) For the purposes of this section, in determining whether any person is acting as an "agent" of another person so as to make such other person responsible for his acts, the question of whether the specific acts performed were actually authorized or subsequently ratified shall not be controlling.

Restrictions on Payments to Employee Representatives

Sec. 302. (a) It shall be unlawful for any employer or association of employers or any person who acts as a labor relations expert, adviser, or consultant to an employer or who acts in the interest of an employer to pay, lend, or deliver, or agree to pay, lend, or deliver, any money or other thing of value—

(1) to any representative of any of his employees who are employed in an industry affecting commerce; or

(2) to any labor organization, or any officer or employee thereof, which represents, seeks to represent, or would admit to membership, any of the employees of such employer who are employed in an industry affecting commerce; or

(3) to any employee or group or committee of employees of such employer employed in an industry affecting commerce in excess of their normal compensation for the purpose of causing such employee or group or committee directly or indirectly to influence any other employees in the exercise of the right to organize and bargain collectively through representatives of their own choosing; or

(4) to any officer or employee of a labor organization engaged in an industry affecting commerce with intent to influence him in respect to any of his actions, decisions, or duties as a representative of employees or as such officer or employee of such labor organization.

(b)(1) It shall be unlawful for any person to request, demand, receive, or accept, or agree to receive or accept, any payment, loan, or delivery of any money or other thing of value prohibited by subsection (a).

(2) It shall be unlawful for any labor organization, or for any person acting as an officer, agent, representative, or employee of such labor organization, to demand or accept from the operator of any motor vehicle (as defined in part II of the Interstate Commerce Act) employed in the transportation of property in commerce, or the employer of any such operator, any money or other thing of value payable to such organization or to an officer, agent, representative or employee thereof as a fee or charge for the unloading, or in connection with the unloading, of the cargo of such vehicle: *Provided,* That nothing in this paragraph shall be construed to make unlawful any payment by an employer to any of his employees as compensation for their services as employees.

(c) The provisions of this section shall not be applicable (1) in respect to any money or other thing of value payable by an employer to any of his employees whose established duties include acting openly for such employer in matters of labor relations or personnel administration or to any representative of his employees, or to any officer or employee of a labor organization, who is also an employee or former employee of such employer, as compensation for, or by reason of, his services as an employee of such employer; (2) with respect to the payment or delivery of any money or other thing of value in satisfaction of a judgment of any court or a decision or award of an arbitrator or impartial chairman or in compromise, adjustment, settlement or release of any claim, complaint, grievance, or dispute in the absence of fraud or duress; (3) with respect to the sale or purchase of an article or commodity at the prevailing market price in the regular course of business; (4) with respect to money deducted from the wages of employees in payment of membership dues in a labor organization: *Provided,* That the employer has received from each employee, on whose account such deductions are made, a written assignment which shall not be irrevocable for a period of more than one year, or beyond the termination date of the applicable collective agreement, which-ever occurs sooner; (5) with respect to money or other thing of value paid to a trust fund established by such representative, for the sole and exclusive benefit of the employees of such employer, and their families and dependents (or of such employees, families, and dependents jointly with the employees of other employers making similar payments, and their families and dependents): *Provided,* That (A) such payments are held in trust for the purpose of paying, either from principal or income or both, for the benefit of employees, their families and dependents, for medical or hospital care, pensions on retirement or death of employees, compensation for injuries or illness resulting from occupational activity or insurance to provide any of the foregoing, or unemployment benefits or life insurance, disability and sickness insurance, or accident insurance; (B) the detailed basis on which such payments are to be made is specified in a written agreement with the employer, and employees and employers are equally represented in the administration of such fund, together with such neutral persons as the representatives of the employers and the representatives of employees may agree upon and in the event the employer may tives of employees may agree upon and in the event the employer and the employee groups deadlock on the administration of such fund and there are no neutral persons empowered to break such deadlock, such agreement provides that the two groups shall agree on an impartial umpire to decide such dispute, or in event of their failure to agree within a reasonable length of time, an impartial umpire to decide such dispute shall, on petition of either group, be appointed by the district court of the United States for the district where the trust fund has its principal office, and shall also contain provisions for an annual audit of the trust fund, a statement of the results of which shall be available for inspection by interested persons at the principal office of the trust fund and at such other places as may be designated in such written agreement: and (C) such payments as are intended to be used for the purpose of providing pensions or annuities for employees are made to a separate trust which provides that the funds held therein cannot be used for any purpose other than paying such pensions or annuities; (6) with respect to money or other thing of value paid by any employer to a trust fund established by such representative for the purpose of pooled vacation, holiday, severance or similar benefits, or defraying costs of apprenticeship or other training programs: *Provided,* That the requirements of clause (B) of the proviso to clause (5) of this subsection shall apply to such trust funds; (7) with respect to money or other thing of value paid by any employer to a pooled or individual trust fund established by such representative for the purpose of (A) scholarships for the benefit of employees, their families, and dependents for study at educational institutions, or (B) child care centers for pre-school and school age dependents of employees: *Provided,* That no labor organization or employer shall be required to bargain on the establishment of any such trust fund, and refusal to do so shall not constitute an unfair labor practice: *Provided further,* That the requirements of clause (B) of the proviso to clause (5) of this subsection shall apply to such trust fund; or (8) with respect to money or any other thing of value paid by any employer to a trust fund established by such representative for the purpose of defraying the costs of legal services for employees, their families, and dependents for counsel or plan of their choice: *Provided,* That the requirements of clause (B) of the proviso to clause (5) of this subsection shall apply to such trust funds: *Provided further,* That no such legal services shall be furnished: (A) to initiate any proceeding directed (i) against any such employer or its officers or agents except in workman's compensation cases, or (ii) against such labor organization, or its parent or subordinate bodies, or their officers or agents, or (iii) against any other employer or labor organization, or their officers or agents, in any matter arising under the National Labor Relations Act, as amended, or this Act; and (B) in any proceeding where a labor organization would be prohibited form defraying the costs of legal services by the provisions of the Labor-Management Reporting and Disclosure Act of 1959.*

(d) Any person who willfully violates any of the provisions of this section shall, upon conviction thereof, be guilty of a misdemeanor and be subject to a fine of not more than $10,000 or to imprisonment for not more than one year, or both.

(e) The district courts of the United States and the United States courts of the Territories and possessions shall have jurisdiction, for cause shown, and subject to the provisions of section 17 (relating to notice to opposite party) of the Act entitled "An Act to supplement existing laws against unlawful restraints and monopolies, and for other purposes," approved October 15, 1914, as amended (U.S.C., title 28, sec. 381), to restrain violations of this section, without regard to the provisions of sections 6 and 20 of such Act of October 15, 1914, as amended (U.S.C., title 15, sec. 17, and title 29, sec. 52), and the provisions of the Act entitled "An Act to amend the Judicial Code and to define and limit the jurisdiction of courts sitting in equity, and for other purposes," approved March 23, 1932 (U.S.C., title 29, secs. 101-115).

(f) This section shall not apply to any contract in force on the date of enactment of this Act, until the expiration of such contract, or until July 1, 1948, whichever first occurs.

(g) Compliance with the restrictions contained in subsection (c)(5)(B) upon contributions to trust funds, otherwise lawful, shall not be applicable to contributions to such trust funds established by collective agreement prior to January 1, 1946, nor shall subsection (c)(5)(A) be construed as prohibiting contributions to such trust funds if prior to January 1, 1947, such funds contained provisions for pooled vacation benefits.

Boycotts and Other Unlawful Combinations

Sec. 303. (a) It shall be unlawful, for the purpose of this section only, in an industry or activity affecting commerce, for any labor organization to engage in any activity or conduct defined as an unfair labor practice in section 8(b)(4) of the National Labor Relations Act, as amended.

(b) Whoever shall be injured in his business or property by reason of any violation of subsection (a) may sue therefor in any district court of the United States subject to the limitations and provisions of section 301 hereof without respect to the amount in controversy, or in any other court

---

* Section 302(c)(7) has been added by Public Law 91–86, 91st Congress, S. 2068, 83 Stat. 133, approved October 14, 1969. Section 302(c)(8) was added by Public Law 93–95, 93rd Congress, 87 Stat. 314, approved August 15, 1973.

having jurisdiction of the parties, and shall recover the damages by him sustained and the cost of the suit.

Restriction on Political Contributions

Sec. 304. Section 313 of the Federal Corrupt Practices Act, 1925 (U.S.C., 1940 edition, title 2, sec. 251; Supp. V, title 50, App. sec. 1509), as amended, is amended to read as follows:

Sec. 313. It is unlawful for any national bank, or any corporation organized by authority of any law of Congress, to make a contribution or expenditure in connection with any election to any political office, or in connection with any primary election or political convention or caucus held to select candidates for any political office, or for any corporation whatever, or any labor organization to make a contribution or expenditure in connection with any election at which Presidential and Vice Presidential electors or a Senator or Representative in, or a Delegate or Resident Commissioner to Congress are to be voted for, or in connection with any primary election or political convention or caucus held to select candidates for any of the foregoing offices, or for any candidate, political committee, or other person to accept or receive any contribution prohibited by this section. Every corporation or labor organization which makes any contribution or expenditure in violation of this section shall be fined not more than $5,000; and every officer or director of any corporation, or officer of any labor organization, who consents to any contribution or expenditure by the corporation or labor organization, as the case may be, in violation of this section shall be fined mot more than $1,000 or imprisoned for not more than one year, or both. For the purposes of this section 'labor organization' means any organization of any kind, or any agency or employee representation committee or plan, in which employees participate and which exists for the purpose, in whole or in part, of dealing with employers concerning grievances, labor disputes, wages, rates of pay, hours of employment, or conditions of work.

TITLE IV
Creation of Joint Committee to Study and Report on Basic Problems Affecting Friendly Labor Relations and Productivity

Sec. 401. There is hereby established a joint congressional committee to be known as the Joint Committee on Labor-Management Relations. . . .

TITLE V
Definitions

Sec. 501. When used in this Act—

(1) The term "industry affecting commerce" means any industry or activity in commerce or in which a labor dispute would burden or obstruct commerce or tend to burden or obstruct commerce or the free flow of commerce.

(2) The term "strike" includes any strike or other concerted stoppage of work by employees (including a stoppage by reason of the expiration

of a collective-bargaining agreement) and any concerted slow-down or other concerted interruption of operations by employees.

(3) The terms "commerce," "labor disputes," "employer," "employee," "labor organization," "representative," "person," and "supervisor" shall have the same meaning as when used in the National Labor Relations Act as amended by this Act.

Saving Provision

Sec. 502. Nothing in this Act shall be construed to require an individual employee to render labor or service without his consent, nor shall anything in this Act be construed to make the quitting of his labor by an individual employee an illegal act; nor shall any court issue any process to compel the performance by an individual employee of such labor or service, without his consent; nor shall the quitting of labor by an employee or employees in good faith because of abnormally dangerous conditions for work at the place of employment of such employee or employees be deemed a strike under this Act.

Separability

Sec. 503. If any provision of this Act, or the application of such provision to any person or circumstance, shall be held invalid, the remainder of this Act, or the application of such provision to persons or circumstances other than those as to which it is held invalid, shall not be affected thereby.

APPENDIX B

[PUBLIC LAW 86-257—86TH CONGRESS,S.
1555 SEPTEMBER 14, 1959]

AN ACT to provide for the reporting and disclosure of certain financial transactions and administrative practices of labor organizations and employers, to prevent abuses in the administration of trusteeships by labor organizations, to provide standards with respect to the election of officers of labor organizations, and for other purposes.

Be it enacted by the Senate and House of Representatives of the United States of America in Congress assembled,

SHORT TITLE

Section 1. This Act may be cited as the "Labor-Management Reporting and Disclosure Act of 1959."

Declaration of Findings, Purposes, and Policy

Sec. 2. (a) The Congress finds that, in the public interest, it continues to be the responsibility of the Federal Government to protect employees' rights to organize, choose their own representatives, bargain collectively, and otherwise engage in concerted activities for their mutual aid or protection; that the relations between employers and labor organizations and the millions of workers they represent have a substantial impact on the commerce of the Nation; and that in order to accomplish the objective of a free flow of commerce it is essential that labor organizations, employers, and their officials adhere to the highest standards of responsibility and ethical conduct in administering the affairs of their organizations, particularly as they affect labor-management relations.

(b) The Congress further finds, from recent investigations in the labor and management fields, that there have been a number of instances of breach of trust, corruption, disregard of the rights of individual employees, and other failures to observe high standards of responsibility and ethical conduct which require further and supplementary legislation that will afford necessary protection of the rights and interests of employees and the public generally as they relate to the activities of labor organizations, employers, labor relations consultants, and their officers and representatives.

(c) The Congress, therefore, further finds and declares that the enactment of this Act is necessary to eliminate or prevent improper practices on the part of labor organizations, employers, labor relations consultants, and their officers and representatives which distort and defeat the policies of the Labor Management Relations Act, 1947, as amended, and the Railway Labor Act, as amended, and have the tendency or necessary effect of burdening or obstructing commerce by (1) impairing the efficiency, safety, or operation of the instrumentalities of commerce; (2) occurring in the current of commerce; (3) materially affecting, restraining, or controlling the flow of raw materials or manufactured or processed goods into or from the channels of commerce, or the prices of such materials or goods in commerce; or (4) causing diminution of employment and wages in such volume as substantially to impair or disrupt the market for goods flowing into or from the channels of commerce.

Definitions

Sec. 3. For the purposes of titles, I, II, III, IV, V (except section 505), and VI of this Act—

(a) "Commerce" means trade, traffic, commerce, transportation, transmission, or communication among the serveral States or between any State and any place outside thereof.

(b) "State" includes any State of the United States, the District of Columbia, Puerto Rico, the Virgin Islands, American Samoa, Guam, Wake Island, the Canal Zone, and Outer Continental Shelf lands defined in the Outer Continental Shelf Lands Act (43 U.S.C. 1331-1343).

(c) "Industry affecting commerce" means any activity, business, or industry in commerce or in which a labor dispute would hinder or obstruct commerce or the free flow of commerce and includes any activity or industry "affecting commerce" within the meaning of the Labor Management Relations Act, 1947, as amended, or the Railway Labor Act, as amended.

(d) "Person" includes one or more individuals, labor organizations, partnerships, associations, corporations, legal representatives, mutual companies, joint-stock companies, trusts unincorporated organizations, trustees, trustees in bankruptcy, or receivers.

(e) "Employer" means any employer or any group or association of employers engaged in an industry affecting commerce (1) which is, with respect to employees engaged in an industry affecting commerce, an employer within the meaning of any law of the United States relating to the employment of any employees or (2) which may deal with any labor organization concerning grievances, labor disputes, wages, rates of pay, hours of employment, or conditions of work, and includes any person acting directly or indirectly as an employer or as an agent of an employer in relation to an employee but does not include the United States or any corporation wholly owned by the Government of the United States or any State or political subdivision thereof.

(f) "Employee" means any individual employed by an employer, and includes any individual whose work has ceased as a consequence of, or in connection with, any current labor dispute or because of any unfair labor practice or because of exclusion or expulsion from a labor organization in any manner or for any reason inconsistent with the requirements of this Act.

(g) "Labor dispute" includes any controversy concerning terms, tenure, or conditions of employment, or concerning the association or representation of persons in negotiating, fixing, maintaining, changing, or seeking to arrange terms or conditions of employment, regardless of whether the disputants stand in the proximate relation of employer and employee.

(h) "Trusteeship" means any receivership, trusteeship, or other method of supervision or control whereby a labor organization suspends the autonomy otherwise available to a subordinate body under its constitution or bylaws.

(i) "Labor organization" means a labor organization engaged in an industry affecting commerce and includes any organization of any kind, any agency, or employee representation committee, group, association, or plan so engaged in which employees participate and which exists for the purpose, in whole or in part, of dealing with employers concerning grievances, labor disputes, wages, rates of pay, hours, or other terms or conditions of employment, and any conference, general committee, joint or system board, or joint council so engaged which is subordinate to a national or inter-national labor organization, other than a State or local central body.

(j) A labor organization shall be deemed to be engaged in an industry affecting commerce if it—

(1) is the certified representative of employees under the provisions of the National Labor Relations Act, as amended, or the Railway Labor Act, as amended; or

(2) although not certified, is a national or international labor organization or a local labor organization recognized or acting as the representative of employees of an employer or employers engaged in an industry affecting commerce; or

(3) has chartered a local labor organization or subsidiary body which is representing or actively seeking to represent employees of employers within the meaning of paragraph (1) or (2); or

(4) has been chartered by a labor organization representing or actively seeking to represent employees within the meaning of paragraph (1) or (2) as the local or subordinate body through which such employees may enjoy membership or become affiliated with such labor organization; or

(5) is a conference, general committee, joint or system board, or joint council, subordinate to a national or international labor organization, which includes a labor organization engaged in an industry affecting commerce within the meaning of any of the preceding paragraphs of this subsection, other than a State or local central body.

(k) "Secret ballot" means the expression by ballot, voting machine, or otherwise, but in no event by proxy, of a choice with respect to any election or vote taken upon any matter, which is cast in such a manner that the person expressing such choice cannot be identified with the choice expressed.

(1) "Trust in which a labor organization is interested" means a trust or other fund or organization (1) which was created or established by a labor organization, or one or more of the trustees or one or more members of the governing body of which is selected or appointed by a labor organization, and (2) a primary purpose of which is to provide benefits for the members of such labor organization or their beneficiaries.

(m) "Labor relations consultant" means any person who, for compensation, advises or represents an employer, employer organization, or labor organization concerning employee organizing, concerted activities, or collective bargaining activities.

(n) "Officer" means any constitutional officer, any person authorized to perform the functions of president, vice president, secretary, treasurer, or other executive functions of a labor organization, and any member of its executive board or similar governing body.

(o) "Member" or "member in good standing," when used in reference to a labor organization, includes any person who has fulfilled the requirements for membership in such organization, and who neither has voluntarily withdrawn from membership nor has been expelled or suspended from membership after appropriate proceedings consistent with lawful provisions of the constitution and bylaws of such organization.

(p) "Secretary" means the Secretary of Labor.

(q) "Officer, agent, shop steward, or other representatives," when used with respect to a labor organization, includes elected officials and key administrative personnel, whether elected or appointed (such as business agents, heads of departments or major units, and organizers who exercise substantial independent authority), but does not include salaried nonsupervisory professional staff, stenographic, and service personnel.

(r) "District court of the United States" means a United States district court and a United States court of any place subject to the jurisdiction of the United States.

TITLE I—BILL OF RIGHTS OF MEMBERS OF LABOR ORGANIZATIONS

Bill of Rights

Sec. 101. (a) (1) EQUAL RIGHTS.—Every member of a labor organization shall have equal rights and privileges within such organization to nominate candidates, to vote in elections or referendums of the labor organization, to attend membership meetings, and to participate in the deliberations and voting upon the business of such meetings, subject to reasonable rules and regulations in such organization's constitution and bylaws.

(2) FREEDOM OF SPEECH AND ASSEMBLY.—Every member of any labor organization shall have the right to meet and assembly freely with other members; and to express any views, arguments, or opinions; and to express at meetings of the labor organization has views, upon candidates in an election of the labor organization or upon any business properly before the meeting, subject to the organization's established and reasonable rules pertaining to the conduct of meetings: *Provided,* That nothing herein shall be construed to impair the right of a labor organization to adopt and enforce reasonable rules as to the responsibility of every member toward the organization as an institution and to his refraining from conduct that would interfere with its performance of its legal or contractual obligations.

(3) DUES, INITIATION FEES, AND ASSESSMENTS.—Except in the case of a federation of national or international labor organizations, the rates of dues and initiation fees payable by members of any labor organization in effect on the date of enactment of this Act shall not be increased, and no general or special assessment shall be levied upon such members, except—

(A) in the case of a local labor organization, (i) by majority vote by secret ballot of the members in good standing voting at a general or special membership meeting, after reasonable notice of the intention to vote upon such question, or (ii) by majority vote of the members in good standing voting in a membership referendum conducted by secret ballot; or

(B) in the case of a labor organization, other than a local labor organization or a federation of national or international labor organizations, (i) by majority vote of the delegates voting at a regular convention, or at a special convention of such labor organization held upon not less than thirty days' written notice to the principal office of each local or constituent labor organization entitled to such notice, or (ii) by majority vote of the members in good standing of such labor organization voting in a membership referendum conducted by secret ballot, or (iii) by majority vote of the members of the executive board or similar governing body of such labor organization, pursuant to express authority contained in the constitution and bylaws of such labor organization: *Provided,* That such action on the part of the executive board or similar governing body shall be effective only until the next regular convention of such labor organization.

(4) PROTECTION OF THE RIGHT TO SUE.—No labor organization shall limit the right of any member thereof to institute an action in any court, or in a proceeding before any administrative agency, irrespective of whether or not the labor organization or its officers are named as defendants or respondents in such action or proceeding, or the right of any member of a labor organization to appear as a witness in any judicial, administrative, or legislative proceeding, or to petition any legislature or to communicate with any legislator: *Provided,* That any such member may be required to exhaust reasonable hearing procedures (but not to exceed a four-month lapse of time) within such organization, before instituting legal or administrative proceedings against such organizations or any officer thereof: *And provided further,* That no interested employer or employer association shall directly or indirectly finance, encourage, or participate in, except as a party, any such action, proceeding, appearance, or petition.

(5) SAFEGUARDS AGAINST IMPROPER DISCIPLINARY ACTION.—No member of any labor organization may be fined, suspended, expelled, or otherwise disciplined except for nonpayment of dues by such organization or by any officer thereof unless such member has been (A) served with written specific charges; (B) given a reasonable time to prepare his defense; (C) afforded a full and fair hearing.

(b) Any provision of the constitution and bylaws of any labor organization which is inconsistent with the provisions of this section shall be of no force or effect.

Civil Enforcement

Sec. 102. Any person whose rights secured by the provisions of this title have been infringed by any violation of this title may bring a civil action in a district court of the United States for such relief (including injunctions) as may be appropriate. Any such action against a labor organization shall be brought in the district court of the United States for the district where the alleged violation occurred, or where the principal office of such labor organization is located.

Retention of Existing Rights

Sec. 103. Nothing contained in this title shall limit the rights and remedies of any member of a labor organization under any State or Federal law or before any court or other tribunal, or under the constitution and bylaws of any labor organization.

Right to Copies of Collective Bargaining Agreements

Sec. 104. It shall be the duty of the secretary or corresponding principal officer of each labor organization, in the case of a local labor organization, to forward a copy of each collective bargaining agreement made by such labor organization with an employer to any employee who requests such a copy and whose rights as such employee are directly affected by such agreement, and in the case of a labor organization other than a local labor organization, to forward a copy of any such agreement to each constituent unit which has members directly affected by such agreement; and such officer shall maintain at the principal office of the labor organization of which he is an officer copies of any such agreement made or received by such labor organization, which copies shall be available for inspection by any member or by any employee whose rights are affected by such agreement. The provisions of section 210 shall be applicable in the enforcement of this section.

Information As To Act

Sec. 105. Every labor organization shall inform its members concerning the provisions of this Act.

TITLE II—REPORTING BY LABOR ORGANIZATIONS, OFFICERS AND EMPLOYEES OF LABOR ORGANIZATIONS, AND EMPLOYERS

Report of Labor Organizations

Sec. 201. (a) Every labor organization shall adopt a constitution and bylaws and shall file a copy thereof with the Secretary, together with a report, signed by its president and secretary or corresponding principal officers, containing the following information—

> (1) the name of the labor organization, its mailing address, and any other address at which it maintains its principal office or at which it keeps the records referred to in this title;
> (2) the name and title of each of its officers;
> (3) the initiation fee or fees required from a new or transferred member and fees for work permits required by the reporting labor organization;
> (4) the regular dues or fees or other periodic payments required to remain a member of the reporting labor organization; and

(5) detailed statements, or references to specific provisions of documents filed under this subsection which contain such statements, showing the provision made and procedures followed with respect to each of the following: (A) qualifications for or restrictions on membership, (B) levying of assessments, (C) participation in insurance or other benefit plans, (D) authorization for disbursement of funds of the labor organization, (E) audit of financial transactions of the labor organization, (F) the calling of regular and special meetings, (G) the selection of officers and stewards and of any representatives to other bodies composed of labor organizations' representatives, with a specific statement of the manner in which each officer was elected, appointed, or otherwise selected, (H) discipline or removal of officers or agents for breaches of their trust, (I) imposition of fines, suspensions, and expulsions of members, including the grounds for such action and any provision made for notice, hearing, judgment on the evidence, and appeal procedures, (J) authorization for bargaining demands, (K) ratification of contract terms, (L) authorization for strikes, and (M) issuance of work permits. Any change in the information required by this subsection shall be reported to the Secretary at the time the reporting labor organization files with the Secretary the annual financial report required by subsection (b).

(b) Every labor organization shall file annually with the Secretary a financial report signed by its president and treasurer or corresponding principal officers containing the following information in such detail as may be necessary accurately to disclose its financial condition and operations for its preceding fiscal year—

(1) assets and liabilities at the beginning and end of the fiscal year;

(2) receipts of any kind and the sources thereof;

(3) salary, allowances, and other direct or indirect disbursements (including reimbursed expenses) to each officer and also to each employee who, during such fiscal year, received more than $10,000 in the aggregate from such labor organization and any other labor organization affiliated with it or with which it is affiliated, or which is affiliated with the same national or international labor organization;

(4) direct and indirect loans made to any officer, employee, or member, which aggregated more than $250 during the fiscal year, together with a statement of the purpose, security, if any, and arrangements for repayment;

(5) direct or indirect loans to any business enterprise, together with a statement of the purpose, security, if any, and arrangements for repayment; and

(6) other disbursements made by it including the purposes thereof;

all in such categories as the Secretary may prescribe.

(c) Every labor organization required to submit a report under this title shall make available the information required to be contained in such report to all of its members, and every such labor organization and its officers shall be under a duty enforceable at the suit of any member of such organization in any State court of competent jurisdiction or in the district court of the United States for the district in which such labor organization maintains its principal office, to permit such member for just cause to examine any books, records, and accounts necessary to verify such report. The court in such action may, in its discretion, in addition to any judgment awarded to the plaintiff or plaintiffs, allow a reasonable attorney's fee to be paid by the defendant, and cost of the action.

Report of Officers and Employees of Labor Organizations

Sec. 202. (a) Every officer of a labor organization and every employee of a labor organization (other than an employee performing exclusively clerical or custodial services) shall file with the Secretary a signed report listing and describing for his preceding fiscal year—

(1) any stock, bond, security, or other interest, legal or equitable, which he or his spouse or minor child directly or indirectly held in, and any income or any other benefit with monetary value (including reimbursed expenses) which he or his spouse or minor child derived directly or indirectly from, an employer whose employees such labor organization represents or is actively seeking to represent, except payments and other benefits received as a bona fide employee of such employer;

(2) any transaction in which he or his spouse or minor child engaged, directly or indirectly, involving any stock, bond, security, or loan to or from, or other legal or equitable interest in the business of an employer whose employees such labor organization represents or is actively seeking to represent;

(3) any stock, bond, security, or other interest, legal or equitable, which he or his spouse or minor child directly or indirectly held in, and any income or any other benefit with monetary value (including reimbursed expenses) which he or his spouse or minor child directly or indirectly derived from, any business a substantial part of which consists of buying from, selling or leasing to, or otherwise dealing with, the business of an employer whose employees such labor organization represents or is actively seeking to represent;

(4) any stock, bond, security, or other interest, legal or equitable, which he or his spouse or minor child directly or indirectly held in, and any income or any other benefit with monetary value (including reimbursed expenses) which he or his spouse or minor child directly or indirectly derived from, a business any part of which consists of buying from, or selling or leasing directly or indirectly to, or otherwise dealing with such labor organization;

(5) any direct or indirect business transaction or arrangement between him or his spouse or minor child and any employer whose employees his organization represents or is actively seeking to represent, except work performed and payments and benefits received as a bona fide employee of such employer and except purchases and sales of goods or services in the regular course of business at prices generally available to any employee of such employer; and

(6) any payment of money or other thing of value (including reimbursed expenses) which he or his spouse or minor child received directly or indirectly from any employer or any persons who acts as a labor relations consultant to an employer, except payments of the kinds referred to in section 302(c) of the Labor Management Relations Act, 1947, as amended.

(b) The provisions of paragraphs (1), (2), (3), (4), and (5) of subsection (a) shall not be construed to require any such officer or employee to report his bona fide investments in securities traded on a securities exchange under the Securities Exchange Act of 1934, in shares in an investment company registered under the Investment Company Act of 1940, or in securities of a public utility holding company registered under the Public Utility Holding Company Act of 1935, or to report any income derived therefrom.

(c) Nothing contained in this section shall be construed to require any officer or employee of a labor organization to file a report under subsection (a) unless he or his spouse or minor child holds or has held an interest, has received income or any other benefit with monetary value or a loan, or has engaged in a transaction described therein.

Report of Employers

Sec. 203. (a) Every employer who in any fiscal years made—

(1) any payment or loan, direct or indirect of money or other thing of value (including reimbursed expenses), or any promise or agreement therefor, to any labor organization or officer, agent, shop steward, or other representative of a labor organization, or employee of any labor organization, except (A) payments or loans made by any national or State bank, credit union, insurance company, savings and loan association or other credit institution and (B) payments of the kind referred to in section 302(c) of the Labor Management Relations Act, 1947, as amended;

(2) any payment (including reimbursed expenses) to any of his employees, or any group or committee of such employees, for the purpose of causing such employee or group or committee of employees to persuade other employees to exercise or not to exercise, or as the manner of exercising, the right to organize and bargain collectively through representatives of their own choosing unless such payments were contemporaneously or previously disclosed to such other employees;

(3) any expenditure, during the fiscal year, where an object thereof, directly or indirectly, is to interfere with, restrain, or coerce employees in the exercise of the right to organize and bargain collectively through representatives of their own choosing, or is to obtain information concerning the activities of employees or a labor organization in connection with a labor dispute involving such employer, except for use solely in conjunction with an administrative or arbitral proceeding or a criminal or civil judicial proceeding;

(4) any agreement or arrangement with a labor relations consultant or other independent contractor or organization pursuant to which such person undertakes activities where an object thereof, directly or indirectly, is to persuade employees to exercise or not to exercise, or persuade employees as to the manner of exercising, the right to organize and bargain collectively through representatives of their own choosing, or undertakes to supply such employer with information concerning the activities of employees or a labor organization in connection with a labor dispute involving such employer, except information for use solely in conjunction with an administrative or arbitral proceeding or a criminal or civil judicial proceeding; or

(5) any payment (including reimbursed expenses) pursuant to an agreement or arrangement described in subdivision (4);

shall file with the Secretary a report, in a form prescribed by him, signed by its president and treasurer or corresponding principal officers showing in detail the date and amount of each such payment, loan, promise, agreement, or arrangement and the name, address, and position, if any, in any firm or labor organization of the person to whom it was made and a full explanation of the circumstances of all such payments, including the terms of any agreement or understanding pursuant to which they were made.

(b) Every person who pursuant to any agreement or arrangement with an employer undertakes activities where an object thereof is, directly or indirectly—

(1) to persuade employees to exercise or not to exercise, or persuade employees as to the manner of exercising, the right to organize and bargain collectively through representatives of their own choosing; or

(2) to supply an employer with information concerning the activities of employees or a labor organization in connection with a labor dispute involving such employer, except information for use solely in conjunction with an administrative or arbitral proceeding or a criminal or civil judicial proceeding;

shall file within thirty days after entering into such agreement or arrangement a report with the Secretary, signed by its president and treasurer or corresponding principal officers, containing the name under which such person is engaged in doing business and the address of its principal office, and a detailed statement of the terms and conditions of such agreement or arrangement. Every such person shall file annually, with respect to each fiscal year during which payments were made as a result of such an agreement or arrangement, a report with the Secretary, signed by its president and treasurer or corresponding principal officers, containing a statement (A) of its receipts of any kind from employers on account of labor relations advice or services, designating the sources thereof, and (B) of its disbursements of any kind, in connection with such services and the purposes thereof. In each such case such information shall be set forth in such categories as the Secretary may prescribe.

(c) Nothing in this section shall be construed to require any employer or other person to file a report covering the services of such person by reason of his giving or agreeing to give advice to such employer or representing or agreeing to represent such employer before any court, administrative agency, or tribunal of arbitration or engaging or agreeing to engage in collective bargaining on behalf of such employer with respect to wages, hours, or other terms or conditions of employment or the negotiation of an agreement or any question arising thereunder.

(d) Nothing contained in this section shall be construed to require an employer to file a report under subsection (a) unless he has made an expenditure, payment, loan, agreement, or arrangement of the kind described therein. Nothing contained in this section shall be construed to require any other person to file a report under subsection (b) unless he was a party to an agreement or arrangement of the kind described therein.

(e) Nothing contained in this section shall be construed to require any regular officer, supervisor, or employee of an employer to file a report in connection with services rendered to such employer nor shall any employer be required to file a report covering expenditures made to any regular officer, supervisor, or employee of an employer as compensation for service as a regular officer, supervisor, or employee of such employer.

(f) Nothing contained in this section shall be construed as an amendment to, or modification of the rights protected by, section 8(c) of the National Labor Relations Act, as amended.

(g) The term "interfere with, restrain, or coerce" as used in this section means interference, restraint, and coercion which, if done with respect to the exercise of rights guaranteed in section 7 of the National Labor Relations Act, as amended, would, under section 8(a) of such Act, constitute an unfair labor practice.

Attorney-Client Communications Exempted

Sec. 204. Nothing contained in this Act shall be construed to require an attorney who is a member in good standing of the bar of any State, to include in any report required to be filed pursuant to the provisions of this Act any information which was lawfully communicated to such attorney by any of his clients in the course of a legitimate attorney-client relationship.

Reports Made Public Information

Sec. 205. (a) The contents of the reports and documents filed with the Secretary pursuant to sections 201, 202, and 203 shall be public information, and the Secretary may publish any information and data which he obtains pursuant to the provisions of this title. The Secretary may use the information and data for statistical and research purposes, and compile and publish such studies, analyses, reports, and surveys based thereon as he may deem appropriate.

(b) The Secretary shall by regulation make reasonable provision for the inspection and examination, on the request of any person, of the information and data contained in any report or other document filed with him pursuant to section 201, 202, or 203.

(c) The Secretary shall by regulation provide for the furnishing by the Department of Labor of copies of reports or other documents filed with the Secretary pursuant to this title, upon payment of a charge based upon the cost of the service. The Secretary shall make available without payment of a charge, or require any person to furnish, to such State agency as is designated by law or by the Governor of the State in which such person has his principal place of business or headquarters, upon request of the Governor or such State, copies of any reports and documents filed by such person with the Secretary pursuant to section 201, 202, or 203, or of information and data contained therein. No person shall be required by reason of any law of any State to furnish to any officer or agency of such State any information included in a report filed by such person with the Secretary pursuant to the provisions of this title, if a copy of such report, or of the portion thereof containing such information, is furnished to such officer or agency. All moneys received in payment of such charges fixed by the Secretary pursuant to this subsection shall be deposited in the general fund of the Treasury.

Retention of Records

Sec. 206. Every person required to file any report under this title shall maintain records on the matters required to be reported which will provide in sufficient detail the necessary basic information and data from which the documents filed with the Secretary may be verified, explained or clarified, and checked for accuracy and completeness, and shall include vouchers, worksheets, receipts, and applicable resolutions, and shall keep such records available for examination for a period of not less than five years after the filing of the documents based on the information which they contain.

Effective Date

Sec. 207. (a) Each labor organization shall file the initial report required under section 201(a) within ninety days after the date on which it first becomes subject to this Act.

(b) Each person required to file a report under section 201(b), 202, 203(a), or the second sentence of 203(b) shall file such report within ninety days after the end of each of its fiscal years; except that where such person is subject to section 201(b), 202, 203(a), or the second sentence of 203(b), as the case may be, for only a portion of such a fiscal year (because the date of enactment of this Act occurs during such person's fiscal year or such person becomes subject to this Act during its fiscal year) such person may consider that portion as the entire fiscal year in making such report.

Rules and Regulations

Sec. 208. The Secretary shall have authority to issue, amend, and rescind rules and regulations prescribing the form and publication of reports required to be filed under this title and such other reasonable rules and regulations (including rules prescribing reports concerning trusts in which a labor organization is interested) as he may find necessary to prevent the circumvention or evasion of such reporting requirements. In exercising his power under this section the Secretary shall prescribe by general rule simplified reports for labor organizations or employers for whom he finds that by virtue of their size a detailed report would be unduly burdensome, but the Secretary may revoke such provision for simplified forms of any labor organization or employer if he determines, after such investigation as he deems proper and due notice and opportunity for a hearing, that the purposes of this section would be served thereby.

Criminal Provisions

Sec. 209. (a) Any person who willfully violates this title shall be fined not more than $10,000 or imprisoned for not more than one year, or both.

(b) Any person who makes a false statement or representation of a material fact, knowing it to be false, or who knowingly fails to disclose a material fact, in any document, report, or other information required under the provisions of this title shall be fined not more than $10,000 or imprisoned for not more than one year, or both.

(c) Any person who willfully makes a false entry in or willfully conceals, withholds, or destroys any books, records, reports, or statements required to be kept by any provision of this shall be fined not more than $10,000 or imprisoned for not more than one year, or both.

(d) Each individual required to sign reports under sections 201 and 203 shall be personally responsible for the filing of such reports and for any statement contained therein which he knows to be false.

Civil Enforcement

Sec. 210. Whenever it shall appear that any person has violated or is about to violate any of the provisions of this title, the Secretary may bring a civil action for such relief (including injunctions) as may be appropriate. Any such action may be brought in the district court of the United States where the violation occurred or, at the option of the parties, in the United States District Court for the District of Columbia.

TITLE III—TRUSTEESHIPS

Reports

Sec. 301. (a) Every labor organization which has or assumes trusteeship over any subordinate labor organization shall file with the Secretary within thirty days after the date of the enactment of this Act or the imposition of any such trusteeship, and semiannually thereafter, a report, signed by its president and treasurer or corresponding principal officers, as well as the trustees of such subordinate labor organizations, containing the following information: (1) the name and address of the subordinate organization; (2) the date of establishing the trusteeship; (3) a detailed statement of the reason or reasons for establishing or continuing the trusteeship; and (4) the nature and extent of participation by the membership of the subordinate organization in the selection of delegates to represent such organization in regular or special conventions or other policy-determining bodies and in the election of officers of the labor organization which has assumed trusteeship over such subordinate organization. The initial report shall also include a full and complete account of the financial condition of such subordinate organization as of the time trusteeship was assumed over it. During the continuance of a trusteeship the labor organization which has assumed trusteeship over a subordinate labor organization shall file on behalf of the subordinate labor organization the annual financial report required by section 201(b) signed by the president and treasurer or corresponding principal officers of the labor organization which has assumed such trusteeship and the trustees of the subordinate labor organization.

(b) The provisions of section 201(c), 205, 206, 208, and 210 shall be applicable to reports under this title.

(c) Any person who willfully violates this section shall be fined not more than $10,000 or imprisoned for not more than one year, or both.

(d) Any person who makes a false statement or representation of a material fact, knowing it to be false, or who knowingly fails to disclose a material fact, in any report required under the provisions of this section or willfully makes any false entry in or willfully withholds, conceals, or destroys any documents, books, records, reports, or statements upon which such report is based, shall be fined not more than $10,000 or imprisoned for not more than one year, or both.

(e) Each individual required to sign a report under this section shall be personally responsible for the filing of such report and for any statement contained therein which he knows to be false.

Purposes for Which a Trusteeship May Be Established

Sec. 302. Trusteeships shall be established and administered by a labor organization over a subordinate body only in accordance with the constitution and bylaws of the organization which has assumed trusteeship over the subordinate body and for the purpose of correcting corruption of financial malpractice, assuring the performance of collective bargaining agreements or other duties of a bargaining representative, restoring democratic procedures, or otherwise carrying out the legitimate objects of such labor organization.

Unlawful Acts Relating to Labor Organization Under Trusteeship

Sec. 303. (a) During any period when a subordinate body of a labor organization is in trusteeship, it shall be unlawful (1) to count the vote of delegates from such body in any convention or election of officers of the labor organization unless the delegates have been chosen by secret ballot in an election in which all the members in good standing of such subordinate body were eligible to participate, or (2) to transfer to such organization any current receipts or other funds of the subordinate body except the normal per capita tax and assessments payable by subordinate bodies not in trusteeship: *Provided,* That nothing herein contained shall prevent the distribution of the assets of a labor organization in accordance with its constitution and bylaws upon the bona fide dissolution thereof.

(b) Any person who willfully violates this section shall be fined not more than $10,000 or imprisoned for not more than one year, or both.

Enforcement

Sec. 304. (a) Upon the written complaint of any member or subordinate body of a labor organization alleging that such organization has violated the provisions of this title (except section 301) the Secretary shall investigate the complaint and if the Secretary finds probable cause to believe that such violation has occurred and has not been remedied he shall, without disclosing the identity of the complainant, bring a civil action in any district court of the United States having jurisdiction of the labor organization for such relief (including injunctions) as may be appropriate. Any member or subordinate body of a labor organization affected by any violation of this title (except section 301) may bring a civil action in any district court of the United States having jurisdiction of the labor organization for such relief (including injunctions) as may be appropriate.

(b) For the purpose of actions under this section, district courts of the United States shall be deemed to have jurisdiction of a labor organization (1) in the district in which the principal office of such labor organization is located, or (2) in any district in which its duly authorized officers or agents are engaged in conducting the affairs of the trusteeship.

(c) In any proceeding pursuant to this section a trusteeship established by a labor organization in conformity with the procedural requirements of its constitution and bylaws and authorized or ratified after a fair hearing either before the executive board or before such other body as may be provided in accordance with its constitution or bylaws shall be presumed valid for a period of eighteen months from the date of its establishment and shall not be subject to attack during such period except upon clear and convincing proof that the trusteeship was not established or maintained in good faith for a purpose allowable under section 302. After the expiration of eighteen months the trusteeship shall be presumed invalid in any such proceeding and its discontinuance shall be decreed unless the labor organization shall show by clear and convincing proof that the continuation of the trusteeship is necessary for a purpose allowable under section 302. In the latter event the court may dismiss the complaint or retain jurisdiction of the cause on such conditions and for such period as it deems appropriate.

Report to Congress

Sec. 305. The Secretary shall submit to the Congress at the expiration of three years from the date of enactment of this Act a report upon the operation of this title.

Complaint by Secretary

Sec. 306. The rights and remedies provided by this title shall be in addition to any and all other rights and remedies at law or in equity: *Provided,* That upon the filing of a complaint by the Secretary the jurisdiction of the district court over such trusteeship shall be exclusive and the final judgment shall be res judicata.

TITLE IV—ELECTIONS

Terms of Office; Election Procedures

Sec. 401. (a) Every national or international labor organization, except a federation of national or international labor organizations, shall elect its officers not less often than once every five years either by secret ballot among the members in good standing or at a convention of delegates chosen by secret ballot.

(b) Every local labor organization shall elect its officers not less often than once every three years by secret ballot among the members in good standing.

(c) Every national or international labor organization, except a federation of national or international labor organizations, and every local labor organization, and its officers, shall be under a duty, enforceable at the suit of any bona fide candidate for office in such labor organization in the district court of the United States in which such labor organization maintains its principal office, to comply with all reasonable requests of any candidate to distribute by mail or otherwise at the candidate's expense campaign literature in aid of such person's candidacy to all members in good standing of such labor organization and to refrain from discrimination in favor of or against any candidate with respect to the use of lists of members, and whenever such labor organizations or its officers authorize the distribution by mail or otherwise to members of campaign literature on behalf of any candidate or of the labor organization itself with reference to such election, similar distribution at the request of any other bona fide candidate shall be made by such labor organization and its officers, with equal treatment as to the expense of such distribution. Every bona fide candidate shall have the right, once within 30 days prior to an election of a labor organization in which he is a candidate, to inspect a list containing the names and last known addresses of all members of the labor organization who are subject to a collective bargaining agreement requiring membership therein as a condition of employment, which list shall be maintained and kept at the principal office of such labor organization by a designated official thereof. Adequate safeguards to insure a fair election shall be provided, including the right of any candidate to have an observer at the polls and at the counting of the ballots.

(d) Officers of intermediate bodies, such as general committees, system boards, joint boards, or joint councils, shall be elected not less often than once every four years by secret ballot among the members in good standing or by labor organization officers representative of such members who have been elected by secret ballot.

(e) In any election required by this section which is to be held by secret ballot a reasonable opportunity shall be given for the nomination of candidates and every member in good standing shall be eligible to be a candidate and to hold office (subject to section 504 and to reasonable qualifications uniformly imposed) and shall have the right to vote for or otherwise support the candidate or candidates of his choice, without being subject to penalty, discipline, or improper interference or reprisal of any kind by such organization or any member thereof. Not less than fifteen days prior to the election notice thereof shall be mailed to each member at his last know home address. Each member in good standing shall be entitled to one vote. No member whose dues have been withheld by his employer for payment to such organization pursuant to his voluntary authorization provided for in a collective bargaining agreement shall be declared ineligible to vote or be a candidate for office in such organization by reason of alleged delay or default in the payment of dues. The votes cast by members of each local labor organization shall be counted, and the results published, separately. The election officials designated in the constitution and bylaws or the secretary, if no other official is designated, shall preserve for one year the ballots and all other records pertaining to the election. The election shall be conducted in accordance with the constitution and bylaws of such organization insofar as they are not inconsistent with the provisions of this title.

(f) When officers are chosen by a convention of delegates elected by secret ballot, the convention shall be conducted in accordance with the constitution and bylaws of the labor organization insofar as they are not inconsistent with the provisions of this title. The officials designated in the constitution and bylaws or the secretary, if no other is designated, shall preserve for one year the credentials of the delegates and all minutes and other records of the convention pertaining to the election of officers.

(g) No moneys received by any labor organization by way of dues, assessment, or similar levy, and no moneys of an employer shall be contributed or applied to promote the candidacy of any person in an election subject to the provisions of this title. Such moneys of a labor organization may be utilized for notices, factual statements of issues not involving candidates, and other expenses necessary for the holding of an election.

(h) If the Secretary, upon application of any member of a local labor organization, finds after hearing in accordance with the Administrative Procedure Act that the constitution and bylaws of such labor organization do not provide an adequate procedure for the removal of an elected officer guilty of serious misconduct, such officer may be removed, for cause shown and after notice and hearing, by the members in good standing voting in a secret ballot conducted by the officers of such labor organization in accordance with its constitution and bylaws insofar as they are not inconsistent with the provisions of this title.

(i) The Secretary shall promulgate rules and regulations prescribing minimum standards and procedures for determining the adequacy of the removal procedures to which reference is made in subsection (h).

Enforcement

Sec. 402. (a) A member of a labor organization—

(1) who has exhausted the remedies available under the constitution and bylaws of such organization and of any parent body, or
(2) who had invoked such available remedies without obtaining a final decision within three calendar months after their invocation.

may file a complaint with the Secretary within one calendar month thereafter alleging the violation of any provision of section 401 (including violation of the constitution and bylaws of the labor organization pertaining to the election and removal of officers). The challenged election shall be presumed valid pending a final decision thereon (as hereinafter provided) and in the interim the affairs of the organization shall be conducted by the officers elected or in such other manner as its constitution and bylaws may provide.

(b) The Secretary shall investigate such complaint and, if he finds probable cause to believe that a violation of this title has occurred and has not been remedied, he shall, within sixty days after the filing of such complaint, bring a civil action against the labor organization as an entity in the district court of the United States in which such labor organization maintains its principal office to set aside the invalid election, if any, and to direct the conduct of an election or hearing and vote upon the removal of officers under the supervision of the Secretary and in accordance with the provisions of this title and such rules and regulations as the Secretary may prescribe. The court shall have power to take such action as it deems proper to preserve the assets of the labor organization.

(c) If, upon a preponderance of the evidence after a trial upon the merits, the court finds—

(1) that an election has not been held within the time prescribed by section 401, or
(2) that the violation of section 401 may have affected the outcome of an election,

the court shall declare the election, if any, to be void and direct the conduct of a new election under supervision of the Secretary and, so far as lawful and practicable, in conformity with the constitution and bylaws of the labor organization. The Secretary shall promptly certify to the court the names of the persons elected, and the court shall thereupon enter a decree declaring such persons to be the officers of the labor organization. If the proceeding is for the removal of officers pursuant to subsection (h) of section 401, the Secretary shall certify the results of the vote and the court shall enter a decree declaring whether such persons have been removed as officers of the labor organization.

(d) An order directing an election, dismissing a complaint, or designating elected officers of a labor organization shall be appealable in the same manner as the final judgment in a civil action, but an order directing an election shall not be stayed pending appeal.

Application of Other Laws

Sec. 403. No labor organization shall be required by law to conduct elections of officers with greater frequency or in a different form or manner than is required by its own constitution or bylaws, except as otherwise provided by this title. Existing rights and remedies to enforce the constitution and bylaws of a labor organization with respect to elections prior to the conduct thereof shall not be affected by the provisions of this title. The remedy provided by this title for challenging an election already conducted shall be exclusive.

Effective Data

Sec. 404. The provision of this title shall become applicable—

(1) ninety days after the date of enactment of this Act in the case of a labor organization whose constitution and bylaws can lawfully be modified or amended by action of its constituional officers or governing body, or

(2) where such modification can only be made by a constitutional convention of the labor organization, not later than the next constitutional convention of such labor organization after the date of enactment of this Act, or one year after such date, whichever is sooner. If no such convention is held within such one-year period, the executive board of similar governing body empowered to act for such labor organization between conventions is empowered to make such interim constitutional changes as are necessary to carry out the provisions of this title.

TITLE V—SAFEGUARDS FOR LABOR ORGANIZATIONS

Fiduciary Responsibility of Officers of Labor Organizations

Sec. 501. (a) The officers, agents, shop stewards, and other representatives of a labor organization occupy positions of trust in relation to such organization and its members as a group. It is, therefore, the duty of each such person, taking into account the special problems and functions of a labor organization, to hold its money and property solely for the benefit of the organization and its members and to manage, invest, and expend the same in accordance with its constitution and bylaws and any resolutions of the governing bodies adopted thereunder, to refrain from dealing with such organization as an adverse party or in behalf of an adverse party in any matter connected with his duties and from holding or acquiring any pecuniary or personal interest which conflicts with the interests of such organization, and to account to the organization for any profit received by him in whatever capacity in connection with transactions conducted by him or under his direction on behalf of the organization. A general exculpatory provision in the constitution and bylaws of such a labor organization or a general exculpatory resolution of a governing body purporting to relieve any such person of liability for breach of the duties declared by this section shall be void as against public policy.

(b) When an officer, agent, shop steward, or representative or any labor organization is alleged to have violated the duties declared in subsection (a) and the labor organization or its governing board or officers refuse or fail to sue or recover damages or secure an accounting or other appropriate relief within a reasonable time after being requested to do so by any member of the labor organization, such member may sue such officer, agent, shop steward, or representative in any district court of the United States or in any State court of competent jurisdiction to recover damages or secure an accounting or other appropriate relief for the benefit of the labor organization. No such proceeding shall be brought except upon leave of the court obtained upon verified application and for good cause shown, which application may be made ex parte. The trial judge may allot a reasonable part of the recovery in any action under this subsection to pay the fees of counsel prosecuting the suit at the instance of the member of the labor organization and to compensate such member for any expenses necessarily paid or incurred by him in connection with the litigation.

(c) Any person who embezzles, steals, or unlawfully and willfully abstracts or converts to his own use, or the use of another, any of the moneys, funds, securities, property, or other assets of a labor organization of which he is an officer, or by which he is employed, directly or indirectly, shall be fined not more than $10,000 or imprisoned for not more than five years, or both.

Bonding

Sec. 502. (a) Every officer, agent, shop steward, or other representative or employee or any labor organization (other than a labor organization whose property and annual financial receipts do not exceed $5,000 in value), or of a trust in which a labor organization is interested, who handles funds or other property thereof shall be bonded for the faithful discharge of his duties. The bond of each such person shall be fixed at the beginning of the organization's fiscal year and shall be in an amount not less than 10 per centum of the funds handled by him and his predecessor or predecessors, if any, during the preceding fiscal year, but in no case more than $500,000. If the labor organization or the trust in which a labor organization is interested does not have a preceding fiscal year, the amount of the bond shall be, in the case of a local labor organization, not less than $1,000, and in the case of any other labor organization or of a trust in which a labor organization is interested, not less than $10,000. Such bonds shall be individual or schedule in form, and shall have a corporate surety company as surety thereon. Any person who is not covered by such bonds shall not be permitted to receive, handle, disburse, or otherwise exercise custody or control of the funds or other property of a labor organization or of a trust in which a labor organization is interested. No such bond shall be placed through an agent or broker or with a surety company in which any labor organization or any officer, agent, shop steward, or other representative of a labor organization has any direct or indirect interest. Such surety company shall be a corporate surety which holds a grant of authority from the Secretary of the Treasury under the Act of July 30, 1947 (6 U.S.C. 6–13), as a acceptable surety on Federal bonds.

(b) Any person who willfully violates this section shall be fined not more than $10,000 or imprisoned for not more than one year, or both.

Making of Loans; Payment of Fines

Sec. 503. (a) No labor organization shall make directly or indirectly any loan or loans to any officer or employee of such organization which results in a total indebtedness on the part of such officer or employee to the labor organization in excess of $2,000.

(b) No labor organization or employer shall directly or indirectly pay the fine of any officer or employee convicted of any willful violation of this Act.

(c) Any person who willfully violates this section shall be fined not more than $5,000 or imprisoned for not more than one year, or both.

Prohibition Against Certain Persons Holding Office

Sec. 504. (a) No person who is or has been a member of the Communist Party or who has been convicted of, or served any part of a prison term resulting from his conviction of, robbery, bribery, extortion, embezzlement, grand larceny, burglary, arson, violation of narcotics laws, murder, rape, assault with intent to kill, assault which inflicts grievous bodily injury, or a violation of title II or III of this Act, or conspiracy to commit any such crimes, shall serve—

(1) as an officer, director, trustee, member of any executive board or similar governing body, business agent, manager, organizer, or other employee (other than as an employee performing exclusively clerical or custodial duties) of any labor organization, or

(2) as a labor relations consultant to a person engaged in an industry or activity affecting commerce, or as an officer, director, agent, or employee (other than as an employee performing exclusively clerical or custodial duties) of any group or association of employers dealing with any labor organization,

during or for five years after the termination of his membership in the Communist Party, or for five years after such conviction or after the end of such imprisonment, unless prior to the end of such five-year period, in the case of a person so convicted or imprisoned, (A) his citizenship rights, having been revoked as a result of such conviction, have been fully restored, or (B) the Board of Parole of the United States Department of

Justice determines that such person's service in any capacity referred to in clause (1) or (2) would not be contrary to the purposes of this Act. Prior to making any such determination the Board shall hold an administrative hearing and shall give notice of such proceeding by certified mail to the State, county, and Federal prosecuting officials in the jurisdiction or jurisdictions in which such person was convicted. The Board's determination in any such proceeding shall be final. No labor organization or officer thereof shall knowingly permit any person to assume or hold any office or paid position in violation of this subsection.

(b) Any person who willfully violates this section shall be fined not more than $10,000 or imprisoned for not more than one year, or both.

(c) For the purposes of this section, any person shall be deemed to have been "convicted" and under the disability of "conviction" from the date of the judgment of the trial court or the date of the final sustaining of such judgment on appeal, whichever is the later event, regardless of whether such conviction occurred before or after the date of enactment of this Act.

TITLE VI—MISCELLANEOUS PROVISIONS

Investigations

Sec. 601. (a) The Secretary shall have power when he believes it necessary in order to determine whether any person has violated or is about to violate any provision of this Act (except title I or amendments made by this Act to other statutes) to make an investigation and in connection therewith he may enter such places and inspect such records and accounts and question such persons as he may deem necessary to enable him to determine the facts relative thereto. The Secretary may report to interested persons or officials concerning the facts required to be shown in any report required by this Act and concerning the reasons for failure or refusal to file such a report or any other matter which he deems to be appropriate as a result of such an investigation.

(b) For the purpose of any investigation provided for in this Act, the provisions of sections 9 and 10 (relating to the attendance of witnesses and the production of books, papers, and documents) of the Federal Trade Commission Act of September 16, 1914, as amended (15 U.S.C. 49, 50), are hereby made applicable to the jurisdiction, powers, and duties of the Secretary or any officers designated by him.

Extortionate Picketing

Sec. 602. (a) It shall be unlawful to carry on picketing on or about the premises of any employer for the purpose of, or as part of any conspiracy or in furtherance of any plan or purpose for, the personal profit or enrichment of any individual (except a bona fide increase in wages or other employee benefits) by taking or obtaining any money or other thing of value from such employer against his will or with his consent.

(b) Any person who willfully violates this section shall be fined not more than $10,000 or imprisoned not more than twenty years, or both.

Retention of Rights Under Other Federal and State Laws

Sec. 603. (a) Except as explicitly provided to the contrary, nothing in this Act shall reduce or limit the responsibilities of any labor organization or any officer, agent, shop steward, or other representative of a labor organization, or of any trust in which a labor organization is interested, under any other Federal law or under the laws of any State, and, except as explicitly provided to the contrary, nothing in this Act shall take away any right or bar any remedy to which members of a labor organization are entitled under such other Federal law or law of any State.

(b) Nothing contained in titles I, II, III, IV, V, or VI of this Act shall be construed to supersede or impair or otherwise affect the provisions of the Railway Labor Act, as amended, or any of the obligations, rights, benefits, privileges, or immunities of any carrier, employee, organization, representative, or person subject thereto; nor shall anything contained in said titles (except section 505) of this Act be construed to confer any rights, privileges, immunities, or defenses upon employers, or to impair or otherwise affect the rights of any person under the National Labor Relations Act, as amended.

Effect on State Laws

Sec. 604. Nothing in this Act shall be construed to impair or diminish the authority of any State to enact and enforce general criminal laws with respect to robbery, bribery, extortion, embezzlement, grand larceny, burglary, arson, violation of narcotics laws, murder, rape, assault with intent to kill, or assault which inflicts grievous bodily injury, or conspiracy to commit any of such crimes.

Service of Process

Sec. 605. For the purposes of this Act, service of summons, subpena, or other legal process of a court of the United States upon an officer or agent of a labor organization in his capacity as such shall constitute service upon the labor organization.

Administrative Procedure Act

Sec. 606. The provisions of the Administrative Procedure Act shall be applicable to the issuance, amendment, or rescission of any rules or regulations, or any adjudication, authorized or required pursuant to the provisions of this Act.

Other Agencies and Departments

Sec. 607. In order to avoid unnecessary expense and duplication of functions among Government agencies, the Secretary may make such arrangements or agreements for cooperation or mutual assistance in the performance of his functions under this Act and the functions of any such agency as he may find to be practicable and consistent with law. The Secretary may utilize the facilities or services of any department, agency, or establishment of the United States or of any State or political subdivision of a State, including the services of any of its employees, with the lawful consent of such department, agency, or establishment; and each department, agency or establishment of the United States is authorized and directed to cooperate with the Secretary and, to the extent permitted by law, to provide such information and facilities as he may request for his assistance in the performance of his functions under this Act. The Attorney General or his representative shall receive from the Secretary for appropriate action such evidence developed in the performance of his functions under this Act as may be found to warrant consideration for criminal prosecution under the provisions of this Act or other Federal law.

Criminal Contempt

Sec. 608. No person shall be punished for any criminal contempt allegedly committed outside the immediate presence of the court in connection with any civil action prosecuted by the Secretary or any other person in any court of the United States under the provisions of this Act unless the facts constituting such criminal contempt are established by the verdict of the jury in a proceeding in the district court of the United States, which jury shall be chosen and empaneled in the manner prescribed by the law governing trial juries in criminal prosecutions in the district courts of the United States.

Prohibition On Certain Discipline By Labor Organization

Sec. 609. It shall be unlawful for any labor organization, or any officer, or any officer, agent, shop steward, or other representative of a labor organization, or any employee thereof to fine, suspend, expel, or otherwise discipline any of its members for exercising any right to which he is entitled under the provisions of this Act. The provisions of section 102 shall be applicable in the enforcement of this section.

Deprivation of Rights Under Act By Violence

Sec. 610. It shall be unlawful for any person through the use of force or violence, or threat of the use of force or violence, to restrain, coerce, or intimidate, or attempt to restrain, coerce, or intimidate any member of a labor organization for the purpose of interfering with or preventing the exercise of any right to which he is entitled under the provisions of this Act. Any person who willfully violates this section shall be fined not more than $1,000 or imprisoned for not more than one year, or both.

Separability Provisions

Sec. 611. If any provision of this Act, or the application of such provision to any person circumstances, shall be held invalid, the remainder of this Act or the application of such provision to persons or circumstances other than those as to which it is held invalid, shall not be affected thereby.